Strategies for Reading
in the Elementary School

Strategies for Reading in the Elementary School

SECOND EDITION

Clifford L. Bush
Kean College of New Jersey

Mildred H. Huebner
Southern Connecticut State College

MACMILLAN PUBLISHING CO., INC.
New York

COLLIER MACMILLAN PUBLISHERS
London

Earlier edition copyright © 1970 by
Macmillan Publishing Co., Inc.

Macmillan Publishing Co., Inc.
866 Third Avenue, New York, New York 10022

Collier Macmillan Canada, Ltd.

Library of Congress Cataloging in Publication Data

Bush, Clifford L   (date)
    Strategies for reading in the elementary school.

    Includes bibliographies and index.
    1.   Reading (Elementary)   I.   Huebner, Mildred H
(date)   joint author.   II.   Title.
LB1573.B898   1979   372.4'1   78–9462
ISBN 0–02–317510–9

Printing: 1 2 3 4 5 6 7 8   Year: 9 0 1 2 3 4 5

Preface

Since 1970 when the first edition of *Strategies for Reading in the Elementary School* appeared, some new emphases in the teaching of reading have surfaced. The questions, "What is reading? How and when do children learn to read?" have been analyzed in some depth by educators, psychologists, linguists and psycholinguists. Their analyses have given impetus to a new round of suggestions for changes in reading instruction—in methods, materials and evaluation.

The task of providing adequate reading instruction requires specific competencies of every teacher. Teachers need to be well-grounded in the practical aspects of effective reading instruction. They need to be aware of the nature of reading and the skills involved, the various methods of planning and teaching efficient reading habits, and the evaluation of children's reading achievement and progress. Classroom teachers of the future will need to feel secure in any situation involving the teaching of reading. Their preparation, therefore, will require a variety of experiences—in the *cognitive* domain, learning about reading programs from books and college professors; in the *affective* domain, acquiring attitudes, values, relationships; and in the *manipulative* or *psychomotor* domain, using the materials of instruction available for teaching reading, through observation and practice in real teaching situations.

How can the prospective teacher best be prepared for the most important task he or she will undertake every day of the teaching career? The authors pose a threefold answer:

1. Provide observation in a variety of good classroom situations.
2. Precede observations by class discussions of the reading text and related books, as well as reading research as reported in professional journals; follow observations with group discussions for clarification.
3. Provide internship experience in reading situations with opportunities for constructive evaluation.

Although the authors firmly believe that these steps are basic in the preparation of the teacher, they also realize that there are complications that prevent any real simplification of the problem. College instructors cannot anticipate for every student the type of classroom and the kinds of children he will meet in his first teaching position. The laboratory school or other student-teaching assignment can provide only limited experience for each prospective teacher. The reading textbook, therefore, will continue to be a very important link between the college classroom and the schoolroom, to produce the knowledgeable, competent teacher of the future.

This book has been based upon the authors' conviction that a new breed of classroom teachers must be developed to keep pace with current changes in curricula, materials, methodology, and the exploration of theory. The educational scene has had an explosion of knowledge, with research reported on many new types of school organizations, electronic equipment, programed packets, and so on. The new teacher, embarking on the first teaching assignment, may be in a traditional or progressive educational setting, or in one of the many intermediate types. The teacher may find himself in a reading program limited to a basal reader, in one that is individualized, in one that is supplemented by many reading materials, or in one that is being tried out on an experimental basis, and will need the confidence that accompanies a broad background of knowledge concerning reading instruction.

The authors have attempted to maintain a readable style in their writing of the various sections. Technical research terminology has been minimized in the interests of readability. Nevertheless, the vocabulary of reading must be brought to the attention of new teachers, just as the vocabulary of cognitive areas must be utilized, so that relationships and implications for reading instruction will be noted. The authors *want* the student to think about relationships to other courses when he is studying his reading textbook. They have therefore incorporated references to other areas so that the student will view his pre-teaching-of-reading course as both practical and functional—somewhere above the level of theory alone!

In the new edition the authors have retained those portions of the book which have proven value, and have changed or expanded some sections. In the decade following the publication of the original book, linguists, psycholinguists and theoreticians * have made strong contributions which have been selectively used to devise our strategies for teaching reading. The teacher of the 1980's is expected to prepare for, and to cope with, the needs of *all* children in an educational environment committed to the concept of mainstreaming. The strategic importance of individualization of instruction has been emphasized throughout the book. Accountability has been defined, and the various aspects treated in the sections dealing with evaluation and instruction.

Part I deals with background information for teachers of reading (theory): Chapters 1 and 2. Part II deals with skills of reading (instructional process): Chapters 3 through 7. Part III deals with planning and organizing effective reading (structure): Chapters 8 through 12. Part IV deals with the evaluation of progress in reading (accountability): Chapters 13 and 14.

Some things to look for in the use of this textbook are the implications of an early start in reading, management systems, programs for culturally

* Whose contributions may be found in *Theoretical Processes and Models of Reading,* Harry Singer and Robert Ruddell, Eds., Newark, DE: International Reading Association, 1976.

and economically disadvantaged, emphasis on individualization of instruction, and the characteristics of good teaching. Lists are included in the book to give an overview of sources—for example, children's encyclopedias. Their use could be that of a reference and selective study of one or two representative samples, to find out the appropriate children's use of the material.

The strategies delineated in the book are procedures that are innovative and different, emphasizing an early start in reading and illustrating with examples of materials that are being developed to reinforce or increase the scope of the program.

At the beginning of each chapter the authors have included specific objectives. By reviewing the objectives one can purposefully read the chapter. The references for each chapter have been updated to give the professor and the prospective teacher selected sources for further study. There is an instructor's manual which includes activities and evaluations for the professor's use.

The authors wish to acknowledge the assistance of Robert Andrews and Frances Kleederman, who each reviewed a portion of the book, Joseph Laronda for his pictures, and Carolin Martin for typing new sections of the book.

C. L. B.
M. H. H.

Contents

Part One:
Background Information for Teachers of Reading
(Theory)

1. The Reading Environment   3
2. Stages of Reading Development   20

Part Two:
Skills of Reading
(Instructional Process)

3. Readiness for Reading   37
4. Language and Vocabulary Development   60
5. Comprehension: Basic Factors   113
6. Comprehension: Skills   145
7. Oral Reading   180

Part Three:
Planning and Organizing Effective Reading
(Structure)

8. Children's Interests   201
9. Reading Programs: Principles for Structure   224
10. Reading Programs: Structure   254
11. Sources of Reading Materials   274
12. Organization of Instruction: Administrative   301

Part Four:
Evaluation of Progress in Reading
(Accountability)

13. Methods of Appraisal   327
14. Challenging Every Reader   363

Appendices

Scope and Sequence Chart   393
Glossary   487
Journals   495
Publishers   497
Name Index   503
Subject Index   509

List of Figures

1 Child Development Chart from Birth Through Sixteen Years 25

2 Characteristics of the Efficient Reader at Several Stages of Reading Development 29

3 A Sample Personal Growth Record Developed for Children in a Transitional Room 52

4 Basic Phonic Elements 78

5 Reading Comprehension Skills 120

6 Variability of Readability in a Seventh Grade Science Test Contrasted with Reading Scores of Sections Using Text 134

7 Students' Grade Level in Reading and Books at That Level 135

8 Work Habits 154

9 Study Techniques 156

10 Oral Reading Checklist for the Classroom Teacher 194

11 Planning Lessons to Help All Readers 235

12 Checklist for a Basal Reading Series 280

13 Assigning Reading Material 291

14 Reading Materials—Six-Year-Olds 292

15 Reading Materials—Seven-Year-Olds 293

16 Reading Materials—Eight-Year-Olds 294

17 Reading Materials—Nine-Year-Olds 295

18 Reading Materials—Ten-Year-Olds 296

19 Reading Materials—Eleven-Year-Olds 297

20 Design Plan 314

21 Meaning Vocabulary 331

22 Norm- *vs* Criterion-Referenced Tests 348

23 Educational Planning Component Model 361

24 Potential Academic Achievement of Children with Various Intelligence Quotient Levels 364

Part One

Background Information for Teachers of Reading

(Theory)

Chapter 1

The Reading Environment

OBJECTIVES

To understand the role of reading in the language arts

To conceptualize the reading process

To consider the importance of reading because of its many benefits

To define reading

To examine the effects of the home, community, and environment on reading achievement

To know the strategies the teacher employs as a reading model

THE LANGUAGE ARTS

The communication skills individuals acquire are a powerful influence on their lives. Their success in education is dependent upon them. Their vocational choice and their success in the vocation are, in most cases, related to communication skills. Even social life and standing among peers and in the community may be heavily influenced by them. It is little wonder, then, that the greatest weighting in the curriculum throughout all formal education is given to the communication skills.

The curriculum area that deals with the development and strengthening of communication skills is the language arts. The subareas of the language arts are (1) listening, (2) speaking, (3) reading, and (4) writing. The last classification includes creative writing, handwriting, and spelling. These basic subareas are interrelated because they all depend on the processes of exchange of thoughts. Because this is true, the focal point in each group of skills is thinking—the organization and reorganization of thoughts. Listening and reading may be classified as receptive or analytical because they represent the process of interpretation of the thoughts of someone else.

Speaking and writing may be classified as synthetic or expressive because they represent the process of sending or the sharing of thoughts with others. All use the same signals—words. The preschool child learns in the home to look, listen, and speak. The child develops some proficiency in these before coming to school, and uses them in developing the skills necessary for the learning of the other language arts—reading and writing. There is a wide range of abilities to handle the initial language arts in the five-year-old because of factors within the child and in the child's environment.

The sound symbols of words that the preschooler hears arouse meaningful thinking and feelings if they are an integral part of the child's experience. If, with parents and friends, he or she has gone on trips, joined in conversations, watched television, heard stories, seen plays, and reacted to parades, the preschooler has enjoyed a rich environment that supports the development of language skills. If the child can get the main idea and supporting information, follow simple directions, understand relationships, and sense emotions, he or she has developed some of the patterns for initial skill development in the language arts. If such children have organized their own thinking to respond to outside stimuli—people, things, places, and events—they may express their reactions in sound elements (some of the words they have heard). They have again moved forward in the skills development of the language arts. In due time, these language skills will be used when they begin to respond to the symbols in print, for the visual elements must be related to the known sound elements to consistently arouse meaning as they read and write.

The language arts skills with all of their variations and aspects require many years of practice, instruction, and self-evaluation.

THE READING PROCESS

Reading is a complex process involving physiological and cerebral activities. Children develop in perception and cognition by attending to their environmental sights, sounds, events, words, and sentences and by responding to them. Concepts develop from children's experiences with the forces in their environment. Those objects, forces, and experiences that have influenced the children's learning are called their "life space." If the child's "life space" has been enriching and favorable and if perception is taking place correctly, he or she has a readiness for beginning reading. If the "life space" has been limited, the child lacks experiences and contact with the language of the classroom, lacks cultural contacts, and/or has been a part of a very narrow learning environment; then the school needs to provide an enriching life space by broadening the child's contacts and assigning labels to objects and experiences. In a sense, this means the provision of models of the perceptual-conceptual process.

The perceptual-conceptual process involves several steps. First, there is the input or sensory recognition, in which there is an awareness of the stimulus caused by the activation of nerve endings, triggering a nerve impulse to the brain. Second, there is the neuroperceptual function, which is a transmittal process. Third, the cognitive decoding or integration process takes place, through which there is derived meaning from the short-term memory store. Fourth, there is a cognitive process whereby meaning is translated into relevant responsive behavior. Fifth, there is an output in which the brain programs an internal response (simply adding to memory) or an external one through glands and muscles in the form of speech, writing, and similar reactions. Last, the feedback occurs whereby the process or outcome is evaluated mentally (acceptance, rejection, disputation, and so on).

Another way to look at the informational processing functioning of an individual is to classify it in three parts—the first is the perceptual-neurological function, or what happens between the stimulus and the cognitive functioning in the brain; the second is the cognitive functioning of identification, association, and selection in the brain; the third is the motor response. To the extent that any of these processes can be broken down into a specific skill, training can be employed to enhance the functioning of that skill. Yet learning takes place *only* when the individual changes in the training process—long-term memory operating by clustering, organizing, chunking of material.

Changes in memory between five and eleven are a consequence of the child's gradual acquisition and mastery of these sophisticated system strategies. The young child usually lacks the knowledge of an efficient means of organizing the information for processing.[1]

There are several elements that make up the school reading situation: some the child brings to the setting; some are independent of the child; some are in the limitations or, better yet, the parameters within which the child can learn. Children bring to the reading situation a certain level of perceptual capability. This is made up of their sensory and neural structures, their conceptual background to date, and their own psychological (affective) characteristics. The program of the curriculum and skill of the teacher present to the child certain skills and content that were selected by others than himself or herself. The teacher can help the child learn only to the

[1] C. Liberty and P. A. Arnstein, "Age Differences in Organization and Recall: The Effect of Training in Categorization," *Journal of Experimental Child Psychology*, 15:169–186 (1973), and H. A. Simon, "On the Development of the Processor," *Information Processing in Children*, ed. Sylvia Farnham-Diggery (New York: Academic Press, 1972).

degree the child's perceptual capability can attend, receive, absorb, and interpret the material that is taught. Children approach the beginning reading task with varying levels of readiness in mental maturity, perceptual skills, language facility (oral, linguistic), concepts, attention, memory factors, motivation, models, and social and emotional adjustment.

The means of organizing information develops through several stages. The *input* stage is a decoding process involving sensoriperceptual discriminations such as the visual, auditory, and haptic (figure-ground, closure, short-term memory, spatial). The *cognitive* process involves long-term memory, discriminations of concrete linguistic, semantic, and symbolic nature and convergent and divergent thinking. The *output* is an encoding stage resulting in phonemic motor responses, activities, speech-gross gestures, writing, drawing, storage, or (sometimes) restructuring activities. What is reading then? From the preceding statements it would seem to be the intelligent response to an interpretation of the symbols stimulus—in more common terminology, bringing meaning to the printed page to get meaning from the printed page.

What then is reading? There are as many definitions as there are people defining the term, from the simple "getting meaning from symbols" to the very erudite complex explanation encompassing most of the known processes involved.

Benefits Derived from Reading

Because purpose plays such an important role in the motivation to read, some of the many benefits from reading are listed. At various times in their learning the skills, children should be reminded of the benefits they gain in mastering the techniques. The more these purposes become their personal goals, the greater is their motivation. Reading

1. Helps satisfy a mood.
2. Aids in meeting everyday needs.
3. Follows the magic of a master storyteller.
4. Puts the reader next to the most creative minds in history.
5. Helps satisfy curiosity.
6. Can be savored at anyone's choice of time and place.
7. Distracts the mind from irritating situations.
8. Allows the reader to try out dangerous or forbidden practices without suffering the direct consequences.
9. Takes the reader to lands he or she cannot physically visit.
10. Gives the chance of sampling ideas as many times as desired.
11. Adds excitement to a dull existence.
12. Helps fill in leisure time.
13. Opens up new interests and follows old interests.

14. Provides knowledge and skill for advancement in vocation.
15. Changes one's level of thinking.
16. Provides a private, secret world.
17. Helps maintain and improve health.
18. Can place ideas of different people in juxtaposition at will.
19. Adds spiritual and personal refreshment.
20. Helps solve problems—social, political, economic, personal.
21. Keeps one abreast of happenings—local and worldwide.
22. Shares the joy of others (writers).
23. Develops aesthetic values.
24. Helps the reader face new situations with greater confidence.

The reader may well ask if he or she has read for all of these purposes lately. A common remark—"I'd better read up on it"—is a testimonial to one's recognition of the value of reading. People who are recognized as well read are usually good conversationalists and thus make friends wherever they go. If readers are strong persons in their field, this usually means they have read widely and applied the knowledge in their particular field of endeavor. In other words, the quantity and quality of a person's reading is reflected in many ways to those around him or her. One of the dangers inherent in the reading task is that an individual will be careless in carrying the process only part way—word recognition and comprehension—without continuing to the mature procedures of reaction and integration into the total experience. For such an individual many of the previously mentioned benefits of reading are never realized, and he or she thus reads only minimally or just enough to get by on.

Another way to look at the reading process is to consider it primarily as a sociological process or as a psychological process or as a physiological or intellectual or perceptual process. The major emphasis seems to be a function of the type of specialist who is defining the term: the psychologist, the reading specialist, the linguist, or the sociologist. The reading specialist and the psychologist focus their attention on the individual who reads; the linguist focuses on the language; the sociologist, on the culture; the man of letters, on the material read. It is wise to examine reading from the standpoint of its relationships in each of the several areas because it is a process involving many skills.

READING IN THE LANGUAGE ARTS

Because all of the language arts are interrelated, successful instruction must deal with the child's total readiness for every stage of learning. Children must be motivated for learning the skills of reading. They come to school with their verbal language experience. In a group of children there is a wide range of linguistic development and eagerness to learn. There is also a wide range of sensory, mental, emotional, and social development. There is a range of previous learnings that make the new task possible. The teacher uses discussion to take advantage of previous learnings and development in order to assure success with the new learnings. Even though reading is presented here in terms of its different characteristics, it must be kept in mind that these must blend to form the background of the individual child. The procedure of grouping children is an attempt to bring together those children who have approximately the same development for the purpose of making instruction efficient.

From psychology we find that there are two major factors in our learning and development: nature and nurture, or inherited genes and the individual's environment. The school can do much about the child's environment to make it favorably supportive of the reading process. The influence of the teacher and the school program should extend into the home and various institutions and functions of the community. This chapter deals with environmental factors that relate to reading success and failure.

THE HOME

Parents set the tone for reading in the home. They are tremendously influential in the young child's desire to read, in his or her use of language that makes the application of visual symbols (words) to the oral language, and in his or her compatibility with books and other reading materials. In the home where the vocabulary is extensive and the use of language patterns is good, there are many different kinds of books, and reading is an everyday occurrence—in this home conditions are favorable for the child's success in reading. There is usually a close partnership with the school program, and cooperation is readily obtained. Unfortunately, acculturation may work both ways—for and against reading. The following quotes convey their own influence on reading: "too busy to read," "too many places to go and things to do," "too busy earning money"; too much parental pressure created by "no play during the week," "do your homework," "bring your books home."

In those homes where reading is never done in any form or where English is not known or spoken, children have a very serious handicap in reading successfully. The five-to-six hour school day may *not be able to offset this handicap.* Gertrude Whipple [2] describes what one teacher did to help the parents learn to read. It is often necessary to establish some form

[2] "A Perspective on Reading for Children Without," *Vistas in Reading,* Proceedings of the International Reading Association (J. Allen Figurel, ed.), 1966, Vol. II, Part 1, pp. 337–38.

of program for parents if their children are to be successful, especially if there are no older siblings who are reading. Where there are older siblings, they may take the place of parents in their influence on the younger child's reading experiences. Of course, sometimes this influence is not good.

Parents might engage in a hobby that naturally involves some reading and get the child interested in it right along beside them. Other suggestions will be made in following sections.

There are some competing agencies that come into the house and both encourage and interfere with reading. The first and most influential is television. This can completely replace reading if there is no supervision of the extent of viewing and the selection of programs. Witty, et al.[3] reports that it overshadows other forms of home recreation. Radio and stereo take their share of time. Do-it-yourself kits and home construction of packaged items are adding to some necessity for reading and following directions.

THE COMMUNITY

Institutions

There are two types of institutions in the community, tax-supported and private, that involve reading, and their influence varies considerably on the child and his or her reading habits. Although the school and its personnel cannot be responsible for all of them, there is a responsibility to work with them as closely as possible; there is a responsibility for the individual teacher to relate the school's reading program cooperatively; and, as a responsible individual, the teacher should wield some influence where the institution or service organization is failing in its standards, type, extent, or unique contribution to society.

Tax-Supported. The first type of community institution is tax-supported. In this classification are the library, children's theater, museums, community recreation department, social agencies, and PTA. The library serving the area of the school may be either a local city-supported one or a state library. The basic feature for adequate functioning is the number, extent, and levels of books available. The accessibility of the books and the proximity of the library are also factors in frequent usage. Parents and children should have library cards and *use* them. Much depends upon the programs of the library and the type of service in lending and help from the librarian. Special programs such as a children's story hour yield great influence in many communities. The classroom teacher should encourage children to use the public library, even to the extent of conducting them

[3] Paul Witty, Alma Freeland, and Edith Grotberg, *The Teaching of Reading* (Boston: D. C. Heath and Company, 1966), p. 45.

there if they are lax in this respect. The teacher should also emphasize, at every opportunity, the desirability of library usage with the parents. He or she can teach library behavior and techniques of book selection, recommend lists, introduce new books, help with book displays, conduct book fairs, and work closely with the local librarian. It is not unusual to find some civic-minded teachers in the political arena supporting library building programs and local financial support.

The second community institution is the children's theater, or any theater group, locally supported. These can result in a tremendous influence on the total language arts. Books are often in demand as the result of a local performance that children have attended. Many youngsters become interested in being performers themselves. These should be fully supported by the schools.

The third institution is the museum—historical, health, science, natural history, art, specialized (antique cars, fire-fighting, baseball, and so on)—and, in the same category, the zoo, botanical gardens, and aquarium. Children can be helped reading captions and learning background for reading. Often they become interested in reading more about what they have seen. The school can conduct trips that contribute to their program and should, by all means, encourage parents to take their children to such fascinating places. Many of the museums have three kinds of services that schools can capitalize on: (1) stationary, permanent, or "don't touch" displays that can be visited; (2) traveling exhibits that can be borrowed by the school, handled, examined, and discussed; and (3) personnel who give programs in the museum prepared for the purpose and sometimes will come to the school for a special program, bringing material with them. A few museums will set up a special exhibit for the classroom teacher in the museum and allow the competent teacher to teach his or her class right there surrounded by the realia of the period (historical).

The fourth institution is the recreation department of the community. It, too, thrives with the full support of the school and its facilities and personnel. Programs typically range from athletics to arts and crafts. Again these programs not only provide recreation, but they also furnish background for reading and the total language arts experience. Teachers are often found participating in these programs in after-school and summer hours.

The fifth institution is the group of social agencies and their service programs. Especially where the physical and mental health and general welfare of the child is in jeopardy, these agencies play a very important role in making the environment of the child conducive to learning. Cooperation with these agencies can bring the success of the child in reading closer to fruition. Some of the agencies with which the schools have cooperated, and which they have found beneficial, directly or indirectly, are listed as follows:

Family and Children's Service

Goodwill Home and Rescue Mission: Child Welfare Section

Mental Health Association

Multiple Sclerosis National Society

Muscular Dystrophy Association of America, Inc.

The state's association for retarded children

The state's society for crippled children and adults

City's day care center

United Community Services

Head Start

Council on Aging

Reading Is Fundamental

YMCA, YWCA

Neighborhood Services Center

Public Housing Authorities

Day nurseries.

The sixth institution is one sponsored by the school as its pipeline to the community. It is the parents' group known in different communities as the Parent-Teacher Association, Room Mothers, Parents' Club, Friends of the School, Home and School Association, or whatever other form it may take. In many communities this group performs a vital task in bringing the members into the school and in providing a forum for the discussion of home and school problems. It is often the best means of getting ideas about reading, the reading program, and types of parent support of the child's reading across to the parents. Complaints and questions can be answered. A reading newsletter can be distributed and discussed. Liaison with the other institutions can be discussed. Current news articles and new developments can be examined to allay parents' concerns and fears and suspicions, and desires.

Private. The second type of community institution is a group of private enterprises that furnish entertainment, programs, services, and/or materials for reading. They are influenced most of the time by public opinion, the membership, and/or patronage. Occasionally, a concerted effort by an individual or group results in a change in practice and/or policy. They can be characterized as reflections of the segment of society they represent. The school system influences them, and they influence the schools.

The first and probably the most influential of the private organizations is the publishing company. The publishers with their retail outlets supply the reading material that is available both in the school and in the community. For the most part they determine their own ethical code and quality of materials. Quantity is related to demand. They meet their competition and increase their profit by merger and by diversification and by increasing the demand for their material by appealing to an additional segment of the population. Sometimes they are regulated or strongly influenced by the courts, a legislature or local government body, a religious group, or a school board, although none of these are very effective because regulation by one of these groups may increase the demand for the material rather than stop it. Books, magazines, and paperbacks are the software products, and the hardware includes machines, which are meant to supply greater need for the software. The number and type of retailers has been increasing in recent years. Besides the mail order business, materials are available in specialty shops, such as the typical book store, drug stores, department stores, supermarkets, book clubs, and, of course, through the traveling salesmen. Paperback books may be purchased in hotels, cigar stores, some gas stations, bus and train and plane stations—in fact, almost anywhere one turns today. In New York City the public library has tried putting miniature lending libraries for browsing in some eating places, in some banks, and in unusual places where individuals may have a few moments of leisure time for browsing. Publishers provide a service to American society; the questions of quality and ethical content are ones for which educators are responsible. If the schools emphasize morality, ethics, and good taste in literature, then the school becomes the model for individuals to make their choices. Censorship does not seem to work; for the young reader an approach of positive guidance is much more effective. Adults should make their own choices based on their moral, ethical, and religious principles.

Toy manufacturers have had an influence on children, and their products, toys, could be considered an important part of the environment. Small tricycles, scooters, pedal cars, and so on, help the child develop motor control. Lincoln Logs, Tinker Toys, and so on, help the child develop motor control, visual copying, and sequence in construction. Number and alphabet blocks and word blocks and games make numbers and words and letters and cubes a familiar part of the child's environment. Children feed, clothe, bathe, walk, talk, and sing to their dolls for language development and for motor and family life development, usually emulating their mothers. Spatial relationships are a part of many of the understandings and skills they develop from puzzles, games, and toys. Visual and auditory experiences are a part of children's play with toy record players, plastic fire engines, plastic drawing sets, toy musical instruments, and so on. As a matter of fact, the toys have been made to appeal to those very same skills and learnings that comprise the reading readiness tests used in kindergarten and first grade. Educators have helped design many of them, even for the preschool child. Toys are used in kindergartens to facilitate the development of these same skills. Toys for older children serve to further reading skills. The child's chemistry set has reading material for the child to follow directions and learn about the interaction of the chemicals. Scrabble, Lotto, and other such games are often used in the classroom. Most of the adult tools and equipment are replicated in smaller size for children.

The second private organization is the religious group. Churches and synagogues are an influential segment of our society in that they run complete educational programs, supplementary programs of education, and community action programs and also provide leadership in many peripheral activities that involve different aspects of the language arts. Bible stories are the first ones that many children hear. A prayer is the first choral speaking that many children learn. A Sunday school class is the first organized group that many children join and from which they learn to be a contributing member to the group. Countrywide, religion permeates the total environment of the young child, his or her home, and neighborhood more than any other institution of those mentioned in this section.

The third private institution is the theater. The movies and the stage provide entertainment for children and adults. Action and adventure are the preferred interests of young children in their choice of movies. These parallel their reading interests. In fact, seeing a movie may cause the child to want to read the book, and vice versa. The drive-in theaters bring families to the movies, and the result is often a discussion of the picture afterwards. Although the theater has taken second place with television viewing far ahead, in a sense they have joined because of the films shown on television screens. The viewer can watch, in the New York City area, a film on television at any hour beginning at 9:00 A.M. and running through the day and night until approximately 6:00 A.M., according to the *TV Guide*. Sometimes the teacher of first and second graders is amazed to hear children discussing a film that was shown at 11:00 P.M. the previous night. Because children have not learned to be selective in their theater and film watching, parents and teachers have an obligation to help them; and, in the case of overindulgence, to limit them. There can be no doubt that the child's language arts and vicarious experiences are broadened by these media.

The fourth private institution is the YM-YWCA and similar organizations, which run varied programs for children and youth. Reading is often involved in their own small libraries, in the rules and regulations they enforce, for their games, in their arts and crafts programs, and in their camping programs. Some of them run book discussion sessions.

The fifth is a group in scouting—Boy Scouts, Girl Scouts, Campfire Girls, Cub Scouts, and so on. Many aspects of these programs involve reading—their manuals, their tests for advancement, their equipment lists, and their laws and oaths. Schools often cooperate with them in providing leadership personnel, sponsorship, and meeting space. Their worth is recognized in building social skills, language arts, group membership, responsibility, and morality.

The sixth private institution is the children's camp. Camping programs are run by individuals (often by teachers), by organizations such as churches and Y's, and sometimes by the school system itself. Camping makes an especially strong contribution to language arts background for city children—often the first time away from home and family. Children love to discuss their camping experiences. These create new interests for reading. Books about nature, birds, insects, and trees are in great demand following a camping experience.

The seventh private institution is the foundation that funds projects that help children directly or indirectly. Examples of such are the Association for the Aid of Crippled Children, Carnegie Corporation of New York, Ford Foundation, W. K. Kellogg Foundation, and National Science Foundation. A list of foundations with their addresses and assets and expenditures may be found in *The World Almanac*. More information about their officers, purposes, and activities may be found at the library in these sources:

> *American Foundations and Their Fields.* New York: American Foundation Information Service (latest edition).
> *Encyclopedia of American Associations.* Detroit: Gale Research Co. (latest edition and supplements).

An example of foundation aid is the financing of a child's diagnostic and remedial treatment at a reading clinic or speech and hearing clinic. Another is the purchasing of corrective glasses for a child whose parents could not afford them. Another foundation recently supported a broad experimental program in several school systems with the ITA and TO (Traditional Orthography) programs compared.

The eighth private institution is the group of clubs formed in most cities, such as the Lions Club, the Kiwanis, and the Rotary International. These have been known to support programs for children in perception, vision, recreation, reading, and many other areas. They also provide a forum for educational speeches and discussions.

All or any of these listed types of institutions have influenced the child's reading success through work with the child directly or through the child's family and associates.

Functions of Community

There are several other functions that take place on occasion that influence children's reading directly or by example. The first is the Great Books Programs, which parents may engage in. Children thereby have a fine example set for them of interest in books, of adult reading, and of adult discussion of books in the home. A second function is a historical celebration of the city or town. Often children take part in these in dramatizations, in reading skits, as guides, and in parades; and they see history as it is interpreted and dramatized. Usually, historical documents and other realia are displayed for all to see.

Federal Support

One final type of program may increase the potential in reading for many children who need extra help. This is the federally supported programs, such as Head Start and U. S. Office of Education Titles I and III. Variations of these programs seem destined to continue for some time. Such programs concentrate on developing language experience in a social setting and broadening types of experiences the children need to supply basics for language development. They give the child who has been deprived experientially and financially an entirely new and enriched environment.

THE SCHOOL

Emphasis on Reading

The kind of school environment that is favorable to reading is sometimes referred to as the reading climate of the school. It is characterized by an observable emphasis on reading in the total school program and a correlation of reading with other aspects of the program. The children show pride in their reading, and they *read.* They progress in reading skill development at their general developmental rate. The program is adjusted to the children rather than vice versa, preparing them for formal reading, developing vocabulary, and developing an appreciation of and an interest in good literature. Emphasis is placed on understanding, interpretation, and meaning.

Personnel

Probably the most important factor in the school's reading environment is the group of personnel who control the environment through their planning decisions and procedures of instruction. The administrators need to show real leadership in this basic curriculum area. For years, the American Association of School Administrators have been emphasizing reading in its annual convention in Atlantic City. Nationally recognized reading specialists have been invited to speak and consult with the superintendents. Other organizations, such as the International Reading Association, the National Society for the Study of Education, and the American Educational Research Association, have held combined meetings with the AASA. Administrators must show real concern for the in-service professional growth and the recruitment of teachers who know the reading field. Their next major responsibility is that of providing budgetary provisions for fully supporting books, reading materials, space, equipment, class size, and additional personnel to make a strong reading program a potentiality.

Supervisory service furnished by the reading specialist should result in coordination of the reading program, planning for changes and regular needs, and arrangements to meet any special needs of children in the program. Coordination is needed, too, to assure an articulated program so that continuous progress may be made by the children through the grades and on into junior and senior high school.

Additional key personnel in the total reading program are the librarian, the reading improvement committee, and special services represented by the medical worker, social worker, psychologist, and reading specialist or learning disabilities consultant.

Curriculum

The reading environment of the school, of course, means the total scope and sequence of the reading part of the curriculum. It is only briefly mentioned here because each phase is more fully treated in other chapters. There is the regular developmental program plus clinical facilities and services to help individuals who are not making normal or expected progress in the regular classroom program. A continuous evaluation of the program is in order and involves a carefully developed testing program, appropriate grouping procedures, and provision for fundamental changes to be made when deemed advisable.

Records

Good cumulative records are necessary if the school system is to examine the sequence quality of its program and is to help each child reach his potential. See chapter 13.

Public Relations

Finally, the reading environment of the school must relate closely to the community. The parents must know what the program is and how their children are doing in it. A public relations program should be in operation so that parental support is continuous and guaranteed, not a parental involvement only when a child is in trouble in his or her reading development. The program must also relate to the community agencies and institutions and functions previously mentioned in this chapter.

The Classroom

The most direct influence of the school's reading environment on the child takes place in the classroom. The teacher is the key to this influence. The

Enjoying Reading

teacher's personality, educational training, creativity, general physical and mental health, and understanding of children are paramount in teaching the child to read, to want to read, and to gain in skills and satisfaction in reading. Next come the procedures that are employed in the classroom to meet the individual's needs adequately and the variety and appropriateness of those procedures. Then come the materials of instruction, their appropriateness and correct usage, the variety of approaches that they encompass, and their attractiveness to the children. After this come the kinds of cultural experiences the children encounter—the types of enrichment that supplement the standard program. Finally, there is the overall setting in which the children are expected to learn—the unhurried, pleasurable but business-like, attractive setting of the modern classroom, where children are fully accepted members of the family of learners, where they are treated with respect and dignity and fully supported in all their learning activity.

The Teacher as a Reader

There are many reasons why the teacher should be an avid reader. First, a little of the teacher's love of reading rubs off on the children and sets the desirable model for them to emulate. Second, it brings a wide range of knowledge into the classroom as a constant resource for enrichment and factual support to discussion. Third, the teacher will know about books, authors, and characters and may make on-the-spot recommendations to children. Fourth, practicing constantly the skills one is trying to teach reinforces the aids passed on to youngsters. Fifth, insights are added to experience that may be helpful in instruction. Sixth, there is the very real possibility that the teacher will be more sympathetic and patient with children's problems of concentration, word attack, and need for help. Seventh, teachers need consistent review and expansion of vocabulary and concepts, especially on an adult level for sustenance. Eighth, the speech of teachers reflects their learning and understanding in a broader sense. Ninth, the continued search for learning impels one toward the researching of ideas and methodology. Finally, a 1980 graduate of a teacher education program cannot afford to remain a 1980 teacher throughout a professional career.

At this point, a statement is appropriate about the strategies of remaining a "growing" teacher. *The Torchlighters Revisited* [4] has some good suggestions for areas of continued professional reading: linguistics, psycholinguistics, dialect, child development, learning characteristics, and variant instructional programs. Research is constantly being reported that can add information and understanding to a teacher's background. Children's literature is a fertile field for understanding children, their problems, and interests. Professional journals are reporting new learning materials, experiments in learning modalities and organizational patterns, and successful programs. The potential is unlimited; the time and place for reading are the individual teachers' election and responsibility. For these sources see *Journals* in the Appendix and Publishers' addresses to which the teacher can write for Publishers' Service Bulletins.

Specifically, as to what should be read—probably everything possible; but, in particular, a minimum reading diet would include a wide range of adult literature, professional literature in one's own and related fields, and children's books. When do busy teachers have time for reading? Probably every chance they get to sandwich it in; but at the very beginning of one's career some time should be scheduled daily for oneself—for reading. Twenty minutes to a half hour per day scheduled for reading, spread over a teaching career, will most likely result in a personable, knowledgeable, and strong professional person—the kind we want in all our schools and classrooms.

SUMMARY

In summary, the reading environment of children is influenced by their home, the institutions and functions of their community, the school system, and their own immediate classroom. Public criticism of reading by popular

---

[4] Coleman Morrison and Mary C. Austin, *The Torchlighters Revisited* (Newark, DE: International Reading Association, 1977), p. 53.

magazine articles written by self-styled experts never look at the overall picture of learning to read and of the frequency and amount and proficiency in reading. We, who teach reading as a skill, must be aware of *all* of the influences on our efforts and their effects. Some of the environmental influences we should capitalize on; some we must attempt to counteract; some we should attempt to change. If we work in the classroom with children, we can adjust our program to meet the needs of individuals with an understanding of their total reading environment. If we work in the larger school system, we can wield greater influence on the total program and the experiences of children through materials, procedures, the teachers, and the organization. As citizens of the community, we can influence directly the institutions, agencies, and functions, even the commercial concerns, through the ballot, through personal contact, through the giving of economic support and of our own energy and time. We can be a model or example of what is right and good in reading through our personal influence. We can even use the power of our professional and social organizations to help children in reading. Many an adult-centered home has been influenced to develop a child-centered island that has helped the child in his or her reading.

SELECTED READINGS

Haber, Ralph, ed. *Information Processing Approaches to Visual Perception.* New York: Holt, Rinehart and Winston, 1969.

Harvard Educational Review Special Issue: Reading, Language and Learning, 47,3 (1977).

Morrison, Coleman, and Mary C. Austin. *The Torchlighters Revisited.* Newark, DE: International Reading Association, 1977.

Mour, Stanley I. "Do Teachers Read?" *The Reading Teacher,* 30,4 (Jan. 1977), 397–401.

NN&Q, News Notes and Quotes, Newsletter of Phi Delta Kappa, 21,5, (May–June 1977).

Singer, Harry, and Robert B. Ruddell, eds. *Theoretical Models and Processes of Reading,* 2d ed. Newark, DE: International Reading Association, 1976.

Smith, Frank. *Psycholinguistics and Reading.* New York: Holt, Rinehart and Winston, 1973.

Chapter 2

Stages of Reading Development

OBJECTIVES

To place child development stages and
reading development stages in juxtaposition
so that the relationship between the two is
clear

To build an awareness of the availability of
literature for children at their various stages
of development

INTRODUCTION

In the preceding chapter the complicated nature of reading and learning
to read was explored. In this section, stages of child growth will be reviewed with the purpose of discovering the relationship between identifiable
growth patterns and reading development.

PIAGET'S STAGES

Piaget has established the following four stages of development.

Age	
0–2	Sensorimotor period
2–7	Period of preoperational thought
7–11	Period of concrete operations
11–14	Formal operations

In the sensorimotor period, reflex reactions to experience are manifest. In the period of preoperational thought, cognitive behaviors of egocentrism, centration, and animistic thought can be observed. The third period is characterized by increases in the ability to classify, to put things in rank order, and eventually to use deduction. In the formal stage the child can manipulate ideas for abstraction, can envision multiple outcomes, and can form logical procedures for problem solving. However, reading development generally falls into six recognizable stages.

THE SIX STAGES OF DEVELOPMENT

Charts of so-called normal development have been devised by psychologists, departments of health, and education specialists. A perusal of any of these will show that there are general, recognizable patterns at each succeeding age level from birth to approximately sixteen years of age. Teachers need to be aware of the implications for teaching and learning that may be gleaned from these studies of human growth and development. There are important generalizations to be observed. Children are alike in many ways at certain ages—in their behavior, their reactions, and their needs. Knowledge of the ways in which children are alike at a given age can help a teacher plan activities and procedures geared to their interests and needs. For example, a teacher can put to good use the knowledge that young children use big muscles, involving the whole body, learning best through active participation and dramatization. Teachers can plan lessons in which children take the parts of characters in simple stories they have read or have had read to them. Their language facility can be increased through such activities, leading to better reading skills as they progress through the grades.

Teachers also need to be aware of ways in which children can differ. Because of the number of factors that can influence an individual child's current progress, a child can exhibit differences from others at his or her current developmental stage. Thus, a history of illnesses or accidents, a mobile family life, a foreign language background, variations among inherent mental abilities, and so on—any of these factors at any point may cause a child to appear to be different from others at his age—in physical development, in skills attainment, or in habit and attitude formation. Recognition of the ways in which Nick or Polly may be different from the expected level of development at a given age will help the teacher plan activities that take into account the individual's current needs. For example, knowing that Nick hears only Italian spoken at home would give his teacher some clues for helping him develop facility in the use of English *before* he is assigned a place in a reading group.

The Prereading Stage—Birth to Level One

Stages of reading development may be identified by the study of the characteristics of children and the reading activities that are typical of children at various ages. The initial stage, from birth to age six, is a period of preparation for the complex, formal act of reading the printed page. Language activities are a natural part of growing up. The child listens to and reacts to the spoken word as an infant. He or she imitates sounds, learns some words, uses short sentences by the age of three or four years. Through television viewing children may widen their vocabulary and concepts. In certain environments they may imitate an observed adult activity —holding a book or magazine and turning the pages. Children may learn to associate the pictures and hieroglyphics with the words they hear as the adult reads to them. A few children teach themselves to read printed words before they enter the first grade classroom.[1]

The Beginning Reading Stage—Level One

The second stage is that of beginning reading instruction, which in schools today may take place in kindergarten or first or second grade. When all factors concerning individuals are identified and recognized by their teachers, it may be considered defensible and appropriate to begin their reading instruction at any of these levels. Readiness for reading, considered at greater length in Chapter 3, is the keynote to the teacher's decision. Some children are *ready* for reading, writing, and spelling near the end of their kindergarten experience. Other children have demonstrated later reading proficiency when their formal reading instruction was delayed until they were in school for several years. A current problem of concern is a large number of disadvantaged children who show readiness later than the average either because of lack of contact with language or because of other factors. With a trend toward nursery school enrollment in public school systems, children may become more sophisticated in formal school activities to the point that more children will be ready earlier for regular reading instruction. Teachers need to be concerned about individual differences, however, rather than adopt a bandwagon stand that because some children do learn to read early, all children should be taught to read by the time they are five years old. Ilg and Ames [2] have studied the characteristics of young children and have advocated developmental testing as the major clue to each child's readiness for reading instruction.

Initial reading instruction involves the recognition of printed words

[1] Dolores Durkin, *Teaching Them to Read* (New York: Teachers College Press, Columbia University, 1966. 2d ed., Boston: Allyn & Bacon, 1974).
[2] Frances L. Ilg and Louise B. Ames, *School Readiness* (New York: Harper & Row, Publishers, 1964).

and the meanings associated with them. Children typically see picture books first. Some of them have explanatory captions or short sentences. Basic reading series provide picture books and easy-reading books that present simple words with the opportunity to practice reading them over and over for retention and understanding in various contexts. Thus *Mother* may be reading to baby sister, preparing lunch, or shopping in a supermarket. *Baby* sister may be playing with a ball, her pet kitten, or eating an ice-cream cone. The words *Mother* and *Baby* appear in print in simple context and with accompanying picture clues as to context. This may be followed with an action word: Mother *cooks* and Baby *plays*. In another picture *Baby* may *help Mother* as she cooks. These are familiar situations to the beginning reader, who now encounters another dimension to his or her language growth—that of deciphering the printed word. Beginning readers may at the same time be writing words they are learning to recognize in print. The processes of decoding (reading) and encoding (writing) are parts of their initial experience in learning to read.

The Initial Stage of Independent Reading—Level Two

A third stage is begun, usually in the first, second, or third grades, again dependent upon the teacher's skill in determining the optimum period for individuals. This is the initiation of independence in reading, when a child can begin to decipher the seemingly unknown printed word on the page. Children are ready to do this when they know words as words and can see likenesses and differences in whole words and in parts of words. Structural and phonetic analysis are techniques that teachers provide at this stage of reading. Children learn parts of words as in *look ing, un hap py.* They listen while looking at initial consonants: *t* ake, *t* eacher, *t* all; they listen while changing *take* to m*ake,* m*ake* to sh*ake,* and so on. Such directed practice prepares the student for doing independent reading in the many supplementary materials and library books provided in classrooms today at every level. (See Chapter 11.)

The Transition Stage—Levels Three and Early Fourth

The fourth stage in reading may occur in grades two, three, or four, as children encounter more reading material in content areas and in the supplementary reading they do by themselves. They need the help of the teacher to break the step between decoding and comprehending the more complex ideas found in their higher level reading. Reading for ideas, in meaningful thought units, will need to be stressed. Teachers need to emphasize the technique of reading a short section silently to find answers to the questions, "Who, what, where, when, why, and how?" (See Chapter 6 for study skills.)

The Intermediate or Low Maturity Stage—Levels Four to Six

The fifth stage has been labeled the low-maturity stage by David Russell.[3] He characterizes this stage as a slow but steady growth in all phases of reading, usually occurring in the intermediate grades, four through six. Children may sharpen their study skills of skimming, reading for main ideas or details, and becoming critical readers. Their comprehension skills become more advanced as they delve into a wider range of reading materials. Teachers need to have available a wide variety of reading materials so that children get a broad background of experience in reading for information, enrichment, and enjoyment.

The Advanced Stage of Reading—Levels Seven and Up

The sixth stage is reached when students, usually in the secondary grades of junior and senior high school, begin to exhibit the characteristics of the mature reader, as delineated by Bond and Tinker.[4] They considered the hallmarks of a good or mature reader to be mastery of word identification techniques, extensive meaning vocabulary, effective comprehension, proficiency in study skills, varied reading interests and tastes, and the acquisition of the foundations for learning the higher level skills needed in secondary school reading.

ILLUSTRATIVE DEVELOPMENTAL CHARTS

The "Child Development Chart" (see Figure 1) represents a composite report of the psychologist and the reading specialist as to the characteristics of children and implications for their reading growth. Teachers can study the chart to learn more about the general characteristics of children in the age range of a particular classroom. Six-year-olds are very active; they like to talk, ask many questions about their immediate environment, and are interested in themselves. They will show an interest in books read *to* them and in pictures. The teacher, however, will find that some six-year-olds also study the captions under pictures, ask, "What's this word?" or happily state, "I can read that." Samples of appropriate books are suggested as the beginning of a list that teachers can compile as they study the interests and abilities of children in their classrooms.

---

[3] David H. Russell, "Reading and Child Development," *Reading in the Elementary School*, Forty-eighth NSSE Yearbook, Part 2 (Chicago: The University of Chicago Press, 1949), pp. 21–22.
[4] Guy L. Bond and Miles B. Tinker, *Reading Difficulties: Their Diagnosis and Correction* (New York: Appleton-Century-Crofts, 1967), p. 39.

Figure 1. Child Development Chart from Birth Through Sixteen Years

---

UP TO THREE YEARS

Physical Characteristics

Rapid gains in weight and height; walks; has 20 teeth

"As a Person"

Very active, exploring his or her environment; plays beside peers

Interests

Immediate environment, himself or herself, parents, some adults, some dramatic plays, oral expression, large muscle activities

His or Her Language Growth

Begins at years 1–2 to say simple words and adds to his or her vocabulary; sometimes speaks in short sentences, understands more than he or she can say

His or Her Reading Growth

Attentive to alliteration; will imitate language heard; like rhymes, likes to listen to stories; will imitate adults' reading habits

Samples of Appropriate Books

Picture books; books that adults can read *to* children:
P. Eastman, *Are You My Mother?*
L. Lenski, *Police Small*
J. Wolff, *Let's Imagine Sounds*
M. Anno, *Anno's Alphabet*

3–5 YEARS

Physical Characteristics

Runs, jumps, climbs, increasingly good coordination

"As a Person"

Cooperative, curious, imaginative, talkative; plays well alone; imitates adults in his or her play

Interests

Immediate environment, himself or herself, parents, some adults, some dramatic plays, oral expression, large muscle activities

His or Her Language Growth

Uses short sentences; tells many stories; asks, "How?" and "Why?"

His or Her Reading Growth

Likes to listen to fanciful, imaginative stories; likes stories that explain the how and why of his or her environment

Figure 1. Child Development Chart from Birth Through Sixteen Years (cont.)

Samples of Appropriate Books

   M. Ets, *Play with Me*
   M. Frisky, *Seven Diving Ducks*
   M. Brown, *The Runaway Bunny*
   L. Fatio, *The Happy Lion's Rabbits*
   T. Tobias, *We're Moving Soon*

AGES 6, 7, 8

Physical Characteristics

   Complete brain size attained; 6-year molars appear; likely to have childhood communicable diseases

"As a Person"

   Active, short attention span; enjoys group play; is competitive

Interests

   Wider interest in environment, community helpers, science

His or Her Language Growth

   Lively conversationalist; asks many questions

His or Her Reading Growth

   Likes adventure stories; continues to like stories of how and why; begins to read on his or her own

Samples of Appropriate Books

   C. Greene, *I Want to Be a Cowboy*
   K. Kuskin, *Just Like Everyone Else*
   M. Rey, *Curious George Flies a Kite*
   E. Keats, *Peter's Chair*

AGES 9–11

Physical Characteristics

   Permanent teeth continue to appear; growth spurt in girls usually appears

"As a Person"

   Is a hero-worshiper; belongs to a gang, Boy Scouts, Girl Scouts; curious about the past and present world and outer space; able to see cause-effect relationships

Interests

   Youth of famous people, adventure, humor, mystery, fairy tales, boys or girls like themselves

Figure 1. Child Development Chart from Birth Through Sixteen Years (cont.)

His or Her Language Growth

Uses slang

His or Her Reading Growth

Mechanics, natural science, and history appeal; begins to enjoy reading biography

Samples of Appropriate Books

J. Blume, *Are you There, God? It's Me, Margaret.*
B. Byfield, *The Haunted Tower*
R. Godden, *Mouse-Wife*
I. and E. D'Aulaire, *Abraham Lincoln*
P. Parish, *Good Work, Amelia Bedelia*
H. Holling, *Paddle-to-the-Sea*
M. Sasek, *This Is Cape Kennedy*

AGES 12–13

Physical Characteristics

Growth spurt in boys usually begins; 24–26 permanent teeth

"As a Person"

Easily embarrassed; girls tend to become spectators—boys, to participate in sports

Interests

Vocational interests, searching for ideals, need for security (family, money, vacations)

His Language Growth

Can discuss abstract ideas—honesty, justice, religion

His Reading Growth

Interested in reading about sports, idealism, religion; peak time for free reading

Samples of Appropriate Books

A. Kelliher, *Life and Growth*
J. Stuart, *The Thread That Runs So True*
E. Forbes, *Johnny Tremain*
P. Green, *Nantucket Summer*
F. Holman, *Slake's Limbo*
A. N. Clark, *All This Wild Land*
G. Goldreich, *Season of Discovery*
S. O'Dell, *The 290*

Figure 1. Child Development Chart from Birth Through Sixteen Years (cont.)

AGES 14–16

Physical Characteristics

Boy's voice deepens; girls usually achieve maximum growth; all permanent teeth, except wisdom teeth

"As a Person"

Concerned about future and life work; self-questioning; wants approval of peers; self-conscious; interested in opposite sex

Interests

Wide and varied; boys and girls diverge in interests

His Language Growth

Argumentative; exaggerates; says what is on his or her mind; can discuss problems with adults

His Reading Growth

Girls interested in reading about romance—boys, sports; boys active, usually with little time or patience for extra reading

Samples of Appropriate Books

S. E. Hinton, *That Was Then, This Is Now*
A. E. Maxwell and I. Ruud, *The Year-Long Day*
I. Noble, *Mahmud's Story*
S. O'Dell, *Carlota*

In the upper grades a study of the individual child and a comparison with the charts will give teachers an indication of his or her development relative to these norms. Children may have interest or social levels considerably below or above what might be expected from a look at their chronological age. Teachers, therefore, may capitalize on known interests (after administering an interest inventory) and upon known reading levels (after administering an informal reading inventory). Both textbooks and supplementary books may be assigned at appropriate levels when teachers are aware of students' achievement and interests.

A PICTURE OF THE EFFICIENT READER AT EACH LEVEL (LISTS)—A SUMMARY

The checklists in Figure 2 provide a generalized picture of the efficient reader at several stages of his development. The classroom teacher who faces a group at any one of these levels will be able to guide the learning

Figure 2. Characteristics of the Efficient Reader at Several Stages of Reading Development

BEGINNING READING STAGE	INITIAL STAGE OF INDEPENDENT READING	TRANSITIONAL STAGE BETWEEN PRIMARY AND UPPER ELEMENTARY LEVELS

Knows some sight words
Uses phonetic analysis:
  initial consonants and
    vowels
  rhyming endings
  blends parts to make a
    new word
Uses structural analysis:
  some syllables
  some endings
Uses context
  to check word
    meanings
  to learn answers
Uses picture clues
Tells stories with
  obvious relish
"Shares" information
  gained from reading
Demands meaning when
  reading
Shows an interest in
  books
Does some self-selection
  in reading
Beginning to be curious
  about immediate en-
  vironment (commu-
  nity, own culture)
	All Previous Skills
	  PLUS:
	Wants a library card
	Enjoys dramatizing
	  stories
	Begins to satisfy his
	  curiosity through
	  reading on his own:
	    community
	    world
	    science
	    animals
	Begins thoughtful
	  reading:
	  wants to know if
	    story is *fact* or *fiction*
	  wants to know *why* a
	    character acted
	    that way
		All Previous Skills
		  PLUS:
		Identifies self with
		  story characters
		Interested in
		  biographies
		Can be challenged to
		  read critically
		Can appreciate good
		  literary style
		Can locate and
		  read additional
		  information in simple
		  reference materials
		Can read aloud skill-
		  fully for an audience

UPPER ELEMENTARY LEVELS	SECONDARY LEVELS

All Previous Skills
  PLUS:
Maintains a zest for learning through
  reading
Has broadened reading interests
Reads newspapers and magazines
Is resourceful in reading and studying
	Has mastered basic reading skills
	  of word recognition and
	  comprehension
	Readily learns a technical vo-
	  cabulary in a new content area
	Is interested in words and word
	  origins
	Uses effectively an organized
	  study attack such as SQ3R[5]

[5] Francis Robinson, *Effective Study* (New York: Harper & Row, Publishers, 1970).

Figure 2. Characteristics of the Efficient Reader at Several Stages of Reading Development (cont.)

UPPER ELEMENTARY LEVELS	SECONDARY LEVELS
Reads for varying purposes	Can use different rates of reading for various types of reading materials
Notes an author's pattern or style of writing	
Can be guided to comprehend at a level below surface meanings: *Why? How?*	Continues to develop the locational skills involved in reading parts of books and in using library facilities and materials

of his or her pupils most effectively after having assessed the reading levels attained by the individual students in the class. Teachers can (and should) make their assessments through the administration of standardized and informal (teacher-made) reading tests. The informal reading inventory will appraise the strengths and weaknesses of individuals for their age and grade level. These techniques of evaluation are important so that the teacher can plan corrective lessons for some, refer severely retarded readers to reading specialists, plan regular grade-level assignments for others, and guide the best readers to materials appropriate for them.

At the same time, the teacher needs to have a point of reference—a composite picture of the efficient reader he or she is trying to develop. Teachers may ask themselves several questions: Is the performance of Jane unusual for a ten-year-old? In what ways can Tom, promoted as a good reader, be helped to be even more efficient in his reading skills? What can I do with this group of students who read only the class assignments? In what ways do the students in my class compare favorably or unfavorably with the composite picture of the efficient reader at this level? (See Figure 2.)

If the lists from the beginning reading stage through the secondary level are studied as a continuum, the teacher will note that in a single classroom some pupils may be achieving at an initial reading stage whereas others may already be exhibiting the skills of a more mature reader. Thus upper grade teachers may become aware of the need to provide, for *some* pupils, a continuance of systematic instruction in basic reading skills. They may note that others can be guided into the grade-level content textbooks and be expected to achieve with minimum teacher instruction. Teachers may note that a few need help with such study skills as surveying an assignment, outlining, summarizing, or interpretation of an author's viewpoint.

Another teacher may note that Bill, a second grade student, has recently asked if a story he has been reading by himself at the library table

"This was a good book!"

"really happened." He wants to read parts of it to the class to see what they think and to get them to read it, too. Where can he get some more books like this one? Bill's teacher, consulting the lists, will conclude that Bill is well into the initial stage of independent reading, selecting stories interesting to him, satisfying his own curiosity, and wanting to share his discoveries with his classmates. In fact, he is ready for his own library card. Bill is an efficient reader at this level. On the other hand, the same teacher may compare another pupil's reading achievement, in the same second grade class, with the items on the checklists. He may note that Ted works laboriously on sounding out words, takes a long time to complete a sentence, and seldom can explain what he has just "read." He is never found at the library table. Often he has forgotten yesterday's vocabulary terms. Ted's teacher rightly concludes that Ted is making slow progress in the beginning reading stage. He will provide for Ted preprimer and primer reading materials and expect progress at a relatively slow pace even though Ted is sitting in a second grade room.

When the lists for the efficient reader are compared with reading interests and reading materials at each level, it becomes apparent to the teacher that good readers *read.* They take pride in their reading accomplishments at each level. The primary grade reader takes home his or her book to read to parents or siblings. Accomplished readers locate material that will give them answers to satisfy their curiosity or zest for knowledge; they find library books and magazines with stories that appeal to their current interests; they become appreciative of good style and literary quality; they *use* their reading for many purposes that seem worthwhile to them. The label *efficient reader* attests to the fact that *practice makes perfect:* the efficient reader is a good reader because he has put to practice the reading skills he has attained at each level.

In the lists are just a few of the many trade books that may affect the child's value development. Among those that provide children with reading experiences that help foster sensitivity to human relations are

> *Are You My Mother?*
> *Just Like Everyone Else*
> *The Hundred Dresses*
> *The Thread That Runs So True*

In the lists are books that help children develop their creative potential, both through opportunities for dramatization and illustration and through class discussions that promote creative and divergent thinking. The teacher who is familiar with many types of literature and knows the interests and reading level of the individual can give the right book to the child. (See Chapter 8.)

> *Let's Imagine Sounds*
> *Stone Soup*
> *Paddle to the Sea*

SUMMARY

The efficient reader will be the product of a school setting in which teachers understand the complexities of the reading process, have access to a wide variety of appropriate reading materials, and provide satisfying activities that foster the *habit* of reading. Thus the teacher may be assured that the components of a good reading program lead to the successful attainment of educational objectives.

SELECTED READINGS

Arbuthnot, May Hill and Zena Sutherland. *Children and Books.* 4th ed. Chicago, IL: Scott, Foresman and Company, 1972.

Chambers, Dewey W. *Children's Literature in the Curriculum.* Chicago, IL: Rand McNally & Company, 1971.

"Classroom Choices: Children's Trade Books." *The Reading Teacher,* 31,1 (Oct. 1977), 6–23.

Elkins, Deborah. *Teaching Literature Designs for Cognitive Development.* Columbus, OH: Charles E. Merrill Publishing Company, 1976.

Fisher, Margery. *Matters of Fact: Aspects of Non-Fiction for Children.* New York: Thomas Y. Crowell Company, 1972.

Gillespie, Margaret C., and John W. Conner. *Creative Growth Through Literature for Children and Adolescents.* Columbus, OH: Charles E. Merrill Publishing Company, 1975.

Huck, Charlotte S., and Doris Young Kuhn. *Children's Literature in the Elementary School.* 3rd ed. New York: Holt, Rinehart and Winston, 1974.

Ilg, Frances I., and Louise B. Ames. *School Readiness.* New York: Harper & Row, Publishers, 1965.

McCann, Donnarae, and Olga Richard. *The Child's First Book: A Critical Study of Pictures and Texts.* New York: H. W. Wilson Company, 1973.

Root, Shelton L. *Adventuring with Books, 2400 Titles for Pre-K through Grade 8.* 2nd ed. Urbana, IL: National Council of Teachers of English, 1972.

Rosenberg, Judith K. and Kenyon C. *Young People's Literature in Series: Fiction. An Annotated Bibliographical Guide.* Littleton, CO: Libraries Unlimited, 1973.

Sebesta, Sam L., and William J. Iverson. *Literature for Thursday's Child.* Chicago, IL: Science Research Associates, Inc., 1975.

Sloan, Glenna Davis. *The Child as Critic: Teaching Literature in the Elementary School.* New York: Teachers College Press, 1975.

Smith, Dora V. "Children's Literature Today." *Elementary English* (Oct. 1970), 777–80.

Part Two

Skills of Reading

(Instructional Process)

Chapter 3

Readiness
for
Reading

OBJECTIVES

To know the readiness factors that lead up to
children's success in reading

To know the factors that affect the child's
readiness for reading

To develop acquaintance with readiness
methodology and materials

To know some strategies for appraisal of
readiness for reading

INTRODUCTION

Those who operate a travel agency have observed that people as travelers
may be divided into several categories. Some who come to the travel desk
are ready to depart by the shortest, fastest route—via jet plane. Some are
ready for a more leisurely trip, scanning timetables for a train that allows
stops along the way. Still others are looking for a scenic tour, a much slower
trip on a bus. Some are preoccupied with preparations, outfits, decisions on
alternate routes, vacillating between several possible destinations—they
will not be ready to start out for quite a while. Some seem to listen to the
agent's descriptions, appear vague about understanding the details, and
after several false starts finally take a guided tour that does not take them
far from home.

Certain similarities may be noted between these travelers and children
starting out in school. When we equate the traveler's journey with the attainment of reading proficiency in the school years, we find certain children
who are ready to depart by "jet plane"—they learn to read very soon and
very well. Some take the "train route"—learning to read in seemingly
measured and continuous stages. Several get off to a slow start, progress at

a very slow pace, yet do get to their destination eventually. Others on the "guided tour" are the children who need careful, patient guidance every step of the way, without very high expectations of academic achievement.

For either type of "journey," time is a very important factor. The successful trip begins with adequate time for preparation—learning at the right time, taking the best route for one's purpose, in order to arrive in good time at the destination. Each child needs his or her own timetable for the trip through school. For each there is the right time to start, a certain amount of time needed for the whole trip, and an estimate of the time when he or she will arrive at his or her destination.

Thus the individual's readiness to start becomes of basic concern to the educator. When should Tom start school? When should he start formal reading instruction? When will he be ready to *succeed* in school and in learning to read? Unfortunately for the educator, there is no single answer to the time question. Too many factors affect the answer. Tom is found to be different from Bill and Mary and Ann in many ways. Research has shown that a child at any one point will differ from others in various aspects that can be measured. These include physical, mental, social, emotional, linguistic, experiential, environmental, sensory, and motor levels of maturity. Any of these factors may contribute to the amount of readiness or lack of readiness a child may experience when faced with school tasks, such as reading.

KEYS TO READINESS

The prospective teacher who examines the reams of literature on readiness, especially readiness for reading, will find that through the years many educators, psychologists, school administrators, and parents have been in disagreement. They have not always agreed on their definitions of readiness and on their subsequent establishment of criteria for admission to school programs.

Definitions

In general, readiness may be defined as a state of preparedness for a task at hand. This state involves the whole individual, his (or her) maturity in terms of his chronological and mental age, his physical and neurological development (health, vision, hearing, and motor-sensory) and his emotional status. Deficits in any of these areas might prevent successful initiation of the new task with subsequent low achievement in the desired terminal behavior. When the new task of children is learning to read, it is important that all of the factors that will affect their achievement are operating in their favor. Prediction of successful achievement on the basis of only one of the factors ignores the possibility of deficits in other areas.

Readiness for reading is an educational concept closely related to children's readiness for learning—their physical well-being, interests, curiosity, memory, and so on. Readiness for reading is a psychological concept when it is viewed in its relationship to children's maturity—their mental maturity, their current level of ability to use their personal background of experience with language and with sensory-motor, perceptual, and cognitive processes. Readiness for reading is a linguistic concept when it is viewed in its relationship to the tasks involved in the reading process, in the encoding and decoding of language symbols.

The interrelationship of these various concepts of reading readiness becomes apparent as teachers study individual children when they first enter school. John returns from a trip with his classmates to the nearby firehouse eager to talk about everything he saw. He contributes details from memory to the teacher's experience chart. He volunteers to participate in the construction of a miniature fire station in a corner of the classroom. He tells the class that his father will bring wood and wheels and paint so that the class can make a "real fire engine." He finds several books on fire engines on the school's library shelves and asks the teacher to "read these books to us" in story time. Bob returns from the same trip and goes straight to the sandbox. He takes no interest in the discussion and looks glassy-eyed when the teacher calls on him for a response to a question on what he remembered or liked about the day's trip. A one-word response is his best contribution—"engines."

When the children cluster around the experience chart the next day, the teacher will have an immediate indication of the reading readiness of both John and Bob. Neither child can *read,* yet one will recognize the chart as a memory clue to an interesting trip. The other will see meaningless hieroglyphics, which remain a puzzle even when several classmates talk glibly about yesterday's trip to the firehouse. John will be ready for formal reading instruction sooner than Bob—as indicated by his language fluency, his interest in his environment, his assurance of his father's cooperation in workshop activities, his knowledge that books contain further information, his demonstrated memory for details, and his awareness that his teacher's chart-writing is "our talk written down."

Chronological Age

In the decades of the twenties and thirties a common cause attributed to poor success in learning to read in first grade was lack of readiness, synonymous with immaturity. It was suggested that "time would heal all." The

Ready for reading

viewpoint of those in the Progressive Education movement was that "the educational environment facilitates development best by providing a maximally permissive field that does not interfere with the predetermined process of spontaneous maturation." [1] Such a laissez-faire attitude led some educators to view readiness as merely a period of time elapsing before learning to read "set in." In the intervening decades the child's birthday has been considered by some as the one key to his or her readiness for reading. Six became a magical number.

Beginning teachers will find that their school system in its philosophy and in its establishment of standards may differ from neighboring communities. Across the nation are cities with preschool and kindergarten classes, whereas other cities have neither. A common requirement for entrance to first grade is the attainment of a certain chronological age, varying usually from five and one-half to six years. In some cities age is the only criterion. Thus, one key to readiness has been established in these school systems. Because first grade has been associated traditionally with the initiation of reading instruction, it is obvious that chronological age has been assumed to be the best criterion for readiness. In the judgment of certain schools, then, all boys and girls at age six are ready to learn to read.

Not only local systems but also most of the states have established entrance requirements based upon chronological age. Currently, children may be as young as five years and seven months to six years of age at the

---

[1] David P. Ausubel, "Learning by Discovery: Rationale and Mystique," *Bulletin of the National Association of Secondary-School Principals,* **XLV**:18–58 (Dec. 1961).

time they enter first grade in all but the seventeen states that have no set policy.[2]

When the one key to admission to first grade and the first grade reading program is age, there will be problems for some children. In a letter published by a New Haven newspaper, a discerning parent posed one of these problems related to the children who are *not* ready, regardless of chronological age:

> Dear Doctor:
>
> We recently moved to this state. And I learned immediately from well-meaning friends that my son Tabor, who will be six in December, is eligible for first grade. I was completely taken aback as he would not have been eligible in our home state and I have never considered a five and one-half year-old ready for the work of first grade.
>
> I couldn't bring myself to register him for the first grade, even though all our friends and neighbors urged it. Instead I started him in kindergarten. To begin with, Tabor is not ready for a full day of school. And in the second place, he is still very babyish. He still enjoys a two-hour nap each afternoon. Still likes to sit on my lap. Is just beginning to show an interest in coloring and cutting out, and his interest span is very short.
>
> I don't mean to imply that my boy is not real bright because he is— bright but babyish. But what have I to lose by waiting? Next year will be quite soon enough for him to go to school all day and to cope with the pressures which first grade brings.

Dr. Louise B. Ames, from the Gesell Institute of Child Development, answered the parent as follows:

> Go to the head of the class, Mother. Your good letter needs no elaboration from us. Would that the day might come soon when all mothers see things as you do and no babyish nap-taking little five-year-old boy is forced to attempt the work of first grade, regardless of what antiquated state and local laws may permit.[3]

This parent has noted facts that some educators and psychologists have been stressing for years. Age alone will not guarantee a child's successful trip through a first grade reading program. *Babyish* is the term the mother used. *Immature* with all its ramifications would be the synonym used by the psychologist and educator. Tabor physically was not ready for a full day—he needed his two-hour afternoon nap. His interest in such school tasks as coloring and cutting would fit him for kindergarten, not formal reading instruction. His short interest span is typical of younger children. His mother's comment that Tabor is a bright boy may go unchallenged (if unproved). His potentiality or capability may be assessed

[2] Frances L. Ilg and Louise B. Ames, *School Readiness* (New York: Harper & Row Publishers, 1964), p. 16.

[3] *New Haven Register,* September 11, 1968.

but will not provide the *one key* to his readiness (as some schools have hoped!).

Mental Age

The influence of mental age in learning to read was studied during the twenties and thirties. The use of intelligence tests [4] led researchers to conclude that a minimum mental age of six years or six and one-half years was a prerequisite to learning to read successfully. Schools began postponing the start of reading instruction. Gates[5] pointed out that the mental age of the pupils was not as important as the methods and materials used to teach them. Through the use of one method a child of five could learn to read; a second child with a mental age of seven might fail when taught by another method. As early as 1937, Gates suggested that teachers use individualized, self-diagnostic materials that could fit the capabilities of individual pupils. Many educators today have reached the same conclusion.

The criterion used by some school systems as the one key to readiness has been the child's intelligence or his or her capability for learning. Some schools have based their predictions concerning children's reading achievement on the administration of a test of intelligence. Those with high scores were expected to do well in reading in grade one, whereas those who scored lowest were considered poor risks, possibly in need of another year of kindergarten, or predicted as failures at the end of grade one. Although a better-than-average relationship has been found generally between intelligence and first grade reading achievement, intelligence has not proved to be the *one key* to predicting reading readiness. Boys and girls with similar scores on intelligence tests do not always achieve at the same level—sometimes because of different interests, or because of physical, emotional, or environmental differences. A high rating on intelligence has not guaranteed a high level of reading achievement—various other factors again act to affect the individual's achievement.

Preschool Reading

Not all children are too immature to get an early start in reading. Another indication of the ways that children may differ as individuals can be found in studies of children who were reading before they entered school. Reports

---

[4] Grace Arthur, "A Quantitative Study of the Results of Grouping First Grade Classes According to Mental Age," *The Journal of Educational Research*, 12:184 (Oct. 1925); Mabel V. Morphett and Carleton Washburne, "When Should Children Begin to Read?" *The Elementary School Journal*, 31:496–503 (March 1931).
[5] Arthur I. Gates, "The Necessary Mental Age for Beginning Reading," *The Elementary School Journal*, 37:497–508 (March 1937).

published by Dolores Durkin and others [6] attest to the fact that some children have learned to read at home or in school at an early age.

Durkin had studied children who were early readers, in California and in New York. She noted that at age four these children had begun to show an interest in written language and in learning to print, as well as in listening to stories and talking about them. She designed a prefirst grade program based upon her studies of the ways children had learned to read at home. She later reported [7] the reading achievement of the forty children who participated in the two-year, prefirst grade language arts program in which writing and reading were taught. She followed the progress of the children through the first four years of elementary school and found that their achievement each year exceeded that of the control group. However, each year the gap between the two groups narrowed. In her concluding statements, Durkin urged schools that provide an early start in reading to alter the reading program for the participating children in later school years. She suggested further research, preferably with children selected because of their interest in writing and reading. She also noted that reports of the success of some children in prereading programs should not cause schools to introduce reading instruction in kindergarten for all children. The criterion for such inclusion should be the child's "enjoyment and greater self-esteem."

Aware that a number of children had learned to read before first grade without instruction, Denver considered a planned instructional reading program in the kindergarten. McKee and Harrison developed beginning reading materials for use with whole classes of kindergarteners. Major findings were as follows: (1) large groups of average kindergarten children can profit from beginning reading instruction; (2) they do not forget what they have learned over the summer vacation; and (3) if the early readers are to maintain their achievement lead over nonearly readers, they must receive an adjusted program in the subsequent grades.

In the Denver project the aid of parents was enlisted to teach their children prereading skills. The parents received instruction via television. The program, "Preparing Your Child for Reading," was developed for Houghton Mifflin by McKee and Harrison.[8] The parents were encouraged to read to their children often. The gains made by the children reflected the amount of time their parents spent in helping them.

[6] Dolores Durkin, *Children Who Read Early* (New York: Teachers College Press, Columbia University, 1966); Susan Gray and Robert Klaus, "The Early Training Project: A Seventh-Year Report," *Child Development,* 41:909–24 (Dec. 1970); Ethel M. King and Doris Friesen, "Children Who Read in Kindergarten," *Alberta Journal of Educational Research,* 18:147–161 (Sept. 1972).
[7] Dolores Durkin, "A Six-Year Study of Children Who Learned to Read in School at the Age of Four," *Reading Research Quarterly,* X,1:9–60 (1974–75).
[8] Anastasia McManus, "The Denver Prereading Project Conducted by WENH-TV," *The Reading Teacher.* 18:22–26 (Oct. 1964).

Sutton reported the findings of a longitudinal study of children who learned to read in kindergarten. Interested kindergarteners were free to choose reading activities and to receive initial reading instruction. The resulting early reading advantage attained by some children continued and increased as they progressed through the primary grades.[9]

That oral language is of prime importance to the young disadvantaged, linguistically different child was pointed out by Martin and Castaneda.[10] Disadvantaged children need to be able to attach meanings orally to objects and experiences. Their ability to express their ideas in writing lags behind their speaking ability. The linguistic and cultural needs of the children must be understood by the teacher who can make oral language a stepping-stone to reading in a program of total language development. The abstract quality of reading and writing poses problems that teachers can tackle by labeling objects in the room. They can record the stories told by the children. When parents and teachers read aloud to the children, they instill a love of reading and a positive attitude toward reading. Martin and Castaneda see the "readiness for reading" program for the disadvantaged as the provision of opportunities for interaction with their environment, for building oral language, and for acquiring a positive attitude toward reading.

Stanchfield[11] reported a study of kindergarten children of varying ethnic backgrounds (Black, Mexican-American, and "other Whites") involved in a structured program designed to teach prereading skills. The six major skills that were developed by the teachers of the experimental curriculum were listening for comprehension of content, listening for auditory discrimination and development, visual discrimination, oral language skills, motor-perceptual development, and sound-symbol correspondence. The Murphy-Durrell Reading Readiness Analysis was given to the experimental and control classes at the end of the school year. The experimental groups scored higher than the control groups, which had regular kindergarten experiences. Stanchfield concluded that a structured, sequential program with appropriate materials can make a significant difference in a readiness program.

As part of the CRAFT (Comparing Reading Approaches in First Grade Teaching) Project, early readers were identified among disadvantaged Blacks as being able to read one or more words in print.[12] These early read-

[9] Marjorie H. Sutton, "Children Who Learned to Read in Kindergarten: A Longitudinal Study," *The Reading Teacher,* 22:595–602 (April 1969).

[10] Clyde Martin and Alberta Castaneda, "Nursery School and Kindergarten," in *Reading for the Disadvantaged,* Thomas Horn, ed. (New York: Harcourt, Brace Jovanovich, Inc. 1970).

[11] Jo M. Stanchfield, "Development of Prereading Skills in an Experimental Kindergarten Program," *The Reading Teacher,* 24:699–707 (May 1971).

[12] Coleman Morrison, Albert J. Harris, and Irma T. Auerback, "The Reading Performance of Disadvantaged Early and Non-Early Readers from Grades One Through Three," *The Journal of Educational Research,* 65:23–26 (Sept. 1971).

ing children were superior in reading readiness at the beginning of first grade and continued to lead for the three years of the study, regardless of the method by which they were taught.

A committee [13] with representatives from several professional organizations reported their concerns about present practices in prefirst grade reading instruction and made recommendations for improvement. Their recommendations included the provision of reading experiences integrated with the communication programs of listening, speaking, and writing; success experiences in communication; evaluative procedures in line with program objectives; the use of the child's own language; adequate preparation of teachers in the language arts; and the encouragement of language learning in the home.

The Will to Learn

The reader is reminded of the basic principles of learning posed by psychologists to analyze the pattern of learning. The general principles are initial motivation or readiness, multiple response, reinforcement, and repetition. For the present section, we might examine further the first of these principles. Why does the child try to learn? When can the teacher get him to learn? The answers lie in the child's desire to learn the task at hand. He or she must be motivated to want to try.

The will to learn has certain factors that appear to be intrinsic motives for learning. Curiosity, the drive to achieve competence, the need for a sense of accomplishment, the striving for identification with individuals and one's society, and the need for social reciprocity (responding to and operating with others)—all become part of a driving force to learn.

When the teacher considers these factors for their relationship to initial reading instruction he may well ask himself, "Which children will have experienced these driving forces?" Other factors can alter the situation for various individuals—their age, sex, intelligence, personality, interests, environment, and so on. An intelligent boy of six may show curiosity in his father's workshop, desire to identify with his father, wish to become competent in taking a motor apart, thus earning his father's approbation. He will be learning about motors at an early age. An intelligent girl of six may show curiosity about books, desire to identify with her mother who reads magazines and books, wish to become competent in reading and earn her mother's approval. She will learn to read at an early age because she has the will to learn. In these two different learning situations each child is *ready* for other parts of the pattern of learning—multiple response, reinforcement, and repetition. The boy will go through a period of trial and error, noting what

[13] "Reading and Pre-First Grade." *The Reading Teacher,* 30:7:780–81 (April 1977).

happens when he is right or wrong, and will do these many times before he understands a motor. The girl will puzzle over letters and words that seem similar, try out words in context, and read many books before she is an accomplished reader. Yet neither would attain their own objectives without the personal will to learn—the initial readiness for the task at hand.

The Teacher's Role

Teachers should examine their own role in the readiness process. They will need to provide situations in which each child can satisfy his own curiosity—experience the satisfaction of exploring some segment of his environment without adult criticism or restrictions. Teachers can provide tasks that the child can master, assuring the child of the necessary sense of competence and accomplishment. The teacher can be a model for the children to imitate and to interact with and can provide other models for identification, real ones—such as community helpers who come in to the class, and book-type models, such as historical heroes and adventurers. Teachers can set the stage for their own main objective—the children's reading readiness—by reading to the children at every opportunity—labels, captions, and *books*. They must provide the readiness situation, so that each child will be motivated to want to try to read.

At this point it should be noted that some children enter school each year already reading.[14] Their motivation apparently existed in their preschool environment—perhaps an insatiable curiosity, a reading model, or a driving need to be like others around them. For these children the teacher's task is to provide reinforcement and practice of the reading skills in appropriate and interesting books. Other children arrive in the classroom from impoverished backgrounds where no one reads, few words are interchanged, and no model or hero-to-emulate has appeared on their horizons. For these children the teacher's task is to provide many opportunities for exploring, listening, interacting, and gaining some competencies they themselves recognize as such. Thus they will eventually arrive at a point where they will want to try to read—their personal readiness for reading instruction.

In the Harvard report on elementary school reading practices, Austin and Morrison[15] noted that among school systems across the country extremely varied criteria were being utilized to determine children's beginning the formal reading program. These criteria were mental maturity, auditory and visual perceptual abilities, physical condition, linguistic ability, emotional and social maturity, reading readiness tests, interest in reading, and chronological age. When combinations of these factors were considered,

[14] Dolores Durkin, *Children Who Read Early* (New York: Teachers College Press, Columbia University, 1966).
[15] Mary C. Austin and Coleman Morrison, *The First R* (New York: The Macmillan Company, 1963), pp. 263–64.

teachers found that variations among children's readiness for learning were more apt to be determined. Adjustments could be made for their initial reading instruction.

RESEARCH IMPLICATIONS

That recent research on reading readiness may have implications for teachers of kindergarten and first grade was pointed out by Rupley.[16] He suggested that practices supported by research findings may improve reading readiness programs. Among the research findings of the seventies that he reported were (1) the identification of such prerequisites to reading instruction as language development and verbal meanings, as well as the skills of perception, attending, listening, and thinking; and (2) the influence of home environment on the level of the child's reading readiness: educational television and parents' criteria for program selection, materials available in the home, and questions prepared for the parent-child's reading. Results of the studies indicated the significance for reading readiness and beginning reading of home environment, parents' participation in guided preschool instruction, and parents' use of packaged materials for teaching the preschool child.

Rosner [17] pointed out that the level of competency of children's perceptual skills can affect children's reading. He defined the perceptual skills as the skills that help a child identify and analyze spatial and acoustical patterns. It is important to determine the adequacy of the child's perceptual skills in order to fit the instructional program to the individual. The beginning reading program may require certain basic skills that some children have not acquired. It is possible to select a program that suits the modality preference of the child. It is also possible to modify the instructional program to make it compatible with each student's perceptual skills. Children with competent auditory perceptual skills can analyze spoken words into their individual sounds, thus noting by themselves many of the sound-symbol relationships of words-in-print that they have heard in conversation. The child with competent visual perception will be able to attack a line of print by fixating on one place, then moving his or her eyes in a jerky movement called a *saccade,* and then going on to the next fixation. With facility in spatial analysis the child will learn letters and will note both letters and words in the line of print. Some children exhibit substandard visual and/or auditory perceptual skills. They may see only a disordered array of elements on the printed page. They cannot analyze the words they hear into structural elements.

[16] William H. Rupley, "Reading Readiness Research: Implications for Instructional Practices," *The Reading Teacher,* 30,4:450–453 (Jan. 1977).
[17] Jerome Rosner, "Adapting Primary Grade Reading Instruction to Individual Differences in Perceptual Skills," *Reading World,* 14,4:293–307 (May 1975).

Rosner made specific suggestions to help teachers adapt to deficits in visual and auditory perceptual skills. For visual perceptual skills deficits, Rosner suggested that teachers begin with capital letters; add a cue, such as a line or color, to one of the two confusing letters such as *b* and *d;* use a system with a minimum number of diacritical marks; have the student use tracing techniques with certain letters; remind the student to start reading at the side of the page where the teacher has drawn a colored vertical line on the left-hand side; and ask direct questions that will help the student to see the story as a series of events.

For auditory perceptual deficits he made several useful suggestions. Teachers should introduce a structured phonics program with only a few sounds at first. Diacritical markings, as of short vowels and key words (ăpple, ĕskimo, and so on), help the student to recall sounds. The students who have satisfactory visual skills could be given an i.t.a. program. The students should watch the lips of the speaker and repeat what they have heard. Their comprehension will be aided when they reread a sentence as a whole after they have decoded the words.

Hall [18] suggested that prereading activities geared for general development of readiness do not ensure a foundation for learning to read. Instead, a reading situation should be considered more appropriate, with activities that involve printed language. Language experience materials that are written expose children to letters, words, and phrases. To be effective, prereading instruction should include experiences with printed language.

Blair [19] suggested that the prepared environment of Montessori techniques can be useful in readiness programs at kindergarten and grade one levels. Teachers would find valuable the Montessori philosophy of freedom for self-development, freedom of choice for the child, and self-motivation. The modern classroom, equipment, and materials could be geared to the developmental tasks of the Montessori classroom. Kindergartens and first grades would have lightweight furniture scaled to the children; wooden puzzles such as interlocking trees, letters, animals; vests with fasteners such as buttons, snaps, or bows; wooden latch frames to be opened and closed; and colored wooden blocks to teach visual sequencing, matching colors, and matching forms. In an informal setting, such as the open space organization, the child may work individually with many of these materials.

Jean Piaget identified four periods in the stage of cognitive development, as described at the beginning of Chapter 2. Cox [20] tested her hypothesis that some children of six and seven have had trouble with reading

---

[18] Maryanne Hall, "Prereading Instruction: Teach for the Task," *Reading Teacher,* 30,1:7–9 (Oct. 1976).
[19] Susan M Blair, "Montessori Materials for Today's Kindergarten," *The Reading Instruction Journal,* 20,1:4, 10 (Nov. 1976).
[20] Mary B. Cox, "The Effect of Conservation Ability on Reading Competency," *Reading Teacher,* 30,3:251–258 (Dec. 1976).

because they were still at the preoperational stage postulated by Piaget. She reported that the results of her study showed that the child who could not conserve and was at the preoperational level had more difficulty in learning to read than the child who could conserve. Six Piagetian conservation tasks of number, area, weight, mass, volume, and length were administered to children ages seven to twelve. An example was the test of conservation of volume. The amounts of water in two identical containers were noted to be the same. When the water from one container was poured into a tall, thin container, the preoperational child stated that there was more water in the tall container than in the remaining container. Another task was conservation of mass. When one of two identical balls of clay was rolled into a snake, the child who noted that the amount remained the same was credited with conservation of mass and was considered, for this task, to have reached the concrete operations stage. Cox suggested that a longitudinal study be made to determine whether conservation at the first grade can be used to predict reading skills at the second grade level. Administering the Piagetian tasks would provide the teacher with information that would show which children were still in the preoperations stage and which had reached the concrete stage of thought. Thus the teacher would have an indication of the child's cognitive status, one of the factors involved in readiness for reading skills.

New research on conservation and reading may affect both the sequence and the methods of teaching beginning reading. To date, it has been suggested that it is useless to attempt to teach reading to a child before he or she has learned to conserve. After a child has acquired developmental competencies, he or she may learn by varied types of instruction. Roberts [21] reported that recent studies on conservation and reading showed a high relationship between conservation ability and reading readiness and also between conservation and reading skills. She reviewed studies that showed that the ability to conserve can be taught. In her conclusions, Roberts indicated that in an individualized program at kindergarten and first grade level certain children might be introduced to reading with initial instruction, using concrete object words and going on to abstract words, according to each child's developmental level.

Several studies [22] in the 1970s supported the theory that initial instruction that favored the preferred modality (visual, auditory, kinesthetic)

[21] Kathleen P. Roberts, "Piaget's Theory of Conservation and Reading Readiness," *The Reading Teacher,* 30,3:246–250 (Dec. 1976).
[22] Patricia N. Daniel and Robert S. Tacker, "Preferred Modality of Stimulus Input and Memory for CVC Triagrams," *The Journal of Educational Research,* 67:255–58 (1974); T. Meehan, "Informal Modality Inventory," *Elementary English,* 51:901–904 (1974); Joseph M. Wepman, "Modalities and Learning," in *Coordinating Reading Instruction,* Helen M. Robinson, ed. (Glenview, IL: Scott, Foresman and Company, 1971), pp. 55–60.

of the individual would correlate with his or her reading achievement. These studies appeared to indicate that teachers should match initial reading methods with the child's preferred sensory modality—as, a visual approach with a child who showed a visual learning preference.

Budin [23] reported an example of modality testing in which six children (out of nine who were discovered not to be succeeding in the school's strong phonetic reading program) were found to have a strong visual modality. When the reading program was changed to one with more of visual emphasis than sound-blending, the majority experienced success in reading almost immediately.

Several other studies [24] concluded, however, that modality preference does not appear to affect reading achievement directly. Teachers should, therefore, do their own research to find evidence that the concept of modality preference is or is not important. They need answers to such questions as, "Do very young children profit from instruction geared to their preferred modality?" "When older children have failed to learn to read, should their preferred modality be checked against the method(s) previously used?"

TRANSITIONAL ROOMS

School systems can make adjustments for the many factors that produce the individual differences among children entering school. When identification through tests and observations has been made, children can be assigned to groups or classrooms where their lessons will be geared to their abilities and needs. A typical adaptation for first grade entrants has been the readiness group. Often this has been a small group within the first grade classroom. Teachers provided lessons that included language activities and the pre-reading lessons in the readiness books of the school's basal reading series.

Some schools with kindergartens found that certain children would profit from typical readiness lessons toward the end of the regular kindergarten year. They also noted the extreme immaturity of some children even after a year in kindergarten. Increased attention to the nature of child development, the appearance of more refined techniques for identifying individual differences, and the population explosion—all contributed finally to an awareness by educators that *more* children than previously observed

---

[23] Marilyn Budin, "Preventive Medicine: Modality Testing in Grade One," *The Reading Instruction Journal*, 17,1:19 (Nov. 1973).
[24] Helen M. Robinson, "Visual and Auditory Modalities Related to Methods for Beginning Reading," *Reading Research Quarterly*, VIII:7–39 (1972); D. A. Sabatino and N. Dorfman, "Matching Learner Aptitude to Two Commercial Reading Programs," *Exceptional Children*, 41:85–90 (1974); R. A. Silverston and J. W. Deichmann, "Sense Modality Research and the Acquisition of Reading Skills," *Review of Educational Research*, 45:149–72 (1975).

could use a *longer* period of prereading activities. They needed to find methods for getting these children into the educational stream. One method has been the provision of preprimary or transitional rooms between kindergarten and first grade. These rooms are an indication that differences in individual growth among children are being recognized, which is especially important when children are beginning their education.

In one town a personal growth record was developed by classroom teachers and the school administration for its transitional rooms. See Figure 3. It reflected their agreement on a basic philosophy concerning the objectives and goals for the children selected. With such a record at hand in personal interview sessions, both the teacher and the parent can study the items that reflect academic, emotional, social, and motor growth. They can observe evidences of change in behavior that will give clues to an individual child's personal growth pattern. The subitems outline possibilities for a program with a close relationship to the carefully considered objectives. For example, there are opportunities for children's experiences: listening attentively, contributing to group discussions, assuming responsibility, playing, interacting, participating, sharing, and so on. All of these experiences are developed through the ingenuity of the teacher who is preparing these children this year for the *formal* instruction of the first grade in the following school year. Here the emphasis is on providing for a readiness for successful educational experiences rather than hopefully expecting the same level of achievement from everyone who enters.

When transitional rooms, the preprimary or junior primary rooms as they are sometimes called, were introduced in the public schools of a Midwestern town in the fifties, one teacher [25] was able to follow the progress of the children who had a full year of a readiness program without any formal attempts at reading instruction. When this class, minus the usual few who moved to other cities, completed the sixth grade and entered junior high, their record was studied. Notable were two facts: not one of these children had ever been referred for remedial reading help, and the girl whose academic record put her at the top of the sixth grade class had been a member of the original transitional room. What was the program for the children assigned to this teacher for the transitional year? The teacher started the program with the information given her by the school system's psychological testing department and the children's kindergarten teachers. These were children for whom the prognosis for any achievement in formal reading instruction was extremely unfavorable. They would need at least a full year of prereading experiences. The teacher was, therefore, on her own, because this was a new program, to provide appropriate types of experiences for a very immature group of children. Ruled out at the start were any of the typical readiness materials, such as the prereading workbooks that accompany basal

[25] Miss Gladys Bannister, Erie, Pennsylvania, Public Schools.

Figure 3. *A Sample Personal Growth Record Developed for Children in a Transitional Room*

Developed for Children in a Transitional Room
TRANSITIONAL GRADE

Personal Growth Record of _____

School _____ Year _____

I. ACADEMIC GROWTH	Satis-factory	Improv-ing	Not Ready
1. Participates in experiences which give meaning to numbers.			
2. Recognizes and verbally identifies objects of a class, shape, size, color.			
3. Is able to retell at least one favorite story.			
4. Listens attentively to stories and music.			
5. Contributes to group discussions.			
6. Is aware of sequential order.			
7. Can predict possible story outcomes.			
8. Can discriminate between sound patterns.			
9. Knows the meaning of left and right.			
10. Is able to follow directions.			
11. Is able to observe and retain scientific principles.			
12. Is developing an understanding of his role in a democratic society.			

II. EMOTIONAL GROWTH			
1. Shows confidence in approaching new experiences.			
2. Shows self control.			
3. Accepts suggestions to improve behavior.			
4. Can assume responsibility beyond own needs.			
5. Respects authority.			
6. Shows no anxiety at separation.			

	Satis– factory	Improv- ing	Not Ready

II. EMOTIONAL GROWTH (Continued)

    7. Respects the rights of others.

    8. Displays stable temperament.

    9. Shows awareness for personal safety.

   10. Capable of responding to change in activities.

III. SOCIAL GROWTH

    1. Performs simple classroom chores.

    2. Shows an awareness of, and an adaptation to, a routine schedule.

    3. Plays and interacts freely with others.

    4. Participates in organized games.

    5. Shares materials and toys.

IV. MOTOR GROWTH

    1. Can cut out simple designs with scissors.

    2. Has use of small muscles to color and form letters within prescribed areas.

    3. Puts on outer clothing independently.

    4. Can tie his shoes.

    5. Attempts to put on his rubbers or boots.

    6. Can use large muscles well in rhythmic activities, play, and games.

V. HEALTH

    1. Has the general appearance that suggests good health. Yes ___ No ___

Milford Public Schools

Milford, Connecticut: Devised Cooperatively by Katherine M. Barrett, Assistant Superintendent, Margaret Aquinas, Elementary Principal, Barbara Gaynor, Barbara McKee, Cora Wetmore, Teachers.

reading series. Even picture reading would need to be delayed until later in the school year. These children needed concrete objects to handle, real-life situations to explore and discuss.

Together teacher and children studied their own room, and became acquainted with the teacher and each other and with the initially austere classroom setting. The teacher had wisely put into the room only a few attractive objects. From time to time during that year these were changed or added to, always with appropriate explanations and discussion.

Gradually, short excursions outside the classroom were begun. The teacher carefully prepared the children for their visits—to the principal's office, to the basement where heating and cleaning devices were explained by a cooperating custodian. The regular first grade teachers occasionally invited this group in for displays and story hours. The playground facilities were explored. As a group the children walked around the school block, which housed a fire station, a grocery store, and several multifamily apartment buildings. Later in the school year, with the help of several parents, the group made several trips on a school bus to a restaurant in a downtown department store where they ordered lunch, to a turkey farm, to a regular farm, and to a city park.

The preceding situations provided extensive opportunities for discussion by the children, who were encouraged to question, to react, to explore in any way that occurred to them. Thus language experiences were abundant. Children literally learned to talk, to express themselves. They were encouraged to draw and color on large papers as part of their daily classwork. They selected the drawings they wished to see on the bulletin boards.

They learned numbers in real situations, counting aloud the paper cups into which juice would be poured, the crackers and napkins that would be needed at each table, and so on. Music and body rhythms were part of the daily program, as was physical education—in the classroom and on the playground, because the old school building had no gymnasium.

Activities that would promote readiness were included in the form of activities and games. The children learned the concepts of *left* and *right*—hands, feet, eyes, ears, and so on. *Up* and *down, top* and *bottom, over* and *under, open* and *close,* and countless other concepts were learned through concrete experiences with the objects they manipulated in the room and on the playground. They were taught to listen—to stories, to adult explanations, to peer discussions, to music, and to everyday sounds around them. Their thoughtful reactions to what they heard were encouraged. They listened to directions, simple at first, a sequence later. They learned to *think* or *listen with comprehension,* as the teacher alerted them before the listening experience to a specific detail they were to discover and checked their understanding by good questions *after* listening.

These children completed a full year of vivid, meaningful experiences before they entered the regular first grade. Later their first grade teacher reported that most of this group began their formal reading easily within the first month of the new school year, with only a few who started somewhat later. *All* were reading in an acceptable fashion by June. And, as reported earlier in this section, all whose progress could be followed continued to *read* and *succeed* in their school work. Thus, it can be seen that *in practice* the establishment of such classes is extremely beneficial not only in preventing reading problems but also in providing appropriate educational experiences that lead to success in later grades.

IDENTIFICATION OF READINESS FOR READING

The importance of the careful placement of children in their early school years has been getting more attention recently. Tests and subtests that might have predictive value for later reading success have been investigated. There are available standardized norms based on tests devised to measure visual and auditory perception, discrimination and memory; learning rate; motor coordination; discrimination of symbols, letters, or words, as well as other areas according to the test used. Checklists for the various behaviors denoting readiness have been devised. A developmental schedule that determines readiness in terms of children's behavior has been suggested by Ilg and Ames. They pointed out that the correct placement of children in their first school years, with the initiation of reading instruction *when children are ready,* would lessen the need for remedial reading help in later school years.[26] Ilg and Ames' conclusions from testing many children in kindergarten were that only 30 per cent of the childern were ready for grade one at age six. Some children needed to progress at a slower rate, paced six months to a year behind others. Ilg and Ames considered unfortunate either the requirements of another year in kindergarten or the requirements of typical first grade instruction that would force these children beyond their current developmental status.[27]

Both the school and the parent need to answer a pertinent question at this point: "How can we be sure which children are ready for the formal reading instruction of first grade and which will not succeed if put into a regular first grade?" The answer is so important to each child's education that it cannot be taken lightly. It becomes the schools' responsibility to put into operation evaluative criteria that will select children who need a period of experiences that will make them ready for first grade instruction.

[26] Ilg and Ames, op cit., p. 337.
[27] Ibid., p. 344.

Developmental Appraisal

Ilg and Ames [28] stressed the need for schools to determine the *right* time to start each child's school experience. They felt that any *one key*—such as chronological age, intelligence, or reading readiness tests—fell short of the necessary evaluation of the individual. In their years of experience they discovered that the most effective evaluation was the determination of the child's current developmental level, an age at which he or she behaves as a total organism intellectually, socially, emotionally, and physically. They developed a battery of developmental or behavior tests that can be used at school entrance and/or for determining promotion to succeeding grades.

In the sixties, Ilg and Ames tried out these tests in several Connecticut school districts—Weston, North Haven, and Cheshire. They developed refined measures for making recommendations for the following school year —promoting to a regular first grade, promoting to a preprimary class, or retention in kindergarten. They trained examiners in a series of two-week workshops at the Gesell Institute to become familiar with the tests, procedures, and interpretations. The Gesell developmental appraisals were found to be useful not only at the end of kindergarten for the placement of children, but also at the end of the following year to determine their readiness for the next level.

Other Techniques

Techniques of appraisal have included teacher judgment, informal checklists, standardized reading readiness tests, and preprimary intelligence tests of mental maturity. They have been used singly or collectively to judge the readiness of certain children for formal reading instruction and to make predictions as to the level of reading achievement children will attain at the end of their first or second year in school. Kindergarten teachers, who observe children in varied activities, are in a good position to note evidences of immaturity. They can make reasonably accurate predictions as to which children would be apt to succeed in the next year and which might need more informal activities before beginning abstract reading instruction. Usually, the teachers want their observations augmented with some more objective data—carefully developed checklists as well as psychological testing.

Checklists of readiness are functional when they reflect the school's philosophy, an awareness of developmental characteristics, and the requirements of the formal reading program. Kindergarten teachers, primary grade teachers, elementary supervisors, and principals can develop a readiness checklist that will be useful at the end of kindergarten, before children are placed in the first grade or in the beginning reading levels of the nongraded primary rooms.

[28] Ibid., pp. 376–84.

It takes some eye-hand coordination

Cooperatively they can decide upon broad areas for observation. Under each area they can raise pertinent questions that will alert classroom teachers to relevant behavior on the part of individual children. Examples of broad areas related to children's developmental growth would be such language patterns as are indicated in their speech, their level of vocabulary and sentence usage; their listening habits, mental ability; physical patterns, such as general health, vision, and hearing; social and emotional habits, such as playing or sharing, self-control; educational or work habits, such as interest in books and classroom materials, participating in classroom activities, listening attentively to stories, directions, and so on; and their background of experience, and ability to deal with their environment. Under each category certain items can be developed for specific observation. Examples might be

Speech

Uses baby talk.
Uses short sentences.
Speaks with good command of vocabulary.

Work Habits

Waits for teacher's directions.
Initiates own tasks.
Works independently.

The writer observed a kindergarten teacher who made excellent use of a readiness checklist tacked to a bulletin board near her work table. Between sessions with the children she would make several checks under the names of certain children. She explained that whenever she saw evidences of certain behaviors or a lack of progress in certain habits, she would immediately check the appropriate column for that boy or girl. With this technique she did not need to trust to faulty memory after a busy day with many children. She could begin to identify certain patterns of immaturity or growth in some children. She could plan activities that would help all of the children because she could see their individual needs. At the end of the year she had objective evidence of trends in their behavior patterns. Some children showed positive signs of readiness for the next step in their education. Others showed that they needed an extended period of readiness activities.

Further information concerning children's readiness for formal reading instruction may be gathered by the school through examining the results of standardized tests of readiness and mental maturity. Examples of these tests and the broad areas they attempt to measure are given in Chapter 13. The tests are useful when considered in conjunction with the teachers' judgement based upon carefully gathered observations of individual behavior.

SUMMARY

The last word has not been said concerning reading readiness. As educators learn more about individual differences, they are realizing the importance of adapting prereading instruction as well as beginning reading instruction to the individual. One recent conclusion from research studies has been the recommendation that the teacher understand and accept the children's cultural and language differences. The educator should "accept" children as they are, the language they bring to school, their developmental level, their modality strengths and weaknesses, their interests, and so on. The teacher's role is the adaptation of the instructional program to the child rather than the adaptation of the child to some preconceived readiness program.

In order to provide the best possible initial instruction geared to individual needs, the teacher will need to keep up-to-date by reading the current research, being selective, and trying out the recommendations of research.

SELECTED READINGS

Austin, Mary C., and Coleman Morrison. *The First R.* New York: Macmillan Publishing Co., Inc., 1963.

Bruner, Jerome S. *Toward a Theory of Instruction.* Cambridge, MA: Belknap Press, 1966.

Chall, Jeanne. *Learning to Read: The Great Debate.* New York: McGraw-Hill Book Company, 1967.

Downing, John, and D. V. Thackray. *Reading Readiness.* United Kingdom Reading Association. Newark, DE: International Reading Association, 1971.

Durkin, Dolores. *Children Who Read Early.* New York: Teachers College Press, Columbia University, 1966.

————. *Teaching Them To Read.* 2d ed. Boston: Allyn & Bacon, Inc., 1974.

Furth, Hans G., and Harry Wachs. *Piaget's Theory in Practice: Thinking Goes to School.* New York: Oxford University Press, 1974.

Gates, Arthur I. "The Necessary Mental Age for Beginning Reading." *The Elementary School Journal,* 37, (March 1937), 497–508.

Hillerich, Robert L. *Reading Fundamentals for Preschool and Primary Children.* Columbus, OH: Charles E. Merrill Publishing Company, 1977.

Horn, Thomas D., ed. *Reading for the Disadvantaged: Problems of Linguistically Different Learners.* New York: Harcourt, Brace Jovanovich Inc., 1970.

Ilg, Frances, and Louise Ames. *Reading Readiness.* New York: Harper & Row, Publishers, 1965.

Jansky, Jeanette, and Katrina de Hirsch. *Preventing Reading Failure: Prediction, Diagnosis, Intervention.* New York: Harper & Row, Publishers, 1972.

Kirkland, Eleanor R. "A Piagetian Interpretation of Beginning Reading Instruction." *Reading Teacher,* 31,5 (Feb. 1978), 497–503.

Latham, William, ed. *The Road to Effective Reading.* Newark, DE: International Reading Association, 1975.

McNally, D. W. *Piaget, Education and Teaching.* Sydney, Australia: Hodder and Stoughton, 1973.

Ollila, Lloyd O. *The Kindergarten Child and Reading.* Newark, DE: International Reading Association, 1977.

Roberts, Kathleen P. "Piaget's Theory of Conservation and Reading Readiness," *Reading Teacher,* 30,3 (Dec. 1976), 246–50.

Rupley, William H. "Reading Readiness Research: Implications for Instructional Practices." *Reading Teacher,* 30,4 (Jan. 1977), 450–53.

Williams, Frederick; Robert Hopper and Diana Natalico. *The Sounds of Children.* Englewood Cliffs, NJ: Prentice-Hall, 1977.

Chapter 4

Language and Vocabulary Development

OBJECTIVES

To be familiar with linguistics concepts and their application to reading-language development

To recognize the factors that affect vocabulary development and the application to language growth

To help children develop vocabulary

To study the use of vocabulary control in beginning reading

To know the several word attack methods, such as phonic, structural, context, and configuration methods

To understand the role of phonics in reading

To know the strategies of phonic and structural analysis

To know the place of sight words in beginning reading

To know how to develop meaning vocabulary

To understand the strategies of developing children's continuing interest in words

To know the means of assessing children's vocabulary

CHILDREN'S VOCABULARIES

Developing Meaningful Vocabularies

The foundation for learning to read is laid in early preschool years. The newborn baby listens to the parent's voice and responds in a sensory motor fashion with crying, smiling, or grunting noises. By the second month the baby makes differentiated sounds for discomfort, hunger, and pain and by the fourth month may be babbling or cooing in pleasure. Between six and nine months the baby may be putting together and repeating *mamma* or *boobooboo*. In nine to eleven months the child may be imitating sounds made by others. The baby listens before learning to speak.

The rate of children's first development of oral language is dependent upon several factors: (1) the development of their central nervous system; (2) the extent of their neural differentiation—sensory modalities and level of conceptualization; and (3) the environment—challenging and interactive motor and verbal and visual stimuli and realia. If the child is audile, of the type where learning is easiest through the auditory modality, he or she may develop oral language rapidly and accurately. We know from experience that the child uses speech as we do, namely, to control and manipulate environment, and subsequent interaction enhances and supports the child's concepts and behavior.

The first word usually appears between the sixth and fifteenth month. There is a close relationship between auditory development and language acquisition. The first words are nouns that have been heard repeatedly. Gradually, the child learns verbs, then adjectives, and then adverbs. The last to be learned are the prepositions, pronouns, and conjunctions. The speech patterns are those of the child's parents and playmates, whom he or she imitates. By the time the child enters school, speech patterns are pretty well established.

Estimates of the number of words in the child's spoken vocabulary by the time he or she enters first grade range from twenty-four hundred to fifteen thousand. Teachers of beginning reading rely upon the child's spoken vocabulary to help make the transition from the spoken word to the printed word.

Parents play a very important role in the child's vocabulary development. They can guide the conversation at the dinner table to a discussion of the happenings of the day, of books and articles read that have interest for all. They can provide a sufficient time scheduled daily for quiet activity, such as reading and conversation, with the child and parents together for this pleasure. They can regularly read to the child from favorite stories and poems. They can show pictures and discuss them. They can answer the child's questions and help him answer questions through experiment and observation and feeling and trying out.

The parents' checklist might include the following activities aimed at supporting vocabulary growth:

1. Build independence—encourage children to gather their own materials, do things for themselves.
2. Build self-confidence—give them experiences in which they can have success with some effort.
3. Challenge them with problem-solving situations that are within their ability range.
4. Give them responsibility—assign regular tasks.
5. Develop careful listening habits—sound and pitch in music, differences in words somewhat similar.
6. Call attention to signs ("Stop," "Go"), posters, license plates.
7. Build on interests through serious treatment of their questions.
8. Name places and things—a trailer, the airport, an airplane, an apartment, a doghouse, a bird's nest.
9. Speak clearly—repeat only if *not* understood.
10. Employ family rules and discuss them.
11. Follow directions—point out procedures.
12. Read to the child.
13. Give him firsthand experiences—talk about them; supply words where he needs them.

When the child enters school, one of the first tasks of the teacher is to evaluate informally the degree of exposure the child has had to these activities. Teachers also may have occasion to present the list of procedures to the parents of preschoolers. The PTA meeting is a good place to discuss the procedures because younger siblings will benefit (parents would not be there if they did not have children in school). Children relate new vocabulary to their past experiences. Experiences become profitable to the degree that the child thinks about them, their meaning, and draws upon them in subsequent speaking, listening, and reading.

CURRENT RESEARCH AND THE TEACHER

Linguistic Concepts and Applications

For the proficient reader, two forms of language exist—one written and one spoken. Written and oral language are alternate surface structures with the same underlying deep structure.

In producing language, the user has alternate sets of rules for producing a signal after having conceived the message. Phonological rules produce a signal that is an oral sequence. Orthographic rules produce a signal that is a graphic display. The reader's job is to get from the graphic display to meaning. It is only in the special case of oral reading that the reader is also interested in producing an oral signal, and, even then, it appears that proficient readers decode graphic language for meaning and then encode (recode) an oral signal.

It is possible with alphabetic writing systems to recode graphic displays as oral sequences without recourse to meaning. This code-to-code shifting does not necessarily yield meaning (as in a foreign language). It is *not decoding;* it is graphic-to-oral *recoding.* It is *not* an essential part of the reading process for meaning. In beginning reading, a focus on phonic recoding skills may interfere with the development of strategies of acquiring meaning from written language.

Types of Vocabulary

Vocabularies may be classified into four general types:

1. Hearing vocabulary—the words a child understands when he or she listens. This is the first to be developed and is the largest.
2. Speaking vocabulary—the range of words a child uses orally and meaningfully. This is the second to be developed. It develops most rapidly from ages one to eight in normal, stimulating environments.
3. Reading vocabulary—the range of words a child can recognize in printed form. Usually, by the end of elementary school, the reading and hearing vocabularies are about equal; the speaking vocabulary is smaller.
4. Writing vocabulary—the words a child uses in authorship activities, such as writing letters and reports. It remains the smallest throughout the school years.

Each of the vocabularies must be cultivated, nourished, and encouraged in every way possible. Children often make mistakes as they experiment with words. Adults may accept this as natural and make children comfortable in their experimenting. They help children to correct their mistakes but do not create tenseness by scolding them or making an issue over the errors. One procedure is very important in its relationship to all the vocabularies. It is recognizing the adults as models—parents, teachers, all adults. Children have a tendency to assign the same importance to each set of words that their parents do. Too high standards for children, too much pressure on them, and they will rebel; establish a model and put it before them regularly, and they will soon cherish it.

Word-count studies have been done on the size of children's vocabularies. The early ones were done by Horn, Thorndike, and Rinsland.[1] The

[1] Ernest A. Horn, *A Basic Writing Vocabulary,* Monographs in Education Series No. 4 (Iowa City: University of Iowa, 1926), and Edward L. Thorndike, *A Teacher's Wordbook of the Twenty Thousand Words Found Most Frequently in General Reading for Children and Young People* (New York: Teachers College Press, Columbia University, 1932), and F. W. Rinsland, *A Basic Vocabulary of Elementary School Children* (New York: The Macmillan Company, 1945).

highest estimates were made by Seashore.[2] He found that the first grader knows twenty-four hundred different words and the eighth grader nearly fifty thousand words. We can safely say that the number of words in the child's vocabulary is enormous. There are problems inherent in assessing children's vocabularies, such as (1) the choice of the group for study, (2) the method used to determine whether or not a child knows the word, (3) the method of sampling the child's word knowledge, and (4) the way a word is delineated (*call, called,* and *calling*—three words or one?). What is most important for instruction is the fact that there are great differences in the size of the vocabulary at any age. If there are thirty children in the classroom, there are thirty different-sized vocabularies. Children with foreign language backgrounds may have a very meager supply of English-language words. Intelligent children may have vocabularies that extend beyond the vocabularies of their teachers in some subjects—especially in science and certain hobbies. Dramatic growth in vocabulary often is wedded to the cultural environment and experiences with reading material, travel, and interesting people.

Recent studies of the vocabulary of children entering school have found that the oral vocabularies have been enlarged considerably as a result of television viewing. Just ask any kindergarten teacher—the children can talk about a TV program they have just seen. Vocabulary development is closely related to maturation and the child's interaction with his or her environment. Children's progress occurs in sequential stages, until they have acquired the basic phonology, grammar, and vocabulary of their language. Before their formal education begins, children can generate an infinite number of sentences and can understand many more complex structures than they can produce.[3] Linguists identify the former as language competence and the latter as language performance.[4] There is considerable variability from child to child, region to region, asd socioeconomic section to section—so extensive that much instruction must be practically individualized to be effective. For this reason the teacher has employed programed material, multilevel materials, and individually used workbook material to aid in supplementing instruction. Sometimes these are the program. Depth of meaning and semantics complicate the picture of how well children know words. Incomplete concepts and vague meanings are common problems. The similes children use are often a reflection of the depth of meaning they apply to words (concepts). The similes they use reveal the associations they have formed with the new words out of their past experience. The fur trim

[2] J. Conrad Seegers and Robert H. Seashore, "How Large Are Children's Vocabularies?" *Elementary English,* 26:181–94 (April 1949).
[3] Frank Smith, "The Learner and His Language," as found in *Language and Learning To Read,* ed. R. Hodges and E. Rudorf (Boston: Houghton Mifflin, 1972).
[4] Dorothy C. Higginbotham, "Psycholinguistic Research and Language Learning," *Elementary English,* 49:811–16 (Oct. 1972).

on their teacher's coat jacket feels like their cat. A small gray plastic elephant looks like a rat they have seen. A pencil is like a stick that writes. Free play is like summer.

Intelligence and Achievement

The verbal factor is an important one in mental ability so far as scholastic achievement is concerned. Vocabulary has been found to be so closely related to intelligence and reading achievement that it is almost always found as a part of tests of each. For example, word recognition and knowledge of word meanings are subsections of the following tests:

Tests of Reading Achievement
Iowa Silent Reading Test (group)
California Reading Test (group)
Durrell Analysis of Reading Difficulty (individual)

Tests of Intelligence
California Test of Mental Maturity (group)
Revised Stanford–Binet Scale (individual)
Wechsler Intelligence Scale for Children (individual)

The child's vocabulary accelerates rapidly during the first decade of life; growth then begins to slow down and starts to level off in the early twenties. This curve is similar to the growth curves of mental abilities. They are related, for the growth of vocabulary depends on the mental processes of perception, remembering, and thinking. Although there is a correlation between intelligence and vocabulary development, we cannot always infer the one from the other, for our reading clinics are full of children with measured intelligence far above their tested vocabulary achievement for one reason or several.

Language of the Disadvantaged

Disadvantaged children have verbal differences (from the standard English of the school) that threaten their success in learning to read unless the teacher and instructional program adapt to their needs. Their range of experiences is often different from those discussed in their textbooks. They usually have not encountered the breadth of objects and ideas that are a part of the formal educational setting of their schools. As often as not, they have been treated behaviorally with language that cuts off response ("Shut up!" "Stop that!") rather than language that encourages interaction ("Why did you think that?" "What would you like to do now?") Much of their vocal experience has been from television where they have been passive observers rather than active participants. These are generalizations, but they apply to too many children to be ignored by the educator.

These children should be provided numerous opportunities for enrichment of vocabulary and reinforcement through language experiences at *all* grade levels, and starting at the earliest possible opportunity—preschool where feasible. Parents and teachers build confidence in children by accepting their thoughts in their own language (dialect). They can get children to talk about things, school, people, feelings, so that their immediate source of learning is not dried up or shut off. Children can listen to stories and poems read by the teacher, play tapes and records, and see appropriate films, and discuss them—the interaction is important to overcome passivity. By the time they have been in school for two or three years they have built some confidence in themselves and should listen to skits done by themselves and their peers in their dialect and to those done in the standard dialect of the school. It is then time to focus on the differences. In the upper grades, fourth through sixth, the child can be imitating the standard dialect with increasing confidence and can move in his conceptualization from the concrete toward the abstract, from the immediate environment to those more removed in time and space.

Summary

This introductory section has shown how meaningful vocabulary develops in its initial stages and the factors that influence its rate of development. The four general types of vocabulary have been listed. Relations between intelligence and vocabulary have been outlined. Finally, the problems that can interfere with the early and rapid development of a meaningful vocabulary have been discussed in terms of the large numbers of disadvantaged children and the family where little or no emphasis is placed on the verbal aspects of their living environment. This section has been presented as background for the discussion of the school's instructional program that follows.

READING VOCABULARY

Readiness for Vocabulary Development

Besides the variations children display in readiness because of intelligence, sex, socioeconomic status, and experience background, there are some other variables. The quality of their vocabulary varies; some children use regularly the same words that the teacher uses in the classroom, whereas others have learned words that are appropriate to neither the teacher's use in the classroom nor to the books they will soon be using. Some children have watched programs on television that may help them with vocabulary in school, whereas others have watched only those programs with a limitedly useful vocabulary because of their parents' interests and choices. Whatever the differences in initial school vocabulary, it is a truism that good teaching tends to widen the differences among children in word knowledge.

The teacher takes advantage of every opportunity to build children's confidence in their use of words in different kinds of situations in school. Children are given a chance to introduce themselves to the class following the teacher's model of an introduction. The child may introduce a friend to the group. After initial contacts they may introduce the nurse, the principal, or his or her parents to the class. Children may report experience(s) or tell about one of their possessions—"What we did this summer." "What we did during vacation." "We had company yesterday." The teacher supplies useful words to help them increase their descriptive terms: the large *fluffy* clouds, the *roaring* wind, the *whirling* baton of the majorette, my uncle's *bright, shiny* new car. The teacher is building a general readiness through the process of giving children a background of information, language facility, and speech development—interpreting objects and events in words. A specific readiness skill is given careful attention during this process—that of the auditory discrimination of speech sounds. This will soon be followed by the visual discrimination of printed symbols so that eventually they will reinforce each other.

The next step is to record the familiar, common experiences of the children in their own words (edited by the teacher) in the short sentences of experience charts. They typically begin with the familiar words of their own speech, such as "We want . . ." "We saw . . . " The teacher places the sentences on the chalkboard as the children dictate and then may transfer them to a chart, after the children are familiar with the sentences, for the purpose of returning to them for subsequent reinforcement. Labels are placed on some objects in the classroom. Names are placed on wardrobe spots or the personal possessions of individual children. Attention is called to these labels.

The signs of readiness for which the teacher watches are that the children:

1. Recognize their own names on the list of today's helpers, labels on possessions, the committee for the Halloween party.
2. Recognize the signs used regularly, such as "Today's Weather," "The News," "Exit," "Library," "Quiet."
3. Show an interest in words, their sounds, or in parts of words.
4. Respond to rhymes and the sounds in rhymes.
5. Repeat words because they like the sound of them.
6. Show an interest in the shapes of words on charts.
7. Show an interest in the key letters of words, in those words that begin as their names do.
8. Recognize words repeated from their previous learning.
9. Remember words from previous titles.

10. Interpret pictures correctly, like to interpret their own drawings.
11. Like to look at pictures and respond to parts of them.
12. Find the title of the books available to them.
13. Follow directions easily.
14. Recognize similar geometric forms, can distinguish differing forms.
15. Have good motor control as evidence of their physical maturity.
16. Readily form associations of related concepts, such as faces, three-ness, hardness, roundness.
17. Evidence emotional maturity in work with their peer group and in individual projects.
18. Attend or concentrate for the usual span of time for their age group.
19. Recall, in both aided and unaided situations, words and broad concepts.

A number of these factors appear in each readiness test. The teacher should examine consecutively several such tests and note the areas included as well as the weighting assigned to each area.

Four conclusions can then be drawn: (1) different standardized readiness tests measure the status of reading differently; (2) none of the tests measures fully the status of children's readiness; (3) some readiness factors are not measurable through standardized testing; and (4) the teacher's judgment must be added to whatever objective measurement is used to round out the truer picture of children's readiness to begin the formal instruction in reading.

Probably the factors that are most important in any classroom program are specific unto the type of program of instruction, that is, basal reading, individualized, and so on.

The child develops word recognition skills through systematic practice. He or she must first have practice in visual discrimination. The teacher starts with this when the child first comes to school. The child learns to discriminate according to color, size, shape, position, and details. Frequent and regular practice builds success in this skill. Along with this skill development comes the understanding of concepts with the use of which the child makes comparison and contrast—small–smaller–smallest; large–larger–largest; little–big; car–truck. The teacher begins to use these concepts to match (and discriminate) objects and then pictures of objects—using words as identification and reinforcement.

Word recognition cannot begin until the child can recognize a word form as the same every time he sees it. The teacher begins this matching of words with large ones that have a distinctive configuration and then gradually moves to small words with a less distinct form. Experience has proved the psychological principle that one can learn to recognize more quickly those forms that are dissimilar before tackling those that are similar

Flannel board practice

in appearance. Drill is not very effective until one recognizes the truly differential characteristics of words.

At first pictures are used with the words so that meaning is enhanced. Meaning should accompany the learning of words, with the possible exception of certain sight words.

After some experience in matching words, children can begin to use letters on the chalkboard. Following this, they use cards with large letters and mimeographed large-type letters. Smith[5] recommends the following order of presentation:

a c u o w s g	easiest letters to match
e v x y k t z l	more difficult
r h f i j n m	still more difficult
b p q d	the most difficult letters to match

Alphabet blocks may be used. Games such as the following are appropriate: Alphabet Talk Flip Chart[6] and A-B-C Game.[7] A teacher-made tachistoscope can also be used very effectively. The Language Master is a useful audio-instructional aid that can be employed in the preceding learnings. The Language Master and its programs are produced by Bell and Howell Company.

[5] Nila B. Smith, *Reading Instruction for Today's Children* (Englewood Cliffs, NJ: Prentice-Hall, Inc., 1963), p. 473.
[6] Juster and Ross, Alphabet Talk Flip Chart. Teachers Publishing Corporation, 23 Leroy Avenue, Darien, CT 06820.
[7] A-B-C Game. Kenworthy Educational Service, Inc., 138 Allen Street, Buffalo, NY.

Practice with a friend can be fun

In summary, when children enter school, they are in various stages of readiness (preparedness) for reading. The teacher has to assess their readiness and then present a program that introduces those commonly needed experiences that will best prepare the children for the formal beginning of reading. Some children need a great deal of preparation and practice; others need little and can begin certain parts of the formalized program before the end of the first year. These latter children can help their peers reinforce their skills as well as strengthen their own if the teacher sets the right environment. The teacher encourages physical-motor development, but cannot speed it up noticeably. Experiences with words and concepts the teacher can regulate. The goal of the teacher is the encouragement of each child to move toward the formal reading process and vocabulary development as rapidly as the child can with attention to his good physical and mental health.

Sight Words

Sight words are the common, frequently used words that form the basis of the child's reading vocabulary. They are learned as wholes so that the child can recognize and pronounce them at a glance. Children do not have to analyze them. They have to know them in order to begin analyzing words and using other word-attack approaches to meaning and recognition. The most frequently used checklist of such words is the Dolch Basic Sight Vocabulary of 220 Service Words.[8] These make up over half of all the running words children read in their elementary textbooks. Nouns, including proper names, are omitted from the list because these differ according to the subject or story. Children obtain these through the teacher's direct telling, or they read the pictures. Hood [9] defines sight words three different ways: (1) words that represent common spelling patterns, recognized immediately as whole words; (2) all the words a child recognizes instantaneously (instant words); and (3) a core of heavy duty words used most frequently (Dolch Core Vocabulary). Mangieri and Kahn [10] studied primer-through-third level of Holt, Rinehart and Winston's *Holt Basic Reading Systems* (1973), Scott Foresman's *Reading Systems* (1971), Harcourt Brace Jovanovich's *Reading Program* (1970), and American Book Company's *Read* Series (1968). They found the Dolch list was *not* irrelevant, that 62 per cent to 76 per cent of the words were drawn from that level and 70 percent of the 220 words appeared at least once; they concluded that many of Dolch words accounted for many of the words in those basal readers.

There are other word studies and vocabulary lists that the teacher should know. Using these, and recording frequently met words at a given grade level, the teacher and children can build their own list. Two extensive word studies are:

Carroll, J. B.; P. Davies; and B. Richman. *American Heritage Word Frequency Book.* Boston: Houghton Mifflin Co., 1971.
Kucera, H., and W. Francis. *Computational Analysis of Present-Day American English.* Providence, RI: Brown University Press, 1967.

Three basic vocabulary list sources are

Dolch, Edward W. *Teaching Primary Reading.* Champaign, IL: Garrard Press, 1960, p. 255.
Johnson, Dale. "A Basic Vocabulary for Beginning Reading," *Elementary School Journal.* (Oct. 1971), EJ 047894, pp. 29–34.
Johns, Jerry L. "Some Comparisons Between The Dolch Basic Sight Vocabulary and the Word List for the 1970's." Northern Illinois University, 1974. ED 098541.

Two oral vocabulary counts are

Moe, Alden, and Carol Hopkins, "The Speaking Vocabularies of Kindergarten, First, and Second Grade Children." Paper presented at

---

[8] E. W. Dolch, *Teaching Primary Reading* (Champaign, IL: Garrard Press, 1960), p. 255.
[9] Joyce Hood, "Sight Words Are Not Going Out of Style," *The Reading Teacher,* 30,4:379–82 (Jan. 1977).
[10] John N. Mangieri and Michael S. Kahn, "Is the Dolch List of 220 Sight Words Irrelevant?" *The Reading Teacher.* 30,6:649–51 (March 1977).

National Council Research on English (March 1975). ED
105465.
Sherk, John Jr. *A Word Count of Spoken English of Culturally
Disadvantaged Preschool and Elementary Pupils.* Kansas City,
MO.: University of Missouri, 1973.

Many reading programs begin with whole words. These words are introduced in meaningful contexts, sometimes by telling or by association with pictures or through the use of experience charts. The words may be reinforced by games and tachistoscopic exercises or by other audiovisual aids. The important point is to get meaning, sight, and sound together so that the child is launched on the road to reading; the sight word response becomes automatic—a direct stimulus-response. Only a few words are presented at a time or in one sitting; their use becomes cumulative as some are added day by day.

By using the children's adventures in common for experience charts, teachers give instruction in sight words by repetition and reinforcement. The teacher creatively varies these adventures in learning with the service words so that the children do not become sated before they ever read the preprimers and equivalent-level trade books. Other forms of reinforcement besides those previously mentioned include (1) word-card matching, (2) keeping a card file of new words, and (3) many published types of self-help material.

Examples of materials are:

Dolch Basic Sight Word Cards—Garrard Publishing Company.
Dolch Picture Word Cards—Garrard Publishing Company.
Picture Word Builder—Milton Bradley Company.
Flash X, A Hand Tachistoscope for Rapid Word Recognition—
    Educational Development Laboratories.
Fry, Edward B., *Instant Words—Line Up* and *Instant Words—Pairs.*
    Learning Through Seeing.

Progress in reading the preprimer from the experience chart involves an intermediate step. From reading their own words children write their words by copying the chart in the same manuscript form that the teacher uses and that they will see in books. They begin to notice that certain words begin alike—*c*at, *c*ar, and *c*alf. The teacher asks the students to point out what is the same in each word; the student writes it, points to it on the chart, identifies it on the alphabet chart over the chalkboards, and says the word. Students begin to notice words and parts of some words. To help them the teacher may ask questions such as "Who went to the park?" "Where does it say that we went to the park?" "Point out the word *walk.*" "Where did we walk?" "Point to the word *path.*" "Is *path* like some other word?" "How are *path* and *pond* alike?"

The teacher is diagnostic in his or her work with the children as they are learning words. He or she observes and makes a note of those words that are difficult to recognize by individuals as they read the charts. The teacher notes the sentences that are particularly difficult, gives individuals or groups extra practice and parallel material, and utilizes a slightly different approach each time. He or she spaces the timing so that repetition and reinforcement will be rewarding and not boring.

One aid the teacher may employ in the analysis of the way the individual child may learn best the sight words is the Mills Learning Methods Test.[11] By administering known words and then teaching unknown words three ways, testing, and retesting, the teacher may find one of these methods slightly more effective: the visual, the phonic, the kinesthetic, or the combination method. Emphasis could then be placed on the method in which the individual, or group, shows the greatest aptitude. The teacher would not, however, exclude the other approaches. A look at the instructional program would show that the teacher is using the varied approach with all the children, with special supplementary emphasis on those approaches for individuals wherein they showed greater aptitude.

In summary, a basic fund of sight words, those that the child recognizes instantaneously, is learned in a meaningful setting to be used in beginning reading. The child is given an opportunity to repeat the words in many different situations in order to be entirely familiar with them. Suggestions have been made as to ways the teacher may approach the task diagnostically, and materials have been listed for the teacher's use. The speed with which the teacher can move in this phase of vocabulary development is dependent upon the abilities of the children. Individualizing and grouping for instruction are necessary to adjust the learning program to the children.

Control of Vocabulary

Vocabulary control is the process of limiting the number of new words presented in each succeeding reading selection so that the child can develop instantaneous word perception through a planned sequential pattern of introducing and maintaining vocabulary. A controlled vocabulary is necessary at the beginning reading stage because (1) children become frustrated by meeting new words in print for which they have not yet learned the methods of getting meaning; (2) their speech vocabulary may be extensive, but they do not yet know the clues to transfer between this and the printed symbols: (3) they need repetition, explanation, and interpretation because they *are immature* in reading, contrary to the way some adults feel about the repetition of what appear to them relatively simple words; (4) they lack the experience in the linguistic sequence of written words to supply unknown (though simple to us) words in a sentence; and (5) established

[11] Robert E. Mills, The Learning Methods Test Kit. (Fort Lauderdale, FL: The Mills Center, 1964).

learning principles indicate that a basic sight vocabulary is a foundation for the child's beginning to read books.

All adults need to do in order to place themselves in the child's position of learning to read is to take a selection written in a foreign language that is new to them and try to read it. Even with their experience with their own language, and possibly a second one, this is a frustrating experience, especially if social pressures demand that they read. Children need to build confidence and interest in written language—not frustration. Children need to practice their few reading skills repetitively before or as they learn new skills. This is the only way to assure the greatest possible retention.

Vocabulary load has increased in basal readers and in most reading programs in the mid-seventies. Beginning reading materials are built according to the principles of learning and child development. Most of the words of the basal readers are the same ones children use orally, and they are pleased to find the same words used by the authors who write for them to read. Each child's maturity, experience and rate of learning dictate how fast he or she can move through the initial stages of vocabulary development and reading. A controlled vocabulary textbook is an instructional tool that the teacher must use wisely. Its use must challenge and interest the child but not frustrate him or her.

Today's basal readers present about 350 to 400 different words in the primary grades. The words in the stories are checked against word-count lists [12] that are based on the frequency of their use in published materials. Harris [13] states that the total reading diet of elementary children includes large numbers of words that are met infrequently; in books recommended for elementary school children there are an estimated sixty thousand different words. One of these words occurs once in about fifty children's books. Of course, the words any particular child will meet in reading will vary widely depending on the choice of books and areas.

The proponent of the individualized method of organization for reading must maintain a control over the frequency of contact with new words. The teacher does this usually through guidance in the choice of reading matter and must also build a sight vocabulary before the child can be expected to read on his own. This teacher must also keep very meticulous records of every child's progress so that the child will not be repeating the skill errors ad infinitum. This requires an experienced, skilled, and knowledgeable teacher, one especially strong in children's literature.

[12] E. L. Thorndike and I. A. Lorge, *A Teachers Word Book of 30,000 Words* (New York: Teachers College Press, Columbia University, 1944), and Arthur I. Gates, *A Reading Vocabulary for Primary Grades* (New York: Teachers College Press, Columbia University, 1935), and Clarence R. Stone, *Progress in Primary Reading* (St. Louis: Webster Publishing Company, 1951), pp. 107–30.
[13] Albert J. Harris, *Effective Teaching of Reading* (New York: David McKay Company, Inc., 1962), p. 220.

Recent research indicates that children seem to prefer language that is less redundant than that presented in their basal readers. If content exerts the motivational influence on the learning process for reading that we assume, children should be allowed free choice of reading material as quickly as possible.[14]

The basal readers with their controlled vocabulary have helped thousands of teachers to teach children to read. These readers can be improved when research has clearly indicated the way. They have to be supplemented with other material to meet the needs of different children. Some children should move more rapidly through the readers and on to other materials where the children can apply their skills. Some children have difficulty reading one basal reader, yet their learning must also have supplemental materials where they are needed.

Word Analysis

When children have learned to recognize a number of sight words, they can use these to relate new words in pronunciation and meaning. The technique by which they determine the printed symbols that represent their familiar spoken words is word analysis. They learn a whole group of skills to help them in word analysis:

1. The configuration—the unique appearance of the word or its parts.
2. Picture clues—as suggestions of what the word might be.
3. Structural clues—prefixes, roots, suffixes, inflectional endings, compound words.
4. Context clues—the narrowing of the choice of possibilities through the meaning of the passage.
5. Phonic analysis—sounding out the word or its parts.
6. Spelling—the letter sequence in graphic representation.
7. Substitution—a word or part that sounds or looks like another.
8. A synonym—a word with a similar meaning to one they know.
9. Cloze—filling in unknown parts with the portion they know.
10. The selective use of several methods.
11. The dictionary—the source or reference they will use throughout their lifetime.

It is a matter of years before children can use all of these methods skillfully to conquer every new word they encounter. Whether or not they will develop and use all the methods depends on many factors—among them two are urgent from the very beginning of their reading experience:

---

[14] Eleanor Gibson and Harry Levin, *The Psychology of Reading* (Cambridge, MA: The M.I.T. Press, 1975), p. 311.

attitudes and values. The teacher is alert to the motivation the child brings to the learning of words for reading with meaning and alert to the richness he or she receives from successes in the initial stages.

Although the following discussions of techniques are presented in neat order according to the type of skill, the teacher is advised to be observant in the classroom for the child's discoveries *as they occur* and to capitalize on them at the moment. When the child notices that two words begin with *s,* the teacher replies, "Yes, they both begin the same; what sound do you hear when you say them?" The group's attention may be called to the discovery made by a single child. The teacher does not miss a good opportunity to challenge the children when two rhyming words have been overlooked by them or when there are two words together that make up a new word or when two words have the same phoneme—one is a word they know, the other in one they have not recognized. An example of the latter is writing the known word *drink* on the chalkboard and pronouncing it; then erasing the *d* and replacing it with the consonant digraph *sh,* again pronouncing the word.

Competent readers have three kinds of information available to them as they read:

1. *Phonological* (spelling-to-sound correspondences) constraints.
2. *Orthographic* (spelling patterns) constraints.
3. *Syntactic* (grammatical structure) constraints.[15]

Children must first be able to break the word into its elements so they can pronounce them. In so doing, children may respond to a letter or a phoneme. Next they must be able to give a reasonable sound equivalent for whatever part(s) of the word they recognize—individual letters, the whole word, syllables, digraphs, blends, prefixes, roots, suffixes, and so on. Third, the child must be able to blend the parts into a recognized whole. Fourth, the child must be able to vary his or her approach from word to word; for example, in *great, bread,* and *mean,* the *ea* represents a different sound. Fifth, children must perform the entire complex task of analyzing the unfamiliar word as they meet it in context, checking its accuracy through the sense of the passage. Sixth, the child must develop the attitudes and skills requisite to the effective use of the dictionary.

For primary school teachers to be effective, they must ask and seek answers to these questions: (1) How does one go about helping children discover the sounds of parts of words? (2) How does one decide which sounds to stress? (3) How can group reading activities be planned to foster word-analysis skills? (4) What help can be given through ongoing classroom activities? (5) What kinds of special practice activities are important?

The usual developmental reading programs follow a systematic ap-

---

[15] Gibson and Levin, op. cit., p. 323.

proach to the various skills necessary in word analysis. The good teacher observes the strengths and weaknesses of individual children as they move through the various stages. With some children the teacher may stop the regular procedure and switch to a greater emphasis on the visual approach, or with some the visual-motor approach, or with some the kinesthetic approach, or with some a more intensive use of phonic analysis to enhance auditory discrimination.

With an emphasis upon the four major aids to word perception— memory of word form, context clues, word analysis (structural and phonetic), and use of the dictionary—the following sections will deal with word analysis techniques first, followed by use of the dictionary skills, and then the synthesis of various techniques. Application will be made to the content fields, and problems (difficulties) will be examined.

Basic Phonics Program. The phonics program, of whatever type, provides that the learner comes into contact as frequently as possible with standard phonic elements. Although Figure 4 is an oversimplification of the extent of the basic phonic elements to be learned, it is helpful in anchoring the many deviations that occur in the English language.

In addition to those listed in the chart, there are symbols for sounds that are not taught until the child has learned to use the dictionary, such as the schwa (ə) sound of the vowel in unaccented syllables (*a*bout, sof*a*, butt*o*n). There are also letters that are silent in some words (*g*nat, *k*now).

Teaching Phonics. The abilities that children must display to be efficient in phonics are (1) to hear and identify consonant sounds, vowel sounds, syllables, and accent (auditory discrimination); (2) to associate the consonant and vowel sounds with letters of the alphabet; (3) to use visual clues that help to identify consonant and vowel sounds, syllables, and accent (visual discrimination); and (4) to blend consonant and vowel sounds into syllables and then into meaningful words (synthesis). Because these steps are necessary, the best approach to the teaching of phonics is to assure a basic sight vocabulary of words first. Children can use the familiar words and sounds to identify similarities and differences, but particularly similarities whereby generalizations can be made. This step makes the learning functional. Phonics taught in isolation, as some publishers' programs do, require a second step—that of making the transfer or application to the actual reading process. This is wasted motion when the phonic generalizations could more profitably be made by the child who already knows the words. In this context teaching family words can be considered an example of wasted time in the child's learning. The process of moving from the whole word to its parts and back to the whole word in context is an analytic process and will be the most useful to the child's total reading experience. A few rules and principles may be derived from the examples encountered by children when they are reading for comprehension. In one sense, this builds readiness for learning phonics, but the teacher has to be

Figure 4. Basic Phonic Elements

CONSONANTS

SINGLE SOUND	MORE THAN ONE SOUND	BLENDS						DIGRAPHS	
b	p	c	candy	bl	blow	pl	play	tw	twin	ch	chap
d	r		face	br	brown	pr	pray	sch	school	gh	rough
f	t	g	game	cl	clean	sc	score	scr	scream	ng	ring
h	v		gentle	cr	crow	sk	skin	spl	split	ph	phone
j	w	s	sad	dl	cradle	sl	slow	spr	spring	sh	she
k	z		lose	dr	drink	sm	small	str	street	th	thin
l			sure	fl	fly	sn	snap			wh	when
m	x		fox	fr	free	sp	speak				
n			exact	gl	glass	st	stand				
				gr	grow	sw	swing				
				lk	milk	tr	train				

VOWELS

SINGLE	DIGRAPHS		DIPHTHONGS					
a	ai	rain	oa	coat	au	cause	ou	house
e	ay	lay	oe	hoe	aw	saw	ow	cow
i	ea	each	oo	roof	eau	beauty	oy	boy
o	ee	week	ui	guide	eu	feud	ui	suite
u	ei	receive			ew	new		
y	ie	believe			i	ice		
					oi	oil		

alert and plan carefully the phonic experiences of those children who need them. Other children will need a minimum of emphasis on phonics because they seem to gain the skills intuitively through their reading. In their manuals, basal reading series suggest the appropriate timing and place for phonic emphasis. The teacher determines which children need extra emphasis on which phonic learnings. Where there are similar needs, children are grouped for this instruction.

The New Phonic Element. The skillful teacher recognizes the appropriate time for the on-the-spot introduction of a new phonic element, where it does not interfere with the continuity of an engrossing story. If it can be done at the beginning of a story, this is ordinarily the best time. For instance, the children have difficulty pronouncing *squeak* in the sentence "The cold seemed to have driven all the air from his lungs but he managed one wild squeak for help before the water closed over him again." [16] The teacher

[16] Robert Lawson, *Rabbit Hill*. New York: The Viking Press, Inc. 1944.

Chart work with phonics

can put on the chalkboard some words, such as *coat, leaf,* and *road,* with two middle vowels. The teacher can have the children pronounce them, identify the vowel that they hear, then make up the rule.

The preplanned program for introducing a new phonic element involves a series of steps that are followed to make the sound recognizable and meaningful in different settings comparable to those that will be encountered in successive reading experiences. For instance, to introduce the initial consonant *b,* the following steps might be preplanned.

1. Present a contextual setting taken from a selection that is to be read. Print the sentence on the chalkboard. Explain that this is a sentence to be read in our new story and that we will develop a way to recognize the last word whenever we meet it.

1. John is playing with a *ball.*

2. To provide visual discrimination in recognizing the initial consonant, some known words are placed on the chalkboard that begin with the initial consonant *b.* "There is something alike in all these words. What is it?" A child is asked to go

2. *boy*
   be
   baby
   Billy
   Bob
   bat

to the board and circle that
which is alike in all the words,
as he or she pronounces each
word.

3. Auditory discrimination is
related or reinforced as each
word is pronounced and the
children's attention is drawn to
the initial sound. The sound of
b is not isolated but is blended
with the vowel sound, or with
the rest of the syllable. Some
other words are added orally for
auditory recognition of those
that begin with *b* and those that
do not.

3. *Betty   John   head*
fish   bat   did
pill   sit   big
box   Dick   doll

4. Picture clues may be used to
reinforce visual and auditory
discrimination by presenting a
picture and several words from
which the children choose the
correct word, pronouncing it.

4. *bird*
coat
dish
bad
coat
cat

5. For application of the skill,
other sentences may be put on
the chalkboard for practice.

5. The (*tell, bell*) is ringing. It
is my turn to (*bat, cat*). He
is a tall (*toy, boy*).

6. Return to the *original sentence.*

6. John is playing with a *ball.*

Some children will need a greater amount of practice and application
than others. Some will need more experience with visual, others with
auditory, discrimination. Even though a lesson is preplanned, it should be
adjusted to the needs of the children with greater or minimum experience
in each step as their needs indicate. This suggests that the teacher evaluate
the success of each step as it is employed. If only one or two children need
further practice, the teacher may proceed through the lesson with the group
and return for individual reinforcement with those who need it.

Order in Which Elements Should Be Taught. Phonics is taught in all
grades of the elementary school. The proper beginning of instruction depends upon the readiness of the children for this experience. They can
progress best if they have a fund of sight words, skill in visual and auditory
discrimination, and a sizeable listening vocabulary. This suggests that the
first few weeks of first grade might well be devoted to the prephonics skills,
and then phonics instruction for some can be begun somewhere between
the sixth and eighth week of first grade. Assuming that phonics is taught
in a meaningful context implies that it has a utilitarian aspect. Another help
in beginning phonics is a recognition or listening stock of words to which
the child learns to relate the visual clues.

Many programs begin with an early emphasis placed on initial consonants and blends, followed by the vowel sounds. Many children need considerable practice in the phonics skills. The goal of phonics is the ability to pronounce new words and be able to recognize and use them. In the second and third grades the phonics skills are strengthened by continued practice.

This is the goal of phonics instruction, limited at first to monosyllabic words. In the second grade much more emphasis is placed on phonics. In the third grade the same skills are strengthened by continued practice. The upper grades continue experiences with the phonics skills and add the application to polysyllabic words. Syllabication must be taught for effective accomplishment of this application. Of course, some children will need a continued emphasis on the beginning stages of phonics and discrimination, and upper grade teachers must diagnose this need in their class.

When children are given words to read, it has been found that fewest errors are made on initial consonants, next on final consonants, and most on medial vowels.[17]

Instruction thus can be adapted to the maturity and individual needs of the children. An examination of various basal reader charts shows that they introduce particular phonic skills at different levels dependent upon the stories used and their use of words requiring those skills. Research has not proved that initial consonants, final consonants, consonant digraphs, consonant blends, consonant irregularities, and silent consonants must be presented in a hierarchy; nor does it suggest that all the consonant digraphs, for instance, must be presented in sequence (*sh, wh, ch, th, nk, ng, ck, qu*). In fact, the good teacher might capitalize on the encounter of a new word to teach any one of the digraphs first, especially if the teacher realizes that the children are going to encounter the digraph frequently. Synthesis of their phonic learnings are most important to children, not the order in which they learn single steps. Context clues help them synthesize the learnings. Sometimes the child starts the phonic analysis and the context makes further phonic analysis unnecessary. In the sentence, "Billy ran and jumped over the fence," the child may read as far as the word *jumped* and start to analyze it. Then he or she notices the rest of the sentence and suddenly realizes that Billy *jumped* to get over the fence.

Syllabication and Inflectional Endings. Breaking words into syllables may serve the learner in several ways. It may help in sounding out the word to pronounce it (a phonics tool). It may help in getting the correct spelling for those words that are regularly phonetic. It may help in writing where a word has to be broken at the end of a line and continued on the next line. A syllable is a pronounceable unit containing a vowel or a group of letters containing a vowel. Letter-sound combinations are based on the

[17] Gibson and Levin op. cit. p. 283.

syllable, not on the word. This must be kept in mind when generalizations are learned. Examples are the vowel diphthong, *aw,* in *aw-ful;* and the same two letters, *aw,* in *a-wake.*

Children have to learn to use a number of generalizations in breaking words into syllables. Some of the more common ones follow:

1. When two consonants, or double consonants, appear between two vowels, the syllable division is made between the consonants.

   lum-ber   sud-den   car-ry

2. There are as many syllables as there are vowel *sounds.*

   be-lieve   dam-age   write

3. A single consonant between vowels usually goes with the second vowel.

   e-lect   de-cide   hu-mid

4. Consonant digraphs and blends are not divided.

   tel-e-phone   weath-er   fish-er-man

5. Prefixes and suffixes form separate syllables.

   un-wrap   life-less   dis-band-ing

6. The inflectional endings *-ible, -cle, -dle, -gle, -ple,* and *-tle* form the final syllable.

   subtle   ta-ble   sta-ple

7. When the letter *x* is preceded and followed by vowels, it is placed in the syllable with the preceding vowel.

   ex-act   tax-i   ox-y-gen

A word should be added at this point regarding the use of the accent in phonic analysis. Accents are stress patterns on a word in a group of words or on the syllable of a word with more than one syllable. The accent in a familiar listening vocabulary is readily recognized when the child's attention is focused on it. In new words the child is dependent upon the teacher until he or she can read accent interpretations in the dictionary. Some clues may be taught as generalizations. See stress and accent generalizations later in this chapter.

Most of the work with accent should be oral and, regularly, attention should be focused on it. This may make the use of generalizations unnecessary, for there are many exceptions to any accent rule. The rules are crutches that help where the child needs concreteness, but they should be de-emphasized as soon as possible.

Phonic Principles and Generalizations. A principle is an accepted or professed rule of action. A generalization is a proposition asserting something to be true either of all members of a certain class or of an indefinite part of that class. There are certain principles that apply to the teaching of phonics. Before one begins phonics instruction, the principles should be examined carefully and applied consistently where they are accepted as valid.

1. Auditory and visual discrimination must be blended. From words that the child recognizes when he hears them, he is taught to recognize them when he sees them. Thus he blends the auditory and the visual processes.
2. The teacher should illustrate a particular sound with as many words as possible. Words and pictures should be used together for reinforcement and association. With the use of pictures, children can furnish additional words illustrating the particular sound.
3. Reliance upon only one method of word analysis is wrong. All the clues should be brought into play.
4. Teachers should direct to the individual child questions that will help him or her analyze the letter-sound relationships. Children vary in this ability and in the ability to generalize from specifics.
5. All elementary teachers should be familiar with the entire phonics program. No matter what grade or level is taught, there must be teaching, practice, reteaching, and review of certain phonic skills, at least with some of the children.
6. Some children need little phonics instruction. Substituting sounds in familiar words or adding sounds to familiar words may suffice for them. Examples of substitution are *ban* for the known *can,* or *bat* for known *cat.* Examples of adding a sound are *farm* where *arm* is known, or *rant* when *ran* is known.
7. By diagnosing the strengths and weaknesses of the class, the teacher determines how much time to spend on phonics and with which children phonic instruction and practice is needed. It is usually a waste of time to teach the whole class or group that which only a few need.

What generalizations should be learned? Only those that have frequent and general use in the children's reading material should be learned, and they should be learned in conjunction with the words put in context. Common generalizations that should be learned follow.

1. In a one-syllable word with a final *e,* the first vowel is usually long and the final *e* is silent; examples: *game, hate, ride.*
2. In a one-vowel word, when the vowel is in the middle of the word, it is usually short; examples: *cat, mad, met.*
3. When two vowels are together in a one-syllable word, the first vowel is usually long, and the second is usually silent; examples: *seat, goat, dream.*
4. The sound of the final letter *y* in a one-syllable word is usually /i/ [18] as in *mine;* examples: *fly, cry.* In a two-syllable word it is usually short; examples: *candy, baby.*

[18] The letter between slanted lines refers to the *sound* of the letter; for example, *cat* begins with a /k/.

5. The letter *c* has a /k/ as in *kite* when followed by *o*, *a*, or *u;*
   examples: *come, cat, cut*. It has the /s/ as in set when followed
   by *e, i*, or *y*; examples: *cent, circle, cyclone*.
6. The letter *g* has the /g/ as in *big* when followed by *o, a*, or *u;*
   examples: *go, gate, gun*. It has the /j/ as in *jump* when followed
   by *e, i*, or *y*; examples: *germ, gingerbread, gymnasium*.
7. The vowels *a, e, i, o,* and *u* in an unaccented syllable all have a soft,
   short sound that is the same, and it is called the *schwa* sound;
   examples: *a*bout, gard*e*n, im*i*tate, cott*o*n, circ*u*s.

Practice in Phonics. Practice in phonics serves the three useful purposes of reinforcement of correct responses in a contextual setting, the
application of learned principles to new situations, and the fixing as permanent learning of that which has been taught. Thinking should be involved
in all instances. The rote process of copying on paper or in a workbook does
not meet these objectives. Some characteristics of good practice are enu-
merated to serve as a guide to the use of practice in the classroom.

Because a single response to a stimulus seldom results in permanent
learning, multiple responses must be provided in the teaching-learning
program. The teacher finds different ways to provide this additional practice.
Usually, the group process is used to fix the response in the majority of the
children. Chalkboard exercises form the mode, but other audiovisual approaches provide the variation and motivation children need in learning.
Flash-cards, hand tachistoscopes, projections on a screen, pictures, games,
and pencil-and-paper exercises are examples of the other approaches. The
tape recorder, the Voice-Master, and the Language Master may also be used.

Workbooks and worksheets may be used, too, but they should be
individualized, and work in them should be done under supervision. Too
often teachers use these tools incorrectly. Children should meet success in
their use but also should be challenged to apply what they have learned.

"My reading teacher and I made a discovery today. We found that *wh*
can say /w/ or /h/, depending upon the word. In *when* and *what,* they say
/w/. In *who* and *whole,* they say /h/.[19] There should be flexible regrouping
for such work, and at times individual help is necessary. At any rate, frequent sampling of the children's work should indicate their readiness to
move on to a higher level of performance. This is, of course, the principle
on which programed materials are devised.

Where a deficiency is observed by the teacher, that deficiency should
get extra attention and practice for correction. Workbooks may furnish
exercises in which this can be done, as long as the exercises are practical,
contextual situations. If the exercises are challenging, the children will be

---

[19] Johnny Mitchell, student, and Bea Roth, director, Downey Reading Improvement
Center, Downey, Calif., "Dear Reading Teacher," *The Reading Teacher.* 30,8:925
(May 1977).

interested in their accomplishment, and they will be building a self-concept that is healthy.

Some General Comments. In any presentation on phonic analysis the dangers and pitfalls might well be brought together for consideration and reiterated so that they are kept firmly in mind as the teacher moves through the day-to-day task of instilling the values, attitudes, and habits in children that will serve them throughout their lifetime.

1. A reader must be able to use sounding techniques to solve words he or she does not recognize as sight words.
2. A reader must not rely completely and solely on phonic analysis. Sometimes other methods are more efficient in promoting fluency and comprehension. Often combinations of methods are most effective.
3. A reader may be using phonic analysis long after the words should be recognized as sight words. This results from overlearning the sounding technique or from sole emphasis on instruction in this technique at the expense of other techniques.
4. Because the English language is complex in its phonetic aspects, many words have to be learned as sight words and should be taught as such.
5. The direct teaching of sounds in regular words is superior to whole-word training—applies only to regular words. Gibson and Levin reported that teaching one-to-one correspondence (grapheme-phoneme) is inferior to teaching several correspondences for each grapheme (set-for-diversity), for example, the grapheme *ough* is /uf/ in *enough* and /ow/ in *bough*. Research is needed in the sounds-approach versus set-for-diversity.[20]
6. Linguistically based methods have tried to maintain natural sounds, so teachers are admonished not to use drills like *b* as in /buh/ because the sound of /buh/ does not occur alone in English.[21]
7. Boredom and disinterest may result from the exclusive use of phonics when it causes slow, laborious reading. Comprehension may not be the only casualty.
8. Finding little words in big words is an inefficient method of word analysis and should be avoided; examples: *in* as in *f-in-e, on* as in *h-on-ey, me* as in *a-me-n.*
9. The public pressure resulting from articles in popular magazines or a Rudolph Flesch book creates problems for teachers who try to put phonics instruction in its proper perspective. Parents should

[20] Douglas Carnine, "Phonics vs. Look-say-Transfer to New Words," *The Reading Teacher,* 30,6:636–40 (March 1977).
[21] Gibson and Levin, op. cit., p. 313.

be told the way phonics is taught in any particular school system and how it fits into the total language arts program.

10. Recent research studies show rather conclusively that the phonics method is not superior to all other methods. They also suggest that its greatest value lies in its use in combination with other methods. This is the position that is taken by the authors of this text. If phonics instruction meets the needs of individuals and small groups of children, it must be taught when they are ready for auditory and visual discrimination, blending, and the application of generalizations. Children must eventually learn to make minimal use of phonics in reading and to throw away the crutch in order to enhance their rate of comprehension.

Justification of Position. A new teacher usually has to begin the instructional process with whatever materials are available. Some current programs are characterized as intensive phonics, such as that of Lippincott, whereas others are graded phonics, such as that of Scott Foresman. Of course, the first step is to recognize whatever phonics materials are available, their place in the local school curriculum, and their general classification as a phonics teaching system. The second step is to add whatever materials and procedures are needed to supplement the current recommended curriculum. The third step is to work on revision of the curriculum so that the program is a desirable one. Fortunate is the new teacher who finds steps two and three not necessary.

Austin and Morrison [22] are quoted here because their comprehensive study covering the whole United States led them to make some generalizations that form a part of the basic philosophy of this section on phonics:

> A variety of sounding systems have been published. They tend to rely strongly on elements of phonic analysis to help children identify the printed word. Some of the materials combine phonic drills and reading materials in a series of paperbound books, while other approaches contain phonic exercises fashioned along "synthetic" principles—that is, children are taught phonemic responses to letters and groups of letters in isolation, after which pupils are expected to synthesize sounds into complete words. Although the current sounding approaches differ in content and methodology, most of them minimize the development of sight words and focus attention early in the first grade on identification of consonant and vowel sounds and on the introduction of phonic generalization. . . . Ironically, the advocates of sounding approaches who decry the development of a sight vocabulary must help children commit to memory an inordinate number of words which do not conform to phonic generalizations. . . . The staff questions the teaching of children to sound out words removed from any meaningful context. . . . Phonics instruction

[22] Mary C. Austin and Coleman Morrison, *The First R* (New York: Macmillan Publishing Co., Inc., 1963), pp. 32–35.

should extend through three to six years of elementary school if needed. . . . All teachers should be well-grounded in their knowledge of phonic principles.

The beginning teacher can take several steps to help in preparing for the teaching of phonics. All the publishers of basal reading series produce a chart of their word analysis program including phonics. These should be studied carefully. There are several booklets that were written to help the teacher understand the teaching of phonics in reading. Among them are those of Durkin [23] and Heilman,[24] which are very helpful. Current college textbooks on the teaching of reading have chapters or sections on word analysis in which phonic analysis is included. Finally, professional journals carry articles on research and experimentation in phonics instruction. The habit of reading these studies will give the beginning teacher insight and perspective concerning his own instruction. The teacher who wishes to examine his own knowledge of phonic analysis may test himself with the *Phonics Test for Teachers.*[25]

Structural Analysis

Structural analysis is a way of analyzing the printed word in order to determine its pronunciation and meaning by identifying its meaningful parts —roots, inflectional endings, prefixes, suffices, and syllables. The syllables are blended into the sound of the word as the individual visually scrutinizes the word. There are relatively simple inflected, compound, and derived forms of known roots, in which the individual identifies the root and inflectional endings as meaningful units. There are also the more difficult derived forms or unknown roots, in which the individual identifies the prefixes and roots as meaningful units and recognizes the grammatical function of the suffixes. Then, finally, there are the most complex derived forms, in which the affixes must be recognized as functional meaning-units: the root must be recognized though it may be changed (derived) in spelling and/or pronunciation, and context may be necessary to determine the pronunciation and meaning. Structural analysis involves the necessity of memory for word form and the imagery of word form so that the reader learns to identify morphemes in words and can see the relationships between inflected or derived forms and their roots. Recognition of words by their configuration, or shape, may help, although children are apt to see minor details to associate with the word or part of a word. Sometimes

---

[23] Dolores Durkin, *Phonics and the Teaching of Reading* (New York: Bureau of Publications, Teachers College, Columbia University, 1962).

[24] Arthur W. Heilman, *Phonics in Proper Perspective* (Columbus, OH: Charles E. Merrill Books, Inc., 1965).

[25] Dolores Durkin and Leonard Meshover, *Phonics Test for Teachers* (New York: (Bureau of Publications) Teachers College, Columbia University, 1964).

Helping each other with word endings

phonics helps in structural analysis, although it may interfere, especially if individual letter phonics has been emphasized too heavily.

A root is a word base that generally remains unchanged or a word part taken from a foreign language; examples: *come—welcome, comely.*

An inflectional form is a word that has undergone change by the addition of an ending for a grammatical reason, such as number, case, gender, person, tense, voice, or mood; examples: *dog—dogs, telephone—telephoned.*

A derivative is a new word developed from another by the addition of a prefix or suffix; examples: *guitar—guitarist, bucket—bucketful, perform —performance.* In each example, the second is a derivative of the first word.

A prefix is a letter or a syllable preceding a root to change its meaning; examples: *in*to, *mal*function, *a*lone, *anti*trust.

A suffix is a syllable added to a word at the end to change its meaning; examples: auction*eer,* western*most,* use*ful.*

An affix is a letter or syllable attached as either a prefix or a suffix; examples: *dis*like, walk*ing.*

The structural analysis program contains some generalizations that should be emphasized. In reading

1. The plural of nouns is formed by adding *s.*
2. When a root word ends in a single consonant preceded by a single vowel, the final consonant is doubled when a suffix beginning with a vowel is added; example: *grab—grabbed.*

3. When a root word ends in *e,* the *e* is dropped when adding an ending beginning with a vowel; example: *make—making.*
4. When a root word ends in *f,* or *fe* in which the *e* is silent, the *f* is changed to *v* before the ending; examples: *knife—knives, wolf—wolves.*
5. When a root word ends in *y* and is preceded by a consonant, the *y* is changed to *i* before the ending; example: *rally—rallied;* except when the ending begins with *i,* example: *rally—rallying.*

An analysis of the teachers' manuals accompanying basal reading series reveals their systematic introduction of the various skills of structural analysis. These skills are maintained throughout the series for practice and reinforcement. On page 90 is an example of such a sequence, condensed from one basal reading series.[26] After each item is indicated the level of the book in which the skill is introduced for the first time. For other sequences, see appendix.

Generally, the teaching of inflectional endings begins in the preprimers, but attention to the root words or roots of words is gradually brought into focus in the second grade. Structural elements are introduced very early and are reviewed throughout the elementary school program. The selection of prefixes, suffixes, and roots to teach is dictated by the reading material and the necessity encountered in writing. In considering the complications of multiple meanings, there seems to be no particular standard that all reading systems follow. Syllabication is the means whereby children break words into their component parts, pronounce these units, and then blend them into the whole word. This helps in pronunciation of the word, in getting meaning when they have heard the word previously, and in spelling and writing where they can visualize the parts of the word.

Research evidence supports the importance of structure within the word and getting the child to notice it. Good readers do this in clusters and relational contexts.[27]

The teaching procedure usually necessitates the following steps: (1) the teacher provides the correct sensory experience—visual and auditory; (2) the children examine the structural pattern under the guidance of the teacher; (3) the children collect and record on the chalkboard words that fit the pattern and use them orally in context; (4) the children generalize the pattern with the help of the teacher; and (5) the children use the learned pattern in other settings on the board, in their reading, in their workbooks, and in their writing. The teacher should be familiar with all of the commonly used prefixes, suffixes, and root words. Some of these are listed for the teacher's review.

[26] *Series r, The New Macmillan Reading Program,* Scope and Sequence Chart (New York: Macmillan Publishing Company, Inc., 1975).
[27] Gibson and Levin, op. cit., p. 297.

STRUCTURAL ANALYSIS	FIRST INTRODUCED
Syllabication	First Reader
Recognizing Word Endings	
Plural ending—*s*	Preprimer
Verb ending—*s*	Preprimer
Possessive ending—'*s*	Primer
Verb endings—*ed, ing*	Primer
Comparative endings—*er, est*	2–1 Reader
es with words ending in *ss, x,* or *ch*	3–2 Reader
Recognizing Word Formation	
Compound words	Primers
Hyphenated words	Primers
Dropping final *e* before adding *-ed, -ing*	2–1 Reader
Doubling final consonant before adding *-ed, -ing*	2–1 Reader
Changing *y* to *i* before adding *ed,* or *es*	2–2 Reader
Changing *y* to *i* before comparative endings *-er, -est*	2–2 Reader
Doubling the final consonant before adding the comparative endings *-er, -est*	2–2 Reader
Contractions	
n't	First Reader
'll, 'm, 're, 've	2–2 Reader
Prefixes	
un-	2–1 Reader
re-	2–2 Reader
in-, dis-, be-	3–1 Reader
im-, micro-, mis-, non-, pre-, semi-, sub-, super-, tele-, tri-, uni-	3–2 Reader
Suffixes	
-ful, -less	2–2 Reader
ish, -ly, -ment,	2–2 Reader
-ness, -ship, -ward	2–2 Reader
-ous, -ion, -able, -hood, -y	3–1 Reader
-ist, -teen	3–2 Reader

Common Prefixes

a-, ab-	from, away from	atone, absent, abstain
ad-	to, toward	admit, adjoin
ante-	before	antewar, antenuptial
anti-	opposite	antidote, antibody, antiglare
con-	together with	consent, concur
contra-	against	contraband, contrabass
de-	from, away	desist, deform
dis-	apart	dismiss, dissuade
ex-	from, out of	exit, exhale
in-	into, not	inside, inactive
inter-	between	interrupt, interscholastic
mis-	wrongly, badly	mishandle, misspell
non-	not	nonchalant, nondescript
out-	beyond	outdistrict, outbound
over-	above	overlay, overboard, overcast
per-	through	persuade, percept
post-	after	postscript, postmarital
pre-	before	precede, prearrange
pro-	forward	proceed, propel
	in behalf of	prowar, pro-American
re-	back, again	repel, relive, remit
sub-	under	submarine, subgroup
super-	above	supersoil, supercharger
syn-	with	synchronize, synonym
trans-	across	transport, transoceanic
un-	not	unlike, unfit

Common Suffixes

-able, -ible	capable of	knowledgeable, feasible
-ace, -ancy	state of being	menace, vacancy
-al, -ial	related to	mental, menial
-an, -ian, -ant	one who	American, musician, servant
-ance	act of	governance, compliance
-ary	relating to	arbitrary, notary
-ate	having the quality of	legate, nitrate
-dom	state of being	freedom, wisdom
-ee, -eer	person who has rights of office	grantee, trustee, engineer
-en	made of or like	whiten, wooden, golden
-ence	action or being	existence, independence
-er, -or	one related to	player, tinner, actor
-ful	much of	flavorful, painful
-hood	condition of	boyhood, manhood
-ic	consisting of	iambic, volcanic

-ion	state or condition	ambition, solution
-ist	one who does	humorist, organist
-itis	inflammation	bronchitis, appendicitis
-ity	condition	acidity, calamity
-ive	quality	active, conclusive
-less	without	thankless, hopeless
-like	resembling	lifelike, catlike
-ly	like	simply, exactly
-ment	condition	amazement, development
-most	superlative	hindmost, foremost
-ness	condition of	fineness, goodness
-ose, -ous	substance of	verbose, cellulose, riotous
-ship	position or condition	hardship, leadership
-some	full of, in all	wearisome, foursome
-ward	in the direction of	toward, leeward
-way	route	biway, highway
-y	like or being	hilly, jealousy

Common Roots

cap, cip	take, cover	capital, capitulate, precipitation
dic, dict	say	diction, edict
duce, duct	lead	conduct, deduce
fact, fic, feit fect	make, do	counterfeit, efficient, manufacture, defect
fer	bear, carry	conference, refer
graph, gram	write	polygraph, telegram
ject	throw	eject, reject
join, junct	join	rejoinder, junction

Common Roots

lat	bear, carry	relate, pallet
leg, lect	read	lectern, ledger
log	word, study	geology, logic
loqu, loc	speak	loquacious, interlocutor
mis, miss, mit	send	transmit, mission
mob, mote	move	mob, motion
pend	hang	dependable, pendant
plit, plex	flex, twist	flexible, pliable
port	carry	report, transportation
pose, pone	place	postpone, depose
scrib, scrip	write	inscription, scribe
sequ, sue	follow	consecutive, sequence, ensue
spec, spic	look	spectator, despicable

sta, sist	stand	static, desist
tact, tang	touch	tangent, tactile
tele	far away	television, telegraph
ten, tent	hold	intent, attend
tra, tract	draw, drag	retract, contract
ven, vent	come	convention, adventure
vers, vert	turn	revert, inverse
voc, voke	call	avocation, invoke

Stress and Accent. Stress is the prominence given to a syllable or word that makes it stand out over the surrounding syllables or words. Accent is the stress given to a syllable. Some of the generalizations that are useful for children to learn are indicated.

1. The first syllable of a two-syllable word is usually accented; examples: *chap'ter, har'vest.*
2. The root of a word is usually accented; examples: *re-duc'ing, dis-pleas'ure.*
3. In compound words, the accent usually is on the first word; examples: *door'way, sail'boat.*
4. A word that is changed to a verb or adjective from a noun has a changed accent; examples: *con'duct* to the verb *con-duct'*, *reb'el* to the verb *re-bel'*, *min'ute* to the adjective *mi-nute'*, *ab'stract* to the adjective *ab-stract'*. Also, suffixes added to a long word often change the accent; examples: *vac'ci-nate* to *vac-ci-na'tion*, *mi'cro-scope* to *mi-cro-scop'ic.*

As was stated earlier, these are general principles, and they can receive lessening emphasis as the child develops vocabulary knowledge. Sometimes the teacher gives the child direct explanations with specific words accompanied wherever possible with additional illustrations. As soon as the skill of dictionary usage is taught, that becomes a major tool to supplement what the child hears.

By starting with regular compound words, moving to root words with their inflectional endings in contextual situations, and having the children listen for syllabication, the teacher takes them through the steps that are necessary for the blending of parts of words into the whole word. The children should arrive at an acceptable procedure for unlocking new words, pronouncing them, and getting their meaning. When children have serious difficulty in reading, the problem may often be traced to their inability to relate the phonic and structural analysis procedures in one total process using both visual and auditory perception. The difficulty could also be traced to the teacher or school curriculum, where the steps are taught discretely with no attempt made to help the child relate them.

The Dictionary

One of the tools that the child must learn to use in the classroom is the dictionary. The types of dictionaries range from the simple picture dictionaries used in the primary grades to the large unabridged editions. Dictionary skills are developmental in nature, and they must be refined and extended as the child moves through the grades.

There are certain prerequisites for successful use of the dictionary: (1) knowledge of the alphabet and alphabetical order, (2) the understanding that a word can have several different meanings, (3) a knowledge of root words and derived and inflected forms, (4) the understanding that letters represent different sounds in different situations, and (5) a knowledge of phonic and structural analysis as approaches to words; (6) use of a key (to pronunciation, etc.).

A listing of all the developmental tasks necessary to dictionary mastery includes the following tasks:

1. Recognize individual letters.
2. Differentiate between letters.
3. Associate letter names with symbols.
4. Know the letters of the alphabet in order.
5. Arrange words in alphabetical order by the initial letter.
6. Extend this skill to the second and third letters if necessary.
7. Approximate position in the dictionary of a word by its initial letter by dividing the alphabet letters into quarters.
8. Use accent marks for the pronunciation of words.
9. Interpret the phonetic spelling used in the dictionary.
10. Use the pronunciation key given by the dictionary.
11. Determine the pronunciation of the word in context.
12. Determine the meaning of the word desired in context.
13. Determine the preferred pronunciation when several are given.
14. Use the guide words at the top of the page for locating a word.
15. Identify the fact that a word should be capitalized.
16. Use the hyphen where the entry calls for it.
17. Determine the linguistic sense of the word (semantics, sequence, and so on).
18. Use cross-references.
19. Identify the parts of speech.
20. Identify and use abbreviations and the key to abbreviations.
21. Identify and use idioms, such as *by the way* and *well-to-do.*
22. Use special sections, such as geographic names, biographical data, and foreign words and phrases.
23. Use etymology facts, such as word derivations in structure and history.

Visual symbols should be taught, such as accent marks: *hap′pen;* diacritical marks: the macron (¯), *date = dāt;* the breve (˘), *ăm;* the schwa (ə), *beckon = bek′ən;* the circumflex (^), *fôr;* the tilde (~), *mak′ẽr.*

The child's language ability, not his or her grade placement, should be the deciding factor in his or her readiness for learning the dictionary skills. However, a general picture of the instructional level of the different phases is helpful to see the program in perspective. The basal readers used or the reading program materials will be influential in the choices of these levels of instruction.

1. Children can make their own picture dictionary and use it in the first stage.
2. Children in the second stage can alphabetize words by their initial letter when they know the letters of the alphabet.
3. The long and short sounds of vowel phonemes can be used in the third stage, and syllables can be used. Children can use the breve and the macron.
4. Children by the fourth stage can alphabetize words through the second and third letters, and they can use the terms *vowel, consonant, accent, synonym,* and *antonym.* They can use syllables, accent marks, page guides, and respellings.
5. By the fifth stage children can also use the terms *diacritical mark, root, stem, prefix,* and *suffix* and understand derivatives (both main and run-on entries), preferred spellings, and preferred pronunciations.
6. By the sixth stage they can also fully alphabetize words, use the abbreviations of the parts of speech, and use unabridged dictionaries.
7. All skills have to be strengthened and reinforced by the seventh stage and from there on.

These stages may parallel the normal grade advancement of children; again they may not, for a child could be delayed in starting formal reading and thus could be in the second grade when in the first stage of dictionary development.

Many classrooms provide children with individual dictionaries. These are usually the elementary ones, which are small, abridged models and are easily handled by the children. This seems to be the best way to encourage the dictionary habit. It is suggested, too, that the school library contain the unabridged dictionary that is necessary for research purposes when the child needs further information than that which his or her small dictionary furnishes. The dictionary is a reference book, although it is used often in directed learning activity.

Some of the standard elementary school dictionaries are

AMERICAN BOOK COMPANY

Webster's Elementary Dictionary—grades 3–6.
Dictionary Discoveries—a programmed book for use with *Webster's Elementary Dictionary.*
Webster's New Elementary Dictionary—grades 3–6.
Webster's New Practical School Dictionary—grades 4–8.
Webster's New Students Dictionary—grades 7–12.

HARCOURT BRACE JOVANOVICH

Harbrace Guide to Dictionaries (paper).

HOLT, RINEHART AND WINSTON

Pixie Dictionary—a readiness picture dictionary.
Very First Words—a picture dictionary for writing and spelling.
Word Wonder Dictionary—a linguistic approach to vocabulary development.
Basic Dictionary of American English—contains gazetteer, nations of the world, Indian tribes of North America.
The Holt Intermediate Dictionary of American English—contains United States presidents, the states, provinces of Canada, countries of the United Nations, weights and measures, signs and symbols, geologic timetable, foreign money units.
The Winston Dictionary for Schools.

MACMILLAN PUBLISHING CO., INC.

My Self-help Dictionary—picture dictionary.
Webster's New World Dictionary, Elementary Edition.
Learning How to Use the Dictionary, plus manual and tests.

NOBLE AND NOBLE, PUBLISHERS, INC.

Picture Dictionary for Primary Grades—paperback picture dictionary.

SCOTT, FORESMAN AND COMPANY

My Little Pictionary—grades 1 and 2, picture.
My Second Pictionary—grades 2 and 3.
Beginning Dictionary—grade 4.
Junior Dictionary—grades 5 and 6.
Advanced Junior Dictionary—grades 7 and 8.
Dictionaries and That Dictionary, softbound.

Programed Materials—Dictionary Skills

CALIFORNIA TEST BUREAU

Lessons for Self-instruction—grades 4–6.

CORONET LEARNING PROGRAMS (CHICAGO)

David Discovers the Dictionary—grades 4–6.

Synthesis and Techniques

Neuwirth [28] said the meaning of a sentence lies in the relationships underlying the surface representation—the syntactically expressed relationship; example: *actor-action-object*—not from a string of isolated words. So, too, in a paragraph or article or a story, meaning is derived not from strings of unrelated sentences, but from the author's underlying organization (with causation, sequence, identification, relationships). Sample grammar and syntax can be developed as a model. Psycholinguistic approaches suggest that the proficient reader can identify surface markers in deriving the underlying relations between words. Syntactic clues the reader uses are (1) word order (sense determined by sequence of words) and the relations these reflect; (2) pattern markers—word inflections and function words; and (3) punctuation (sets off phrases, clauses, and the completed sentence). The skilled reader uses the redundancy and predictability of syntactic surface markers to "chunk" information. "Chunking" means fewer units to store in memory.

When readers develop some sophistication in their reading, they may recognize certain clues to the unknown word in a passage. These may be language-rhythm clues or picture clues, or they may be context clues. These clues narrow the possibilities of what the word might sensibly be, and they help the readers decide whether they must use the other forms of word attack and which ones they should use. They may start to use phonic or structural analysis or configuration and not have to use one of these completely before they know what the word is. They may suddenly know the word because it makes sense in the context or meaning of the sentence or passage.

There are several context clues that should be taught when the appropriate occasion arises in the reading experience. The thoughtful teacher makes sure the occasion does arise, for the use of context clues is a very effective tool in rapid reading for meaning. These are the most frequently encountered context clues:

1. *Definition.* The unknown word is defined in the passage. "Although the surrounding land area was green, we saw that the high range of _____ was covered with snow as we flew over."
2. *Synonym.* A word that means the same as the unknown word is given in the passage, and instead of a repetition of the known word, another one is used in its place. "You certainly are a pal; you will be my lifelong _____."

[28] Sharyn Neuwirth, "A Look At Intersentence Grammar," *The Reading Teacher,* **30**, 1:28–32 (Oct. 1976).

3. *Familiar expression.* (context clues) Everyday expressions with which the reader is familiar help him identify the unknown word. "That pan has several holes; it leaks like a _____."

4. *Comparison or contrast.* That which is unknown is compared to or contrasted with a word that is known. "The engine of that lawn-mower _____ like the engines of an airplane revving up for a takeoff."

5. *Experience.* The unknown is recognized through the reader's former personal experiences or reading. "The young foxes are _____ just as kittens or puppies do with a piece of string."

6. *Word order.* Linguistically, certain words have a tendency to be in a certain sequence. "He has just awakened from a deep _____." "He did not _____ that he was too close to the machine until his tie caught in it."

7. *Reflection of a mood.* The situation provides a mood or tone that the unknown word must reflect: "All were happy and smiling as they danced _____ around him."

8. *Summary.* The unknown word summarizes the several ideas that precede it. "As he stood before his audience, his hand shook, his voice was husky, and perspiration appeared on his forehead, for he was very _____."

If the preceding context clues appear in the reading material, the teacher should stop and have the children identify them. If they do not appear, then the teacher can make up exercises leaving out the word to be furnished by the children. Another way to accomplish the recognition of clues is to make up riddles about the unknown word, using the clues. A final method would be to plant clues in the children's own stories and conversation and then to discuss them.

Children will probably always have trouble with some types of expressions until they have built some experience with them. The teacher should help them in direct encounter with idiomatic expressions, as in the sentence "The dam will be built to *harness* the river"; with abstract terms, such as the *forest belt* or the *shrinking world;* with figurative terms like the *raging wind* or *dancing eyes;* and with new connotations for previously known words, such as *ruler,* meaning the leader of a country, or *brothers,* meaning members of the same group or race. Children's magazines often help children become accustomed to new figurative language, such as the *bamboo curtain,* the *cold war,* a *busman's holiday, dollar diplomacy, horns of a dilemma,* and the *squeaking wheel.* One clue should be taken from the fact that children who live on a military base or next to an airport quickly pick up the specialized jargon of their parents. To them a vacation is a leave; a store may be the PX. Proximity and the frequency of hearing these terms make them easily learned. Teachers in the classroom can use proximity and frequency in their instructional planning to assure success.

Content Fields

In 1940, Luella Cole prepared *The Teacher's Handbook of Technical Vocabulary,*[29] in which are listed the essential elementary terms and concepts in thirteen school subjects, together with their frequency of occurrence. The classroom teacher would find it worthwhile to examine the lists in the various subjects taught and then to accumulate his or her own list of words that children find difficult. These words could be taught in anticipation of reading assignments. Most teachers seem to be only vaguely aware of the precise difficulties their children encounter in reading in the content fields. Good instruction involves preparation for reading in any subject. An analysis of the types of vocabulary children face in content areas will result in more effective instruction.

There is the specialized vocabulary of each subject. Words such as the following have to be learned in their contextual setting so that the concept is clear: *terrarium, divisor, equator, shelter, century, mores, region, production, abolition, hemisphere, the Middle East, ancient, civilization.* Some words have multiple meanings and must be recognized in a new context from that previously known. Children know a lion as an animal of the cat family, which they have seen at the zoo or on television. In their reading they encounter a man called a lion because of his courage or excessive cruelty; or a social lion, one who is the object of curiosity and interest; or the constellation Leo. These are new meanings for the children, and for them they must build associations that are new. They may know the man as their father; then encounter the same word meaning any male, an adult, or all human beings, past and present. Some specialized vocabulary involves broad concepts, such as society, religion, government. Then, too, there are little words that had almost no meaning that suddenly develop very specific meaning, as in "3 and 2 are 5," where *and* becomes *plus,* and *are* becomes *equal.*

In the social studies many new words are being added to an already heavy vocabulary load. Such new words are *grassroots, blitz, goldbrick, rabbit ears, snow* (TV), *supermarket, kudos, greenspan, ads,* and *deductible.* New names for geographic places and people suddenly spring into the limelight; at the present writing they are towns and states in Africa. In science there are unfamiliar uses of such words, such as *ocean of air* or *sandwich of rock* or *air,* and words never encountered before, such as *troposphere, emulsion,* and *leptons.* In mathematics, added to the new vocabulary of terms

[29] Luella Cole, *The Teacher's Handbook of Technical Vocabulary* (Bloomington, IL: Public School Publishing Company, 1940).

such as *set* and *base,* there are the symbols that must be learned, such as +, −, ×, >, <, and =. A whole group of abbreviations are added: *lb., hr., ans., pt., doz.* Then, too, there are the formulas, which are a new language themselves. In English there is the formal writing vocabulary, which may differ considerably from that which children are used to. Also, they frequently encounter terms that are no longer used in our present-day vernacular and thus, in effect, become new terms to the children.

The teacher must find some way to relate new words to the past experience of the children. In teaching new words, the teacher has the children pronounce them, use them in discussion, use them in reporting, hear them in the reading of stories, and use them and use them. Meaningful practice is the only way the children will become familiar with the words.

Vocabulary Difficulties

A number of difficulties common to classroom instruction are presented here because they will occur in spite of the best planning of the program.

Word Calling. This is a frequent problem in beginning reading, and the teacher should very early say to the child, "Have you heard someone say, 'I saw him'?" "How would she say that?" "Say it again." "What do you mean?" The total approach is to get the child to recognize that reading stands for talking and to want to get the meaning from what he or she is saying. Meaning is the important aspect from the very beginning. Word-by-word reading may be due to habit, an excessive use of phonics, a short fixation span, material too difficult, or too low intelligence. The solution to some of these causes is quite obvious. When correction can be handled in the classroom, the teacher starts with phrases that are familiar to the children in their listening vocabulary and has them repeat them in the reading context; then they move on to less familiar ones and attempt to read those with the same ease of expression. If excessive phonics usage is the problem, then the teacher must move the child gradually into sight-word reading—seeing the whole word at once. Some form of tachistoscopic exercises or word and phrase games may be helpful at this stage.

Substitution. Some children guess a word from context and substitute their own guess for the correct word without paying attention to the configuration or the initial blend of the word. The teacher patiently calls attention to the word itself in such cases. Where there are many and frequent substitutions, the teacher must use judgment in deciding what to do about it. If spontaneously correcting the error would interfere with the meaning of the passage, the teacher should not stop the reader. If corrections are necessary frequently, easier reading material should be selected. The teacher might allow the child to finish reading the passage and then go back and correct the substitutions by calling the child's attention to the wrong word. If it were an occasional oversight, the other children might be asked to correct it. Rereading should be done if the meaning has suffered because of the substitution.

Omissions. Letter or word omissions should receive special attention. The teacher first determines the type of problem. Is the child not paying attention to the endings of words? Is he skipping whole words? How does this affect the meaning of the passage? Is he depending too much upon context? The solution may be simply calling the child's attention to the sequence of the words or to endings or to syllabication.

Reversals. If the child reverses words, the teacher calls attention to the word and its meaning in the selection or to the selection itself. The most common reversals are of the words *was* and *saw* and of *no* and *on.* Great emphasis and time should not be placed on correction of these reversals, for the child, in most cases, outgrows them as he blends letters from left to right. Letter reversals, such as *b* and *d, m* and *n,* are best handled by focusing attention to meaning in the context of the whole word. Practice may be enhanced by the use of familiar sight words.

Losing the Place. Poor readers often have difficulty following the line of print or in the return sweep to the beginning of the next line, causing confusion, and regressions. If the material is of an appropriate level for the reader, the lighting and the position of the book should be examined. If these are correct, the child may need a line guide, which he will discard as soon as feasible. Finger-pointing should be discouraged, because children should be trained to see (or read) in phrases rather than to isolate syllables or words in the line of print.

Misconceptions. Homographs and homonyms give children a great deal of trouble in their reading until they have gained a sufficient experience to understand words from context. A homograph is a word with the same spelling as another word but with a different meaning and origin, such as *mail,* meaning *armor* or *letters.* A homonym is a word with the same pronunciation as another but with a different meaning, origin, and, often, spelling, such as *principal* and *principle.* Probably all of us have experienced sometime in our reading the sudden insight we gain when we discover that a word such as *animated* does not mean *like an animal* but *full of spirit* or *vigorous,* as in an *animated discussion.* Children frequently have misconceptions of the words in series that they have heard but have not actually seen visually. Many illustrations, humorous to adults, have been given from children's Pledge of Allegiance, or from church prayers: "Lead us not into Penn station. . . ."

Figurative Expressions. Children encounter expressions that they can read orally but have difficulty interpreting unless they have heard them used in the same context. Examples of these are (1) the quarterback *barked* his signals; (2) night *fell* on them suddenly; (3) the woodchuck is very, very fat, but doesn't *care a pin* for that; and (4) John *lost his head* when the fire started.

Foreign Language. The English-speaking child has difficulty with foreign words and phrases, and these must be taught as he encounters them. The bilingual child has other kinds of difficulties: (1) English word sequence may be different from that of his language spoken at home; (2) English words may not be used frequently enough for him to get accustomed to them; and (3) the idioms do not fit the individual word meanings he or she is trying to learn. When both mono- and bilingual children are in the same classroom, they may help each other. Otherwise, the teacher must provide patience and frequent practice sessions to help these children.

INTEREST IN WORDS

The teacher continually has three programs for encouraging the children's interest in words. A time and a setting for wide reading is the first method, for that puts to work the skills that children are learning. Second, direct instruction in word analysis and word meanings is a continuous process. Third, incidental instruction builds a running vocabulary and conveys to the children the adult's interest in words. This latter is important as an attitude and habit builder. In the classroom, children should build their own personal list of new words, especially those with which they have some trouble or seldom meet in their reading. In the middle grades it is not too early to point out a system whereby the children can build their personal glossary in the back of their own books. This should result in the establishment of a lifelong habit. A reading vocabulary becomes permanent as it is transferred to the writing, speaking, and thinking processes.

Word Origins

One method of direct teaching should be mentioned here as a technique for motivating an interest in words. It is the study of word origins. An interesting start can be made in the middle grades with the first names of the children. They can investigate the meaning and derivation in the back of a dictionary in the section called "A Pronouncing Vocabulary of Common English Christian Names." From their books on local history children are interested in the way certain nearby places got their names. This interest may be expanded to a study of the derivation of other names of places. They may then move on to a study of the derivations of other words. For example, one child has become interested in the source of the word *doctor.* This is what he or she reports to the class:

> doctor—Latin, *docere, doct-,* meant to lead, to teach; hence (from the adjective Latin, *docilis,* easily led) Eng. *docile.* That which is taught is a *doctrine,* and *indoctrination* is a form of teaching opposed to education; *cp. destroy. (For induction, see duke.)*

The Latin term *doctor,* learned, was used in the medieval universities as the title for their degrees; we still use it thus, esp. for M.D. (*doctor* of medicine) and D.D.S. (*doctor* of dental surgery). There are many more.

The *Physician* draws his name from Gr. *physike,* knowledge of nature, from *physis,* nature, from *phyein,* to bring forth, cognate with Eng. *be.* The ending is *-ian,* one skilled in, after a word ending *-ica: mathematician; politician* (and other words of analogy).[30]

Another child reads about the meandering river. He is curious about the reason *meandering* means *wandering.* This is what he reports to his classmates:

meander—there is a river, called the *Meander,* in Asia Minor, of which Ovid wrote: "The limpid *Meander* sports in the Phrygian fields; it flows backwards and forwards in its varying course and, meeting itself, beholds its waters that are to follow, until it fatigues its wandering current, now pointing to its source, and now to the open sea." Do you wonder that we speak of meandering?[31]

The teacher may wish to examine the following materials for a range of ideas about interest in words at different levels:

Happy Bears (K–1). Champaign, IL: Garrard Press.
Hayes Duplicating Reading Series (K–2). Wilkensburg, PA: Hayes School Publishing Company.
Let's See (1). St. Louis: Webster Publishing Company.
Eye and Ear Fun (1–3) and (4–6). St. Louis: Webster Publishing Company.
Origins of Words, Robert G. Forest, Curriculum Associates, 1973.
William and Mary Morris, *Dictionary of Words and Phrase Origins,* Volumes I and II, Harper and Row, 1962, 1967.
S. Epstein and B. Epstein. *The First Book of Words.* New York: Franklin Watts, 1954.
Marguerite Ernst. *Words.* New York: Alfred A. Knopf, Inc., 1951.
Magic World of Dr. Spello (4–9). St. Louis: Webster Publishing Company.
Vocabulary Builder Series (6–12). Cambridge, MA: Educator's Publishing Service.
Word Study for Improved Reading (7–12). New York: Globe Publishing Company.
Making Friends with Words (7–12). New York: Globe Publishing Company.
Graded Words and Phrases in Speed-I-O-Strip Series (4, 5–6, 6–8). Filmstrips. Chicago: Society for Visual Education, Inc.
Austin M. Works. *A Vocabulary Builder* (6–12). Cambridge, MA: Educators Publishing Service.

[30] Joseph T. Shipley, *Dictionary of Word Origins* (Ames, IA: Littlefield, Adams and Company, 1955), p. 121.
[31] Ibid., p. 227.

Edward C. Gruber. *2300 Steps to Word Power.* New York: ARC Books,
   Inc.
Joel S. Weinberg. *Word Analysis;* and Lee C. Deighton. *Vocabulary
   Development.* New York: Macmillan Publishing Company, Inc.
Janet M. Rule. *The Structure of Words* (7–12). Cambridge, MA:
   Educators Publishing Service, 1963.
Elmer W. Cavins, *Orthography* (7–8). Chicago: Follett Publishing
   Company, 1961.

There are many other possible types of sources, such as the *Readers Digest's* "It Pays to Increase Your Word Power," crossword puzzles, and anagrams. The only limitation the authors would place on these emphases of interest in words is the slight danger of "word worship" in a perfectionist kind of atmosphere. This is an extreme that few teachers need fear. If the children are prepared or ready for an increase in their vocabulary horizons, the teacher should be prepared to help them.

MEANINGFUL PRACTICE

Teachers who use the basal readers have the accompanying teachers' manuals to guide and assist them in their instruction. The teacher, though, is the one who must recognize individual differences and provide appropriate extra practice for those children who need it. College courses in child development and the psychology of learning provide the bases for making such judgments. Through these courses future teachers recognize the reasons for providing extra practice in the form of repetition, reinforcement, motivation through variety, transfer of training in writing, and supplementary exercises in critical reading. Knowledge of the sources of materials and of their correct use, then, becomes an objective of preparing to teach reading, and in this subarea, vocabulary, *The First R* suggests[32] that teachers do not adequately use the manuals. If this is characteristic of many teachers, then they must rely heavily upon their own knowledge of and the availability of the materials that will selectively supplement their classroom instruction in word analysis and total vocabulary power.

   In teaching by drill, be sure that (1) the learning experience is appropriate for the learning mode, (2) it produces the desired outcome, and (3) it has reliability as a tool for reading.

   To enhance word acquisition, there are many and varied approaches. In the first grade children enjoy matching words on cards with words on the chalkboard, a chart, or in a book. They practice framing words and phrases as they pronounce them singly or in chorus. They may locate words that are repeated. They use a word(s) to create new stories. They use a

[32] Austin and Morrison, *op. cit.,* pp 29–32.

"This is the way I see it."

word(s) in discussion. The teacher obtains new material by examining trade books for common words and calls the attention of the children to them for reading experience. Children with the help of the teacher can build a word box file and keep word cards in it for review.

Teacher-prepared materials can be developed to serve almost any need in the classroom and can be duplicated for group work. Word cards can be made or purchased. Examples of sources of commercial word cards are:

1. Dolch, E. W. *Basic Sight Vocabulary Cards.* Champaign, IL:
2. Dolch, E. W. *Popper Words.* Garrard.
3. Dolch, E. W. *Picture Word Cards.* Garrard.
4. Mountain, L. *Word Family Fun.* Buffalo, NY.: Kenworthy Education Service.
5. *Picto-Word Flash Cards.* Dansville, NY.: F. A. Owen Publishing Company.

Children enjoy keeping their own word notebook with each new word they have put in it, along with their own sentences using the word correctly in context. This can be a great source of pride for the child. The teacher may call attention to the collection of words by asking the following questions in respect to the story about to be read:

1. Choose a word (or more if desired) that has more than one meaning. What are its different meanings?
2. Which words are used in the plural form?
3. Which words give you trouble?
4. Which words give you a happy feeling?

5. Which words indicate a great deal of action?
6. Which words would help you describe a person and identify him?
7. Which two words rhyme?

Words can be fun. Many games are used to enhance the learning of vocabulary and the gaining of experiences with new words. *Guessing Riddles* is a good example, wherein the word is described by one child and then another child or the class tries to guess the word. Word Wheels are commonly used in classrooms to relate parts of words:

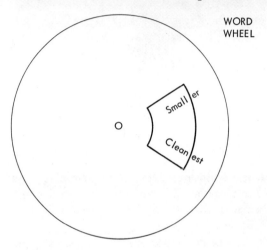

WORD
WHEEL

Another form for accomplishing the same result is

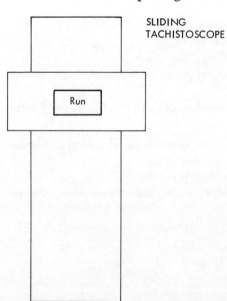

SLIDING
TACHISTOSCOPE

Word Lotto and *Word Bingo* are other examples of games used to reinforce skill with words. Many publishers, such as Garrard, Milton-Bradley, and Webster now produce a great variety of word games played with cards.

Motivation to learn words is not confined to books and games in the classroom. There is a rapidly increasing science of "hardware" that includes machines that will aid vocabulary development. They include the *Tach-X* and *Flash-X* of Educational Development Laboratories, *The Language-Master,* the tachistoscopes of Keystone View Company and Lafayette Instrument Company, the *Speed-I-Scope* of the Society for Visual Education, and the SRA *Tachist-o-Flasher,* and others. Although they are not typically found in classrooms, they do appear in some, and federal aid has made it possible for more schools to furnish such materials.

Children's newspapers furnish an opportunity for word growth in a number of ways. They contain questions and word games, rhymes, cross-word puzzles, and other forms of varied approaches.

Teachers should not overlook the materials that most publishers will furnish with the basal reading series—workbooks, filmstrips, tests, pocket charts, and large books for group work.

One of the fine resource booklets that teachers have found very helpful suggests teacher-made vocabulary games and divides at elementary and secondary levels.[33]

Meaningful practice must be examined carefully from time to time by the teacher to see that it is a balanced word-attack program and that the forms of experiences are balanced in the total language arts. Attention to single words should never overshadow the meaning of the passage. Speaking, writing, and reading ideas are the appropriate goal.

The classroom environment should be arranged so that groups of children may interact with each other, allowing language input, practice, and feedback. Concrete experiences that provide extending activities, add depth to known vocabulary, and bring children in contact with new items or processes linked to verbal descriptions are important. Conversations with adults that center on the content of the child's remarks create the opportunity for practice and for mature language input. Surrounding children with a wealth of oral language, meaningful for them to hear and use, seems to be a significant step to culminate in mastery of another language form—the written word.

[33] David H. Russell and E. E. Karp, *Reading Aids Through the Grades* revised (New York: Bureau of Publications, Teachers College, Columbia University, 1965).

EVALUATION

Informal

Children's vocabulary development should be examined continuously. The rate of development in word knowledge and use is related to intelligence and environmental contacts with words. The teacher regulary checks to see if they know what a word means and asks them to use the word in a sentence that shows that they know its contextual relationship. The informal reading inventory often starts with a wordlist chosen from the books at each level. Only carefully graded words are chosen for this purpose, and a child's performance on the wordlist gives a quick indication of the book level at which the informal reading inventory should begin (see Chapter 13).

Another procedure is the classroom use of a sight wordlist on cards, such as the Dolch Basic 220 Word List. This may be used as an indicator for beginning reading or as a review for a child's current status at any stage in the first few years of reading.

The teacher must constantly be alert for the symptoms of causes of word-by-word reading. Teaching vocabulary in isolation is not the method for producing good readers, for poor readers cannot relate vocabulary in meaningful sequence. Some children are slow word-by-word readers even though they know meanings for a considerable number of words.

Following are some ways in which word-by-word reading may be caused.

1. Confusing quantitative and qualitative miscues (surface level decoding; overall test score grouping; inappropriate materials).
2. Placing students at wrong level (frustration level; too stringent IRI criteria—teacher should use Powell's 1971 revised criteria; types of errors).
3. Not providing language match (matching similar patterns of language structure by reader and materials without experience charts using children's language) or syntactically too difficult material even if overall readability is satisfactory.
4. Assuming that the print carries meaning (meaning is supplied by the reader; thought grouping is by syntax, not visual).
5. Assuming that children are cognitively mature enough to handle concept load (Piagetian—have not reached level of maturity to handle abstract words)
6. Overloading the memory system (new information infringing on old; making word-perfect reading the objective).
7. Not providing opportunity for discussion of ideas.[34]

To appraise the child's progress after instruction the teacher may develop informal tests on endings of common root words—-*s, -ed, -ing,* and

[34] Victor Froese, "How to Cause Word-By-Word Reading," *The Reading Teacher,* **30,** 6:611–15 (March, 1977).

so on: *seated, jumps, walking.* The same may be done for contractions: *I'll, we've;* for compound words: *everyone, raincoat;* for derived forms; *slowly, safety;* and for syllabication: *re-mem-ber, beau-ti-ful.* These would be developed from second grade on through the elementary school. Informal auditory discrimination exercises can be devised by the teacher for evaluating growth. Directions: Have the child listen and respond with the word that does *not* belong:

Skill	Words			
Hearing initial consonants	toy	tall	hall	tack
Hearing initial blends	blue	blow	bank	black
Hearing vowel sounds	joke	lock	note	snow
Hearing word endings	sack	neck	knit	kick

These informal techniques may also be used for the purpose of regrouping for instruction as well as determining the success of instruction.

Students moving into a different basal series or program encounter many words they have not previously been introduced to. Assessment of these words is needed before proceeding. Word-attack skills should also be assessed. The meaning of words, as well as pronunciation, is important. One good procedure would be to keep a record of words introduced at each level to provide as much continuity as possible to the childs' program.

One other informal procedure should be mentioned: the use of the teacher's observation of the child's performance in word games and the one-to-one interaction of children in different settings—formal classroom and informal play and playground situations.

Formal Testing

Vocabulary is very important in reading comprehension, and therefore most silent reading tests include a separate section for measuring vocabulary status. The teacher should examine several tests to be sure that the one chosen will yield an indication of the skills desired. The teacher might profit from an examination of the vocabulary section of some of the following tests:

READINESS TESTS

1. American School Readiness Test K—1, Public School Publishing Co.
2. Clymer-Barrett Prereading Battery K—1, Personnel Press, Inc.
3. Gates Reading Readiness Test K—1, Teachers College Press.
4. Lee-Clark Reading Readiness Test K—1, California Test Bureau.
5. Van Wagenen Reading Readiness Scales K—1, Psycho-Educational Research Laboratories.

PRIMARY TESTS

1. Bond-Hoyt-Clymer Silent Diagnostic Reading Test 1–3, Lyons & Carnahan.
2. Botel Reading Inventory 1–3, Follett.
3. California Reading Test 1–2, California Test Bureau.
4. Coordinated Scales of Attainment 1–3, Educational Test Bureau.
5. Detroit Word Recognition Test 1–2, Harcourt Brace Jovanovich, Inc.
6. Dolch-Gray Word Recognition and Word Attack Tests 1–3, Scott, Foresman and Company.
7. Doren Diagnostic Reading Test of Word Recognition Skills 1–4, American Guidance Service.
8. Durrell-Sullivan Reading Capacity and Achievement Test 2.5–4.5, Harcourt Brace Jovanovich, Inc.
9. Gates Primary Reading Test 1–2.5, Teachers College Press.
10. Gates Advanced Primary Reading Test 2.5–3, Teachers College Press.
11. Manwiller Word Recognition Test 1–2, Harcourt Brace Jovanovich, Inc.
12. Metropolitan Reading Tests 1–2, Harcourt, Brace Jovanovich, Inc.
13. Pressey Diagnostic Reading Test 1A–2A, Public School Publishing Company.
14. SRA Achievement Series: Reading 2–4, Science Research Associates.
15. Stanford Primary I and II Reading 1.5–2.4 and 2.5–3.9, Harcourt Brace Jovanovich, Inc.
16. Stroud-Hieronymus Primary Reading Profiles 1–2, Houghton Mifflin Company.

UPPER ELEMENTARY TESTS

1. American School Achievement Tests 2–3, 4–6, 7–9, The Bobbs-Merrill Co., Inc.
2. California Reading Test 4–6, California Test Bureau.
3. Durrell-Sullivan Reading Capacity and Achievement Test 3–6, Harcourt Brace Jovanovich, Inc.
4. Durkin-Meshover Phonics Knowledge Survey all grades, Teachers College Press.
5. Gates-MacGinitie Reading Tests K–12, Teachers College Press.
6. Gates-McKillop Reading Diagnostic Tests all grades, Teachers College Press.
7. Holley Sentence Vocabulary Scale 3–12, Public School Publishing Company.

8. Hoyt-Clymer Developmental Reading Tests 4–6, Lyons & Carnahan.
9. Iowa Every-Pupil Tests of Basic Skills 3–9, Houghton Mifflin Company.
10. Iowa Silent Reading Test 4–8, Harcourt Brace Jovanovich, Inc.
11. Metropolitan Reading Tests 3–4 and 5–7.5, Harcourt Brace Jovanovich, Inc.
12. McCullough Word Analysis Test 4–5, Ginn and Company.
13. Nelson-Lohmann Reading Test 4–8, Educational Test Bureau.
14. Roswell-Chall Auditory Blending Test, Essay Press.
15. SRA Achievement Series: Reading 4–6, Science Research Associates.
16. Stanford Achievement Test: Reading 5–6, Harcourt Brace Jovanovich, Inc.
17. Thorndike Test of Word Knowledge 4–9, Teachers College Press.

OTHERS

1. Detroit Tests of Learning Aptitude, ages 3⁺, The Bobbs-Merrill Co., Inc.
2. Illinois Test of Psycholginguistic Abilities, ages 2–10, University of Illinois Press.
3. Learning Methods Test (Mills), K–3, Mills Center, Inc.
4. Slosson Oral Reading Test, K-H.S., Slosson Education, Inc.

SUMMARY

For a complete description of the tests and the reactions of some users to the tests, see the *Mental Measurements Yearbooks.*[35] Publishers regularly put out bulletins, flyers, and catalogs with descriptions of their newest revisions of the tests, as well as any new tests that have been placed on the market. A specimen set of any test can be purchased for the teachers' perusal by the school system at nominal cost. There is really no good excuse for teachers' not being familiar with appropriate tests in their field. Familiarity with a test means that the teacher knows (1) the type of test, (2) what the test measures (preferably by taking the test oneself and studying its parts), (3) by which means it measures vocabulary (preferably in a contextual setting), (4) what kind of norms are presented and how they were derived, (5) the appropriateness of the levels of difficulty of the test, (6) the available forms of the test, and (7) any other characteristics important to the teacher's educational setting.

[35] Oscar K. Buros, *First through Eighth Mental Measurements Yearbooks* (New Brunswick, NJ: Gryphon Press).

Tests represent one important phase of a continuous process of evaluation. They give an indication of the status of one child in relation to other children at any given time in development of the child's vocabulary skills. The data should be recorded carefully so that information concerning the child's progress can be studied along with other evidence at any time.

SELECTED READINGS

Barnard, Douglas P., and James De Gracie. "Vocabulary Analysis of New Primary Reading Series." *The Reading Teacher,* 30,3, (Nov. 1976), 177–80.

Bush, Clifford, and Robert Andrews. *Dictionary of Reading and Learning Disabilities.* Los Angeles, CA: Western Psychological Services, 1978.

Buros, Oscar K. *First* through *Eighth Mental Measurements Yearbooks.* Highland Park, NJ: Gryphon Press.

———. *Reading Tests and Reviews.* I (1968) and II (1975). Highland Park, NJ: Gryphon Press.

Drever, James. *A Dictionary of Psychology,* revised. Baltimore, MD: Penguin Books, 1964.

Durkin, Dolores. *Phonics in the Teaching of Reading.* New York: Teachers College Press, Columbia University, 1965.

Gibson, Eleanor, and Harry Levin, *Psychology of Reading.* Cambridge, MA: The M.I.T. Press, 1975.

Heilman, Arthur W. *Phonics in Proper Perspective,* 3d ed. Columbus, OH: Charles E. Merrill Publishing Company, 1976.

Hull, Marion. *Phonics for the Teacher of Reading.* Columbus, OH: Charles E. Merrill Publishing Company, 1976.

Lamb, Pose. *Linguistics In Proper Perspective,* 2d ed. Columbus, OH: Charles E. Merrill Publishing Company, 1977.

Leonard, Laurence B. *Meaning in Child Language: Issues in the Study of Early Semantic Development.* New York: Grune & Stratton, Inc., 1976.

Mazurkiewicz, Albert J. *Teaching About Phonics.* New York: St. Martin's Press, Inc., 1976.

Ruddell, Robert D. *Innovations in Reading—Language Instruction.* Englewood-Cliffs, NJ: Prentice-Hall, Inc., 1974.

Russell, David H., and E. E. Karp. *Reading Aids Through The Grades, Revised.* New York: Teachers College Press, Columbia University Press, 1975.

Chapter 5

Comprehension: Basic Factors

OBJECTIVES

To understand the concepts of comprehension and reading comprehension

To understand the basic factors affecting the development of comprehension skills

To learn specific comprehension skills

To learn the strategies of questioning for ensuring adequate reading comprehension

INTRODUCTION

Seven-year-old Bobby looked up from his easy-to-read book and told his teacher, "This is a funny story. I never heard of a canoe on a hill." She discovered that he had come to the word *knew* and read it as *canoe.*

Tom, aged eleven, had just read the twenty-fourth item on a fifty-item multiple-choice social studies test when the bell rang for dismissal. He had one error and received a failing mark on his paper.

The casual observer in either of the above situations might very well see each child as a reader in trouble. How serious is the problem in each case? What can the classroom teacher do about each one? These children and their counterparts may be found in elementary classrooms at any time. Teachers who diagnose before teaching examine each of these situations with the purpose of determining why each child is reacting thus before deciding what to do for each of them.

Bobby is a bright boy, obviously demanding meaning when reading. He lacks some of the word analysis techniques that would put him on his own more effectively. He lacks the technique of checking his reading in context. With specific help from a skilled teacher, Bobby will eventually be working out such "funny" errors by himself.

Tom is a slow, word-by-word reader. His permanent record cards show an intelligence quotient in the superior range. One error in twenty-four would give him an excellent score, if there were only twenty-four items! With excellent reading comprehension, bright Tom is penalized by his inefficient reading habits. He could not read the entire test in the time allotted. His score becomes a reading score rather than a history score. Diagnostic teaching, for Tom, means breaking his word-by-word habits and substituting the concept "read for ideas; go in with a question and come out with an answer—fast." Tom's teacher gave him some individual attention each day for several weeks to help him acquire more effective reading techniques. Together they attacked a history book, one paragraph at a time. The teacher raised a question. Tom was told to skim quickly until he found a phrase that would answer the question. They progressed to the point where Tom could find a more complicated answer, such as a reason why some event had occurred. Tom was then encouraged to raise his own question before he turned a page. He then read to find his own answer. Thus Tom learned to overcome his slow habits, through the process of setting a purpose for reading even short selections, then reading to find answers as quickly as possible. With some mechanical aids, such as phrases flashed with a tachistoscope, Tom could have had additional help in reading meaningful phrases to break his slow word-by-word reading habit.

The anecdotes related above represent real children at different stages of reading comprehension. The teacher's considered plans to help each student represent a diagnosis based upon as complete knowledge of each child as could be obtained—more, in fact, than is presented in the brief accounts given here. In each case, however, the teacher's knowledge of the child's intellectual capacity or his potential for thinking while reading, gave a clue to methods and materials for his reading improvement.

The good classroom teacher cuts across the knowledge gained in various college courses to arrive at an understanding of the nature of reading comprehension. In psychology courses college students of education learn about children's development—physically, mentally, emotionally, and so on. They learn how children think—how concepts are formed, proceeding from the concrete to the abstract. They study the laws of learning, their effective use and limitations. And they investigate the interests of children from preschool age through adolescence.

In linguistics classes college students learn about communication skills. They discover that the individual learns language in almost the same way the race learned language—oral communication through the imitation of sounds, and written communication through the coding and decoding processes.

In speech courses they learn how accurate speech sounds are produced, and their graphic representations. In linguistic classes they study in detail the language they speak, write, and read. In sociology and social science children are studied as part of the human race, with a heritage of many centuries in the past, and with implications for the present and future. In literature classes students review the folk tales, poetry, stories, and books of their culture.

Often the "new material" of a course is presented in a pattern that appears to be repetitious—the various levels of mental ability of children, the developmental levels of children, and their interests and needs at various ages.

In the very practical setting of the classroom teachers discover the advantages of such repetition. They find that the more they call upon their knowledge of all fields, the better they are able to cope with the problem at hand—providing the best educational experience for each child in the classroom. Thus they can look at the individual (Bobby, for example) as part of an age or grade group, yet as an individual with his own background of experiences, language, native ability, interests, and achievement. They can bring to the solution of Bobby's present reading problems the insights gained through all the information they have at hand about Bobby. And, very significant for Bobby's improvement, his teachers understand the nature of reading, the factors affecting reading comprehension, and the effective methods of teaching reading comprehension skills.

LEVELS OF READING COMPREHENSION

What are the basic comprehension skills? What sequential pattern is involved in their development? What comprehension skills does the mature reader possess? In the balance of this chapter and the succeeding one, these questions will be investigated. The implications for the teacher of reading at the various developmental levels will be considered.

Definition

Current definitions of reading comprehension reflect the thinking of educators, psychologists, linguists, and psycholinguists. Although some definitions of reading and reading comprehension reflect a decoding emphasis, usually those who define reading comprehension go beyond the step of deciphering the graphic representation of sound (print) to some consideration of the meaning implied by the writer of the symbols.

Reading comprehension has been variously defined as (1) an interpretation of written symbols, (2) the apprehending of meaning, (3) the assimilation of ideas presented by the writer, and (4) the process of thinking while deciphering symbols.

In the first definition the assumption is made that symbols for sounds, when written down, can be understood by someone other than the writer. In the second, the reader responds to the printed symbols with a mental image that has meaning because of some direct or vicarious experience associated with the symbols. In the third, the reader digests and makes a part of himself or herself the ideas gleaned from the translation of the writer's words. In the fourth and most inclusive definition, the process of deciphering symbols has been subordinated to the process of thinking. The reader's thinking may take the form of some personal involvement with the ideas presented, some evaluation of the ideas (critical reading), or some creative activity, such as devising a different story ending, a dramatization, some hypothesis for further testing, and so on.

In the process of analyzing reading, Smith has written extensively about reading comprehension. He defined "meaning" as the relevance that can be imposed on an utterance.[1] He considered that children make sense of language when they can bring meaning to it. They also need to understand that what they see on the printed page is meaningful. In *Understanding Reading*,[2] Smith made several cogent statements that add up to a novel way of thinking about comprehension: "I shall define comprehension—or the extraction of meaning from text—as the reduction of uncertainty" (page 185); ". . . Comprehension—the identification of meaning in a passage—may be regarded as a process that results in the elimination of alternatives" (page 194); "Reading for meaning entails making use of information simultaneously at both the surface and deep structure of language—using elements of both visual and semantic information" (page 207); and ". . . knowledge can be acquired of what differences are significant only through experience" (page 209). When we examine these statements, we can conclude that as the reader *reads,* he discriminates visual features (words, groups of words), calls upon one's past experiences, and uses one's personal experience with language (grammar, semantics) to attain meaning from the printed page. Thus one who practices reading, one who always reads and reads, becomes eventually the efficient reader. Such readers become the good readers who read with comprehension when their environment provides many opportunities for reading and for feedback, for questions and discussion to clarify their thinking about their reading and the knowledge they gain from it.

How Children Think

As children grow in reading skill, they can be taught to think about the content of the reading material, while they are reading, as well as after they have read a selection. In terms of intellectual capacity, some children of low potential will be limited to a factual, concrete level of thinking.

[1] Frank Smith, *Comprehension and Learning* (New York: Holt, Rinehart and Winston, 1975).
[2] Frank Smith, *Understanding Reading—A Psycholinguistic Analysis of Reading and Learning to Read* (New York: Holt, Rinehart and Winston, 1971).

They may learn the *who, what, when,* and *where* answers to be found in the content of reading material. Others may be taught to call upon their personal experiences to produce additional insights into the ideas they meet in print. In addition to learning the *who, what, when,* and *where* of the reading material, they may detect the *why* and *how* implicit in the content. Some may be taught to be alert to emotionally toned writing and to be aware that preconceived attitudes may be brought to the reading material. Thus they may evaluate the content in terms of the writer's purposes for writing as well as their own purposes for reading. Those who are capable of more profound thinking about the material they are reading may be taught to do the stratified type of reading that characterizes mastery of the skills of reading comprehension. Involved in stratified reading skills are the abilities to read between the lines, to plumb the depths of the author's purposes, and to find themes applicable to life as a whole. David Russell [3] illustrated this quality of reading comprehension with an analysis of a familiar piece of literature:

> *Tom Sawyer*—on the surface, a story of a boy's adventures; at a second level, an account of life on the Mississippi a hundred years ago; on the third level, a more universal theme—the tug between respectability and the raffish life which we all experience; with respectability exemplified by Aunt Polly and the ne'er-do-well by Huck Finn and his father.

The Stratified Concept

Children in upper elementary grades may employ the stratified concept in their reading of the varied materials they encounter daily. Thus they may learn to read certain sections of a newspaper quickly and superficially while scrutinizing other sections (headlines, editorials, and so on) for examples of documented evidence, biased writing, editorial policy, and so on. They may learn to draw conclusions from their reading of certain textbooks, to form sound judgments based upon wide reading rather than on one writer's viewpoint, and to look between the lines in evaluating some sections of social studies and science selections and raising questions concerning the competency of the writer, the time when the section was written, and so on. Obviously, these are skills that will not be mastered in the elementary grades, but they may be initiated with superior readers in these grades. The teacher's function is to detect which children are capable of reading at the deepest level of comprehension, then to teach the skills involved. Thus children can be taught to note humor, irony, deep emotion, biased writing, fantasy, and so on.

[3] David H. Russell, "Reading for Effective Personal Living," *Reading for Effective Living.* International Reading Association Conference Proceedings, Vol. III (1958), p. 16.

Specific Comprehension Skills

The previous section has dealt with the definitions of reading comprehension as thinking while reading. In this section specific comprehension skills useful to all children, from the slow-learning to the superior student, will be analyzed within the framework of a sequential pattern for their development. (See Figure 5, "Reading Comprehension Skills.")

In Chapter 4 the importance of meaningful vocabularies was presented. The development of an adequate vocabulary was shown to be basic to the ability to read with good comprehension. While children are attaining independence in word recognition and analysis, they are taught to perceive words, phrases, and sentences as meaningful units. Thus they are getting ready for understanding the paragraph, the short story, and the textbook chapter—getting meaning in context from connected prose. All of the steps in Figure 5 under "Meaningful Vocabularies" are fundamental to the attainment of efficient reading comprehension. Teachers need to know that the next steps in the sequence are the thinking skills that they want children to develop while they are reading. When the mechanical aspects of word recognition are learned, children are ready to think while reading.

It was pointed out in Chapter 4 that children bring different levels of experience and different levels of vocabulary development to the initial stages of learning to read. Teachers first help children in these areas before they can expect high-level reading comprehension. Possibly the first skill then, which *all* readers can be taught, is to relate the reading activity at hand to their own background of experience. Teachers foster this ability to relate self to reading when they ask children questions such as, "Has anything like this ever happened to you?" and "How did *you* feel when you had your first party?" and "How does *corduroy* feel when you run your hand over it?"

Main Ideas. Determining the main idea of a paragraph or short story may be taught in primary grades. It is a skill that will be helpful throughout the grades, as well as in college and in personal reading. A teacher focuses attention on the main idea when asking primary grade children, "Why were the squirrels hunting for nuts?" Another teacher asks an upper grade group, "Why does the author give us all these details about the main character?" and "Now that you have read this section in history, what purpose do you think the writer had in presenting it this way?" Usually, in English classes teachers point out the design of good paragraphs, with a topic sentence expressing the main idea. Often this sentence is found at the beginning of the paragraph, with accompanying illustrations and explanatory details. Sometimes the writer presents the illustrations first, leading to the punch line—the topic sentence that pulls the ideas together. In upper grades students will sometimes encounter several paragraphs of illustration following a topic sentence. Too often children have learned about topic sentences in the isolation of an English class and have not learned to make the concept functional in all of their reading. Reading teachers and all content area teachers need to stress the importance of finding the main idea in paragraphs and longer selections. Teachers are reminded of a point made in modern psychology classes: Transfer is not necessarily automatic. Common elements among various subject areas must be pointed out and taught by teachers in each of the areas concerned.

In an art gallery a visitor approaches a masterpiece, seeing from afar a seascape with a ship tossed about on a dark and angry ocean. Thus he or she has an overall idea about the tone of the composition and nears the painting to see how the artist produced this effect. Closer inspection shows the details of the painting, the force and slant of brush strokes, the effect of color boldly applied here, masterfully withheld there, and the devices used by the artist to capture attention upon the focal point of the canvas.

Specific Details. Children can be taught to see the same artistry in well-composed paragraphs and stories. A main idea or theme has been developed by the writer with much attention to details. Teachers draw attention to the details by asking, "Where was the bunny when the farmer first saw him?" "When did the United States buy the Alaskan Territory?" "How does the author let us know that Harry was displeased?"

Sequence. Many writers give their readers clues to a particular sequence of facts, times, events, or other ideas. They may number the series or use such word clues as *first, second, next,* or *last.* Additional illustrations of a main point may be signaled by words such as *moreover, further, then, another example, in addition,* and *finally.* That the writer has given illustrations or reasons leading into the main idea may be indicated by such words as *for these reasons, therefore, consequently,* and so on. Good readers who are alert to such words as connectives learn to follow the author's sequence of ideas as they are reading. Excellent readers take pride in anticipating the sequence or flow of ideas. Thus they are pleased to find the writer presenting what they had predicted or are surprised when the writer presents a different point or outcome. In either case, comprehension is high. In primary grades teachers may ask, "What do you think will happen next?" Other examples of questions that focus attention on sequence are "In what order did Betty prepare the ingredients for the recipe?" "What did Columbus do to get ready for his trip across the ocean?"

Outcomes. Attention and comprehension are high when the teacher asks questions that set purposes for further reading. "What will happen if . . . ?" "If Bill goes ahead with his plan to mix these ingredients in the test tube, what do you expect will happen?" "What else could happen if . . . ?" Teachers know that discovery is one of the best ways of learning and of attaining understandings. In the situations just posed, the teacher knows what outcomes can be predicted but wisely refrains from telling the students. Children who are led this way to conclusions and outcomes feel

Figure 5. Reading Comprehension Skills

Meaningful Vocabularies

Listening, understanding
Speaking
Word recognition
  Sight words
Word analysis
  Structural
  Phonetic
  Blending or synthesizing
Semantics
Dictionary
Word origins

Specific Comprehension

Relating reading to experience
Selecting main ideas
Noting specific details
Following and anticipating sequence
Predicting outcomes
Gaining sensory impressions
Recognizing feelings and moods
Following directions
Locating, evaluating, and using pertinent information
Drawing conclusions

Analysis During Reading

Noting paragraph patterns
Topic sentences
Author's signals

Determining Author's Pattern of Writing

Introduction
Main points
Illustrations
Conclusions

Anticipating Author's Pattern of Presentation

Evaluating Content

Interpreting facts in the reading material
Personal association and experience
  Personal opportunities for applying knowledge gained
  Making comparisons with other materials
Challenging writer's authority

Creative Reading Skills

Interpreting author's purposes
Detecting author's point of view

Figure 5. Reading Comprehension Skills (cont.)

Distinguishing between fact and fiction
Detecting propaganda devices

Synthesis Following Reading

Sensing universal truths
Recognizing new ideas with universal applications
Recognizing new ideas to integrate into a personal philosophy
Recognizing uses or applications of the new ideas acquired
Recognizing possible need for further research
   Suspending judgment
   Summarizing
   Using or applying information gained

---

that they themselves have made the discovery. They know and retain their knowledge longer when taught in this manner.

Sensory Impressions. Reading with effective comprehension involves more than visual clues. Practical firsthand experiences with the ideas in print will help ensure understanding. Memories and strong mental images may be called upon to help involve readers in their reading activity. All of the senses play a part in evoking the sensory impressions called up by words in print. Teachers can prepare children for reading by providing such experiences as handling *fuzzy* peaches, *smooth-skinned* apples, *soft* cotton, *sandpaper, rubber* bands; smelling *buttery* popcorn, *burning* leaves, *apple blossoms;* tasting *sour* cherries, *puckery* lemons, *acidy* vinegar, *sweet* molasses; moving at various gaits, such as *running, hopping, skipping, hobbling* along, *sliding* into the base; and finally more abstract sensory impressions, such as empathy with storybook or historical characters "who were once your age, too."

Feelings and Mood. Children may be reminded of their own feelings at certain times—when they were given birthday presents, when they first saw snow, when their pet was hurt. They may become aware of what triggered certain moods they experienced—sad or happy or excited—listening to certain music, looking at pictures, or starting out on a vacation. Thus they gain insights into the feelings and moods of others as they read about storybook characters or real people in the news or in their history books.

Following Directions. Reading to follow directions is a very practical activity, one that many will be following into adulthood. This activity provides an immediate test of reading comprehension—because the end product will prove how well the person read. Children can be taught this reading skill as soon as they know some words by sight: "Color this red." "Draw a man." "Paint the house white." "Draw two toys." These are examples of exercises children may do to good advantage if they read these directions

"What does it say right here?"

by themselves. They are truly on their own in reading when, prepared by such early practice, they bring home library books from which they learn personal hobbies. Girls may make salads or puddings, following written recipes. Boys may make model planes or kites, following written directions.

Locating Information. Curiosity plays a part in motivating learning. Reading about a new idea can stimulate a student to learn a great deal more that he or she has found in the initial source. Teachers, therefore, need to provide students with such locating skills as using the library, the index, the table of contents, graphs, and charts. Here purposes play a major role. Gifted students, on their own, may literally exhaust the subject. On the other hand, when the students' purpose is to prepare their contribution to a group project their procedure will be different. They will be hunting for information pertinent to their own more limited topics as part of a broader presentation. They will need to evaluate books and articles, scanning them for items that relate to their interests. In both cases, the skills of locating will be useful.

Drawing Conclusions. Elementary students may be led to form conclusions based upon their reading. They need to recognize which of the facts presented would contribute to an acceptable summary or conclusion. They may also note which facts do not apply or add to the evidence needed. Teachers give practice in this skill when they say to students at a critical point in a story or textbook chapter, "From what the author has presented so far, what conclusions can be drawn? Jot down your answers. Then check to see if you agree with the author's conclusions." "What points did the author make that would warrant his drawing this conclusion?"

Analysis During Reading. With considerable practice on each of the aforementioned specific skills, able students in the upper grades will be ready to analyze the structure of printed material while they are perusing it. They can begin to think while reading, "I have found the first topic sentence. Here is an example the author is giving to illustrate the main idea. Now he's going on to another topic sentence. It's an important point. This time he says there will be three illustrations and he's numbering them." Thus the students are transferring to reading the information they have gained in their English class about the structure of paragraphs. Reading in different subject areas, they may discover that one author has a standard pattern for writing paragraphs, presenting a topic sentence followed by explanatory details or illustrations, but that another author may vary his paragraphs, sometimes concluding with a topic sentence, sometimes writing several paragraphs with a single topic sentence. Students will become alert to the word clues used by an author to express interrelationships among his ideas. As they read a paragraph with such words as *moreover* or *further,* they will see this as a clue to an idea similar to one in the previous paragraph. If they come to the phrase *on the other hand* or words like *but* or *however,* they realize they are being given some contrasting facts. As they continue they may encounter clues such as *therefore, consequently,* or *as a result,* which the author has used to indicate his conclusions. As they are reading they are following the author's pattern of organization. They are analyzing the structure, concentrating on obtaining the author's main ideas and supporting details, and consequently finishing the chapter with good comprehension.

A Pattern of Writing. The classroom teacher needs to make children aware of authors' patterns of writing—how they introduce new topics; define terms; and present main ideas, illustrations, summaries, or conclusions. In writing a textbook for children in a content area, an author typically presents a multitude of facts about his subject. He plans the presentation of these facts in a particular pattern or sequence. For example, the writer of a geography textbook may develop a chapter with a brief introduction to a country. He may use maps and aerial photographs to show the natural topography of the region. Throughout the chapter he presents pictures depicting the native costumes, food, occupations, modes of transportation, and so on. In the text are many definitions and illustrations. The summary statement reviews the main points to be noted about this country and the way in which the immediate environment has influenced the customs of the people.

Teachers may help pupils discover that the basic pattern of one chapter is quite similar to that of other chapters in the same book. Children may note the familiar plan of an introduction, maps, photographs, explanatory text, and summary statements. Thus in each succeeding chapter of this textbook readers can anticipate the author's pattern of presentation. In previewing the next chapter, they will be looking for the expected pictures and maps. They will note that the author has again provided both an introduction and a summary in which important points are pulled together. With a feeling of satisfaction that they understand how the author presents his information, children will be ready for thorough reading about another country or geographical region.

Evaluating Content. As children progress in their ability to analyze an author's patterns of writing and of presenting thoughts on a subject, they may begin to think about other aspects related to effective reading. They may think about themselves and their own personal experiences, noting similarities and differences as they encounter situations and characters in print. They may think of characters as "just like me" or "just like my father." They may relate an incident in a story to a happening in their own experience—painting a fence, exploring an island, or repairing a lamp.

Personal Associations. They may follow their reading of a science book by applying the knowledge they gained to incidents in their own lives. Having learned that heat causes expansion and that cold will cause objects to contract, a child may pull apart two glasses seemingly fused in her mother's hot sudsy dishwater. A child may set up a basement laboratory after reading about scientific experiments. The child wants firsthand experience viewing objects under a microscope or mixing test tube ingredients to obtain a new effect or product.

Comparisons. Some children may compare the material at hand with other books and articles they have previously read. Their comparisons may lead them to raise some good questions. Why did one author condemn a general's action in history whereas another praised it? Why did two geography books differ in reporting the population of a certain country? Of two stories just completed, which was based on fact and which was fiction?

Challenging Writer's Authority. Readers are coming close to independence when they are able to challenge a writer's authority. They look for evidence that the author has sought original, reliable sources to back up the facts presented. They expect to find documentation through footnotes and acknowledgment of authentic sources and authorities. They will be unable to accept the ideas presented by some one who presents no evidence of having done research where it would be appropriate. They will become selective in their reading—using library techniques for locating authentic material when preparing reports or otherwise seeking information.

Evaluating the content of reading material is a valuable skill, which can be acquired by the majority of students. Reading skills may be considered effective when the student has acquired the ability to relate reading to his or her own experience and to interpret the abstract in print through associations with personal as well as vicarious experiences. Because basically these skills are thinking skills, intellectual capacity plays an important role in their attainment. The teacher's aspirations for his or her students' acquisition of high-level comprehension skills need to be tempered by knowledge of each student's level of intellectual functioning or learning potential. The creative reading skills of interpreting the author's purposes, detecting points of view and various propaganda devices, and evaluating material critically are obviously not to be expected of the dull or subnormal individual. All others need these skills in order to function effectively in a world where they are constantly bombarded with ideas in print—the biases, the editorial convictions, and other studied reactions of many writers.

Author's Purposes. Children can be taught to react to the printed message with pertinent questions: "Why did the author write this?" "What is he trying to tell me?" "Is he writing to provide entertainment, humor, information, or his own point of view?" "Is he trying to convince me or change my thinking on this subject?" Early detection of an author's point of view will be valuable as readers go through a written article, chapter, or book. They may thus hold themselves in readiness for learning new facts that will give them desired answers to questions raised for a personal or class project. They may sit back and let the author entertain them with a light story about other children in amusing situations. They may attempt to ascertain how soon after an historical event the author chronicled the happening; how the information was acquired; whether he or she gave his or her own viewpoint or the reactions of others, and so on. They may skim before reading to see if the material at hand is fact or fiction or some combination of both, as in a novel that may be conscientiously true to life or historical fiction. It should be pointed out that teachers in content area subjects such as history as well as those in literature courses need to emphasize the techniques for distinguishing between fact and fiction. Familiarity with historical and biographical sources will give students the background needed to make such distinctions when they encounter new material on their own. Such familiarity can be acquired as teachers provide students with opportunities to enter such source material with definite purposes and to locate answers to questions they themselves raise. Children can discuss with their peers the facts they found as well as their reactions to ideas presented in the reading material.

Propaganda Devices. All of the senses are constantly being bombarded through various media in this century by persuasive sales persons. We are reminded on television and radio of the fine taste and aroma of certain commercial items; invited to eat, drink, and smoke other products; and cajoled into hearing forceful speakers or viewing the larger sizes and finer qualities of one product versus Brand X. Persuasion is the key in the salesman's hand.

Children and youth today need defenses against such persuasive tactics as well as basic techniques for detecting the propaganda devices used by such salesmen. They need to know that certain people sell ideas, too. They need some measuring devices or criteria with which to make good judgments. Basically, these are tools for thinking or reasoning, which will be effective in reading as well as listening.

Propaganda has been defined as any organized effort or movement to spread particular doctrines, information, and other ideas. As early as 1623 a College of Propaganda was instituted by Urban VIII to educate priests for missions "to disseminate or spread the faith." If, several hundred years later, some of us evaluate such a movement, we can see that the immediate purpose behind this type of propagandizing was "good" as far as the intentions of the group so engaged. When a specific form of government spreads the word concerning its beliefs and ideas, it is also engaging in a form of propagandizing. Those who are convinced of the values of their particular beliefs may form a group to spread their concepts far and wide. Sometimes, however, they have used force in an attempt to convince others.

The concept of the term *propaganda* today has been affected by the judgment of those who have viewed the results of both well-intentioned and narrowly conceived efforts at propagandizing. Certain governments have been forceful in spreading their cause; certain religions have been militant in spreading their tenets; certain individuals have been fanatics in spreading their beliefs, practices, and messages. Propaganda, as a result, has been seen as a device for influencing people's thinking and actions. Whether this influence has an effect that is advantageous or adverse is a matter of judgment on the part of the listener or reader exposed to the propaganda. Too often the person fails to recognize the message as propaganda. For some, anything in print is reliable, believable, and to be accepted without question. It is important that the reader be taught to recognize others' attempts to influence thinking, practices, buying habits, and so on. He or she can learn to withhold judgment that this attempt will be advantageous or adverse to him until he or she has (1) examined the writer's competency and apparent purposes, (2) considered his own background of experience and familiarity with the subject, (3) noted the extent of information covered or withheld, (4) contacted other sources for further information as needed, and (5) decided to accept or reject the ideas offered.

The various devices that have been used to influence the thinking and decisions of others should be understood and identified by all pupils. In the elementary grades children may study examples of these devices in order to be familiar with them. As early as 1937 seven types of propaganda were identified by Clyde Miller.[4] These were name-calling, glittering generalities, transfer, testimonial, plain folks, card-stacking, and band wagon. Basically, these devices attempt to influence the listener or reader by slanting

[4] Clyde R. Miller, "How to Detect Propaganda," *The Publications of the Institute for Propaganda Analysis,* Vol. I (Nov. 1937).

their thinking along certain lines—omitting some pertinent information or concentrating on one aspect, favorable or unfavorable.

A positive approach to propaganda can be detected in some: a cause or service or product is presented with glittering generalities, words that are typically associated with "the best" in idealism, democracy, and religious or national beliefs. The transfer device is an effort to cause people to accept something because it has been approved by some acceptable agent like a church or country. The testimonial is a similar device, calling upon well-liked figures in sports, politics, and so on to endorse a product. To be one of many who have already learned its appeal, readers are urged to get on "the band wagon" and use a certain product. Those who would persuade sometimes label themselves "plain folks" just like yourselves in order to appear acceptable.

A negative approach to propaganda may be detected in such devices as name-calling and card-stacking. In these attempts at persuasion the propagandist emphasizes negative qualities, uses words with bad connotations, and deceives by intentional omissions and distortion of facts.

Students who examine the various devices used by propagandists will note that all such techniques violate a general principle of good research and accurate reporting—that of presenting fairly all available information pro and con that might have a bearing on the formation of any conclusions. Students, therefore, need practice in detecting propaganda as well as practice in discussing the various aspects related to their reading of such techniques—why the device was used, how it was done, what effects it could have upon unwary readers, and why it may not be accepted in general.

Many people at one time or another have had the experience of listening to a spirited march, a heartwarming folk song, or a moving concerto played by a fine orchestra. The listener is stirred by the music—sometimes to the point of tears, sometimes to clap for an encore, and even at times to a great desire to learn to play a musical instrument with similar skill. Music has done something to the listener.

A parallel situation may occur when a reader has completed a book— he or she may be moved emotionally to the point of tears, laughter, or anger; may immediately look for another book by the author; and at times may even be spurred on to creative writing or to active research on a topic suggested or discussed in the book. Reading has done something to the reader.

When readers have arrived at the point where they are capable of high-level comprehension while reading, they will be able to synthesize ideas gained from their reading. This is the point where they delve deep beneath the literal or factual surface. They are aware that the author had several purposes in writing, some of which may not be immediately apparent and some of which may have impact only upon a few of those who read the book. The reader asks himself or herself any one of several questions: "What is there in this article (or book) for me? What has the author given me that I want to keep as part of my own personal philosophy? What is a basic or universal truth that I can distinguish and possibly integrate into all the knowledge I have acquired so far? How can I use this new idea, or this new knowledge?" The reader may, however, feel the need to know more about a new idea presented in the book. Rather than adopting the new idea as his own or rejecting it forthwith, he may recognize the advisability of suspending judgment until he has located further information. Later, summarizing all of the information that he has gained from various sources, he may form a judgment valid for him; he may use the information in a personal or group project; or he may see the personal or universal application of the information he has gained.

In summary, it may be noted that the highest levels of reading comprehension skills are dependent upon the individual's successful completion of skills at each level of development. Simple word meaning in listening vocabulary precedes word analysis in his reading vocabulary. Practice in the use of context clues to meaning is another step toward independence in reading. Thinking while reading puts the reader on one of the highest levels—ready to do the critical, creative reading demanded of effective citizens today.

FACTORS AFFECTING COMPREHENSION

Personal Factors

Several children in one class may read the same historical selection with varying degrees of comprehension. One understands some of the factual content only; another finds the vocabulary difficult and subsequently answers few questions of comprehension correctly; another skims through the selection, mentally drawing comparisons with another chapter he has read on the same subject; still another child may suggest that his group draw a frieze depicting the adventures of the main character, whom he admires to the point of hero worship.

Why does one reading selection produce such a variety of reactions? The answers lie in certain factors that influence reading comprehension—personal or internal factors, external factors, and learning factors.

Intelligence. Each reader brings to the printed page variations among the personal factors that may affect reading comprehension. When reading is defined as thinking, it is important to remember that different children bring varying levels of *thinking ability* to the reading act. The moron and imbecile are not expected to react to the printed page as well as the superior and gifted boy and girl. Between these two extremes is a wide range of intellectual abilities from low average to high average. Thus expectancy levels are different—borderline defectives may be taught, after considerable time and attention, to read words with which they can associate some meanings as in *Go, Stop,* and so on. Gifted children may be expected to read quite abstract material—the new mathematics or ancient and medieval history—with a high level of conceptual ability. They may give their reactions to the author's purpose in writing, contrast one author's views with another, or proceed to write a new and more satisfactory conclusion to a story they have read. In between are the children with the mental ability to grasp the main facts of the writer's presentation and retain enough information for subsequent discussion. Native intelligence plays a role in determining the quality of the reader's comprehension of printed material.

Experiential Background. When children hold a book in their hands, it should convey something familiar to them—a picture of a familiar object or a sentence with language they themselves speak. Beyond this, the book should whet their curiosity—provide a puzzle or a problem for which they will have an answer when they unlock its mysteries—when they *read* it.

When children are at the picture-reading stage, they need language or a speaking vocabulary to express their reaction to what they see. At the same time, they need to *think* about what they see. They must call upon their background of experiences to tell them what this small flat object represents —to associate it with something concrete in their own background. Otherwise, how can they think about it or talk about it?

When they are *ready to read,* they must be able to express whole ideas or sentences, so that they can reproduce the whole idea or sentence the author has put on the printed page. Many opportunities to use vocabulary, both in listening and in speaking, will enable students to decode others' ideas in print. A lack of opportunity to listen and use vocabulary will hinder them in their initial attempts to read the printed page.

The home, the community, and the school ordinarily provide the occasions for vocabulary development. They also provide important experiences in handling concrete objects—personal items like shoes and sweaters, toys like dolls and tops, food like milk and bread, and so on. They may also provide opportunities for other types of learning—such as *happiness* in acquiring a pet or other present, *fear* of fire, *sharing* with a brother or sister, *fun* at a picnic, *surprise* at an unexpected event like a birthday party or sudden snowstorm. The school often provides opportunities for children to discuss their experiences with such objects and events as these. Many opportunities for discussion need to be provided when children have not been encouraged to talk in their home or community environment. Oral communication thus precedes written communication and presumes a background of the experience necessary for any type of communication.

Physical Factors. Physical conditions can affect the level of achievement in children. Good general health allows harmonious development, whereas its absence may mean inattention, sleepiness, absence, and so on. Excellent visual acuity will make educational tasks comfortable, whereas anything less than good may result in discomfort or the inability to attend to such tasks as reading books or chalkboard assignments. Both teachers and children talk about the various lessons throughout the school day. When children have difficulty in hearing, they may miss important points or make inexplicable errors, if their problem is undetected. Reading comprehension can be affected by any of these conditions.

Emotional Adjustments. Occasionally, emotional tensions and maladjustments affect a child's learning in school. The child who is having difficulty in completing assignments in reading orally to the group or in silent reading often shows emotional tension and antisocial behavior. These, in turn, affect success in reading. The teacher cannot expect him to succeed unless his problems, both personal and academic, have been attacked by the school and the specialist.

Interests. Children in general have a natural curiosity about many things. Their interests abound, and reading may well serve the purpose of answering their countless questions. Teachers who understand the interests of children at each age level can provide the reading material appropriate to their age and grade so that children will read to satisfy their curiosity. Fortunately, children's interests can be developed as well as channeled. Pictures, films, and television bring many ideas to children's attention— broadening their horizons and directing them to many sources of information as well as to books for fun and enjoyment. Certain children have an insatiable curiosity—they will exhaust all sources before they move on to another topic. Others read widely and develop a fine background of knowledge on many topics. Thus curiosity may cause a child to acquire backgrounds of information that contribute to highly effectual comprehension of new reading material.

Purpose for Reading. It is likely that no truly high-level comprehension of reading material can occur without a strong purpose for reading. One adult stated, "I would not read *anything* unless I knew *why* I was reading it." Why does a person read? One may be motivated to read for information, for recreation or enjoyment, and for certain other related purposes —such as reading to ascertain directions (map-reading), to follow a recipe, to determine an editor's bias, to learn about a politician's viewpoint, and so on. For the reader, these become intrinsic purposes—his own set for perusing a chapter or book. In the schoolroom the teacher sets the stage for this ultimate goal by asking questions preceding reading. Thus extrinsic reasons are established by the teacher for the reader: "How was America first discovered?" "How did Jack find the Giant?" "Why do you think the editor has chosen this topic to write about today?" Familiarity with such purposes and the satisfaction of finding one's own answers promote the eventuality of the reader's asking questions before attempting to read anything in print.

External Factors

At the same time, there are external factors that play a part in the individual's attainment of an optimum level of reading comprehension. These include the reading program and the reading materials to which he or she is exposed.

The Reading Program. What type of reading program produces readers who demand of themselves a high level of comprehension? First, everyone who in involved in establishing the reading program has analyzed the objectives of education and the aims of instruction in relation to the reading program. Second, the classrooms have been organized so that individual differences among students will be recognized and provided for. Instruction will be geared to the abilities and achievement levels of each child. Third, teachers will be highly competent in content or subject matter as well as in current methodology. They will be knowledgeable in the area of child growth and development, as well as in their understanding of the laws of learning and their effect on children's levels of achievement. In professional meetings from time to time, teachers will review critically their goals, the types of organization, current methodology, and the instructional materials in use. They will give serious consideration to the latest research and reports of studies in reading, looking for implications for their own program.

Reading Materials. In what ways do the reading materials affect the reader's level of comprehension? Once more, teachers' competencies play an important role. Selecting appropriate books for children involves a study of their current reading levels and reading skills, their interests and capabilities, as well as information concerning the content, interest level, and readability levels of available reading materials.

Basal reading materials supply a continuing program for the development of reading skills. Supplementary books, library and trade books provide reading material for the practice and utilization of the skills. Textbooks in content areas provide additional reading skill practice although their major function is informational. Here again, the teacher's skill in raising thought-provoking questions will affect the student's level of comprehension of any of these materials.

The availability of many types of attractive, interesting reading material must also be considered. On several occasions the writer has heard panels of high school and college students, selected because they were excellent readers, explain their own reading success: "I think I'm a good reader because I have always read a great deal." *Good* readers read, and then they become excellent readers. The accessibility of good reading materials for all classrooms is, therefore, essential so that the children will read.

Someone has said, "Nothing succeeds like success." When children have successfully read a book, their feeling of satisfaction in accomplishment will make it easy for them to go on to another book. How can a teacher ensure the child's successful reading of a book? Knowledge of the child's current level of reading achievement must be supplemented with knowledge of the readability of the books in which the child might be interested. The child cannot successfully read a book that is too difficult for him or her right now. The difficulty may be caused by unfamiliar concepts, by many new hard words, by long, involved sentence structure, and so on. Such a difficult book would be frustrating for the child at this point, yet he may read it with ease two or three years hence, if present reading material is geared to his current achievement level. Every book successfully completed paves the way for more reading at succeedingly higher levels.

The Readability of Materials. Information concerning the readability of the reading materials used at various grade levels can be obtained by teachers who try to match children and their reading level with an appropriate textbook or supplementary reading book. Spache has listed the approximate readability level of books elementary and junior high students read.[5] An objective estimate of the reading difficulty of many of these books was obtained through the use of several readability formulas. Teachers who wish to apply such formulas to children's books and other reading materials may study the instructions for the use of the Dale-Chall, Lorge, Spache, and Fry formulas.[6] The Fry formula is a currently popular and easily used scale and is used by professors and publishers for judging the readability level of their books. Klare [7] has presented a comprehensive study of the many readability formulas.

When textbooks have been analyzed by readability formulas, several conclusions important for teachers have been found. Varying degrees of difficulty are often found from page to page within a textbook. The beginning of the book is often not easier to read than successive chapters. A series of textbooks in content areas frequently do not show gradation in difficulty from one grade level to the next.

"Graded" materials are sometimes found to vary from the grade level designated by the publisher. Pagan and Walter [8] studied the Ginn 360 Program. They presented a table with the readability estimates by levels

[5] George D. Spache, *Good Reading for Poor Readers* (Champaign, IL: Garrard Publishing Company, 1972).

[6] Edgar Dale and Jeanne Chall, *A Formula for Predicting Readability* (Columbus, OH: Bureau of Educational Research, Ohio State University). Reprinted from the *Educational Research Bulletin*, 27:11–20, 37–54 (Jan. 21 and Feb. 17, 1948); Irving Lorge, "Predicting Readability," *Teachers College Record*, 40:404–19 (March, 1944); Edward Fry, *Fry Readability Scale* (Providence, RI: Jamestown Publishers, 1978).

[7] George Klare, "Assessing Readability," *Reading Research Quarterly* X,1:62–102 (1974–75).

[8] Judith Pagan and Richard B. Walter, "Informal Reading Inventories Plus New Basal Readers Equal Misplaced Pupils," *Reading Instruction Journal*, 19:68–71 (June 1976).

and pointed out the variations in grade-level designations. For example, Level 12, used for the fifth grade, had material ranging from fifth to ninth grade. They suggested that using an informal reading inventory to find pupil's reading levels may not help the teacher assign a new textbook accurately.

Teachers who have assessed the reading levels of students within their classes can use the information gleaned through readability analysis of textbooks to good advantage. They can assign textbooks of known readability levels to students whose reading ability is above the difficulty level of the textbook. They can also help certain students with the more difficult passages and pages in a given textbook. They can avoid assigning a difficult textbook to students or sections with lower reading levels.

Teachers in in-service programs might use to good advantage a technique employed by the writer of a master's thesis at Kean College. Eva Shatkin [9] analyzed data obtained through testing seventh and eighth grade students and applying readability formulas to the science textbooks they were using. She contrasted the variability of readability found within seventh and eighth grade science texts with the reading scores of sections using the texts. See Figure 6. In another unpublished thesis, Rita Gerace [10] studied the appropriateness of the reading material found in a second grade classroom. She assessed both the students' grade placement and the readability of the texts and supplementary reading material. (See Figure 7). Teachers should analyze both the reading ability of students and the readability of the available reading materials. They can then assign to students the appropriate materials for their various abilities. Adequate comprehension of content material as well as supplementary reading will be better assured when such measures are taken.

Laws of Learning

When recommendations for improving reading programs are examined, it is noted that they are often phrased "children are taught" or "as children learn . . ." It is especially important that teachers understand the ways in which children learn in order that they may plan effective teaching procedures. The different kinds of learning to which students are exposed will be affected basically by their learning capacity and the modifications attempted by their teachers. The teachers can affect a student's satisfactory attainment of learning objectives only to the extent that they are knowledgeable concerning learning capacity as related to personal factors, and modifications as reflected in external factors and learning theories.

[9] Eva Shatkin, *Readability of Science Textbooks in the Junior High School.* (Union, NJ: Kean College, 1968), pp. 32–38.
[10] Rita Gerace, *A Study of Readability of the Materials in a Second Grade Class.* (Union. NJ: Kean College, April 1968).

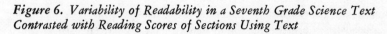

Figure 6. Variability of Readability in a Seventh Grade Science Text Contrasted with Reading Scores of Sections Using Text

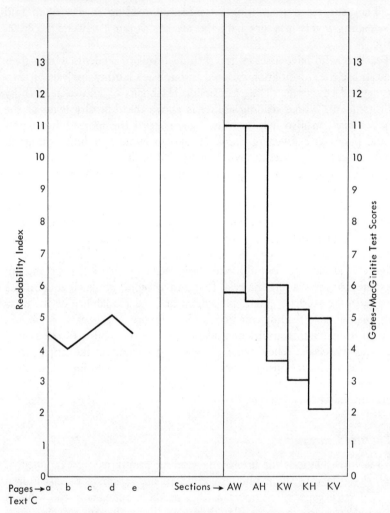

In the previous section personal factors and external factors were examined in regard to the manner in which they may affect the reader's attainment of effectual comprehension in the act of reading. Personal factors are the individual's own makeup. These factors must be known by the teacher in order that a real learning situation may be provided for everyone in a class. External factors are those within the reading situation; reading programs and materials influence the level of comprehension a reader attains. How well a student eventually reads will to a large extent depend

Figure 7. Students' Grade Level in Reading and Books at That Level

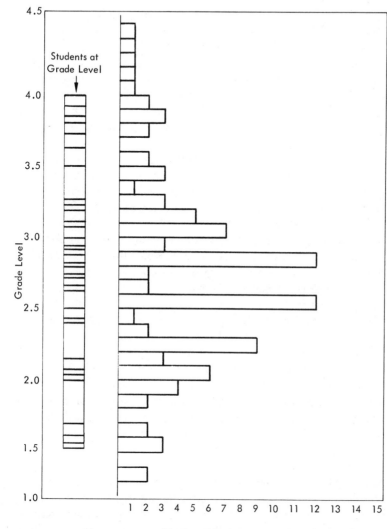

Number of Books

upon the ways in which he or she was taught and whether the methods used were appropriate.

How do children learn? In the last half century various theories have been advanced. In this section these theories will be reviewed briefly for the purpose of relating them to teaching and learning the techniques of effective reading comprehension.

The prospective teacher in current college psychology courses has examined the most prominent theories of learning. Thorndike, Skinner, and others have postulated stimulus-response theories of learning. Tolman, classical *Gestalt* psychologists, and Lewin have posed cognitive theories of learning. Snygg and Combs have explored the nature of intelligence in a perceptual or phenomenological frame of reference.

Stimulus-Response. Edward L. Thorndike's learning theory of connectionism is the original S-R or stimulus-response psychology of learning. He referred to three laws—readiness, exercise, and effect. The law of readiness stated that when a conduction unit is ready to conduct, it is satisfying to do so and annoying or frustrating not to do so; if not ready but forced to conduct, frustration or annoyance also occurs. The law of exercise referred to the law of use (strengthening the S-R bonds through practice) and the law of disuse (weakening the bonds or forgetting through discontinuance of practice). The law of effect referred to the consequences of satisfaction (increasing the strength of the connection) and of dissatisfaction (decreasing the strength of the connection).

Thorndike's theory of S-R bonds leads to a definition of intelligence as one of capacity—bright children having a greater quantity of bonds available than dull children. Bonds are strengthened through practice when the connections are rewarded. Understanding is the outgrowth of earlier, appropriate habits. Transfer occurs when certain elements in a new situation are identified as identical or partly identical with elements in old, familiar situations.

Thorndike stressed the automatic strengthening of specific connections. He stated that the child could read if the words were known. Thorndike studied the frequency of words used by all kinds of people, arriving at a count of the most frequently used words. He proceeded to publish these lists so that teachers could teach the words most needed. He stressed the importance of drill and habitual associations to the extent that insight and understanding were subordinate to them.

The stimulus-response theorist considers that with repetition a habit of response is formed. The cognitive theorist considers that what is learned is a fact, something now known or recognized when met again. In the former, trial and error will be resorted to when past habits are not sufficient to solve a problem. In the latter, a perceptual structuring of the problem leads to insight, or an understanding of the relationships involved in the solution. Thus it is necessary to look beyond Thorndike's theories for an explanation of meaning and understanding as related to learning theories. How does the individual develop an insight into a situation? How does he grasp the meaning of reading material at stratified levels?

The Gestalt. The *Gestalt* theorist considers the importance of the law or organization. When all aspects needed are open to observation, insight into a situation becomes possible.

In the laws of organization can be found principles from perception applied to learning. The law of Pragnanz is the guiding principle, suggesting the direction of the organization or *Gestalt*. Four laws subordinate to it are the laws of similarity, proximity, closure, and good continuation. The law of similarity is a principle of perception concerning the formation of groups—similar or homogeneous pairs are learned more readily than heterogeneous pairs. The law of proximity is the principle in perception that favors the learning of groups or patterns because of the nearness of parts, contiguity or recency. According to the law of closure, the direction of behavior in a problem situation is toward completion as a satisfying goal. The law of good continuation is a principle of perceptual structuring whereby learning is facilitated when it is observed that pairs fit or items are noted as parts of a recognized whole—as an arc's being part of a circle.

Snygg and Combs have also presented a perceptual point of view. According to their theory, the phenomenal field is "the universe of experience open to the individual at the moment of his behavior." [11] Within a perceptual frame of reference, the intelligence of an individual will coincide with the quantity and quality of the perceptions possible to him at the moment of measurement. Perception may be limited by such anomalies or maladjustments as physical handicaps, prenatal or birth injuries, or central nervous system disorders; lack of opportunities in the environment; and, such individual factors as a low self-concept or the presence of threat in the learning situation. To the extent that any of these anomalies may be actual restraints upon effective perception, the individual's intelligence may be tested as considerably lower than true capacity. Snygg and Combs suggest that intelligence may not be as immutable as some have thought. Providing opportunities for adequate perceptions, removing restraints such as threat, improving physical and environmental conditions—all might have a significant effect upon the individual's capacity for effective behavior.

What are the implications for teachers of reading? They will need to be guided in their own aspirations for each student—how much they can expect an individual to learn—that is, to change or modify their behavior. The teacher needs to be alert to indications of intelligence—the level at which the student operates or could operate effectively in learning situations. The teacher's knowledge of prevailing learning theories will provide clues to the ways by which an individual's capacities for learning may be modified.

Teachers need to select learning experiences in which the student is led, through careful structuring, to note relationships that are significant to ultimate understanding or insightful learning. The teacher may provide an overview of new material, emphasizing main points. An overall orientation to a new subject or unit will prepare students for better understanding and retention of the content.

[11] Ray Loree, *Educational Psychology* (New York: The Ronald Press Company, 1959), p. 123.

Teachers prepare for the new learning situation by presenting material that has an intrinsic interest for the child, because of its size, shape, color, or form. It may be related to his or her previous experience or to age-group experiences known by the teacher. It may appeal to the basic drives of the children. Thus, teachers try to build motivation in the individual through association with some of these materials. They try to build the bridges that will cause the child to be motivated, or motivated to read.

Motivation is a concomitant result of success experiences, those which have been strengthened through practice and those through which the individual gains satisfaction. Individuals differ in their propensity toward motivation. Teachers find some children easy to motivate because they have natural interests in many things. Teachers find other children almost impossible to motivate, as if they cannot get through to the child—an invisible barrier is in the way. Most children range between these two extremes in their propensity to be motivated.

Because of individual differences in learning capacity and in propensity toward motivation, it is imperative that teachers know each pupil—for example the pupil's background, current level of verbal functioning, even the degree of curiosity displayed in classroom situations.

A basic component in teachers' plans for providing adequate motivation for learning, in reading situations, is the quality of their questions. The type of questions markedly affects the level of comprehension attained by the student. As teachers study the laws of learning, they will note implications for effective comprehension in the nature of the questions they raise for each student. The kinds of questions teachers ask reflect what they know about learning theory.

Knowing that certain children have a natural curiosity concerning the things about them as well as about the unknown, far removed from their immediate environment, teachers ask, "What kind of animal is the beaver? How does he use his flat tail?" They may also ask at another time, "What is it like to be in a spaceship? How do astronauts feel when they are in outer space?" Either set of questions, used by the teacher for motivating purposes, will be followed by the statement, "Read to find your answers."

The questions teachers ask may serve many purposes. Children need the meaningful practice and repetition that makes learning more permanent. They need to be encouraged to use their newly acquired reading skills and knowledges. Teachers may employ selectively a variety of types of questions in planning effective lessons.

Thorndike's Theory of Connectionism. As previously stated, teachers motivate children to read when they set the stage for learning. They may use bulletin board displays, library corners with books and book jackets, tables with objects related to a new subject, films, filmstrips, and so on. Children's curiosity is thus aroused. They themselves ask the how, why, when, and where questions. Good teachers supply the place to find the answers: "Read to find out, in this story or this book or this magazine." Thus stimulated, children are ready to read. They find satisfaction in accomplishment. The more often they do this, the better able they are to find their own answers: "How did you find out about beavers? Where could you go to learn what you want to know about porcupines?" The boy who has had success in finding his own answers can be guided to further learning on his own.[12] Thus the laws of readiness, use, and effect are put into practice by the skillful teacher.

Cognitive or Insightful Learning Theories. In order to ensure children's effective grasp of the meaning in reading materials, teachers need to guide the reading experience through a careful selection of questions. Some of these questions precede actual reading; some lead to a clarification of what has been read; still others lead the reader to raise additional questions that can be answered by further reading.

Questions Preceding Reading

1. *Observation.* Questions can be raised that will help children to use direct observation immediately in order to arrive at an answer: "How did the Indians frighten the buffalo?"
2. *Definition or explanation.* Questions can be raised to show children that definitions or explanations may be found in context: "What does the author mean by a mountain *gap?*"

Questions Leading to Clarification

1. *Recall.* There are numerous questions that clarify details in a reading selection: "Who? What? When? Where? How much?" These can be answered on the basis of memory of what has been read. They may be extended further to more complex types of recall—selecting the best of several answers: "Which of his tools does the archeologist value the most? Why?" Both questions are specifically answered in the story.
2. *Statement of aim.* In upper grades children can be led to find the author's purpose in the selection or arrangement of materials: "Why did the author tell us first the age of the fawn?"
3. *Summary.* Teachers may ask students to recall several main points: "What are the four characteristics of arable soil?" "In your own words, what were the three main facts the author pointed out?" "How can you summarize the history of the Plains Indians?"
4. *Outline.* In order to point out the relationship among main ideas

---

[12] Elaine Schwartz and Alice Sheff, "Student Involvement in Questioning for Comprehension," *The Reading Teacher,* 29,2:150–154 (Nov. 1975).

and subordinate details, teachers may ask, "How would you outline the plan the general proposed to head off the enemy?" "If you had been the author of this story, what would have been the outline from which you wrote?"

5. *Comparison or contrast.* The law of similarity refers to the principle of perception concerning the formation of similar groups. Children may be asked to note likenesses after they have read: "What did you notice about the customs of Eskimos that is very much like some other people we have studied?" "When have you ever felt the way Tom did in this story?" "In what ways are honeybees and bumblebees alike? How is a drone different from a bumblebee?" As students are guided in their reading, they may note the relationships among seemingly isolated illustrations or events and the author's main ideas. They may begin to see why the author chose certain illustrations, or where the reader is being led. In some situations they may make comparisons with previous work by the same author or note differences or likenesses between this writing and that of other authors: "In what ways do you get a different picture of Benjamin Franklin from the one you had of him in our last story?" Or: "What similarities do you note in the writing style of these two authors?"

6. *Decision for or against.* Teachers may ask students to indicate a choice after weighing certain factors that were noted as they read a selection: "Would you do the same as Tom if you found yourself in the same position? What do you think you would do differently?" "How sensible was Bill's decision? In what ways did he make mistakes?" These questions are to get the child to weigh and rank support for different sides of an issue.

7. *Classification.* In noting similarities and differences, students may be led to do more complex thinking—as placing several items or facts, based upon their relationships, in certain groups: "Which of following are mammals?" "Can you identify the deciduous trees in this picture?"

8. *Relationships due to cause and effect.* When children are reading in science textbooks and supplementary materials, their attention may be directed to relationships that might otherwise go undetected: "How do ocean currents affect the weather of places miles inland, away from the sea?" "In what ways may ocean currents affect deep-sea fishing?" "How does the Gulf Stream affect icebergs?" Cause and effect relationships may be noted in other areas besides science, as teachers ask questions such as, "Why did the fawn's mother put him in a clump of heavy bushes?" "How did Marco Polo's travels affect the lives of people in Europe?"

9. *Application in new situations.* Teachers can find in stories, those

that are fact as well as those that are fiction, some common truths or principles that could operate in the lives of children. Stories of success, courage, happiness, and so on may have implications for readers. Teachers, therefore, need to raise the type of questions that may help a child to see that certain knowledge may be employed in new situations: "How did Margaret Bourke-White use her mother's advice about facing fear? How could *you* use the same advice?" [13] In these days of great mobility, children may be finding difficulty in adjusting to new surroundings or new schools. Trade books at various grade levels deal with some of these problems. Teachers may help certain children to see that others have common problems and to make some application to their own lives. This may be done with individuals or groups: "What do we learn from Janey that we can remember when we move on to another place with our parents?" [14] "What can we learn from *The Hundred Dresses* [15] that will help the next girl who moves into our neighborhood or into this class? Would you want a class to do the same if *you* were the new pupil?"

10. *Criticism.* Teachers need to make children aware that criticisms are judgments as to the adequacy, correctness, or relevancy of a situation or statement. Judgments should be made after many observations, after the gathering of as much relevant data as possible. Teachers may point out how authors arrive at their critical judgments; they may ask students to make a tentative judgment; they may suggest comparing one artist's picture with another or one author's presentation with another: "What type of person is well suited to be a bullfighter?" "After reading two different authors who wrote about the discovery of America, who do you think was correct in his account? Be critical of both writers."

11. *Formulating new questions.* Teachers need to encourage children to develop new questions or raise new problems based on other material with which they are familiar. In the case in item 10, where readers are comparing different accounts of the discovery of America, some imaginative thinking may be brought out, as children develop their own new questions: "What else have I read about the discovery of America? How can I go about finding proof of these theories?" "If the author had stopped with Jim's arriving home, how would I write an ending to this story?"

12. *Discussion.* Discussion for the purpose of clarification is essential

[13] Margaret Bourke-White, "I Had to Learn Courage," *Reading Skill Builder* (Pleasantville, NY: Reader's Digest, 1960), pp. 11–15.

[14] Doris Gates, *Blue Willow* (New York: The Viking Press, Inc., 1940).

[15] Eleanor Estes, *The Hundred Dresses* (New York: Harcourt, Brace Jovanovich, Inc., 1944).

to nearly every instructional period. In discussion periods children may raise their own questions to be answered if possible by their peers. Teachers prepare for these periods by having questions at hand to be considered if children are not yet adept at raising questions. Discussion is profitable only after preparation on the part of the children, so that they have *facts* on which to base their discussion or to raise their questions. Talking without previous preparation can be classified as conversation—unstructured, lacking a major goal. Discussion implies both preparation and structure. If children discuss a story or an issue, reading should have preceded the discussion.

Discussion may very profitably follow the return of test papers. Individually or in small groups, students who have answered multiple-choice type questions may respond reflectively to the teacher's question, "Why did you choose that answer?" This question may also follow the typical *true-false, yes-no* items in a test. For the open-ended, short-answer, or essay types of tests, teachers may ask the student, "Why did you answer that way? Why do you think that is the best explanation? Where do you find any information that proves you are right?" Eventually, children can be taught to question themselves and their reasons for making choices and judgments—all in the name of a higher level of understanding and retention of knowledge.

13. *Inference.* Students can be guided through the formulation of questions of inference to use data previously observed or learned to arrive at some conclusions. They may note the author's pattern of presentation and raise questions as to the facts selected—pertinent, sufficient, or insufficient—to arrive at the conclusions or principles presented. They may question the author's reasons for writing a selection—a newspaper article, an editorial, a story, a novel, or a chapter in a book of science or social studies. Some of the questions that may be raised by the teacher are "What was the writer's purpose in telling this story (or writing this editorial)?" "What has happened so far that gives us a clue to a possible ending for this story?" "How does the author show the reader that Ted had great courage?" "How does the author inform us that he considers exploring caves to be either dangerous or merely adventurous?"

Teachers should develop variety in their questions. They should periodically evaluate them. Because thinking while reading is an ultimate goal in the instruction of reading, the teacher should be alert to learning situations that supply problem-solving experiences. In an atmosphere devoid of threat or emotional tension, the student may be encouraged to be flexible and creative in his or her thinking, to offer new and imaginative solutions and answers to problems. As they read, readers who have been encouraged to be original thinkers may anticipate the author's conclusions, or make up their own. Schaefer [16] emphasized the need for high level questions to help students develop the ability to think. Questions that promote thinking on the part of the students are an important responsibility of the teacher. That teachers do not always persist in effective questioning techniques was pointed out by Tinsley.[17]

SUMMARY

In summary, classroom teachers can find no higher goal in their teaching than ensuring for each child in their classes the highest level of reading comprehension of which the student is capable. Inferred in this statement are the importance of the teacher's understanding of all of the personal factors mentioned above for each child, as well as all of the external factors that may be affecting the child's progress at any one point in his educational development. In addition, the teacher must understand how children learn, in order to use methods and techniques that are appropriate for the individual. There are factors that we are not always able to measure and identify that can affect comprehension. Teachers can do little about such causal factors. In these cases, the only way the teacher can be effective is to teach the major skills rather than to attempt to determine causal factors. This chapter has stressed the importance of high-level reading comprehension. About 90 per cent of a student's work in school involves reading. Other media of communication do not give students opportunities to review, to slow down or speed up as they might wish, to encounter material at will (rather than when commercially available as on radio or television), or to browse undisturbed when personal needs and interests spur them on to further learning. Once attained, an optimum level of reading comprehension will remain a useful tool for personal enjoyment and for the acquisition of information throughout the lifetime of the reader.

SELECTED READINGS

Almy, Millie. *Young Children's Thinking.* New York: Teachers College Press, Columbia University, 1966.

Downing, John. *Learning to Read With Understanding.* Wynberg, Cape, 7824, Republic of South Africa: Juta and Company Ltd. 1976.

[16] Paul J. Schaefer, "Effective Use of Questioning," *Reading World,* **XV**,4:226–230 (May 1976).

[17] Drew C. Tinsley, "Use of Questions," *Educational Leadership,* **XXX**:710 (May 1973).

Gerhard, Christian. *Making Sense: Reading Comprehension Improved Through Categorizing*. Newark, DE: International Reading Association, 1975.

Henry, George H. *Teaching Reading as Concept Development: Emphasis on Affective Thinking*. Newark, DE: International Reading Association, 1974.

Klare, George. "Assessing Readability," *Reading Research Quarterly*, X,1, (1974–75), 62–102.

Smith, Frank. *Comprehension and Learning*. New York: Holt, Rinehart and Winston, 1975.

————. "Making Sense of Reading." *Harvard Educational Review*, 17,3 (1977), 386–395.

————. *Understanding Reading: A Psycholinguistic Analysis of Reading and Learning to Read*. New York: Holt, Rinehart and Winston, 1971.

Spache, George D., and Evelyn B. Spache. *Reading in the Elementary School*. 4th ed. Boston: Allyn & Bacon, Inc., 1977.

Stauffer, Russell G. *Directing Reading Maturity as a Cognitive Process*. New York: Harper & Row, Publishers, 1969.

————. *Teaching Reading as a Thinking Process*. New York: Harper & Row, Publishers, 1969.

Chapter 6

Comprehension: Skills

OBJECTIVES

To understand the insights children need
in order to learn how to read with meaning

To learn implications of research related to
teaching reading comprehension skills

To understand children's purposes
for reading

To learn how to analyze instructional
material as an aid to teaching
comprehension skills

To understand how to help the pupil
prepare for reading and study

To learn the study and work habits children
need in order to understand the reading
materials they encounter

To develop strategies for helping pupils
read for meaning in the content areas

INTRODUCTION

Varied techniques and approaches are utilized in schools today to initiate
children's learning of man's vast accumulation of knowledge. Children
learn through many avenues—through nonverbal and verbal techniques,
as well as by many audio, visual, and multisensory approaches. There are
pictures, photographs, and objects such as the abacus, the calendar, globes,
maps, and microscopes, to name a few of the many devices utilized in classrooms. There are audiovisual devices such as motion pictures, audio-film-
strips, videotapes, television, the Language Master, and others now commercially available. These educational devices serve to supplement the
student's universal source of knowledge—words in print.

Man's knowledge from its limited origins to its present extensive state has been disseminated by means of written language for several thousands of years. Over four thousand years ago the Egyptians recorded their medical knowledge on papyrus. Later the Greeks and Romans recorded their histories on parchment and tablets. European monasteries preserved some of the early writing. And, finally, the invention of the printing press coupled with the use of paper made possible the book as it is known today. Through such printed media as textbooks, reference materials, and trade books, the modern student has the wealth of all recorded knowledge, verbal and graphic, at one's disposal.

Thus, although human beings have developed many supplementary tools and techniques for ensuring effective learning on the part of students, they have perpetuated the use of a common tool, books in print. It has been estimated that schools today are 90 per cent reading schools. Regardless of the subject involved, the student will be reading to gain the information sought.

Faced with the fact that students will be acquiring a major portion of their knowledges and understandings through reading, teachers are becoming increasingly aware of the fact that effective reading skills play a significant role in contemporary education. The nature of assignments in textbooks and in collateral and reference materials has emphasized the need for independent reading skills on the part of each student.

What can be done to produce effective independent readers? Smith and Smith have pointed out that cybernetic or feedback research has implications for education:

> The broad outlines of a new scientific approach to human learning became apparent more than twenty years ago when the research effort of wartime training psychologists laid the foundations for the discipline known as human engineering. The central idea that emerged was that performance and learning must be analyzed in terms of the control relationship between a human operator and an instrumental situation. That is, learning was understood to be determined by the nature of the behaving individual as well as by the design of the learning situation—an understanding that structured the human factors approach to training research.[1]

In terms of the reading comprehension, implications of this research for the reading teacher are twofold: (1) The teacher must thoroughly understand the nature of the reader (factors affecting comprehension, as discussed in Chapter 5), and (2) the teacher must analyze the design of the learning situation (readability, format, design, and so on). Modern teachers will be effective when they exercise directional control of each student's learning—that is, they will provide systematic teaching and training adjusted to the student's maturational level. They will, moreover, pro-

---

[1] Karl U. Smith and Margaret F. Smith, *Cybernetic Principles of Learning and Educational Design* (New York: Holt, Rinehart and Winston, 1966), p. vii.

vide for the involvement of the students in their own learning so that the students can gain control over their own actions in the learning situation.

The key ideas here are directional control on the part of the teacher and involvement on the part of the student. Possibly the best single illustration of these ideas is the study technique developed by Francis Robinson,[2] the SQ3R method for reading and studying an assignment. This method, described more fully in a later section, provides for systematic teaching and learning as well as for learner involvement.

The varied reading skills necessary for effective reading in any of the content areas can be acquired by students when teachers are aware of all of the learning phenomena involved—the personal factors as well as the specific reading skills required for comprehension in any subject area. In the following sections methods for acquiring effective reading comprehension techniques are examined. Various facets of efficient study habits are pointed out. Included are such work habits as student preparation, motivation, concentration, and retention; study skills such as SQ3R, outlining, and note-taking; the use of a flexible reading rate; and the development of specific skills for reading in the content areas.

THE TEACHER'S PREPARATION FOR TEACHING COMPREHENSION SKILLS

Analyzing the instruments that will be utilized by the learner will give the teacher much-needed insights into an important facet of the contemporary educational program. In addition, the use of some of the procedures of task analysis will help the teacher to structure efficient performance on the part of the learner. Thus the modern teacher can combine knowledge of both the learner and the tools of learning when planning effective lessons.

Instrument Analysis

In education today books remain the indispensable tool. Both the neophyte and the experienced teacher in making assignments draw upon the content of the textbook and the reference materials that they find at hand in the classroom and on the library shelves. Occasionally, they have had the use of certain programed materials and educational hardware, which have been developed in the last decade. Thus students have been provided with many avenues of learning within the classroom setting. These instruments provide vicariously some of the concrete experiences that are educationally desirable but not always feasible.

[2] Francis P. Robinson, *Effective Study*, 4th ed. (New York: Harper & Row, Publishers, 1970).

Because they cannot provide firsthand experiences for all of the student's basic learning, teachers need to be thoroughly familiar with the nature of the abstract teaching tools available in the classroom. Pressey has analyzed the common textbook as an aid to understanding content material:

> For a learner with reading-study skills, conventional textual matter orders and structures its contents in paragraphs and sections and chapters, exhibits that structure in headings and tables of contents, makes all readily available in index with page headings and numbers. The learner thus has multiple aids to the development and structuring of his understanding. If need be he can, with a flick of the finger, move about in the material; he can skip that already known, turn back as a result of a later felt need, review selectively.[3]

A specific content area textbook is thus seen as a logical structure of organized subject matter. Authors have presented their knowledge and ideas of their subjects in a framework of main ideas and supporting details. They have organized their own thinking about their topics under specific headings and subheadings. They (or their editors) present these partitions as chapters subdivided by typographic devices. These may be in the form of indented, capitalized headings, underlined topics or subtopics, marginal headings, italicized definitions, numbering of sequential data, and so on. They often add to the book's usefulness as a learning tool by including pictures, maps, and graphs that emphasize details that are important for reinforcement, deeper understanding, and retention. The author usually writes captions and a verbal description of the nonverbal material for further clarification. The intended use of a graph, for example, is explained by the writer to ensure the reader's comprehension of the specific information thus supplied.

The content and sequential arrangement of subject matter differ from one school course to another. This is obvious to the teacher who examines a textbook or course of study in mathematics or social studies, for example. One textbook is narrative in form; another presents much information with graphs and tables. The teacher, therefore, needs to analyze the particular textbook for the course as well as all collateral material for the types of organizational pattern the students will encounter when assignments are made. See in this chapter "Reading for Meaning in Content Areas."

When supplementary material for a unit includes films or filmstrips, the teacher needs to preview each with specific questions in mind. How has this film been organized? For whom does it appear to be geared—the teacher, older or younger children? How does it fit into the sequence of learnings related to the current topic? Would it reinforce or review specific learnings or skills developed in other ways? Is the vocabulary suitable?

[3] S. L. Pressey, "Teaching Machine (and Learning Theory) Crisis," *Journal of Applied Psychology,* 47:1–6 (1963).

What questions can I ask, what concepts can I develop, before showing this film or filmstrip? Which children would benefit from seeing the film more than once? And, basically, what does this film teach better than any telling I can do?

The teacher who has previewed a film has done the survey step of SQ3R for the students. He or she then can raise pertinent questions, in proper sequence, to set the stage for good comprehension of the film's content. He or she can provide discussion periods immediately following the film, help students relate what they saw with reading they have previously done, occasionally rerun the film to clear up points that were missed or misunderstood, and help students raise questions that could be answered by further reading. Thus understanding can be structured, but only after careful analysis of the film's content, previewed by the teacher and viewed by students with their attention alerted through questions.

Task Analysis

In the course of a week an elementary teacher may set the following tasks for a group of children:

1. Read an assignment.
2. Study a map.
3. Solve a mathematical problem.
4. Contribute to a social studies project.
5. Get the main ideas from a film.
6. Try a science experiment.

The teacher's preparation for teaching effective comprehension must include not only an analysis of any piece of material (the instruments of instruction), but also a careful analysis of the task involved for the students.

Knowledge of individual differences among the students will play a part. The task at hand may be difficult for an individual or group within the class—so that the teacher will need to recognize whether a step-by-step instructional procedure will be needed. For example, a required textbook may be at the instructional reading level for some students who will need the teacher's guidance with vocabulary, concepts, and comprehension checks. The same textbook may be easier reading for another group of students who will be reading it at an independent level, with minimum guidance by the teacher. Such knowledge of students, their reading levels, and the reading difficulty of a textbook or supplementary book will also aid the teacher when homework or school-study assignments are made. Certainly, such assignments should be made at independent reading levels, when the purpose is to master content in subject areas. At more difficult reading levels the students will need the supervision of the teacher.

What is involved in the reading of a map in the social studies book?

The teacher needs to analyze the task, to note whether certain necessary skills have been previously taught or are new at this grade level. Examples are the use of a key or legend, using the scale of miles, or understanding maps drawn to different scales. The interpretation of a map needs careful introduction by the teacher, with attention drawn to the explanation given within the text, so that students become aware that the author typically presents an explanation of the map he has included. Intensive instruction in map-reading is presented in Michaelis.[4]

The reading of a mathematical problem presents another set of tasks for the reader, who may be taught to read and reread for various purposes before attempting to do the computation required. One purpose is to see the problem in its total setting, to get a mental image of the story involved before setting down the facts provided and attempting to find a solution. The teacher needs to alert the student to the power of such words as *sets, premises, are equivalent,* and so on in modern elementary mathematical problems.

When the task at hand is to make a contribution to a social studies project, students are faced with several problems. One is locating necessary sources of information. Where are the reference or supplementary books that hold some of the information they need? How will they find them? How will they select suitable facts from among the many they will certainly find in the library? How will they organize their information for presentation to the group? The teacher again needs to do the preliminary structuring of this lesson—previewing the unit; alerting the librarian of the topics to be covered; collecting many types of materials from such sources as the library, curriculum center, and possibly other community resource people. Thus the teacher makes it possible for all students to meet success as they become involved in a project they consider their own, with resulting high-level understanding and assimilation.

When the assignment is to get main ideas from a film, the teacher must analyze the students' involvement in this task: they have not seen it previously; they cannot survey it before viewing it; they may or may not have a background of understanding the content to be presented; they may not be able to grasp everything in one viewing. The teacher's preparation then must be to preview for the purposes of surveying, raising questions, assessing the quantity and quality of the concepts involved, and preparing the students with some discussion that will ascertain their level of sophistication for this particular film. Then the teacher can raise key questions to alert the students to the main ideas they will be facing in the film.

Laboratory experiments in science need to be carefully analyzed by the

[4] John U. Michaelis, *Social Studies for Children in a Democracy,* 5th ed. (Englewood Cliffs, NJ: Prentice-Hall, Inc., 1972), pp. 424–41.

teacher well in advance of pupil participation. How much observation and reading should precede actual involvement in a specific experiment? How meaningful would observation and reading be without personal involvement? What cautions will be needed? What materials will be needed? How well can these pupils evaluate the experiment? Teachers who analyze the tasks involved in any assignment—seatwork, group lesson, or homework—will provide the motivation and individual help students need for successful achievement in any content area.

THE PUPIL'S PREPARATION FOR READING AND STUDY

Reading Motives

When we look at the achievement of boys and girls at the time they leave school, we are aware that some have developed into efficient lifetime readers, whereas others have found reading a chore and a bore. A factor analysis of reading habits and achievement of both good and poor readers reveals that a common denominator accounts for both types of students—purpose (or lack of purpose).

Why read? Try this question aloud with the varying inflections of the enthusiastic scholar, the indifferent student, and the older nonreader. The first knows why he reads—to find out something he is vitally interested in knowing, to follow certain directions, to get a central idea, even to stimulate some personal thinking on a subject of deep interest. The second may read when prodded to answer the teacher's questions, to do his homework, or occasionally to find an answer when there is no one to tell him what he needs to know. The third has not learned to read; therefore he considers reading as impossible or unnecessary or completely frustrating; he cannot, so he does not read for any purposes. There are, of course, many children who may be found at intermediate points on the continuum from the efficient reader to the nonreader. They may read for a literal interpretation of a teacher's question or for a set of facts. They may occasionally read for momentary enjoyment. Their reasons are transient and very often extrinsically developed.

The attitude of reading for meaning is a personal one. Demanding meaning of oneself while reading is basic to efficient reading—whether in the functional reading of content areas or in recreational reading. The classroom teacher, therefore, might profitably explore ways and means of developing in students the habit of reading for meaning.

Personal reasons for reading are the ultimate goal in reading instruction. Teachers prepare students for this goal by providing the type of setting that makes reading a successful and satisfying occupation for everyone. The reading program is successful when children acquire the reading skills they need; it is satisfying when children can fulfill their natural curiosity by reading on their own.

Teachers at any educational level prepare students for reading and study when they help students set purposes for reading. Primary grade children are asked to read a story in a basic reader or trade book "to find out how Bob and Sue got to the party on that stormy day." Intermediate grade students are instructed to illustrate the locks of a canal by studying a section of the geography book with pictures and text. Junior high students are told to be prepared to "read the parts" for a tryout for a play to be produced at an up-coming assembly.

These varied goals for reading, previously set by the teacher, serve to prepare students for the occasions when they are studying or reading independently. The readers are setting their own purpose when they think while reading an adventure story, "I wonder if the hero will find the jewels before the pirates return," then read to find out. They are setting their own aims when they open the model airplane kit and read the directions before assembling the plane. They are setting their own aims when they turn the heading of the new chapter in their book *Clipper Ships* into a question, "What are clipper ships?" before reading to learn the answer.

Thus the traditional assignment of certain content area teachers, "Read from pages 92 to 147 for the next lesson," may be evaluated as both meaningless and worthless. The goals for neither the teacher nor the pupil can be detected in such an assignment. Even when students dutifully read the pages assigned, they often emerge from the exercise with such statements as, "I'll have to read it again as I didn't get much out of it" and "I wonder how much of that she'll expect me to know."

Mature, efficient readers will not read anything, from a small newspaper article to a full-length novel, without having their own reasons well in mind. When they complete the reading, they will know what they have read, why they have read it, and how much they want to remember and use.

How is the efficient reader developed? He or she is the product of a carefully planned, sequentially developed program that has provided him or her with opportunities to acquire work habits and study skills that are effective in the various content areas as well as in any type of reading he or she may undertake.

Work Habits

Habits of many types play a part in everyday life. Statements such as the following appear in advertisements by savings banks: "Save a little regularly for a secure future." School savings programs were devised on the premise that, if children begin saving early, habit would cause many to continue the program of thrift.

In the schoolroom the satisfaction that comes from accomplishment, of work well done is a strong motivation for continuing the habits that assure satisfactory accomplishment. Thus even the smallest increments of success build the solid foundation that ensures future progress.

Several moments in Fred's school career may illustrate the positive force of habits. When he was six years old, a smiling teacher put a star on his completed workbook as a stamp of approval. Later in the fourth grade his teacher complimented him on his report to the class, garnered from an encyclopedia and several books in the library. His sixth grade teacher commended him for the highest history test mark he had ever earned, as evidence of his improved techniques of review and study. In each case, Fred had experienced the satisfaction of approval for successful achievement. Several important work habits underlined his success—completion of a project, either short- or long-range; independent study or research with attendant locational skills; and personal attention to improving his skills of review and study as he advanced in the grades. His knowledge of his own success played an important part. The groundwork was thus laid for a pattern of success rather than failure in his attainment of higher level work and study habits.

Good work habits, however, are not attained incidentally, as might be inferred from the above example. Rather they result from strategies employed by skillful teachers. Patterns of work and study may profitably be initiated early in the lives of children. Students will then reap the benefits of efficient habits during their school (and possibly college) careers as well as over the span of their lifetime.

It is unlikely that all children in today's heterogeneous classrooms have established good work habits when they come to school. (See Figure 8.) Teachers have the opportunity to guide children's work habits in the school setting. They can point out and recommend the ideal home setting for study (homework, usually). In parent conferences and through bulletins sent home periodically, they can explain the appropriate environment for encouraging study at home.

In primary grades teachers may provide a short period daily for supervised study. This "study period" for the children, guided by the teacher and evaluated by the teacher and children together for accomplishments, sets the stage for future profitable study sessions in upper grades. Elementary schools that have planned time for study as part of their regular program have found this more successful than unstructured, unsupervised homework assignments.

Homework assignments vary greatly in schools across the country. Some schools assign homework in every grade, first through twelfth. Some reserve homework for the secondary grades. When teachers investigate how children accomplish homework assignments, they discover great variations among the children. Some children have no place of their own to study.

Figure 8. Work Habits.

SPECIAL TIME RESERVED FOR STUDY

SCHOOL	HOME
One period (minimum) for *supervised* study	Appropriate times
Same time daily	Before school
Guided with questions	Directly after school
Evaluation (of time and effort)	Directly after supper
	Time limits
	Setting a time
	Setting time limits

SPECIAL PLACE RESERVED FOR STUDY

SCHOOL	HOME
Special corner of room	Desk or table
Near reference material	In child's own room
Tables, chairs	In study or den
Appropriate tools	Separated from home distractions
Study room	
With reference material	
Tables, chairs	
At own school desk	
With no distractions	

CONCENTRATION FOR EFFECTIVE STUDY

SCHOOL	HOME
Comfortable temperatures	Comfortable temperatures
Appropriate lighting	Appropriate lighting
Minimum of distractions	Minimum of distractions
	Television, radio, telephone removed, "home" noises
Materials for study at hand	Materials for study at hand
Selected materials	Selected materials
Reference materials	Reference materials
Tools for study	Tools for study

They may be making an attempt to study in a room with several other people, with television and the radio blaring away at the same time. Some children are discouraged with their own attempts to produce an acceptable piece of homework. They draw upon a parent or older sibling to do the work for them. Some children have a room of their own, reference and other

We work together on this reading workbook

materials always at hand, and encouragement from parents to "do the best you can with your own work."

Study Skills

When students are in the appropriate environment for study, with all of the materials and tools they will need close at hand, they need further skills in order to study or read efficiently their assignments. At this point they need to call upon effective study habits. The teacher is in a key position to develop in the student a sequential pattern of study techniques that will eventually result in the student's involvement in independent study techniques. (See Figure 9).

SQ3R. One of the most effective techniques for an organized pattern of study was devised by Francis P. Robinson [5] for college students.

As indicated in the beginning of this chapter, Robinson's SQ3R method may be considered an illustration of a technique that emphasizes involvement on the part of the student in his or her own learning. Thus he or she controls his or her own actions in the learning situation. The steps in this procedure may be analyzed in terms of student involvement.

SURVEY—Students are taught to look where they are going. They are shown the importance of the overview, knowing beforehand the length and breadth of their assignment (as a chapter in a content area textbook). They are taught to examine the main headings for the author's presentation of

[5] Robinson, op. cit.

Figure 9. Study Techniques.

EFFECTIVE STUDY HABITS ARE DEVELOPED WHEN TEACHERS	INDEPENDENCE IN STUDY TECHNIQUES IS ACHIEVED WHEN STUDENTS
1. Arouse curiosity by setting the stage with pictures, displays, visitors, and so on.	1. Turn naturally to reading to satisfy their curiosity, for pleasure, and so on.
2. Ask a motivating question to prepare children for a short reading selection (sentence, paragraph, or single page).	2. Ask themselves what they hope to learn from a reading selection; then concentrate on reading to find answers to the questions they themselves raise.
3. Relate the new lesson to children's experience or to previous lessons when applicable.	3. Note any relationships between the reading at hand and experience (personal or vicarious) that seem applicable.
4. Set a reading task that can be completed in an amount of time reasonable for the age and ability of the children.	4. Set a reasonable time for studying; then complete the task.
5. Raise additional questions to emphasize the main points, details, sequence of ideas, conclusions (if any).	5. Record in their own words the main ideas, supporting details, illustrations, conclusions, and so on.
6. Review at regular intervals for reinforcement to assure retention.	6. Review notes taken in step 5 immediately; review again before class and before examinations to aid retention.
7. Plan opportunities for students to use the information gained through reading (whenever possible).	7. Develop self-confidence through the use of information gained in reading; keep alert to situations in which new information may be put to use.
8. Alternate reading lessons with big muscle activity to prevent fatigue.	8. Develop psychologically varied approaches to homework—planning, spacing, and timing.
9. Make new sources available; encourage creativity.	9. Work on their own, or go beyond requirements in initiating a learning activity.

several main ideas—usually not above a half dozen in a single chapter. They read the introductory paragraph as well as any summary or concluding statement. They also read the captions of the illustrations, graphs, and maps.

At this point the students are no longer on a rudderless ship, afloat on an unknown sea. Instead, they are at the helm, in control of the situation. In other words, they are no longer like the countless students who open a book to the assigned page and start to read, with no idea about the material other than the fact that it is the new lesson. Having made a survey, the reader may make certain personal decisions—to read slowly and thoroughly a chapter with much unfamiliar material and vocabulary or to go rather quickly through a section containing easy vocabulary and material on which he or she has previously done much reading. Or, noting an excessively long chapter, he or she may decide to break the chapter into two or three sessions, stopping at the end of one of the main sections.

These decisions, of course, depend upon the reader's maturity and reading experience. Elementary grade teachers prepare students by doing this preliminary survey with them—looking over the new textbook chapter for new vocabulary and concepts, the length of the assignment, and so on. They help the students see any relationship between the new lesson and the children's previous experiences; they build curiosity for learning the new by asking questions to be answered by reading. They help the students to see how they can raise their own questions: "What would you like to know about . . . ?"

QUESTIONS—This step calls for the very active involvement of the students as they turn each heading into a question that will be meaningful for them. They may want to know what is meant by a heading "Turning Point in History," who brought about the turning point, how the turning point was effected, or why the author called the event a turning point in history. As they change the heading into a meaningful question, they have given themselves a reason for concentrating, at least until they have come up with an answer. They will be alert for any main ideas that will afford them the answers, as well as any supporting details and illustrations.

READ—Having raised their own questions, they have now given themselves a reason for reading the new section. While reading the section "Turning Point in History," they may think, "The author is going back over events from the last chapter. Now he is telling what really happened. . . . Oh, this is why he considers it a turning point in history. I want to make some notes on this." Students who have thus attacked their reading assignment have gone in with a question and come out with an answer. They now have an organized plan of attack that will keep them alert and interested in finding the answers the author is giving, right up to the end of the assignment. They take each heading, change it into a question, then read to learn the answers.

RECITE—At the end of each section readers stop to contemplate the information supplied them. Did they get the answers to the questions they had raised? Was there a point they missed? If so they can go back at once and look for it. Then in brief summary form they can put down on paper in their own words the answers they find appropriate. Some students tell aloud to a buddy what they found in reading a section. Teachers ask elementary children at this point to share with the class what they have found by the reading. This step, whether oral or in writing, gives the readers a cue as to their level of comprehension of their reading. Putting down their answer on paper supplies them with the material they will need for their next review.

REVIEW—Students can take an active interest in their review of an assignment when they realize the extent to which review prevents much natural forgetting. When they go over their notes immediately upon completing a textbook chapter, they can see the whole in a form shorter than the chapter. They can see interrelationships among the author's main points, and they can test themselves by looking away from their notes to see if they remember all the items or at least the main ideas. They now have notes that they can reread just before the next class and again before an examination on the subject. When they ask themselves, "What will the teacher ask on the test?" they can go over their own notes and predict many of the questions. The test maker is certain to include main points, which are the headings that the reader has learned to turn into questions.

Elementary grade teachers provide the review step as they show students how to recall main points and supporting details, how to connect the new section with what went before. They provide frequent short tests with opportunities to look back in the book to find the place where the author provided an answer. Thus they build the student's confidence that he can locate the author's main points and remember them. Analogous to SQ3R is the SQR [6] technique, which has been used successfully with elementary grade children.

Concentration. "Know thyself" is as good advice to the student about to sit down for a session of study as it was when first suggested by an early philosopher. To be in control of the situation, the boy (or girl) must be aware of any poor habits—daydreaming, procrastination, a tendency to take on too many tasks at once, and so on. A sincere desire to spend study time to good purpose is the next step. Knowledge of better habits to substitute for inefficient ones is imperative. Finally, putting good habits into practice must follow.

Students who are aware of tendencies to daydream or to think of almost anything but the reading assignment during the period set aside for study need to pay special attention to methods of learning better habits. Deciding upon a time when they will be free to give their attention to their dreams, personal problems, or other distracting thoughts is the practical attack. The students are then ready to use their study period to good advantage. Pitching into the first steps of a good study technique such as SQ3R reinforces their ability to concentrate. They become occupied with discrete tasks, such as raising a good question, reading to find their answers,

---

[6] *Handbook for Elementary Reading Laboratory* (Chicago: Science Research Associates, 1958).

then summarizing their answers in notes for future reference. Upon occasion, this plan of procedure has engaged the interest of the students to the extent that they have attained the good concentration they had been striving for.

Teachers help elementary pupils to attain good habits of concentration by providing such practice as asking questions that can be answered by the reading of a single paragraph, followed by discussion. They repeat this procedure for each paragraph in a short selection but do not spend so much time on one lesson that students mentally withdraw. Active participation in the discussions also aids student concentration on the lesson at hand.

Procrastination is often due to the feeling of frustration that accompanies the awareness of too much to do. In such a situation students often feel they cannot concentrate on a reading assignment because there are too many demands for their attention. They put off their studying for the free period that never seems to materialize. Once they have become aware of the nature of this problem, they can establish some new habits. They can set aside certain times for study, then keep to their schedule. Within the allotted time they can line up a reasonable number of pages to cover, then read with the intention of completing this assignment and have a few minutes to organize their next lesson. Little by little they will be accomplishing more within the same amount of time as they consciously try to do better than their own previous record of accomplishment—ten pages yesterday, twelve pages today.

Elementary grade students need teacher supervision for their study periods, so that they do not acquire habits of procrastination, daydreaming, and the like. Definite tasks that can be completed in short periods, in an atmosphere conducive to study, such as the classroom desk or work table, will help students develop effective work habits and the ability to concentrate on the task at hand.

Retention. Readers at any age from early childhood to college level have at times had the bewildering experience of having read a selection without being able to recall much of what they read, either immediately or at a later date. How can this happen? For some, at a late hour or after much reading, fatigue had set in—the eyes moved obediently across the lines and down the page, but no real comprehension took place, hence, no recall. For others, the reading had proceeded blindly—that is, without the conscious direction that accompanies an alert search for answers to questions. Therefore, little comprehension meant little opportunity for recall.

Some have said with confidence, "There, I've read it!" only to discover on the following day that they could recall nothing that they had read the day before. An analysis of their behavior during reading revealed (1) no organized pattern of reading, such as the SQ3R method; (2) their attempt to read the whole lesson in one session; (3) no review of the material; and (4) no attention, while reading or immediately thereafter, to ways in which the ideas gained in reading could be put to use. Personal involvement was at a minimum or completely lacking. Good retention of essential facts could be better assured if they would break the lesson into several sessions, summarizing each time the ideas gained in their own words, then reviewing several times. Elementary grade students practice this process when teachers follow manuals or plan lessons in the content area subjects.

Students are working toward the goal of good retention when they put several skills into operation. They need to read with attention to the various comprehension aids (for main ideas, supporting details, and so on). They need to read with the intention of remembering certain facts or ideas (main points, illustrations, and items related to previously learned materials). Their retention is further aided by frequent reviews in which they attempt to note relationships between fragmented lessons and a unit as a whole (for example, the various segments of the westward movement may be interwoven to form a whole picture).

Locational Skills

Library Techniques. Contributing to the reader's level of comprehension is his or her ability to locate pertinent information. Children need to become familiar with library techniques early in the elementary school. They need to know sources of information, such as various supplementary and reference materials as well as card files in the library. School librarians can teach basic library procedures to primary grade children and more involved procedures in upper grades. Library research can be carried on by some elementary children when facilities are made available to them within the school building.

The pupil is prepared for reading and study in any content area to gather pertinent materials for the topic at hand and use them efficiently. He or she can use first the books, magazines, and reference books in the classroom, and then use the library resources for further information.

Teachers help students to become independent in locational study skills when they teach the use of the various parts of books and the specialized uses of reference materials and also give children experiences in library use with the help of the school librarian.

Knowledge of the parts of a book is basic to the pupil's acquiring further locational skills. In the primary grades the teacher calls attention to the title of the book and the names of the stories or chapters. The table of contents is used to find the pages on which stories appear. Later, as stories appear in units, children are made aware of the concept of main topics and subtopics as they are outlined in textbooks in the table of contents. They learn to see the table of contents as a valuable bird's-eye view of the book as a whole.

When children begin reading in a textbook, they can learn to note the name of the author and the date the book was published. They can examine other sections, such as lists of maps, figures, or tables, as well as the appendix, glossary, and index.

Children find a practical use for their acquaintance with the alphabet as they enter the glossary and index of content textbooks. They can note that terms in the glossary are listed in alphabetical order. They find topics in the index also in alphabetical order, often with further alphabetized subtopics appearing under certain main topics. They may be taught the use of cross-references, which often appear under topics in the index: "See also . . ."

When children need further information beyond that supplied in the basic textbook, they are ready to use the additional locational skills needed for reference materials and library usage. The use of the dictionary is a basic tool. See Chapter 4. Classroom projects, the development of a unit, individual research, simple curiosity on the part of an individual—all require some independence in locating answers. Reference books and supplementary materials within the classroom may be examined first. Students need to think through their own questions to discover key words that will be clues to main topics in an encyclopedia or in the index of a supplementary textbook.

In many elementary schools today students have access to a library with a full-time librarian. They learn simple library techniques in the primary grades, such as the location of books and magazines, checking out and returning books, and the care of library materials. Further locational skills are taught as children can use them, especially the use of the card catalog and the *Reader's Guide.*

The teacher and librarian can plan experiences with many of the resources in the library. In the course of studying a unit, children may find answers in several encyclopedias, yearbooks, almanacs, magazines, and periodicals. They may be directed to sources of biographical references, atlases, directories, and other guides. Effective and continued practice in going to multiple sources will help students become independent readers, able to do critical and creative thinking after acquiring a background of knowledge on a subject of current importance to them.

Rate of Comprehension

Appropriate Materials. The student needs to have control over rates of reading. To have one reading rate, either a very slow or a very fast rate, is unsatisfactory. Material that is easy or familiar may be read at a faster rate than material with unfamiliar vocabulary terms or with concepts never previously encountered. Students who plod through every type of reading at a very slow rate often spend a great deal of time rereading. They have forgotten the material at the beginning of the chapter by the time they come to the end. Some students who race carelessly through an assignment also are destined to rereading if they want to understand the lesson—they missed too many of the main points and details in their hurried reading.

Students show an interest in their own reading habits when they ask, "How fast should I read?" Although it contains no magic numbers like five hundred or twelve hundred words per minute, there is one basic answer to this question: "You can learn to read as fast as you can think while reading in a specific subject or piece of reading material." This statement is at the heart of the whole problem of speed reading or improved rate of comprehension.

Very few primary grade teachers talk about improving the pupil's speed of reading. They are concerned with the task of helping children acquire the tools for reading or the mechanics of reading: recognizing words, analyzing words, understanding a reading vocabulary, understanding the mechanics of the communication arts—decoding and encoding the English language. Up to a point, the mechanics of the process may interfere with children's reading for meaning and reading with meaning. When children know how to read and can think about the author's ideas while reading, they are ready to acquire these ideas at a faster pace. Some children are able to think faster than other children. Some children know a great deal about a certain subject so that they can read and think faster on that subject than on other less familiar topics.

When teachers help students increase their speed of reading, they select materials that will not present such difficulties as unfamiliar vocabulary and concepts and long, involved sentences. They expect the pupils to improve one skill, rate, without the presence of other difficulties. They, therefore, select easy reading materials for practicing rate of comprehension, with checks of comprehension. *Reader's Digest Skill Builders*[7] and rate cards in *SRA Reading Laboratories*[8] are graded and provide materials for practice in elementary and secondary grades.

Analyzing various aspects of reading for their contribution to effective, flexible reading rates would be profitable for both teacher and student. Vocabulary is the first to come under scrutiny. A command of sight vocabulary is essential to speed reading. Techniques of word analysis must be mastered and automatic. Expecting help from the context for an occasional unfamiliar word helps the student to be self-reliant and speeds up reading.

At first the student will give careful attention to meaningful units on the line of print—dividing a sentence into phrases: "Boys and girls/like to eat / cookies and candy / after school." In time, taking several words at a glance becomes automatic, if the student is taught to think while reading a sentence, "Who did what, where, when, and why?" Note the following

[7] *Reader's Digest Skill Builders, I–VII* (Pleasantville, NY).
[8] *SRA Reading Laboratories,* Science Research Associates (Chicago, IL).

sentence: "Teddy / put the plug / into the wall socket / after school / in order / to watch / the ball game / on his television set." Both comprehension and rate of reading are involved when the reader gets a workable mental image as he reads, "A boy like me wanted to see a game on television, but first he had to plug it in. I did that last week when Mother pulled out the plug when she was vacuuming."

The next key to improved rate is practice in finding answers to questions. These are first posed by the teacher, to be found quickly in the reading material. Later, children pose their own questions, as they consider what they would like to find out. They learn to turn headings into questions and read to find answers. Skimming, a very rapid method of reading, may be defined as looking for something as quickly as possible—a predetermined reason for looking through an article, chapter, or book. Scanning is similarly rapid reading, but with a different purpose, to get an overview of the material. Thus, purpose plays an important role in improving one's rate of reading.

The basic key to improved reading rate is thinking while reading. The elementary teacher sets the stage by asking, "Before you turn the page, what do you think it will say?" Mature readers have done a great deal of reading. They have prepared themselves for faster reading by becoming aware of the pattern of sentences, paragraphs, and the author's organization of the chapters. As they read, they anticipate ideas and endings of paragraphs. They expect the author of a social studies book to present the chapter on "Life Among the Incas" in the same pattern as the previous chapter, "Life Among the Aztecs." They can, therefore, think faster while reading succeeding chapters in a social studies book, for example, because they can anticipate the author's pattern of organization.

Flexibility. It is important that teachers and students recognize the fact that comprehension should not be sacrificed in any attempt to acquire a fast rate of reading. Teachers can point out to students that, when they have set their purposes for reading, when they have a question in mind before reading, they may then ask themselves, "How fast can I find the answer?" Thus speed of reading and speed of comprehension are faced at the same time. In some materials students will find themselves able to read along quickly and locate the answers they are seeking. In other content areas, they may find difficult vocabulary, a complicated problem to solve, a puzzling cause-effect relationship, or an author's unusual style of writing—any of which may preclude the possibility of attaining a fast rate of reading.

In the elementary grades the teacher surveys the materials and notes the possible reading difficulties for students. If the material is supplementary to an assignment already completed in a textbook, the teacher may encourage the students to skim quickly to find additional facts, similar presentations, or contradictory information. If the material has answers to questions children have raised but presents difficult vocabulary and an unfamiliar style of presentation, he may suggest that they read slowly, looking for one answer at a time.

Students who have learned the SQ3R technique may make their own decision concerning the rate at which they will read a selection. After the survey step they should be sufficiently aware of the readability of the selection for them, so that they can use the rate that will best assure their comprehension of the new material. They can use a rather fast rate for material that looks familiar and a slower pace for material with new or technical vocabulary or with content for which they have little background.

Teachers provide opportunities for students to practice varied rates of reading when they point out the differences in the nature of content areas and the purposes for reading in each. Science and mathematics at upper grade levels require careful, thoughtful reading, even rereading at times. In literature a short story may be read quickly for its plot. Another may be read more carefully to detect the author's details of characterization and setting. In social studies several sources may be skimmed quickly to locate additional information on a topic. Other social studies sources, however, may be studied more thoroughly and read more slowly when the assignment calls for an evaluation in terms of historical accuracy.

To help students in upper grades overcome a tendency to read all materials at one rate, the teacher may provide some opportunities to read under the pressure of time. Timed selections appear in *Reader's Digest Skill Builders* [9] and *SRA Reading Laboratory* kits. [10] Practice in materials at independent reading level will help the good reader to be aware that he can be flexible in his rate of reading and still attain a reasonable level of comprehension.

The slowest reader is usually the one who shows no difference between his oral and silent reading rates when timed on tests of both types. He is perpetuating his slow rate of oral reading even when he is supposedly reading silently. Many high school and college students have not broken the habit of reading out loud silently to themselves—subvocalizing and thus retaining the slow rate at which people read aloud.

Some of the mechanical devices found in reading centers can help the older students. Tachistoscopic materials [11] help them realize that they can see words and phrases instantaneously. Certain films and filmstrips [12] provide reading materials at a controlled rate with questions to show them the quality of their comprehension.

---

[9] *Readers Digest Skill Builders,* op. cit.
[10] *SRA Reading Laboratories,* op. cit.
[11] *Keystone Tachistoscope* (Meadville, PA); and *Tach X,* Educational Development Laboratories (Huntington, NY).
[12] *Controlled Reader.* Educational Development Laboratories.

Harris [13] reported a study in which a group of nine-year-olds were trained to vary their reading according to purpose. He suggested that early reading instruction be varied according to the needs of students. Lloyd and Lloyd [14] reported a study in which fifth and sixth grade students received instruction daily for five weeks in digital exercises, word recognition, and comprehension. This experimental program increased the subjects' rate and accuracy, with little change in vocabulary and comprehension.

In summary, it may be noted that teachers can encourage flexible reading rates among students. In any reading lesson they may ask students to locate quickly a word, a date, a phrase, or an answer to a question in a limited section of a lesson. They may point out the familiarity of a selection and suggest that it be read quickly for a set purpose. They may, however, suggest a slow reading of another assignment because of the large number of new vocabulary terms and the sequence of events with which students will need to be familiar. Teachers may provide certain students with timed practice in easy reading material to improve their rate of comprehension. They may provide mechanical devices for older students who have made a habit of a slow rate in all types of reading. In these and other ways, teachers are assuring flexible reading rates for all students—with good comprehension as the main goal.

They help the student become independent in deciding upon their own purposes and the rates they will use in varying types of materials.

READING FOR MEANING IN CONTENT AREAS

The learning situation consists basically of objectives (the why?), knowledges (the what? who? where? when?), and the vehicles for learning (the how?). All of these become the components of the program in that area— for the duration of the pupils' school career, for the year's offerings, for the weekly program, and for the lesson of the day.

Each of the components assumes importance, first for the teacher at the helm, guiding the learning of children with their wide range of abilities, backgrounds, and interests; and second, for each child at the helm, when he is in control of his own performance in that content area. Responsibilities for teaching and learning become shared experiences at a high level when instruction in a content area has been analyzed for effective involvement of the teacher and the learner.

[13] Theodore L. Harris, "Reading Flexibility: A Neglected Aspect of Reading Instruction," *New Horizons in Reading,* Proceedings of the Fifth IRA World Congress on Reading (Newark, DE: International Reading Association, 1976), pp. 27–35.
[14] Bruce A. Lloyd and Rosalin C. Lloyd, "Paradigm and Reading Flexibility," *Education,* 92:57–65 (1971).

In examining objectives, the teacher first notes the relationship of a content area to the entire curriculum. The course of study provides long-range, overall objectives—the whole in relationship to its parts. It also delineates more immediate objectives (units, weekly and daily plans) or the parts as they relate to the whole area. The objectives become the why question as teachers ask themselves, "Why teach?" and the students ask themselves, "Why learn?" this particular subject or this particular lesson. When each gets to the point of asking this question it is a critical one. Motivation is engendered by a positive answer to the question. It is imperative that significant reasons be in evidence for both teacher and student in order that real learning take place. Thus the teacher looks for valid reasons for teaching the material of the program, and the children look for their own reasons for attention to the activity at hand. The challenge for the teacher is the provision of meaningful experiences and activities that fulfill objectives in a manner satisfactory to the teacher and the students.

Knowledges in various content areas may take the form of language development, skills such as phonetic analysis or mathematical computation, creative expression, the acquisition of a sequential body of facts, and so on. The basic purpose in any content area may be seen to be the development of individuals through the appreciations and attitudes they acquire as they gain knowledge of this particular aspect of the curriculum. For example, the student who takes part in a panel discussion in social studies first acquires a set of facts, puts them into the framework of the topic as a whole for his creative contribution to the topic, then expresses his ideas to the class. This experience may develop awareness of the need to know the subject, to give one's listeners several viewpoints rather than a single one, and even to defend one's ideas as the class reacts to the presentation. With many such experiences the student will improve his social attitudes, independence in thinking through a topic, and ability to express himself or herself in a creative manner. Thus knowledge fosters growth in several aspects of worthwhile educational objectives. The students' confidence in their own knowledge and ability is developed when they are aware that they have at their fingertips the answers to the *What? Who? Where? When?* of a particular subject. They can then think through the more complicated questions, *How?* and *Why?* with their background of facts.

The vehicles for learning (and teaching) a specific content area need to be examined. How can students have at their fingertips the answers they need? Much of what they learn in school the students will find through reading their textbooks, collateral reading material, reference materials, newspapers, and periodicals. Although these sources may consist entirely of words in print, many publications recently have added visuals—illustrations such as photographs, artists' drawings, graphs, maps, and the like.

In any one content area the teacher will need to be aware of the design of the materials—the organizational pattern of each textbook, variations in the pattern of presentation in other sources such as trade books or reference materials, and the provision (or lack) of visual aids. Teachers ask themselves how the pupils will be expected to learn content in their subject. The answer may be through the sole medium of the textbook; preferably it will be through many media, through activities that are multisensory in approach. An analysis of the typical textbook reveals an organized structure based upon the author's outline of main topics and subtopics. Some books have marginal notations of short headings or summary statements to point the way for the reader. Bold-face type and underlined phrases are often used to note main and subtopics. Chapters usually have introductory and concluding statements, and several main sections are clearly indicated. Sequence of presentation may be noted with numerical or alphabetical designations so that the author's outline may be detected during the survey and reading of the chapter. Textbooks in some content areas add further aids to comprehension with maps, graphs, and tables. They are often used to present ideas. They may give a picture or summary of facts and data for a better overview of certain relationships in the material. Responsibilities in terms of the vehicles for learning are clear-cut for the teachers. They must help students with all aspects of these devices, to see how they have been constructed and to know how they can best be studied and interpreted.

The reading skills requisite to the student for good comprehension in the various subject areas of the curriculum may be determined through such an analysis of anticipated objectives, knowledges, and the vehicles of instruction. In general, these skills are

1. Setting one's own purposes.
2. Acquiring the special or technical vocabulary of the subject.
3. Understanding the concepts specific to the content area.
4. Noting main points and supporting details.
5. Noting sequence and interrelationships in the presentation of ideas.
6. Being alert to ways of making the new learnings functional in one's own life.

How good a student he or she is depends upon how well these skills or techniques are mastered.

In the next sections, comprehensive skills for efficient reading in several content areas will be examined. With the variety of textbooks and supplementary materials on the market today, teachers will need to examine the specific materials available to them, within the framework of objectives in their own course of study.

English

The elementary teacher of English finds that he or she is responsible for the teaching of the communication arts—speaking, writing, and reading.

Thus the teacher assists children in learning correct oral and written expression—proper grammatical construction in oral speech and written composition. The teacher provides experiences in the reading and evaluating of others' compositions and in such literary works as poems, short stories, essays, novels, and plays.

The teacher of reading will recognize a familiar pattern—the development, in terms of communication, of speaking skills, followed by writing skills, with the subsequent need of reading skills to interpret the written expression of ideas.

Textbooks in elementary English classes typically include an English grammar, a speller, and workbooks for written composition. Additional materials in upper grades may include story anthologies, poetry anthologies, biographies, and novels. Literature reading in elementary grades may be limited to selections, such as the short stories and poetry in basal readers, and trade books from a room library or central library in the school.

Possibly the most important task facing the English teacher, in terms of the grammar, speller, and composition book, is that of making each meaningful and functional in the lives of the children. In the grammar are exercises that provide necessary practice in the use of parts of speech, punctuation marks, types of sentences and paragraphs, and so on. Directions for their correct usage need to be read by the students. They need to write answers; proofread what they have written; discuss the different sections; and attempt to make the various language learnings functional in their own speaking, writing, and reading. Teachers provide instruction as they themselves become good models of English usage and encourage children to apply the information they gain in their textbooks in the practical situations of talking and writing.

In the primary grades children are given many opportunities to relate personal experiences. They listen to the stories others tell in the classroom. They listen to the teacher and to the stories the teacher reads to them. Thus they are informally building an understanding and appreciation of thoughts expressed in words—sentences that in a certain sequence produce an understandable experience.

As children gain in their abilities to express themselves in writing, they need the additional skills of spelling, grammar, and punctuation. By this time the teacher has usually provided textbooks and workbooks, which children will need to read with understanding. Teachers will need to be familiar with these textbooks—to know whether or not children will be able to read them independently or only with teacher supervision. They can point out the author's use of bold-faced type to set off directions. They could use the cloze techniques (elimination of every n'th word) in sentences as a device to help the student to think of the best word to complete the thought or of the best synonym for the word in parentheses, and so on. They can teach the use of the dictionary to determine various meanings of words or the unfamiliar usage of a previously learned word. They can point out exercises that will help the children better understand the use of various punctuation marks as aids to reading comprehension.

An appreciation of literary works can be developed as the teacher carefully selects different types that are appropriate to the children's maturity. The children can be encouraged to look for points of similarity and difference in their own experiences and those of the characters in a short story or novel. They can learn to assess the author's purpose in writing a selection. They may prepare a summary—a review, interpretation, or evaluation of their reading, to be shared with the class.

Thus children become involved in the improvement of their own communication skills. They become aware of good language patterns in their own and others' speaking, writing, and reading.

Even children who have previously shown no interest in language activities, in reading or writing have been reached by a set of books developed by the Hunter College Project English Curriculum Study Center. The *Macmillan Gateway English* [15] soft-back books and workbooks present true-to-life tales that stimulate reluctant upper grade students to read and write.

Record albums are features of this literature and language arts program for culturally disadvantaged youth. Regional variations in dialect can be heard in recorded songs and poems.

The manual of a level one anthology provides an assignment relating the student's writing to both life and literature: [16] "Write a composition called either 'A Gift for _____' (someone in your family or a friend) or 'My Most Valued Possession.' This is a *first draft*. It will be rewritten in class."

The teacher follows the next day's lesson with the statement, "Now we will hear each other's compositions as if they were riddles and try to guess what objects have been written about." The suggestion is made in the manual that students substitute the word *blank* for the name of the object as they read their composition aloud.

Students with such an assignment have been motivated to write, to read, and to listen to others' compositions. If a selection of stories were to be made subsequently for a school newspaper, there would be adequate motivation for learning proofreading techniques.

Social Studies

The area of social studies for children in the elementary grades usually includes history, geography, and civics. Human relationships and interactions

[15] New York: Macmillan Publishing Co., Inc.
[16] *A Family Is a Way of Feeling,* Macmillan Gateway English Series (New York: Macmillan Publishing Co., Inc.), p. 35.

are studied within the context of these areas. The heritage of man's past is studied for its effects upon the present and future.

The importance of high-level reading and thinking skills will be evident to any teacher who studies the numerous objectives of teaching social studies. Michaelis [17] groups objectives in new social studies programs under four headings: (1) knowledge objectives, such as understanding data, concepts, items, and generalizations; (2) affective objectives, such as developing attitudes, values, and appreciations; (3) inquiry objectives, such as developing the ability to inquire by means of analysis of topics, formulation and the use of criteria for making judgments, and the use of systematic observation techniques; and (4) skills objectives, to develop competencies in skills such as using multiple sources, interpreting graphic material, reading critically, and so on. Objectives in curriculum guides are being stated in terms of observable behavior. Knowledges are analyzed in terms of such cognitive objectives as facts, concepts, generalizations, and such affective objectives as awareness of values and attitudes like respect for others and fair play.

Vehicles for learning in the social studies are *all* of the avenues of learning—directed attention to acquisition of knowledge through all of the senses. Children learn by listening to authorities and to peers; by looking at the world about them, at pictures, and at the printed page; by taking part in activities that give them kinetic experience—feeling, smelling, tasting, touching, drawing, moving about as in marches and dances. By discussing their reactions to all of the above activities, children learn to know themselves and others. They have opportunities to comprehend and evaluate their experiences.

In Chapter 5 the types of questions teachers might use to develop comprehension were explored. In the social studies, or in any subject, children can read not only to find answers to teachers' questions, but also to answer questions they themselves raise as they become interested in the problems of people who attempted or attempt currently to find solutions. Children can be helped to develop critical thinking skills as they read in various sources. [18]

Teachers need to be aware of the many ways children are learning about the world in which they live—its people, its cultural heritage, and its emerging future. Specifically, in elementary schools teachers need to analyze the reading skills children will need in order to profit from the many facets of social studies instruction to which good schools expose them today.

[17] Michaelis, op. cit. pp. 7–13.
[18] James A. Banks and Ambrose A. Clegg, Jr., *Teaching Strategies for the Social Studies* (Reading, MA: Addison-Wesley Publishing Company, 1973); Jack R. Fraenkel, *Helping Students Think and Value: Strategies for Teaching Social Studies* (Englewood Cliffs, NJ: Prentice-Hall, Inc., 1973); Ellen L. Thomas and H. Alan Robinson, *Improving Reading in Every Class* (Boston: Allyn & Bacon, Inc., 1977).

Teachers can find more attention given to reading skills for social studies in current manuals than was given a decade ago. College textbooks for teachers preparing to teach the social studies have recently included sections related to the teaching of reading skills in this content area.

Michaelis [19] has devoted a chapter to the types of reading materials and reading skills requisite to effective learning in the social studies area. The reader is recommended to this chapter for a comprehensive review of such topics as (1) types of reading materials, (2) planning for differences in ability, and (3) using textbooks effectively. An intensive section on skills includes building vocabulary and identifying concepts; reading to interpret meaning; skimming; forming sensory impressions; discovering relationships; and reading critically, creatively, and appreciatively.

What aids for reading effectively are incorporated in the classroom textbook? The teacher can examine the textbooks and supplementary books available to class for their format and readability as well as for clues to reading provided in the guidebooks.

Living in Our Times [20] prepares children by starting with their immediate environment and spreading out into other times and places. *Learning About Our Country* [21] has many illustrations in black and white as well as color. Its text in large print concerns various sections of the United States and its cities—large and small, old and new, in various parts of the country. It includes a geography dictionary. It informs the teacher that the words used are geared to the reading level of the third grade reader. An examination of the sixth book in the series [22] shows that the format has changed to smaller print with a two-column arrangement on each page. Each chapter has a short introduction with main headings and subheadings centered in bold-faced type. Each chapter concludes with questions for review and suggested activities.

The teacher's manual states that a social studies program in the intermediate grades should give children a knowledge of people and help them to think about and value the people of the world. It suggests that the teacher provide activities through such means as using community resources, visitors, trips, maps, globes, and creative experiences. It lists for the teacher the various skills and concepts maintained from grades four and five and introduces the new skills in the text, such as identifying cultural or physical regions on maps, identifying regions in one's own community, and so on.

The manual [23] points out the need for reading skills on the part of the student:

[19] Michaelis, *op. cit.,* pp. 363–92.
[20] Allyn & Bacon, Inc.
[21] Allyn & Bacon, Inc.
[22] Allyn & Bacon, Inc.
[23] Ibid., *Teacher's Manual.*

A maximum use of the carefully planned illustration in each text will enable the slower readers to gain directly from the illustrations many of the ideas developed there. Frequent discussion of the pictures will help these children to gain skill in interpreting graphic materials. Careful attention by the authors to sequence of ideas and the organizing devices provided by headings and subheadings will help children to follow more easily the entire exposition. . . . The use of committees of reading-mate pairs will help slow readers keep pace with the group. . . . Questions used as guides for study will be a further help. It is important to help the slower readers use supplementary, teacher-made, printed, kinaesthetic, visual and auditory materials, so that they can make a contribution to the class.

Another aid to reading in the social studies classes is the appearance on the market in the last decade of materials written in considerably easier style, yet attractive and interesting to the older pupil who has trouble reading the textbook at grade level. An example of a book written specifically to be read with social studies units is *The Big City and How It Grew*.[24] Its manual states that it was designed to be used by the independent younger reader and the retarded older reader, as well as by seventh graders "who are unable to read the textbooks on New York City's history designed for their age level." [25] There are black-and-white drawings and photographs on every page. The pictures and text together would furnish a basis for much discussion with subsequent clarification of the vocabulary and concepts involved.

Science

Certainly, in this technological age the question, "Why teach science?" never rears its head. Teachers of science can almost glibly recite reasons: to help students to develop a scientific attitude and outlook; to develop powers of observation; to train students in the problem-solving techniques of forming hypotheses, gathering information, experimentation, drawing conclusions, and so on. Objectives of teaching science are usually clearly formulated.

Knowledges pupils are expected to acquire typically include an understanding of the technical vocabulary, concepts, and generalizations in the various science areas; the acquisition of a science background; and the development of a stock of functional scientific information.

The vehicles for learning science in the elementary school are predominantly the textbook and experimentation (through observation, performance, or both). Even in a subject that lends itself exceptionally well to the theory of learning by doing, pupils are being taught primarily through the reading of the textbook.

Teachers need to be well acquainted with the science textbook at their

[24] Follett.
[25] Ibid.

particular level. They need to analyze it for its burden of technical vocabulary and the number of concepts developed in a paragraph or page. They need to be aware of the possible familiarity of the children with these vocabulary terms and concepts. A chapter may be easy reading to a group of children who find the concepts familiar and simple to understand. It may prove to be difficult reading for a group of children whose background (suburban or urban) does not provide experiences in the area under study.

Teachers need also to look at the textbook to assess the amount of difficulty certain children will have when reading (1) to find important generalizations, (2) to follow the directions related to a scientific experiment, (3) to answer questions raised in a problem-solving situation, and (4) to interpret accompanying diagrams and graphic representations of various technical processes. They must also be familiar with the outside sources of information to which children will go, such as reference materials, scientific books, and magazines. Many of these sources are more difficult to read than the textbook in the classroom. Better readers can be guided to their use, whereas poorer readers must be helped to find science material at a suitable reading level.

A perusal of science series currently on the market for elementary schools will show the classroom teacher that today there are built-in helps to aid teachers and students for adequate comprehension of scientifica materials. One series [26] provides in its *Guide for Teaching* suggested procedures for developing a lesson plan: attention to important concepts and generalizations, ways to clarify principles, ways to encourage independent thinking, additional experiments, science background (resource section), and vocabulary summary. The teacher is told to use the same techniques that he or she is accustomed to using in reading lessons to introduce new science vocabulary. Discussion with the children will help to make new words meaningful and readable. The use of context clues is encouraged, because the manual points out that in the primary grades illustrations are used to help define words, whereas in the intermediate grade books new words are italicized and accompanied by a built-in definition. Units in Book I are developed through the use of pictures and short sentences: [27] "Here is another airplane. What makes it go?" In Book II children are introduced to five procedures: (1) observation, (2) experimentation, (3) discussion, (4) recording data, and (5) reading science books. Book III introduces the control experiment. Students are expected to be careful and persistent in repeating experiments. Book IV defines the hypothesis in problem-solving. Book V from the very first unit shows students the importance of trial ideas, the forming of hypotheses, the developing of new ideas, the gathering of information, and the ultimate using of ideas.

[26] Harper & Row.
[27] Harper & Row.

In a unit on "Rocks and the Earth"[28] fourth grade students are told to solve the problem of testing soil to see if it is weathered rock. They are given a method, with guided observation and experimentation, followed by questions, vocabulary terms, and suggested books to read. One example is Miriam Selsam's *Birth of an Island*.[29]

The teacher who examines science textbooks and follows the suggestions in the guide books will be teaching the student to read efficiently in science materials. With the mobility of families today, the glossary of terms will be useful because some students will not have met some of these terms in earlier books of this science series.

Mathematics

A brief analysis of the teacher's edition of a book on elementary mathematics[30] will show that current textbooks provide the prospective teacher with a mathematical background through numerous suggestions for activities and discussion. The concepts of numbers and operations on numbers are included. Students are encouraged to state their discovery, thus participating in the solving of problems. Motivation is provided through a variety of techniques, such as special exercises and puzzles, as well as through application to real-life situations. The page format for the student shows double columns with many pictures and drawings, for the purpose of clarifying abstract number concepts. In the teacher's manual each page for the children has an accompanying page for the teacher with purpose, pre-book teaching, and procedure for that page carefully delineated.

It is important that the teacher recognize the basic problem involved in teaching the reading of mathematics today. It may be simply stated as learning to think while reading. The processes involved, however, are not simple. Thinking while reading a mathematical problem requires the student to differentiate among the symbols presented, to identify each with a meaning derived from past experiences, and to manipulate the whole to arrive at or discover a satisfactory solution.

The vocabulary of mathematics needs to be carefully studied by the teacher. There are technical terms specific to the subject that children need to learn. There is a mathematical language unique to the subject, which can be translated into a way of thinking or reasoning. Certainly an oral facility with the vocabulary and attendant meanings is prerequisite to reading in mathematics. Real experiences that help children see common patterns, likenesses, and differences while using mathematical language are fundamental to the teacher's objective—guiding children to the point where they can be on their own when they face mathematical problems, en-

---

[28] Harper & Row.
[29] Harper & Row.
[30] Harcourt Brace Jovanovich.

countered either as written symbols for problems in their textbooks or as real-life situations that demand mathematical reasoning.

Thus, readiness for reading in mathematics can be structured by the teacher who sets the stage by providing real experiences with concrete objects, by using the language of mathematics, and by promoting oral facility with this language before children encounter mathematical symbols in the textbook.

Other Subjects

In the modern classroom children study textbooks, pore over supplementary references, and read teacher-made worksheets and tests in each content area. Through the reading of their assignments, children are expected to extract meaning, note interrelationships, relate past knowledge with present information, and make application of new knowledge to their own lives and experiences. Carefully structured lessons in any content area will help children toward the ultimate attainment of these objectives.

Teachers need to analyze the school's curriculum, previously prepared courses of study, and the textbooks and other teaching instruments available for a particular subject—all in relation to the kinds of children in the classroom at a given moment. Teaching the children to read efficiently in any content area involves, in addition, a detailed analysis of the reading skills required of the children. Common factors are vocabulary and comprehension. Vocabulary can be explored in terms of the children's familiarity with the concepts they will encounter as they study the subject. New meanings for previously learned words will be discovered. Ways to think about the new concepts will be studied. For example, syllogistic reasoning in mathematics has implications for thinking in other areas. An author may be using deductive reasoning by presenting major and minor premises leading to stated conclusions. Such learning cannot be incidental but must be the result of carefully structured lessons on the part of perceptive teachers. Thus teachers can help children deduce an author's subtlety, irony, deviousness, ingenuity, or skillfully prepared arguments.

Teachers can help children recognize such organizational patterns as a historically based presentation, the sequential development of a theme, or the author's use of varied illustrations to clarify a new concept. They can help children learn to restate in their own words the main ideas and supporting details they grasped in their reading of an assignment. In any content area in which children are expected to read to learn, the skills involved in the SQ3R approach to study (see the section about SQ3R in this chapter) can be utilized to good advantage—to see the whole and the parts related to the whole, to relate the new to the old, to note implications for utilization, and to aid the retention of useful knowledge gained in reading.

Teachers need to provide for discussion—preceding and following the assigned reading. These periods are especially useful for clarification. It is important that children do not form misconceptions from partially under-stood reading. When the reading material is too difficult for some children, they may read at the verbalizing level—not understanding and not con-ceptualizing. The resultant rote learning is not functional. It is, therefore, during discussion periods that teachers can note which children need further explanations, more review, or more concrete presentations. In these discus-sions certain children may discover meanings and relationships that they had not previously understood in their own reading by listening to peers and teachers. How they may put new vocabulary and new concepts to use in their own lives would be a point for discussion in these sessions.

Literature

In the last fifty years in the books written on children's reading habits and children's literature, one can usually find the statement "Literature will en-rich the lives of young people." The statement is seemingly innocuous, but is it realistic? Are its implications borne out in the lives of both children and adults? Do adults read and thus enrich their lives? How much did they read as growing children? Why *don't* some adults read? What do they miss by not having the reading habit? What part do curriculum and instructional strategies play in producing the reading adult?

Recent research has given educators some significant information re-garding reading comprehension and the reading of literature. Benjamin Bloom [31] reported that the International Association for the Evaluation of Educational Achievement (IEA) has engaged in research related to the study of educational problems in twenty-two countries, including the United States. The findings of the IEA showed three variables of importance in accounting for differences in curriculum success, namely, opportunity to learn, competence of teachers, and time or the number of hours devoted to instruction in a particular area of the curriculum. The IEA generalized from interrelations for literature, science, and reading that (1) learning in both science and literature is highly related to reading comprehension, and (2) reading comprehension is more highly related to literature than to science. Thorndike [32] reported in the IEA study of reading comprehension that the three most important variables related to students' level of reading com-prehension are reading resources in the home, socioeconomic status (father's

[31] Benjamin S. Bloom, "Implications of the IEA Studies for Curriculum and In-struction," *Educational Policy and International Assessment* (Berkeley, CA: Mc-Cutchan Publishing Corporation, 1975), pp. 65–84.
[32] Robert L. Thorndike, *Reading Comprehension Education in Fifteen Countries: An Empirical Study,* International Studies in Evaluation, **VIII,** (New York: John Wiley & Sons, Inc., 1973).

occupation and parents' education), and parents' interest in the child's education and the encouragement they give him to read.

Contributions of both home and school to reading achievement must, therefore, be recognized. When teachers realize the importance of parents' reading habits, over which they at that point have no control, at best they can point out that the child of today is the parent of tomorrow—and provide reading instruction and reading opportunity in the classroom. "It is unlikely that students can learn much from teachers who do not thoroughly understand the subject they are teaching." [33] Implications of this statement are clear-cut. Because literature cuts across nearly all areas of the curriculum, teachers need to be familiar with all types of books for children's reading in the classroom and in their leisure time.

The IEA has pointed out the significance of "parents who read" in the education of young people. Let us now look at the possible contributions that teachers and librarians can make toward producing the willing and avid reader. At the grass roots level teachers and librarians have the opportunity to introduce children to the various genres of children's literature that will become a bridge to the vast world of traditional and modern literature for adults—biography, fiction, poetry, to name a few. Just as adults' lives are enriched by their reading of classical and current literature, so children benefit from experiences with the literature developed just for them. In content area subjects, literature can broaden children's concepts and make each subject live. For example, the history text will be more meaningful to the student who is exposed to biographies or autobiographies. One can learn about interesting and admirable personalities, their ways of life, their place in history, their influence on that history, and their accomplishments and contributions to society.

Teachers and librarians who have enjoyed wide reading and have encountered children and young adults who have found literature exciting and rewarding, at the same time are well aware that there are countless numbers of children and adults who do not read and are, therefore, denied imaginative excursions into the adventure, humor, characterization, and information that can be found between the pages of a good book.

Side-by-side throughout their lives go the nonreader and the reader. The first reads not and cares not (usually). The second has read as a child as an adolescent, and as an adult. How can we account for the differences between the reader and nonreader? The authors' tenet is that knowledgeable parents, teachers, and librarians make the difference. Parents who like to read and who read to their children set the stage for the youngsters' predilection for reading. Teachers who have a wide acquaintance with literature, who read to children and teach skills for efficient reading, provide a reading

[33] Bloom, op. cit., p. 70.

Illustrating the story

environment conducive to building enduring reading habits. Librarians who understand children's abilities and interests can provide both story hours and books appropriate to the ages and needs of young people. See Chapter 2 for suggested literature reading.

SUMMARY

Teachers need to be aware of the many factors that modify or clarify students' reading comprehension. As they examine the reading materials in content areas, through the procedures of task analysis, they can structure the type of lessons that will result in advancing the reading comprehension of each learner. They can go beyond the textbook by directing each student's attention to supplementary types of reading—trade books, magazines, reference materials, audiovisual aids, any or all of which may extend the student's knowledge of subject matter in content areas.

The student's successful reading for meaning in any content area is the result of such strategies as initial preparation on the part of the teacher and students, motivation for reading through the teacher's and/or pupils' questions, the student's grasp of study skills, his ability to think while reading, his involvement in subsequent discussion for review and clarification, concepts extended through varying supplementary aids, and the projected utilization of the new knowledge he has gained in the content area.

SELECTED READINGS

Berger, Allen, and James D. Peebles, comp. *Rates of Comprehension, Annotated Bibliography.* Newark, DE: International Reading Association, 1976.

Burros, Arnold, and Amos L. Claybough. *Using Reading to Teach Subject Matter: Fundamentals for Content Teachers.* Columbus, OH: Charles E. Merrill, 1974.

Earle, Richard. *Teaching Reading and Mathematics.* Newark, DE: International Association, 1976.

Howes, Virgil M. *Individualizing Instruction in Reading and Social Studies.* New York: Macmillan Publishing Company, Inc., 1970.

Kottmeyer, William. *Decoding and Meaning: A Modest Proposal.* New York: McGraw-Hill Book Company, 1974.

Laffey, James, ed. *Reading in the Content Areas.* Newark, DE: International Association, 1972.

Merritt, John E., ed. *New Horizons in Reading.* Proceedings of the Fifth IRA World Congress on Reading. Newark, DE: International Reading Association, 1976.

Robinson, Francis R. *Effective Study.* 4th ed. New York: Harper & Row, Publishers, 1970.

Robinson, H. Alan. *Teaching Reading and Study Strategies: The Content Areas.* Boston: Allyn & Bacon, Inc., 1975.

Ruddell, Robert B. *Reading-Language Instruction: Innovative Practices.* Englewood Cliffs, NJ: Prentice-Hall, Inc., 1974.

Schulwitz, Bonnie S. *Teachers, Tangibles, Techniques: Comprehension of Content in Reading.* Newark, DE: International Reading Association, 1975.

Smith, Frank. *Understanding Reading—A Psycholinguistic Analysis of Reading and Learning to Read.* New York: Holt, Rinehart and Winston, 1971.

Thelen, Judith. *Improving Reading in Science.* Newark, DE: International Reading Association, 1972.

Thorndike, Robert L. *Reading Comprehension Education in Fifteen Countries.* Newark, DE: International Reading Association, 1973.

West, Gail B. *Teaching Reading Skills in Content Areas.* Orlando, FL: The Sandpiper Press, 1974.

Chapter 7

Oral Reading

OBJECTIVES

To know the purposes and appropriateness of oral reading in the classroom

To know what skills are involved in effective oral reading

To know the place of oral reading in the program

To plan strategies for providing oral reading practice

To know how oral reading instruction should differ from silent reading instruction

To learn how to evaluate correctly oral reading

INTRODUCTION

Oral reading is the process of reading printed or written material aloud. Most of us read silently much more often than we read orally. When we do read orally, there is a significant purpose attached to the reading. We read some material we have especially prepared to our professional group or to the PTA or to our church, political, or social organization. We may read an announcement, a short book review, some poetry, a dictionary definition of a word, or a phone message. We listen every day to the reading of announcers, entertainers, and news commentators on the car radio and on television.

There seem to be four major purposes for oral reading in adult life: (1) to convey information, (2) to create a mood, (3) to entertain, and (4) to gain personal gratification or social development. Sometimes purposes are combined, as in the case of candidates for office who may tell a few jokes to get their audience in a receptive mood, give some personal anecdotes to sell their own personality, and then speak to the issues and present their platform and their party's platform by conveying information.

The candidates may read orally a portion of their presentation; they may interpret orally after quickly scanning notes that they have before them; they may read a quotation of another author. They have learned to use skillfully variations in their voice, stress and intonation patterns, a considerable eye-voice span, adjustment to their audience, gestures, and other forms of expression to convey their message to the people in their audience. Their speed may increase or decrease to enhance the meaning or stress of their message. The pauses may be long or short as the occasion demands. In other words, they adjust their oral reading to fit the situation.

These skills have to be learned and practiced if one is to be proficient and effective in oral reading. The purposes for oral reading arise naturally in the school classroom. The teacher should capitalize on them and use them appropriately rather than try to create artificial situations where tension is often associated with the process of learning the skills of oral reading. In considering the place of oral reading in the total reading and language arts program, the question is not whether it should be in the program; rather it is a question of the role it plays in the individual's language arts development. This chapter presents in detail the various phases of the oral reading process, the techniques of teaching, examples of good practice, and methods of evaluating oral reading. The preceding examples were meant to show that oral reading contains educational, cultural, personal, and social values.

PURPOSE OF ORAL READING IN THE CLASSROOM

Beginning Reading

A group of children read aloud their experience charts to associate printed words with their spoken words, familiar because they are their own oral interpretation of experiences, their own words. Oral language is basic to written language. This oral reading helps the children relate symbols and meaning. They establish habits that are common to both oral and silent reading, such as clustering words in thought units. The teacher accepts the sentence or thought unit only as it would be said to a friend; thus the conveying of meaning is paramount, with good speech patterns and expression characterizing the children's oral reading.

As soon as word recognition has advanced to the point where words are perceived accurately at a glance, silent and independent reading begins. From this point on everything does not have to be read orally, but only for specific purposes instead of the general one of combining the two senses of visual and vocomotor in the perceptual learning of word forms. Vocalizing, which at first is helpful in learning to read, may later become a handicap. Like a crutch, children must discard it when they are ready to read silently. At this stage of their learning, children usually like to read orally in order to demonstrate their success in learning to read. They gain reinforcement and personal satisfaction.

Sharing Information

Probably the most common use of oral reading in the classroom is the practice of having the child read a selection to share with others a source that is scarce. Examples of this are a single library book, an encyclopedia reference, a magazine or newspaper article, and a supplementary book. Sometimes it is an excerpt that settles an argument, proves a point, clarifies an idea, quotes an authority, or presents a different point of view from the current one. To support the general affairs of the classroom, a child may read an announcement, a committee report, meeting minutes, or directions to be followed in case of a fire or an air raid. Emphasis is placed on accurately and correctly conveying the meaning of the scarce material.

Providing Pleasure or Entertainment to Others

There is full justification for oral reading in school to serve the purpose of entertainment. It builds a group feeling of appreciation of literature that is contagious. It permits individuals to share their literary enthusiasm. Audience behavior and correct listening habits can be taught as a good way of learning. Interests can be broadened to different forms of literature. Plot and characters can be discussed as they become more real through hearing the characters speak throughout the story. To be fully appreciated, certain

An appreciative audience

types of literature, such as poetry, must be heard. Literary tastes can be developed. All profit, reader and listeners, when a selection is read that contains beauty of language, a colorful and unusual use of words, and skilled authoring of imagery and description. The oral reading of humor teaches the reader how to successfully get humor across to others. The listeners benefit from the entertainment as a break in the serious process of learning, whether it be in a small group, a classroom, or the school assembly. The teacher's serial reading to the children may serve several purposes—acquainting them with literature, a quieting period after more rigorous physical activity, teaching a plot—and through this daily process the teacher develops a pleasurable association with books, stories, and characters. Eventually, this serves as an incentive for the child to read independently.

Personal Improvement

Correctly taught, oral reading helps children develop naturally in their speaking habits and personality traits before an audience. It helps them develop confidence and poise in facing a group of people. It may establish desirable language patterns, vocabulary, voice production, and articulation. Some children gain much-needed approval from the group and develop a sense of personal worth through oral reading. It has helped some in overcoming minor speech defects. As soon as children develop competency in oral reading, they are ready to move to the next step of combining oral reading and speaking from notes. Eventually, they arrive at the stage where they are comfortable enough to use the skill of oral reading easily and naturally in any social situation for whatever purpose they desire.

Evaluate Reading Skills and Speech

The teacher has children read orally in order to determine the strength and extent of their reading skills, including comprehension. As an evaluation instrument this is handled mostly in private. They are questioned so that they can be helped and supported in their reading. This is a continuous, if not a daily, process as the teacher needs more than a single sampling to determine the instructional needs of the child. An oral informal reading inventory may be the first step in the evaluation process to get the child started at the correct level. The teacher listens for word reversals, omissions, repetitions, attack methods, and substitutions and mispronunciations; and determines *why* the child may not get meaning or inference or analogy. The child may not be phrasing correctly or responding to punctuation marks or placing the emphasis properly. Instructional and grouping procedures are then adjusted to suit the child's needs.

Because speech difficulties are often related to reading problems, the speech characteristics of the child are examined at the same time. The teacher listens for (1) articulatory disorders (lisping, clumsy speech, baby talk, sound substitutions); (2) voice disorders (nasality, monotony, weakness); (3) rhythmic disorders (poor coordination of the speech apparatus); (4) symbolic disorders (poor grammatical relationships); and (5) delayed speech (average for speech development). In the case of speech difficulties the teacher may refer the child to the speech specialist and adjust instruction to help the child.

Oral reading is used as an evaluative procedure whereby the teacher can improve the instructional method by individualizing the reading approach. The purpose is to help the child make normal progress in reading skill development for him or her. In this case, there is an interaction between oral and silent reading and the other language arts. Silent reading tests may indicate certain errors the child is making, but it often remains for oral reading and questioning to discover *why* the mistakes are made.

TEACHING THE SKILLS FOR EFFECTIVE ORAL READING

Types

There are several types of oral reading. Some are focused on instruction for the process itself; others are focused on the communication of information, ideas, or entertainment; and some emphasize the personal development of the individual: (1) sight reading or oral reading of new material, not previously seen; (2) oral reading that follows silent reading—an instructional process for the reinforcement or the checking of skills; (3) reading to an audience that does not have the material before it; (4) private oral reading (usually with the teacher) where work is progressing on specific skills; (5) dramatic reading (interpretive reading) by a group taking the parts of characters; (6) choral reading where a group reads in unison; and (7) oral reading to a recording device for evaluation purposes, classified as a separate type because there is occasionally a reaction known as mike fright.

Characteristics of Good Oral Reading

Because oral reading is a social experience, as contrasted with silent reading, it involves the child's total reactions to other people. The attitude of the audience must be kept favorable if the reader is to gain success and get a feeling of pleasure from the reading. Good readers use a conversational tone without embarrassment. They display their comprehension of the material by communicating the meaning clearly as the author presents it. They avoid errors of substitution and omission. They read fluently in thought units, and speak clearly so that their total audience can hear easily. They give full attention to the transmission of the author's writing.

The Place of Oral Reading in the Program

The initial contact of children with reading involves oral reading exclusively. Someone reads to them: parents, other children who read, teachers, or a reader on television. They eventually move from being a passive listener to being a reader, usually under the direction of the teacher. They learn that they can transform the print to oral speaking. They do a great deal of this in learning to read so that the meaning can be heard, the letters and printed words can be associated. From experience charts to words to books is a gradual transition for most children. Television watching is a mediating process of reinforcement for certain words. As silent reading begins, oral reading continues, but becomes less frequent and more incidental. However, except for the specific sight reading experiences in instruction and evaluation, silent reading precedes the oral reading before an audience. If the teacher expects comprehension, fluency, and accuracy in oral reading, the child must be given adequate preparation for such oral reading. Oral reading must continue a specific part of the language arts program throughout the elementary school with a wide variety of materials and instruction in its skills.

In the first and second grades, probably about half of the reading time is spent on oral reading. After the second grade, oral reading time is considerably less. One way to assure its retention is to set aside a specific time for the sharing of appropriate literature. This might include the teacher's reading of stories and poems *and* the children's reading of their preferences.

Emphases in Instruction

With the teacher setting the example of the best oral reader in the classroom, work sessions may be devoted to developing the children's skills in oral reading. Standards are set cooperatively for reading "just as the character would say it"; one child helps another; results are analyzed in terms of the standards. Corrections are made tactfully by the teacher or help is obtained from another child on a word or an expression. The teacher suggests correct posture and book holding, materials at appropriate levels of readability for each child. Sometimes the teacher puts on the chalkboard what the child said, and they compare it with the printed selection; the teacher may demonstrate how to break the sentence into thought units. When the teacher recognizes a new interest, a book may be used to capitalize on that interest. When a child misreads a statement by a character, the teacher may read it two or even three different ways and ask the group or the child: "Which way is the correct one?" Words that are consistently missed must later be taught, probably not at the time they are reading; but surely later. A small pad or notebook may be needed so that the teacher will not forget to do this. The later drill should involve the word in context, usually in a series of short

Oral reading to share a story: utilization of word recognition skills

sentences employing correct context. Teaching the word in isolation may not help the child. Simple rhymes or stories are very helpful.

The basal readers and their manuals supply practice material for oral reading. Good teacher orientation to the material helps the child with new words encountered. Varied materials and approaches to the content are what some children need. The linguists suggest that children need to develop a sensitivity to language patterns and that they have to learn rising-tone patterns such as those in rhythmic songs and games. The child can be taught the latter by practicing rising tones throughout the sentence with falling tone only at the end of the sentence. Children who read word by word or with a series of heavy stresses need this help. The child can be taught to emphasize words in the sentence with relative stress, loudness, and elongated pronunciation or higher pitch.

When one prepares for an audience situation, there are several processes that should be kept in mind. The children will find stronger purpose in work that they prepare themselves. They need the teacher's guidance in

1. Selection of the appropriate material.
2. Selection of the story to present.
3. Ways to shorten a story for presentation.
4. Choice of the places to break a story if there are different readers.
5. Choice of what to present if it is a special events program.
6. Use of the dictionary.
7. Pronunciation of difficult or irregular words.

8. Arrangement for practice sessions and time.
9. Use of their own writing.
10. Choice of standards for oral readers and listeners.
11. Determination of what should be read versus what should be told.

They may even discuss a censoring process for their own presentation in terms of taste, excellence, personal feeling, jokes, and so on. Sufficient practice should assure a creditable presentation, but not a polished production. The teacher should exercise some careful judgment in this respect. This usually results in a selection appropriate in type and difficulty, recognized purposes on the part of readers and listeners, and silent reading followed by oral reading practice for fluency and vocabulary and expression.

The oral reading is thus correlated with the other language arts, such as writing and listening. It may form the basis for other creative or expressive arts—drama, drawing and painting, music. It may use as content some of the academic fields of literature, social studies, and science. This work with language can strengthen the child's personality and cultural and social traits so that he is free from unnecessary restraints throughout his lifetime.

Where disabled readers are supposedly being helped with extra attention on phonics, a caution is necessary. They tend to function better with concrete ideas; therefore, the highly abstract phonics treatment should be related directly to concrete meaningful activities. It would be a good idea to work the phonics instruction into the experiences of the child's own language and life-style; otherwise, the child will be doing pseudoreading, calling out the sounds of the words and not using the deep structure for meaning acquisition. The child who thus uses surface structures is more apt to make syntactic and semantic errors.[1]

EXAMPLES OF GOOD PRACTICE

Choral Reading

Choral reading is the practice of a group reading in concert. This is helpful in the classroom that has a range (but not too great) of reading abilities represented. The better readers help the slower ones. Shy children develop greater confidence. Those with expression encourage the others to speak similarly. The teacher can alternate with the children or speak in chorus with them. The teacher may help an individual child by reading in chorus with him or her. Choral reading of poems can be especially effective. Variations of choral reading, which may help certain children, are the singing of ballads and group oral reading where the whole class is divided into

[1] William D. Page. "Are We Beginning to Understand Oral Reading?" *Reading World*, **XIII**,3:161–70 (March 1974).

groups and each member reads a section for the others. The best oral reader sets the standard for the rest of the group to emulate. In adult life, choral reading is used in church services and in various entertainment media.

Drama

Dramatization is a form of oral reading that is pleasing to children. The children read the story or play silently first. Then they select scenes if it is too long. Characters are chosen. Any props or scenery are decided on and responsibility allocated. A narrator or introducer is chosen. Readers then prepare their parts. The very shy child may, at first, take a behind-the-scenes role or a nonspeaking role. It is best to choose a play that has short, simple parts rather than long ones. Dramatization may be the answer to the teacher's question, "How would he say that?" or "Show us how Columbus would have stepped onto the shore and taken possession in the name of the queen." Dramatization may be a play or choral reading done for the rest of the class, the neighboring classroom, the school assembly, or for a parent group. It should be kept in mind that the goal remains the same for the child—the expressive interpretation of the selection, not a polished performance. Material for dramatization is to be found in the basal readers, juvenile literature books, teachers' journals, commercial company publications, and social studies books and may be the creative writing of the children themselves with the encouragement of the teacher. *Reader's Theatre* is an example of drama where there is selective use of scenery and costumes, readers may sit on stools or boxes of different heights and face different directions, action is merely suggested, imagination supplies the audience with scene and movement, a narrator establishes the situation, the reader uses a physical script, and the readers establish direct, close relationship with the audience. Many think *Reader's Theatre* is oral reading at its stimulating best.[2]

Good Example Set by Adults

The teacher has several obligations in reading orally to children. The first one is to read well, with enthusiasm and emotion. The second is to select appropriate literature, usually a little above the reading level of the group, and to be perceptively aware of the acceptance of the piece of literature, so that a change is made where necessary. Not all stories will be received well by a particular group. A variety of readings is necessary and should be a regular part of the day's program with the setting and environment conducive to listening. The third responsibility is the necessity of gearing the reading to the group by prereading to cut unnecessary or inappropriate

[2] Martha L. Larson, "Reader's Theatre: New Vitality for Oral Reading," *The Reading Teacher,* 29,4:359–60 (Jan. 1976).

sections and to determine interesting places to stop in serial reading by introducing the story and by planning a follow-up program of discussion or creative expression or dramatization or whatever. The teacher should avoid moralistic preaching. Usually, the children should be comfortably grouped around the teacher, as close as reasonable in the setting of the classroom with comfort. The final responsibility of the teacher is the provision for encouragement of others to read to the children.

Parents may get help from the teacher in the form of suggestion pertaining to (1) what to read, (2) sources of good material, (3) the frequency of reading, (4) the duration of the reading session, and (5) suggestions for a neighborhood exchange of books and story hours at the public library. The PTA can provide a good forum for these ideas to be presented to parents. Individualization can be handled in parent-teacher conferences.

The librarian and the teacher are more effective if they work together on the above procedures. The librarian can also help in arousing interest in good books by the selective oral reading of interesting passages in presenting library books. Many run a regular story hour, which the teacher can encourage by providing the children with the opportunity to get there and advising parents about possible car pools and so on for getting children to weekend and summer programs of the library.

Recordings

Besides the tape recorder in the classroom for the children to read and listen to their own oral reading, some classrooms have the videotape for audio-visual use. Tapes may be made of an individual reading or of a class session. Discussion could then point to ways to improve the reading. A child can recognize where practice in speech, enunciation, or fluency is needed.

Another possibility is the use of records available from commercial sources, libraries, and so on. The following is a partial list of sources that the teacher will want to investigate in order to bring good oral reading samples of literature to the classroom:

1. The American Library Association.
2. Caedmon Records—Houghton Mifflin Company, Boston.
3. The Children's Book Council.
4. Folkway Records.
5. Landmark Enrichment Records and Filmstrips—Enrichment Teaching Materials, New York City.
6. Society for Visual Education.
7. Commercial companies' catalogues.
8. Public libraries' lists of records.
9. Television and radio stations—program records and scripts.

10. Many professional journals in the areas of English, reading, and language arts.

Miscellaneous Practices

In a reading lesson oral reading is often interspersed with silent reading for a specific purpose: (1) to verify facts; (2) to demonstrate sequences; (3) to answer a question by reference to a passage; (4) to practice under guidance intonation, phrasing, expression, or vocabulary; (5) to clarify a detail; or (6) to illustrate a humorous incident. In a corner of the classroom a child can read orally to another child and can seek help from the other child or the teacher only when needed. This is especially effective when the child is reading a story written by himself. In such a case he will seldom need help.

An uncommon practice is that of the whole class reading orally simultaneously. Children learn quickly to mask the sounds of the others' reading while the teacher tunes in on the individual child by moving close to him. Each child reads his or her own book. Although it sounds chaotic to an outsider stepping into the classroom, it can be effective as a technique for those who are accustomed to it. Visitors would have to stay long enough to get the total picture to understand it. The process is not very different from home life where the radio or TV is running, father's electric drill is heard, the family dog is barking, and, while siblings are tuned in to the TV, the child is sitting reading aloud to his mother. This is a procedure possibly expedient for evaluating oral reading when the group is excessively large, much oral reading practice is needed, and insufficient time seems to be available for individual evaluation.

Some classrooms have a corner containing a calendar, the weather report, and a brief news item, which the children read to the class each morning in turn. This furnishes a good audience situation providing the teacher makes certain the child is prepared. Sight reading probably would defeat the purpose of audience reading, if the child were not prepared for the vocabulary. He should read it silently first; some children might read it softly to the teacher first.

There are many practices that the innovative teacher can provide for the reinforcement of oral reading skills in the classroom. A little planning is required to integrate them with the regular routine.

COMPARISON WITH SILENT READING

Oral reading requires all the skills that silent reading requires. In addition it requires concern for the audience of one or more, for getting the full meaning across, for pronouncing words correctly and enunciating clearly, for interpreting punctuation effectively, and for the reader's appearance and manner. It is slower than silent reading because of the necessity for the eye-voice span. Except in the testing situation, it requires some previous contact with the material to assure familiarity with terms and ideas and to promote fluency. Thus it is considered a more difficult task than silent reading. The teacher should keep in mind that the quantity of oral reading is not nearly as important a factor as the quality of experience with oral reading. This requires instruction and practice plus instruction and opportunity for practice. The purpose is communication of the author's ideas, mood, and feelings to the audience.

Oral reading is slower than silent reading, with longer fixations and pauses and usually more regressions. Speed should not be emphasized in the instructional procedure. That should be left to the proficiency stage of silent reading. Oral reading should resemble talking as closely as possible in manner and expression.

The child has to learn both processes because silent reading is a see-and-think activity whereas oral reading is a see-say-and-think activity involving vocalization as one of the mediating processes.

EVALUATION OF ORAL READING

Classroom Technique

Progress in oral and silent reading is interrelated. The experienced teacher can often judge the one from the other. Some skills, however, can only be pinpointed by listening to the child read orally. Speech habits and pronunciation and expression fall into this category. Children who get meaning mainly from context may skip words or substitute and add words. They need to be slowed down and to have their attention drawn to specific details, such as individual words or endings. If the children's posture is poor or they hold the book incorrectly, they may be tense, and they may need more easy material or shorter selections before their voice and speech can become natural and appropriately pleasing.

A variety of questions is the responsibility of the teacher if the question is whether the child is interpreting meaning, getting facts straight, drawing logical inference, relating dispersed ideas, and following sequence. Of course, the success of children's oral reading is whether their audience can answer these questions after they have read the selection to it. If instruction seems necessary, it usually precedes or follows the oral reading, but is not given during it, as that reduces its effectiveness as a process of communication. In the individual session there are several areas that frequently require special work: (1) if the child has trouble such as word-calling, stress the talking aspect of reading; (2) if the eye-voice span is too limited for the background and experience, a tachistoscopic device may be used so that one sees the print and then says what *was* there; (3) if one seems insecure reading to the group of children, have the child read to the teacher alone or to a single other child as a beginning, then move to a larger group when ready to do so without embarrassment; (4) if children embellish the author's actual words, have them slow down and read the actual words as the author presents them; (5) if they repeat, the teacher needs to find out why, and this may have any of a number of different causes or a combination thereof; (6) if word attack is the chief problem, the child needs help with sounding, blending, parts of words, and syllabication; (7) if expression is the problem, he or she and others might practice making the voice sad, mean, demanding, spooky, and happy; (8) if punctuation is not interpreted correctly, the teacher or the class in chorus may say, "Pause" for commas and "Double-pause" for periods.

Along with the oral reading it is necessary to develop the attitudes, habits, and skills of good listening. The one can truly reach no success without the other. Good listening begins with an attitude that this is the way to share with others, to profit from others' experiences, to discover new ideas, to develop in discrimination, and to learn easily. Listening skills start with this receptivity, then develop into a means of quickly adding to our sum total of organized knowledge. Discussion often follows the listening process as a means of relating knowledge to experience and as an evaluation process. It is sometimes amusing, but more often disconcerting, to observe or participate in a discussion session following oral reading and find that only a small portion of what was read was assimilated by the listeners. Children need a great deal of practice in this skill. If the children are to be worthy audience members, they must have the attitudes and skills to assume the role. Their books should be closed as they listen to the oral reader. *No round robin reading!*

The best way to be sure each child in the class is progressing in oral reading skills is to develop an oral reading checklist and frequently rate each child on its criteria

The checklist would include such errors as additions, omissions, substitutions (semantic variations), reversals, dialect variations, and so on. The list might vary slightly according to grade level, but comprehensive lists may be examined in the following sources:

Heilman, Arthur W. *Principles and Practices of Teaching Reading.*
        4th ed. Columbus, OH: Charles E. Merrill Publishing Company
        (1977), pp. 337–338. A Reading Behavior Record.
Spache, George D., and Evelyn B. Spache. *Reading in the Elementary
        School,* 4th ed. Boston: Allyn & Bacon, Inc. (1977), pp. 345–50.
        Fluency, Word Attack, Posture, and Interpreting Errors.
Austin, Mary C.; Clifford Bush; and Mildred Huebner. *Reading Evalua-*

tion. New York: The Ronald Press Company (1961), p. 67.
A Speech Checklist

The tape recorder can be used to record errors after the session in a more leisurely and precise manner, or it can be used as a before-and-after instruction record of progress. The main point is that the teacher should have a record of the individual's deficiencies and progress rather than rely on memory in a busy day-to-day schedule.

Tests

Testing the child's oral reading involves three major factors: (1) the appropriate level of the author's material, (2) the child's ability to communicate the printed material to an audience, and (3) the audience's receptive response to the communication. To measure one factor accurately, one must hold the other two constant.

The informal reading inventory provides graded levels of reading material to ascertain how the child performs at each level. The tester starts with easy reading material for the subject, then moves to increasingly difficult material. In this way, the tester can judge the approximate grade level for the child's performance in independent reading, instructional level (computed), and frustration level. Reference to published informal reading inventories may be found in Chapter 13. The teacher might use graded selections from basal readers to get a rough estimate for his or her guidance in working with the child. In this case, the teacher's own observations and questions of the child reading orally would form the bases for temporary analysis. It should be emphasized here that most, if not all, testing situations are measuring sight reading, not prepared audience reading. Daily classroom routines might more accurately measure the latter.

Standardized oral reading tests yield a grade level score and should be interpreted along with tests of mental ability and standardized silent reading tests. They are most appropriate when used in research and surveys as a part of group data. When used to arrange remedial work or referral of the individual child or for grouping or adjusting the instructional program for the individual child, the teacher's observations should be taken into consideration along with the test results. In other words, the reliability of such tests for decisions about the individual child must be checked very carefully. In a complete diagnosis the standardized oral reading test adds valuable information to the data gained from the child's cumulative history and other tests.

Some of the oral reading tests that are frequently used are listed as follows:

Durrell Analysis of Reading Difficulty. Harcourt Brace Jovanovich, Inc.,
New York. Grades 1–6. Oral reading section for individual
diagnosis, requires teacher's practice and skill in administering.

Figure 10. Oral Reading Checklist for the Classroom Teacher

Place a checkmark (√) next to item to note that it appears to be a problem when the child reads orally. Continuous classroom evaluation with follow-up practice in needed areas will result in each child's progress.

PROBLEM	POSSIBLE INTERPRETATION
1. Fluency	
____ Slow, word-by-word reading	Material too difficult; possibly low fund of sight vocabulary
____ Poor phrasing	Needs practice in finding meaningful thought units
____ Hesitation	Lack of confidence; uncertain of word analysis techniques
____ Ignores punctuation	Too involved in decoding process; not attending to reading as a thought-getting process
____ Repetitions	Insecurity
____ Too rapid reading	Tension; forgetting audience
____ Eye-voice span	Lacks previous silent reading of selection; lacks practice in reading for meaning
____ Habitually uses finger as a guide	Immaturity; lacks practice in phrase reading; material too difficult
2. Use of Voice	
____ Nervous	Lacks practice and motivation
____ Volume—Too loud or soft	Forgets audience; Too embroiled in deciphering the print
____ Pitch—Too high or low	Insecurity; tension; habit
____ Word endings missing	For some, cultural; for some, more attention to word parts
____ Dialect	Cultural; reading model needed
3. Word Recognition and Analysis	
____ Small sight word fund	Needs practice in easy reading materials
____ Omissions	Material too difficult; poor word analysis techniques; carelessness
____ Reversals	Immaturity; lack of practice in looking at words from left-to-right; possible learning disability
____ Substitutions	Carelessness; guessing; inability to attack unknown words
____ Lacks persistence	Too dependent on adults help; not motivated
____ Ignores errors	Not reading for meaning
____ Additions	Significant *if* meaning is changed, as in adding *not*

Figure 10 (Continued)

PROBLEM	POSSIBLE INTERPRETATION
Graphic Analysis	
____ Spells, letter-by-letter	Uneconomic, useless as a technique in reading
____ Sounds out, blends	Possibly helpful technique if blending sounds results in a word recognized to be within his own experience
____ Attends mainly beginnings	Needs help with word parts
____ Attends mainly endings	Lacks good left-to-right attack on words
____ Sees words within words	Poor technique; useful only with parts of compound words, and with roots and affixes
Semantic Analysis	
____ Guesses from context	Insecure but willing to try
____ Uses words with similar meaning	Reading for meaning, but lacking effective word attack skills
____ Uses irrelevant words and phrases	Not reading for meaning; guessing
4. Attitude	
____ Dislikes oral reading	Work too difficult; has met with little or no success
____ Gives up; defiant, uncooperative	Frustrated by too difficult material and lack of necessary skills
5. General	
____ Squints, frowns, cocks head	Possible vision problem; material too difficult
____ Moves book, holds at wrong distance	Vision problem; good habits not yet formed
____ Ignores audience	Insecurity; difficult material; purpose for oral reading not understood
____ Is easily distracted	Child's own purpose not developed; possibly learning disabled

6. *Summary:*
   A. Types of errors
   B. Prescription (kinds of instruction needed)
   C. Strengths

Gates-McKillop Reading Diagnostic Tests. Bureau of Publications, Teachers College, Columbia University, New York, Grades 1–8. Oral reading section for individual diagnosis.

Gilmore Oral Reading Test. Harcourt Brace Jovanovich, Inc., New York. Grades 1–8. Comprehension, rate and accuracy in individual diagnosis.

Goodman and Burke Reading Miscue Inventory. Manual, Procedure for
   Diagnosis and Evaluation. Macmillan Publishing Co., Inc., New
   York.
Gray Oral Reading Tests. The Bobbs-Merrill Company, Inc., Indianapolis.
   Grades 1–12. Thirteen short passages arranged in order of increasing
   difficulty. Teacher records number and types of errors.
Gray Standardized Oral Reading Check Tests. Public School Publishing
   Company, The Bobbs-Merrill Company, Inc., Indianapolis. Grades
   1–8. Measures rate and accuracy.
Slosson Oral Reading Test, Slosson Educational Publications, East Aurora,
   New York. Grades 1–8.

The *Gilmore Oral Reading Test,* the *California Reading Test,* and the
IRI are compared as to types of errors they measure and on what basis a
final score is derived in current articles. An example is one such article by
Kaufman.[3]
   Young adults, in high school, college, and daily and civic life, reflect
the educational training when they get up before a group of people to read
some printed material. If they have developed a proficiency in such oral
reading and the poise necessary for a good presentation, they will not
hesitate to make their social contribution. The elementary school has an
obligation to incorporate this kind of training in its regular curriculum and
to evaluate its degree of success regularly.

SUMMARY

Oral reading is different from silent reading; it requires additional skills.
Oral reading necessitates fluency and attention to stress and juncture as in
silent reading, but the reader must also attend to and react to the audience
in order to be effective. Oral reading should always be purposeful—to share
information, to give and harvest pleasure, and to provide the vehicle for
evaluation of speech and reading skills. Sight reading should be limited; the
major emphasis should be on prepared oral presentation. Choral speaking
and drama, radio statements, and records are good examples. The best form
of evaluation of oral reading is self-evaluation, using taping sessions and
checklists. Proficiency and poise in oral reading can be developed through
practice. Such practice starts in the informal atmosphere of the elementary
school classroom.

[3] Maurice Kaufman, "Measuring Oral Reading Accuracy," *Reading World,* XV,4:
216–26 (May 1976).

SELECTED READINGS

Austin, Mary C., Clifford Bush, and Mildred Huebner. *Reading Evaluation.* New York: The Ronald Press Company, 1961.

Chan, Julie M. T. *Why Read Aloud to Children?* An IRA Micromonograph. Newark, DE: International Reading Association.

Duffy, Gerald G., and George Sherman. *How to Teach Reading Systematically.* New York: Harper & Row, Publishers, 1973, pp. 37–51.

Goodman, Yetta M. "Reading Diagnosis—Qualitative or Quantitative?" *The Reading Teacher,* 26, (Oct. 1972), 32–37.

Harris, Albert J., and Edward Sipay. *Effective Teaching of Reading.* 2d ed. New York: David McKay Co., Inc., 1971, pp. 178–179. Reading Analysis Checklist.

Heilman, Arthur W. *Principles and Practices of Teaching Reading.* 4th ed. Columbus, OH: Charles E. Merrill Publishing Company, 1977, pp. 331–55.

Kaufman, Maurice. "Measuring Oral Reading Accuracy." *Reading World,* XV,4 (May 1976), 216–26.

Larson, Martha L. "Readers' Theatre: New Vitality for Oral Reading." *The Reading Teacher,* 29,4 (Jan. 1976), 359–60.

Page, William D. "Are We Beginning to Understand Oral Reading?" *Reading World,* XIII,3 (March 1974), 161–70.

Spache, George D., and Evelyn Spache, *Reading in the Elementary School.* 4th ed. Boston: Allyn & Bacon, Inc., 1977, pp. 345–50.

Part Three

Planning and Organizing Effective Reading

(Structure)

Chapter 8

Children's
Interests

OBJECTIVES

To be familiar with the varied bases
of children's interests

To understand the role of teachers
in motivating children's interests

To become acquainted with the
variety of children's materials

To learn and put into practice formal and
informal strategies for assessing
children's interests

INTRODUCTION

If people give their attention to an object or activity, they display an interest.
If, through pleasure or success or satisfaction, they continue to give attention to the same object or class of objects or to the same activity, they display
a continuing interest. They obviously consider it worthwhile and may move
on to related objects or activities. This continuing, developing interest is
related to the values, attitudes, and tastes they assign to the objects or
activities. Values and attitudes refer to their feelings, whereas tastes represent the quality of the choices or experiences. In reading, tastes would be
their free choice of the quality and character of writing. Interest seems to
be the basis or generator of voluntary reading activity. In reading instruction,
two processes are important: (1) the discovering of interests that the individual brings to the instructional setting based on past experience, and (2)
building or capitalizing upon those interests to aid reading skill development and to develop new and continuing interests in reading. Current interests can be used to aid reading instruction; but unless they are expanded,
the individual stands little chance of becoming a regular and continuing
reader. The latter is the school's ultimate goal: continued reading for pleasurable leisure-time activity, for learning more about oneself and one's

world, for aesthetic development. There is an interaction of interests and reading that the school nurtures.

To explain more fully the relationship between these two, this chapter presents the psychological bases of interests, the role of society and culture in the development of interests, the instructional program, the use of materials, and the evaluative procedures for the assessment and use of interests.

PSYCHOLOGICAL BASES OF CHILDREN'S INTERESTS

Psychologists indicate that interest is a fundamental motivational factor in the learning process. Rewards and satisfaction accompany the satisfying of needs through brain stimulus and social approval. When reading is associated with satisfying physiological and psychological needs, it becomes a meaningful activity that the child is apt to repeat. This repetition can result in a continued motivation to read. Reading itself becomes interesting. Thus interest in reading is acquired by people, based on their constitutional nature, their personality, and their set of unique experiences. They find pleasure in the use of their mind and organs and learned ability. Maslow[1] has presented a psychological theory of the prepotency of needs and their satisfaction that may be helpful in understanding the responsibility of the teacher in creating the classroom environment that will favor intellectual activity and aid in interest motivation:

1. The physiological needs.
2. The safety needs.
3. The love needs.
4. The esteem needs—self-esteem and esteem of others.
5. The need for self-actualization.
6. The need to know.

This hierarchy of needs must be met if the child is to develop a continuing interest in reading.

The repetitive satisfaction in self-esteem, security, belonging, success, and curiosity results in habits being formed. These, in turn, are lost as the habit itself becomes self-propelling, creating an anxiety that requires the individual to attend to it. The interest is born in the object or activity and becomes self-sustaining.

[1] A. H. Maslow, "A Theory of Human Motivation," *Psychological Review*, L:370–96 (July 1943), and A. H. Maslow, "A Preface to Motivation Theory," *Psychosomatic Medicine*, V:85–92 (Jan. 1943).

Intelligence

The level of intellectual functioning of the child seems to be related to interest in reading and to the type of reading interests. Children with lower mental age prefer to read simple stories about activities that are familiar to them. Children with high mental ability choose books that represent a wide variety of interests, and they read adult books (so-called). These children have what we would call a higher level of interests, and they have a tendency to read whatever they can find when they are pursuing a topic if they can read it.

Age

Age is a factor in reading interests. Younger readers can be interested in all kinds of stories and topics and types of writing, being heavily influenced by example, recommendation, and emulation. As they get older, they gradually develop choices and will choose reading according to likes or dislikes, according to authors whom they like, according to type of story, poetry, or subject. Although research studies done by teachers and librarians have linked this factor of book selection with age, probably other factors are more important and account for the reasons, such as reading ability, experiences, basic and secondary needs, and so on. The age of children is a help to the schools in knowing the types of free reading materials to have on hand; the age alone of a given child may be of little help in knowing what will be chosen. Reports of studies follow later in this chapter.

Sex

Sex differences in reading interests begin to emerge as soon as the children are reading on their own. However, sex is not as important a factor as maturity in development and in reading skills until grades three and four. Girls are more interested in reading than boys from the very beginning. Their choices of reading material differ considerably after the primary grades just as their choice of play and recreation activities differ in our culture, probably culturally induced. Generally, boys move in the direction of sports, science, and adventure, whereas girls generally move toward romance and related literature involving sentiment. Girls generally read more than boys as boys use more active leisure-time activities to evidence their interests. Once again, in working with children, one finds a wide range of choice within the sexes. Boys and girls seem to be moving closer together in their interests, especially in sports and science. This may be due to increased emphasis on study of sex roles in schools, to adult programs, and to television addiction.

Self-concept

Among the psychological bases of children's interests probably no other factor is as important as the individual child's self-concept. This point is reiterated here because it must be considered in juxtaposition to mental ability, maturity, age, and sex. If children feel secure in their personal life, in their learning in school, in their reading development, they will read any (if not all) material available in their free time for pleasurable reading. A child will pick up an available comic book, a magazine, a trashy paperback, an adult book lying on the table, or whatever.

Thinking

One other dimension is important in our concern over interests that continue throughout one's lifetime. It is the type of thinking that children are taught and encouraged to engage in for learning and accomplishment. If they read to find *the* answer to a question, *the* way something should be done, *the* person to quote, *the* response that fits, *the one solution,* then they are engaging in convergent thinking. Almost all of our school instruction is concerned with the one correct solution to the problem. On the other hand, divergent thinking deals with situations for which there are many reasonable solutions, and it calls for fluency and imagination. The school should concentrate its efforts more than it has in the past on the interests that will cause the child to read widely and find multiple solutions to problems, to integrate ideas that are widely dispersed, and to use imaginative ideas. In other words, if interests are to be developed and used, they should lead the child to the divergent thinking approach to his problems and their solutions.

CULTURE AND SOCIETY

Social Setting

Whether they are aware of it or not, children emulate parents, teachers, and other individuals in their immediate social environment. There is a tendency for their interests to develop in common with those of the society surrounding them. Their immediate subculture is made up of the social institutions to which they belong: family, church, school, play groups, work groups. They seek the approval of their social contacts—adults and their peer group. Their interests are shaped by the goals these groups set for them. Starting with their own constitutional determinants, they assume a specific role in each of the social groups. There are situational determinants that influence these roles: an older child, in a family where the father or mother is absent, is apt to assume a more adult role sooner in life. In such a case he or she matures quickly in matters that are important to the family. A child in the role of "youngest child" may mature more slowly.

Cultural Setting

Children are often caught up in rapid societal changes, as in the case where their family and neighbors are fighting vigorously for the social acceptance of a minority group. Every institution to which they belong may be in turmoil over this change. Their reading interests may be centered in this problem. As a part of a rebelling society they adopt the attitudes, interests, and rebellion of this society. Their vocational interests may be influenced strongly by this situation. They may develop a conflict of interests out of this situation. Their loyalties are challenged; their curiosity is aroused about many factors in his society. They are in a prime state of anxiety for reading interests to be channeled constructively along paths that will help them solve problems, temporarily escape from the realities of their difficult world, and develop an interest in reading for many purposes. They hear language used for persuasion and can begin to use language effectively for their own purposes. When the folkways, or customs, of their group reach the stage where they become regarded as necessary for the group welfare, they are known as *mores.* Children are particularly susceptible to these changes, and their behavior and interests change quickly in line with the mores, often taking the extreme positions on them. Teachers who are studying the various subcultures within the United States, in order to capitalize on the interests of the groups find that the similarities are greater than the differences among them, and the variations within a group may be greater than the differences between or among the groups. An example is the reported study by Jung[2] where he explored the relationships between leisure activities (outdoor play, TV viewing, reading, and so on) and socioeconomic status and ethnic group for 574 middle- and lower-class Caucasian, black, and Oriental fifth and sixth graders. The subjects recorded for one week in diaries their leisure activities, which were later tabulated. Also, a questionnaire was administered to determine their preferences and the extent of participation in the activities. The most popular out-of-school activities were TV viewing and outdoor play. Girls showed a higher interest in reading than boys. The Oriental children reported reading books, newspapers, and comic books more often than black and Caucasian children; but Jung found that the differences between socioeconomic or ethnic groups were not significant.

[2] R. Jung, "Leisure in Three Cultures," *Elementary School Journal,* 67:285–95 (March 1967).

There are several factors in culture and society that tend to standardize the interests of children. A first is the culture itself and the respect for tradition. A second one is standardized testing where importance is attached to certain types of knowledge and skills. A third is the school and the education of its teachers and administrators. A fourth is law and uniform codes. A fifth is mass communication where a national convention, an election candidate, a sports event, a catastrophe, or a special on driving habits is seen by millions of people across the country simultaneously. A sixth is bigness where individual personal contact is limited. A seventh is federal support where single standards are set for compliance in order to obtain funds. An eighth is the mobility of people and families.

Interaction

Most of the forces that operate in the other direction, toward variation and difference, seem to emanate from the individual in society: the desire to excel, the level of aspiration, effort and energy, the individual's personal needs, local unique needs, competitive spirit, and of course native and learned ability.

INTERESTS AND READING INSTRUCTION

The Teacher

The motivation of interests in children requires preparation by the teacher. Before systematic instruction can be presented, there are cerain characteristics and procedures in which the teacher must be competent. Most important is the teacher's contagious love of children's literature and books. If teachers feel the need, they should take additional course work in children's literature and appreciation of the related art and music areas. They should go to the library and get some of the good books on the art of the storyteller and study them. They should be thoroughly familiar with the works of Nancy Larrick, Mary Hill Arbuthnot, Leland Jacobs, and others in the field of recommendations and analyses of children's literature. They should read children's books, develop interesting and provocative questions on them, know their characters. They must learn how to listen to children, accept their reaction in a respectful permissive manner, and lead them into their own correct responses. This requires good rapport with the youngsters. They must have the right books available, in both quantity and quality. Knowing the interests children bring to the instructional situation helps them know where to begin to build new interests. A teacher might become the "scribe of his children and listen and record their words and sentences." [3] Sandberg has good suggestions on inciting children to talk about their reading.

One way the teacher can capitalize on experience to develop new interests in children is to gather realia, maps, pictures, and stories on his or her own trips, and form a display of these in the classroom, tell the children of incidents that happened, and relate these to stories or books where similar types of happenings appear. Many teachers have introduced social studies lessons this way and developed children's interests in the literature, art, music, geography, and people of a particular region. In this manner, the teacher creates a favorable environment for correlating the various subjects of the elementary school in an interest-arousing unified approach. The teacher's own enthusiasm and thorough preparation will be the key to the success of the approach.

The Physical Environment

The physical environment can be conducive to the encouragement of reading interests. It has to be a comfortable setting. The child should be surrounded with books. Shelf space should be adequate. Movable tables and plenty of space are helpful. Good, changing, attractive bulletin boards in which the children participate under guidance, along with realia and audio-visual equipment make the setting interesting. The chance to display and share experiences for a period of time creates a personal atmosphere that makes the child feel right at home. A place of one's own to keep his materials is imperative. The physical environment must encourage the child to learn, not detract from ongoing interests.

The Curriculum

The reading curriculum contains endless opportunity for creative methodology in respect to children's interests from the readiness stage of the kindergarten to the technical research techniques of the upper grades. Evidence of the child's readiness for beginning reading is interest in stories, reciting poetry, browsing in attractive books, labels and signs and words. The first grade teacher often starts with the child's own books and experiences and language. Poetry is enjoyable when it is read well in brief and frequent encounters; when it is a part of rhythmic games and songs; when it contains action, story line, humor, personal experience, and fanciful

---

[3] Herbert H. Sandberg, "Needed: Teachers to Vitalize Reading," *College Reading Association Proceedings,* 1967, 8 (Fall 1967), pp. 135–39.

Story illustrations

experience; when it creates memorable characters; and when it is geared to the child's maturity and current interests.

Balanced reading curricula that build and sustain reading interests have certain practices in common. They emphasize developing interests rather than a specific quantity of books read. They bring children and books together, for exploration, for discussion, for the researching of topics. They allow freedom of choice according to the child's personal goals in line with his abilities. There is a flexible grouping of children according to their interests. There is a sharing of interests and experiences. There is a constant accumulation of concepts and a relating of them to each other and to the total accumulation of learnings. The library is a part of the program, with each child using a library card, and with frequent visits to the classroom, school, and public library. There is a reasonable degree of pupil management and selection of books. There are book programs utilizing radio, TV, assemblies, and other audiovisual aids. Book Week activities and book fairs are a part of the curriculum. Reading is closely allied with other projects and studies, such as dramatics, writing, art, construction, music, and social studies. Current events are read in magazines and newspapers and discussed. Many forms of self-evaluation are employed, which may be progress charts, personal diary, book trees, "My Reading Design," or a file card on the window sill.

To stimulate reading interests, teachers have provided children successful and satisfying experiences in other ways. Some have used sports and comics to capitalize on a current interest of some of the children. A multimedia kit on Spider-man [4] with sound films, story cards, and a comic book is an example of a commercial attempt to motivate reading interests of elementary grade children. A display of pictures of the children reading their favorite books draws a great deal of attention and pride in their reading. A classroom book club has been successful in some instances. A recommendation by an older child of a good book to a younger child (for whom it is appropriate) is very effective; the child tells the younger one why he or she liked the book and one interesting episode to pique the younger one's curiosity. This has been done on an interclass basis in some schools. Sometimes a puppet show based on well-liked books is rewarding in developing art, oral reading, interpretation, and writing, as well as an interest builder. Some children have developed hobby reading lists, interviewed other children or teachers or known personalities regarding their hobbies, and reported to the class on the interviews. Of course, one of the most common interest-getters is the display of book jackets in classroom, library, and hall cabinets; but this must be supervised carefully, for the display should be simple, short-lived, and attention-getting. To be effective, some use should be made of the display rather than simply having it blend with the background. In the middle and upper grades, an illustrated talk by the child on a travel book is rewarding where pictures, maps, (and realia) have been gathered to share with classmates. Some teachers have found that having the child make a paper cover for a book and then listing the names on the cover of those who have read the book make the reading of that book a challenge to other children. Occasionally, such extrinsic motivation is justified, although it is not recommended for general practice.

Relevance

Children of today live in a pluralistic society. They are taught in a "pluralistic classroom." [5] In the modern classroom can be found children whose background is different from others in many ways—cultural, ethnic, racial, linguistic, economic, to name a few. They are boys and girls, rich and poor; black, yellow, or white; with standard and nonstandard dialects; from inner cities, suburbia, and farms—to list a few notable differences. How can the

---

[4] Spider-man Reading Motivation Kit. McGraw-Hill Films, 1975.
[5] Leona M. Foerster, "Teaching Reading in Our Pluralistic Classrooms," *The Reading Teacher,* 30,2:146–150 (Nov. 1976).

teacher make learning meaningful to each child? The most effective answers lie in the definition of relevance—knowing each child as an individual, personalizing his or her learning experiences, and making his or her textbooks, projects, and recreational reading meaningful and enjoyable to him or her.

Teachers can provide for each child some reading materials that are relevant and enjoyable. Bresnahan [6] established criteria for the selection of books about black children. She compiled a basic list of thirty-seven books that would promote a positive understanding of blacks among all children in the elementary classroom. "Asian Americans in Children's Books" is the theme of a recent issue of Interracial Books.[7] Included are guidelines for selecting nonracist, nonsexist books and reviews of books for children on Asian American themes. A new minority group, farm children, was detected by Roggenbuck.[8] She pointed out that stories in their reading textbooks lack relevance for children who live on small farms or large mechanized farms. Farmers are often depicted as stereotypes, and their occupations are distorted. To counteract the negative effect of the presentations in basal series, teachers will need to provide library books on modern farms to give farm children an incentive and an interest in reading.

A book for primary grade children [9] with story and pictures about different racial and ethnic backgrounds is an interesting addition to classroom libraries, as it allows children to consider and discuss openly differences in themselves and others. For primary grade children, it encourages positive thinking and acceptance of differences.

Mullins and Wolf [10] have annotated more than a thousand books that deal with handicapped people. The handicapped child can be led to read about others like himself or herself in books of autobiography, biography, and fiction. Other children who read these books can learn to understand and accept the handicapped person.

In summary, by studying each child, the teacher can gain insights into the significance of individual differences and the need to supply instructional materials that are relevant to the various children in the classroom. When the teacher knows the child—his or her background, interests, aspirations —he or she can match the child with the right book at the right time.

[6] Mary Bresnahan. "Selecting Sensitive and Sensible Books About Blacks," *The Reading Teacher,* 30,1:16–20 (Oct. 1976).

[7] *Interracial Books for Children Bulletin,* Volume 7, Numbers 2 and 3, 1976 (New York: Council on Interracial Books for Children).

[8] Mary J. Roggenbuck, "Motivating Farm Children to Read," *The Reading Teacher,* 30,8:868–874 (May 1977).

[9] Norma Simon, *Why Am I Different?* (Chicago: Albert Whitman, 1976).

[10] Jane Mullins and Suzanne Wolf. *Special People Behind the Eight-Ball: An Annotated Bibliography of Literature Classified by Handicapping Conditions.* Johnstown, PA.: Mafex Associates, Inc. 1975.

MATERIALS AND MEDIA

Variety

Few classrooms have the range of materials for reading that will continuously challenge and provide enjoyment for every child annually passing through its portals. The teacher starts the year with a range of reading materials and adds to them from time to time, studying the children and their needs, studying various sources of information about the materials available, using the library and audiovisual sources, and building their own resources. The cumulative supply should include appropriate books, magazines, short stories, informative articles, pictures, puzzles, games, poems, songs, and audiovisual equipment and supplies. The variety of material would thus pique each child's curiosity and challenge his abilities and interests. If there are children from the lower socioeconomic classes, the teacher will get ideas from reading the literature in professional journals. An example of one such article is the description of materials applied to individual children in the article "If Only Dickens Had Written about Hot Rods" by Charles Speigler in the April 1965 issue of the *English Journal.*

Illustrating a book report

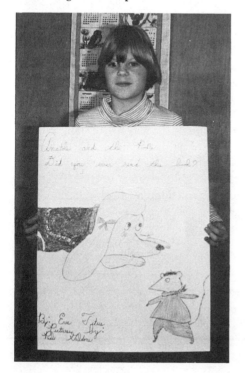

If the children are Puerto Rican or Mexican-American and Spanish is their first language, then some Spanish-language books should be there, and provision should be made for use of the books and some instruction in reading in their language. Such a Spanish program is discussed in Dick Yoes, Jr.'s article "Reading Programs for Mexican-American Children in Texas" in the January 1967 issue of *The Reading Teacher*. For the boys in the classroom a good assortment of supplementary books and stories, along with concrete and manipulative objects that appeal especially to boys, is a necessity if their interests are to be challenged.

Books

If the children are to read independently in the classroom and if this is to be a part of the school curriculum as it should be, then the teacher must remember that interest in reading is associated with the availability of books. Every classroom should have at least one hundred books at all times; about half of them should be a permanent collection and the others rotating. Some should be above the grade level; some at; some below. Some should be classified as humorous (example: E. B. White's *Charlotte's Web*), fanciful tales (example: *Alice in Wonderland*), animal stories (example: *My Friend Flicka*), biography (example: James Daugherty's *Abraham Lincoln*), a boy as main character (example: Krumgold's *And Now Miguel*), aesthetic appreciation (example: McCloskey's *Homer Price*), problems related to minority groups (example: Sidney Taylor's *All-of-a-Kind Family*), humorous folktales (example: *The Talking Cat and Other Stories of French Canada*), interracial friendship (example: *Steffie and Me*), and so forth. Selections can be arranged by consultation between the child as class librarian and teacher by theme, type, topic, subject, and so on.

The teacher must be familiar with all the good sources of what children like to read, the types of children's literature, and the readability level of the books. Only examples of sources of information are listed here as Chapter 11 deals specifically with such sources. First, there are the previously mentioned anthologies of children's literature; second, there are specific books written to guide the teacher in children's book selection, such as Nancy Larrick's *A Teacher's Guide to Children's Reading;* third, there are similar books addressed to parents, such as Josette Frank's *Your Child's Reading Today;* fourth, there are publications of the American Library Association (Chicago) and the Children's Book Council (New York); fifth, the teacher's professional journals carry feature articles on children's literature (example: in *The Reading Teacher*, January 1968, Dorothy Bracken's feature section, "Literature for Children," has an article by May Hill Arbuthnot, "Of Other Worlds—Fantasy Part II: Highlights of Modern Fantasy," and in the March 1968 issue Bracken has Robert Whitehead's "Scent of the Rose: Poetry Books for Children"); sixth, there are the book

Listening to a story

lists revised each year, such as *Best Books for Children* (R. R. Bowker Co., New York); seventh, *The Horn Book;* and eighth, *Top of the News.* Not to be overlooked are the book clubs for children:

1. The Arrow Book Club, Scholastic Magazines, Inc., New York.
2. Junior Literary Guild, New York.
3. Young Folks' Book Club, Brooklyn, New York.
4. Weekly Reader Children's Book Club, Middletown, CT.

Magazines

Children's magazines that the teacher may want available are

American Girl
The Beaver
Boys' Life, Boys Scouts of America
Child Life
Children's Digest
Children's Playmate
Humpty Dumpty's Magazine
Jack and Jill
National Geographic World
Ranger Rick
Sprint Magazine

Teachers can become acquainted with the variety of children's magazines by consulting lists such as Ladley's revised editions of sources.[11]

In 1966, Norvell[12] analyzed the responses of approximately six thousand children in grades three to six to a questionnaire about the degree of their interest in each of thirty-one magazines. He found that the pupils were acquainted with an average of ten magazines. Among the four most popular with boys, three are edited for adults, whereas only one of the highest on the girls' list was adult-oriented. Boys and girls showed quite different interests, with the girls' more expansive. In comparing the children's magazine interests with those of a similar study in 1936, Norvell concluded that children's interests in periodicals has decreased. This may be true, not only for children, but for the general population, because of the competition for reader interests and time from paperbacks and television. From one aspect, this is to be lamented, because those who find books too long and too challenging might read shorter selections—witness the popularity of the *Reader's Digest*—and some may thus never get out of the comic book level of reading habit.

Comics

Comic books may be used as a starting point of interest building with some children because they will read them. They should be analyzed to build discrimination on the part of the children for interesting points, variety of humor, wholesomeness, and relation to reality. Children should recognize that some emphasize crime, violence, and revenge. There are good, well-illustrated comics; some are developed by church organizations. Comics contain action, adventure, excitement, humor, pictures, and brevity and could be used as a stepping-stone to the good literature of books, rather than simply letting them be the untouched competition. The teacher's goal is to build taste and discrimination in literature.

Paperbacks for Children

Many schools and colleges are using paperbacks where student ownership or intermittent loan is involved. The Arrow Book Club for ages nine to eleven issues paperback editions of favorite children's books. Some of the children's classics are in paperback edition. Good, colorful books of birds, insects, flowers, and boats, and resource books, such as dictionaries and

[11] Winifred C. Ladley, *Sources of Good Books and Magazines for Children: An Annotated Bibliography* (Newark, DE: International Reading Association, 1973).
[12] G. W. Norvell, "The Challenge of Periodicals in Education," *Elementary English,* 43:402–408 (April 1966).

The World Almanac and others, are now available. They have the advantage of being less expensive than clothbound books, easy to handle, small in size, with colorful covers. Their big disadvantage is lack of durability under children's normal wear-and-tear handling. It is no longer unusual to observe a man pull one out of his pocket while waiting for a train or a haircut or for a woman teacher to pull one out of her handbag while waiting for her graduate classes to begin. They are certainly most mobile. Children and adults even pack them in their luggage to take to summer camp. Research studies, using control and experimental groups, have found that they have value in the school program. In this age of multimedia just note the tremendous success of such publications as Avon, Bantam, Berkley, Dell, Fawcett, New American Library, Pocket Books Inc., Popular Library, and Pyramid, to name but a few—paperbacks by the thousands. Paperbacks are books, and the function of the teacher, again, is to bring children and books together.[13] If taste in literature is developed, children can do this as readily with paperbacks as they can with clothbound books. The teacher therefore will use paperbacks to supplement the library books available.[14] Children should be in contact with both.

Newspapers

Childrens' newspapers serve the general purpose of providing information and understanding about current events. This is again a two-way street. There is intrinsic interest in the people and activities of today; at the same time the newspaper is an excellent medium for expanding the interests of the child. Popular children's newspapers include *Current Events, The Junior Review,* and *My Weekly Reader,* among others, as well as sections of the great modern adult dailies. Recognizing that much academic content is contained in children's newspapers, the teacher can use them not only for their short story and literature material, but also for the correlating of current information on science, social studies, music, art, and other areas of the curriculum. Skills in newspaper use can be taught as a part of the reading program in an interesting manner—interpreting headlines and captions, classifying articles, relating facts, analyzing differing opinions and propaganda techniques. Interest can be aroused in children in scanning articles for examples to illustrate a given point. Because of the newspaper reading propensity of present-day Americans, interest and skills can be readily integrated in the newspaper.

[13] William H. Rupley, "Reading Interests: Motivating Students to Read for Personal Enjoyment," *The Reading Teacher,* 30,1:118–121 (Oct. 1976).
[14] M. Jerry Weiss, Joseph Brunner, Warren Heiss, eds., *New Perspectives on Paperbacks,* Monograph No. 1 (York, Pa.: Strine Publishing Company, 1977); Beatrice Simmons, ed., *Paperback Books for Children* (New York: Citation Press, 1972).

Audiovisual Aids

The present-day teacher can be most effective only if informed about modern media and uses modern media to relate sight and sound in children's learning. Marshall McLuhan, in his book *Understanding Media*,[15] indicated how strongly the message is influenced by the medium, how the medium reaches the individual and does something to him or her, how the medium affects society and may in time reshape culture and civilization. What are the media that relate sight and sound? They are the audiovisual materials: sound films, filmstrips and records, recordings, tapes, television, and electronic talking machines. Chapter 11 indicates the sources of these materials. Here the purpose of mentioning them is to relate them to their effect on interest and vice versa. They are no longer supplementary enrichment aspects of the curriculum. They are necessary to make book reading alive and interesting, to make learning an active rather than a passive process.[16] Many are common in the homes of children and, therefore, must be included in their learning at school. Teachers *use* them, along with books preceding or following their use. A child who reads the book wants to see the movie; a child who sees the movie is inclined to read the book. It is on this basis that the films by Radnitz, Weston Woods Studios, and Legacy Library [17] are re-presenting children's literature classics. Publishing companies in recent years have seen the wisdom of amalgamating with electronics companies to produce A-V materials in coordination with reading materials. Teachers cannot ignore this trend any more than they can ignore the enthusiasm generated by a TV program the children saw last night and want to discuss and relate to their school program. If the school system is slow in allocating funds to this particular medium of instruction, the teacher must take the initiative in requisitioning and insisting upon A-V purchases. The huge exhibits of instructional materials at teachers' conventions and the annual American Association of School Administrators has been steadily changing in the direction of audiovisual aids (particularly electronic aids) in recent years. There are not fewer books on display, significantly—just many more A-V aids. Teacher education programs may have lagged behind in the preparation of new teachers for this instructional revolution, in which case the new teacher must study the catalogues of the publishers and commercial concerns (usually obtainable in the administrator's offices), visit learning centers and classrooms where they are in use, attend demonstrations of their use, spend some time in the library studying such sources

[15] New York: McGraw-Hill Book Company, 1964.
[16] Joan T. Feeley, "Interest Patterns and Media Preferences of Middle Grade Children," *Reading World*, 13:224–237 (March 1974).
[17] See Mark Taylor, "An Accumulation of Excellence," in the feature section "Literature for Children" by Dorothy Kendall Bracken, *The Reading Teacher*, 20:573–578 (March 1967).

as *The Educator's Guide to Free Films*,[18] and take a course in modern audiovisual aids or request an in-service institute.

EVALUATION OF CHILDREN'S INTERESTS

Research

The professional literature that reports studies of children's interests is extensive. It is difficult to assess because of the many variables in the methodology, the numbers of children, the grade levels, the numbers of each sex, socioeconomic levels, and other factors. There are, though, certain common findings and certain trends developing in recent studies that are summarized. Some studies are listed because they appear to be soundly conducted and reported and seem to be representative of the more frequent findings. The most noticeable trend is the overwhelming lead that television viewing has taken in children's leisure-time activities and the resulting number of studies that deal with this phenomenon. A second trend is the continuously rising amount of interest in science when all the various areas of that field are lumped together. A third trend is of a slightly different nature, but is very important for the classroom teacher to know and utilize: educational research studies are being increasingly funded by foundations, the federal government, the states, and the research allotments of school budgets. Several important results are developing: (1) larger number of children are sampled in the studies, thus (one hopes) making the sample more representative of the population; (2) the standardization of hypotheses, variables, and methodology yields more reliable and comparable generalizations; (3) the dissemination of findings is improved through publication in journals, their annual research summaries, and clearinghouses such as ERIC.[19]

This section reports first the broader, general interests of elementary school children and then the methods of evaluating the child's specific interests in the classroom.

Studies of Children's Interests, Primary. Byers[20] classified by topic the tape-recorded contributions of 1,860 first grade children during sharing periods for six months in thirty-four communities of fourteen states. The choices in order were science, possessions, personal experiences, home and family activities, outdoor recreation, books, clothing, events involving

---

[18] Educators' Progress Service, Randolph, Wis. Annually revised.
[19] Educational Resources Information Center, Reading and Communication Skills, 1111 Kenyon Road, Urbana, IL 61801.
[20] Loretta Byers, "Pupils' Interests and the Content of Primary Reading Texts," *The Reading Teacher,* 17:227–33 (Jan. 1964).

friends, movies and television, and music. The implications she drew for
beginning reading books were as follows: (1) readers should emphasize
the immediate environment; (2) increased emphasis should be given to
science; (3) real-life drama needs emphasis, especially for those from lower
socioeconomic groups; (4) boys' interests should be reflected; and (5)
special experiences, language, and materials are needed for culturally
deprived children.

Witty [21] reported the activity interests of boys and girls in first and
second grades as very similar. They both ranked in order their first three
choices: (1) play outdoors, (2) watch TV, and (3) go to the movies. This
study shows the contrast with the studies of the late sixties, which show
almost without exception that watching television ranks first in the choices
of first and second graders.[22] Witty [23] also reported the reading interests of
first and second graders, which showed a discrepancy between boys and
girls in their first three choices. Both chose books about animals first; then
the second and third choices of boys were stars, planets, space and pilots.
The second and third choices of girls were children of other lands and
children at home. Obviously, a sex difference in reading interests develops
early in the school years, and, too, the interests of young children change
with the times and types of leisure-time activities available to them.[24]

Children's Interests, Intermediate and Upper Grades. Curry [25] asked
43,979 fifth grade children from fifty states through a questionnaire to rank
preferences for nine school subjects. Reading ranked fifth for both boys
and girls. Boys chose art, arithmetic, spelling, health and physical education ahead of reading, whereas girls chose spelling, art, music, and
arithmetic in that order.

Greenblatt [26] asked 300 children and their ten teachers to list their
favorite subjects in order of preference. Only art and arithmetic came ahead
of reading. The boys preferred science whereas girls preferred music. There
was no significant difference between achievement in reading and their
preferences. Brighter children chose art, arithmetic, and reading, whereas

---

[21] Paul Witty, "Studies of Interests of Children," *The Packet,* 16:15–23 (Winter,
1961–62).

[22] Jung, op. cit., and Paul Witty, et al., The Teaching of Reading, op. cit., p. 43.

[23] Witty, "Studies of Interests of Children," op. cit.

[24] L. F. Ashley, "Children's Reading Interests and Individualized Reading," *Elemen-
tary English,* 47:1088–1096 (Dec. 1970); Sara G. Zimet and Bonnie W. Camp,
"Favorite Books of First Graders from City and Suburb," *The Elementary School
Journal,* 74:191–196 (Dec. 1974).

[25] Robert L. Curry, "Subject Preferences of Fifth-Grade Children," *Peabody Journal
of Education,* 41:23–27 (July 1963).

[26] E. L. Greenblatt, "An Analysis of School Subject Preferences of Elementary
School Children of the Middle Grades," *Journal of Educational Research,* 55:554–
560 (Aug. 1962).

less bright pupils chose art, reading, and spelling. The preferences of the teachers and their bright pupils (IQ 110 plus) were in high agreement; this was not true with the other pupils. Evidently, teachers have failed to make reading the number one area of interest in school.

Both Stanchfield [27] and Ramsey [28] compared good and poor readers in the middle and upper grades and their reading interests. The former used one-hour interviews and the latter a questionnaire. Stanchfield found strong similarities among fourth, sixth, and eighth graders and among the high and low achievers. The boys chose, in order, outdoor life, explorations, sports, and games. Their least-interest categories included plants, music, plays, art, family life, and poetry. Ramsey used fourth, fifth, and sixth graders and found that poor readers chose adventure stories, whereas good readers chose biography and adventure equally. The difference between choices of good and poor readers among girls was negligible. Ramsey concluded that good and poor readers do not differ in preference for school subjects, leisure-time activities, or choice of reading topics. We would conclude from these studies that reading ability does not greatly influence choices of type of reading.

One study of newspaper reading of 564 pupils of grades four, five, and six seems to have found rather typical interests in this medium at the middle grade level. Johnson [29] through a questionnaire, found that 70 per cent of the children read the newspaper irregularly, 24 per cent read it regularly, and 6 per cent did not read it at all. The percentage of readers increased from grade to grade. Preference for parts of the paper showed in order: funnies, first-page news, sports, and television. They knew what the other parts of the paper were, though they did not read them. Seventy-five per cent indicated that newspaper reading was a help in school subjects—reading, current events, and social studies.

Witty [30] and Norvell [31] have conducted extensive studies of the reading interest of children in grades three to six. Witty listed the types of reading that the pupils liked and the kinds of stories they liked with their first choices ranking as follows:

[27] Jo M. Stanchfield, "Boys' Reading Interests as Revealed Through Personal Conferences," *The Reading Teacher*, 16:41–44 (Sept. 1962).

[28] Wallace Ramsey, "A Study of Salient Characteristics of Pupils of High and Low Reading Ability," *Journal of Developmental Reading*, 5:87–94 (Winter 1962).

[29] Lois V. Johnson, "Children's Newspaper Reading," *Elementary English*, 40: 428–32, 444 (April 1963).

[30] Paul Witty (director of project), "A Study of the Interests of Children and Youth" as reported in Paul Witty, et al. *The Teaching of Reading, op. cit.*, pp. 41–51.

[31] George W. Norvell, *What Boys and Girls Like to Read* (Morristown, NJ: Silver Burdett Company, 1959).

BOYS		GIRLS	
KINDS OF READING	STORIES	KINDS OF READING	STORIES
Fiction	Adventure	Fiction	Mystery
Articles in	Westerns	Poetry	Adventure
newspapers &	Mystery	Plays	Animals
magazines	Science-	Articles in	Humor
Biography	Fiction	newspapers &	
Poetry		magazines	

Norvell found that boys liked adventurous action, physical struggle, human characters, animals, humor, courage and heroism, and patriotism. The boys disliked descriptions, didacticism, fairies, love stories, sentiment, girls as leading characters, and physical weakness in male characters. Girls liked lively adventure, home and school life, human characters, domestic animals, romantic love, sentiment, mystery, the supernatural, and patriotism. They disliked violent action, description, didacticism, younger boys and girls (except babies), and fierce animals.

It is obvious from these extensive studies that the interests of middle and upper elementary children vary according to sex, though boys and girls do have reading interests in common. Some studies have shown that girls will read boys' books (those directed predominantly toward boys' major interests), but boys do not like to read girls' books. The teacher who is acquainted with the major studies and keeps up-to-date on current studies of children's interests can help children choose good reading material.[32] The one further step the teacher should take is that of carefully identifying the interests of the particular children under present guidance.[33]

Individual Interests

The interests of the individual child are often fleeting, elusive, and un-recognized. They may evidence themselves in subtle ways so that the teacher is unaware of them in the daily routine of the classroom. Some methods are necessary that will assure that the teacher can correctly identify each child's interests continuously, can evaluate them, and can use them to moti-vate the child's reading and to enlarge interests in new areas. One factor the elementary schoolteacher must keep constantly in mind is that the goal is the building of a permanent, lifetime interest in reading. Two steps are necessary to get a true picture of children's interests: (1) employing regular

[32] Helen M. Robinson and Samuel Weintraub, "Research Related to Children's Interests and to Developmental Values of Reading," *Library Trends,* 22:81–108 (Oct. 1973).
[33] Jerry L. Johns, "Reading Preferences of Intermediate-Grade Students in Urban Settings," *Reading World,* 14:51–63 (Oct. 1974).

informal classroom techniques of a varied, ongoing nature; and (2) employing an occasional formal instrument to get the overall picture of the individuals and the group for guidance in instruction, book requisitions, and planning.

Informal Classroom Techniques. Observation by the teacher is the first informal classroom technique employed, beginning in kindergarten and continuing right on through the school years. The teacher carefully observes the behavior of the children in play activities and all uses of free time. He or she observes the types of books and specific choices they browse through. In connection with this process, there must be some anecdotal recording of individual's choices—their frequency and type.

The second form is listening by the teacher in free time; in conferences, where the individual child talks about interests and choices, likes and dislikes, and opinions about specific books and materials; in play activities; in group discussions of books and characters, television programs, and movies.

A third procedure is to tape children's responses about their reading and about their interests in general. This provides a permanent record that may be used to refer back to later. It also saves the teacher from having to take notes daily. If tapes are used, erased, and reused, the teacher should take notes, at leisure, of the salient points.

There are several procedures whereby the children can record their own interests in the classroom—or at least reflect their interests: (1) the teacher can have them write on a simple question or two such as "What I like to read" or "What I have enjoyed reading most" or "What I hate to read"; (2) the children can write an autobiography of their reading experiences (this may yield a clue to their developing interests); (3) titles of potentially popular books may be read and the children may record the ones they think they would like best; (4) "Three Wishes" has often been used successfully as an interest indicator; and (5) children can keep the actual record of their reading in a file card, on *My Reading Design,*[34] in a notebook, on special book jackets, or in any other number of creatively designed ways.

One technique that has been helpful is to ask the children to tell the class of some of the best reading of their previous year. This may give a clue to the types of stories the children like best.

Formal Techniques. There are various forms of the interest inventory that can be administered to groups of children. There is the standardized test, such as Thorpe's *What I Like to Do: An Inventory of Children's Interests.*[35] Then there are the interest inventories that individual teachers devise

---

[34] G. O. Simpson, *My Reading Design* (North Manchester, IN: Reading Circle, Inc.).

[35] Louis P. Thorpe, Charles E. Meyers, and Marcella R. Sea, *What I Like to Do: An Inventory of Children's Interests* (Chicago: Science Research Associates, Inc., 1958).

to meet the needs of their own school and children. Samples of such inventories may be found in the following books:

MARY AUSTIN, CLIFFORD BUSH, and MILDRED HUEBNER. *Reading Evaluation.* New York: The Ronald Press Company, 1961, p. 85.

GUY L. BOND and EVA BOND WAGNER. *Teaching the Child to Read,* 4th ed. New York: Macmillan Publishing Co., Inc., 1966, p. 293.

LILLIAN GRAY. *Teaching Children to Read,* 3d ed. New York: The Ronald Press Company, 1963, pp. 404–06.

ALBERT J. HARRIS and EDWARD R. SIPAY. *How to Increase Reading Ability,* 6th ed. New York: David McKay Co., Inc., 1975.

PAUL WITTY, ALMA FREELAND, and EDITH GROTBERG. *The Teaching of Reading.* Boston: D. C. Heath & Company, 1966, pp. 41–42, 406–10.

These inventories are actually questionnaires that use the standardized interview or written response to measure typical behavior on the basis of the child's introspection or chronicling of activities. Most of them have open-ended questions and allow the child plenty of time to respond. These instruments can be very helpful, but they do contain one drawback—there is the tendency for children to respond to authority (the teacher usually) in the socially acceptable manner. In other words, they may respond the way they think the teacher wants them to. In this case, the validity of the instrument would be questionable.

No single method of ascertaining the child's interests is infallible, and teachers will want to vary their approaches and uses of the information gained. The important fact remains, however, that some conscientious efforts should be made to utilize the current interests of the children in their instructional program so that they are actually involved in the program, not simply recipients of it.

SUMMARY

It has been shown that teachers must identify the interests of children and capitalize on them to stimulate the children's interests toward varied, complex, permanent, and worthy reading interests. To do this the teachers must radiate interest themselves; must make attitudes and interests in literature an integral part of their curriculum, not just a free time adjunct; must present stimulating models of reading; and must know the cultural and psychological bases of interests. In short, teachers must know (1) the research studies' findings of age and sex characteristics of children's interests; (2) the children's actual current interests and abilities; and (3) the literature—its characters and authors—to match to the children. The teachers must have available (1) the variety of literature suitable to their children, and (2) the audiovisual materials that enhance children's interests in literature. Finally they must love books and be able to spark this same love of books in children.

SELECTED READINGS

Johns, Jerry L., and Linda Hunt. "Motivating Reading: Professional Ideas." *The Reading Teacher,* 28,7 (April 1975), 617–619.

Kujoth, J. S. *Reading Interests of Children and Young Adults.* Metuchen, NJ: The Scarecrow Press, Inc., 1970.

Landeck, Beatrice. *Learn to Read/Read to Learn: Poetry and Prose from Afro-rooted Sources.* New York: David McKay Co., Inc., 1975.

Mullins, Jane, and Suzanne Wolf. *Special People Behind the Eight Ball: An Annotated Bibliography of Literature Classified by Handicapping Conditions.* Johnstown, PA: Mafex Associates, Inc., 1975.

Roeder, Harold H., and Nancy Lee. "Twenty-five Teacher-Tested Ways to Encourage Voluntary Reading." *The Reading Teacher,* 27 (Oct. 1973), 48–50.

Roggenbuck, Mary J., "Motivating Farm Children to Read." *The Reading Teacher,* 30,8 (May 1977), 868–874.

Rupley, William H. "Reading Interests: Motivating Students to Read for Personal Enjoyment." *The Reading Teacher,* 30,1 (Oct. 1976), 118–121.

Sadker, Myra and David. *Now Upon a Time—A Contemporary View of Children's Literature.* New York: Harper & Row, Publishers, 1977.

Sebesta, Sam L., and William J. Iverson. *Literature for Thursday's Child.* Chicago, IL: Science Research Associates, Inc., 1975.

Simon, Norma. *Why Am I Different?* Chicago: Albert Whitman, 1976.

Tanyzer, Harold, and Jean Karl, eds. *Reading, Children's Books and Our Pluralistic Society: Perspectives in Reading No. 16.* Newark, Delaware: International Reading Association, 1972.

Trela, Thaddeus. *Getting Boys to Read: Ideas for Individualizing Reading for Boys.* Palo Alto, CA: Fearon Press, 1974.

Chapter 9

Reading Programs: Principles for Structure

OBJECTIVES

To describe the elementary reading
program and its purposes

To develop the strategies for planning a
program, a unit, and the
daily reading lesson

To understand the in-service teacher
education program and its purposes and needs

To learn how to develop the techniques
to assure growth in reading programs and
their effectiveness

To know the role of the teacher, parent,
administrators, librarian, and consultants
in the ongoing reading program

To know the sources of help in program
evaluation and development—professional,
community, and financial

INTRODUCTION: READING IN THE TOTAL CURRICULUM

The new classroom teacher is plunged directly into an ongoing program. It
may be traditional or progressive; it may or may not be caught up in current
pressures for change. Although their immediate responsibility is to plan
today's lessons, new teachers have a broader responsibility—to the educational system, to the students, and to themselves—to be fully cognizant
of the total curriculum and of the organizational pattern or patterns in
which the schools are operating.

All school personnel need to be aware of the many facets of the total educational picture in their own school system. These include the objectives of instruction; the expectations of the school, the community, and the students; the curriculum; the organizational framework in which instruction is carried out; the status of reading instruction; and their roles in interpreting the purposes and objectives of the program. They need a good perspective of the total program in order to be effective in the segmented, day-by-day instruction of the students.

Administrators and staff need to be aware of the changing emphasis in education, so that they can plan an effective curriculum through implementation or improvement from preschool through junior college. Those who analyze curriculum offerings note areas that have remained relatively the same in the last half century, other areas like science and mathematics that have undergone noticeable curriculum changes, and areas in which pressures for changes are being made. Research in psychology has caused many curriculum planners to give consideration to the nature of the learner and the learning process. The interests and needs of students of varying abilities and backgrounds have been investigated. The role of the school in society has been studied.

An all-pervading factor in contemporary society is change. As schools today face this challenge they ask, "How can we prepare every child for effective living in a changing world?" School personnel attempt to find answers by studying educational objectives, the nature and scope of curriculum practices, and the current organizational structure. They face many pressures from both the community and the educational profession to make changes in the school's organization of curriculum practices. To maintain equilibrium, the administrator must analyze the pressures, study pertinent research data, and make decisions that reflect an internal consistency.

For over a century schools in America have followed a graded type of organization. Children progress through schools in a sequential pattern, typically spending a year in each of the grades, one through twelve. The concept of grade has been developed in textbooks as well. Examples are the "fifth grade history text," the "preprimer and primer" basal readers (early first grade), the "primary" dictionary (early grades), and so on. Thus, children are exposed to a content structure of increasing difficulty as they progress through the grades.

During this past century many educators have become aware of the dangers inherent in the lockstep of rigid grading. Increased knowledge of child development patterns and of individual differences among children has led to attempts to institute changes. Some innovative procedures have been designed for the purpose of differentiation in organizational patterns, in curriculum offerings, in pupil progress rates, in teaching methods, and in instructional materials.

Differentiation in organization has been adopted on a schoolwide basis as well as in a single classroom. The typical graded pattern has been the self-contained classroom with one teacher who has the responsibility for all subjects at grade level. This pattern has been modified in some schools by the addition of special subject teachers in art, music, and physical education and/or adopting the departmentalized pattern. Both modifications result in more content-centered instruction than in the self-contained classroom where a child-centered philosophy could more readily be followed. Thus, when educators have thought through their basic instructional objectives, they need to study their organizational pattern for its effects upon the curriculum and upon pupil success.

In an educational yearbook devoted to a study of innovation and change in reading instruction, Sartain [1] reviewed the various patterns of schools and classrooms for reading instruction. Both new and experienced teachers will find a detailed review of the traditional and innovative patterns that have been developed, as well as criteria for judging their effectiveness. The following are organizational patterns that have emerged at the elementary level:

1. Self-contained classrooms.
2. Departmentalization.
3. Team teaching.
4. Nongraded patterns.
5. Various combinations: (a) Joplin interclass grouping; (b) dual progress plan; (c) continuous progress plan.

Within some of these organizational structures certain modifications, because of instructional methods or materials, have been introduced:

1. Individualized instruction.
2. Individually prescribed instruction.
3. Pupil-team study.

Reading has been taught within the framework of each of the preceding organizational designs. Various techniques for teaching reading that have been developed include the following:

1. Whole-class instruction by one teacher (basal readers, typically).
2. Intraclass grouping within a single classroom: (a) basal instruction (achievement, ability); (b) skills instruction (special needs); (c) activity grouping (interests, research, projects).
3. Individualized reading (differentiation within the classroom).

[1] Harry W. Sartain, "Organizational Patterns of Schools and Classrooms for Reading Instruction," *Innovation and Change in Reading Instruction.* Yearbook of the National Society for the Study of Education (1968), Part II, pp. 195–236.

4. Joplin interclass grouping (homogeneous sectioning in several classrooms).
5. Reading as a special subject (one teacher in a departmentalized structure).
6. Reading taught by a team (cooperative teaching).
7. Teams of pupils.

Further innovations in the teaching of reading may be noted in certain modifications because of specially devised materials, equipment, or approaches. These include the following:

1. i.t.a. (a modification in orthography).
2. Linguistic approach (language signals related to the structure of language).
3. Language-experience approach (all communication skills taught simultaneously).
4. Programed reading (developmental sequences in prescribed increments, often utilizing newer hardware).
5. New Castle plan (filmstrips accompanying reading texts).
6. Montessori plan (a prepared environment of materials specially constructed to provide experiences leading from the concrete to the abstract).
7. Color coding (a system of color-coded sounds).
8. Talking typewriter (exploratory approach with young children).
9. Numerous phonetic approaches (systematic teaching of consonants, vowels, blending, and so on).

SCOPE AND SEQUENCE OF THE READING PROGRAM

Developmental reading has been defined in terms of the acquisition of a sequential pattern of the reading skills needed at each level from initial reading instruction through the junior year in college. It includes the habits, skills, attitudes, and appreciations characteristic of the good reader. Any student may be termed a good reader when he has achieved the highest level of reading skill of which he is currently capable and at the same time uses his reading skills effectively for personal reasons.

The effective reading program takes into account individual differences in children, their interests, their learning rates, their present levels of attainment, their potential achievement levels, and any other factors that may influence their development. It provides readiness activities, varied types of reading material geared to children's age and their language-experience backgrounds, and an instructional pace appropriate to each child. It helps children to read efficiently in context textbooks and supplies them with the reading-study skills they need at each succeeding level through the upper grades. It provides children with a well-rounded curriculum with individual and integrated learning experiences that lead them to read for various purposes such as recreation (children's literature), information (work-study), and utilization (how-to-do-it).

Because of the many factors that influence educational progress, some children do not achieve a year's progress in a year's time. Some schools provide a plan of continuous progress, which allows the children to go ahead at their own rate. Thus, if they are slower than others, they will not be considered a failure. In the nongraded schools children are not expected to progress within the lockstep of yearly grades; they may proceed at a faster or slower pace without penalty. The philosophy underlying this concept of developmental reading is a promising one because of its positive approach and its implications for improving reading instruction.

Many schools make provision for corrective and remedial reading programs for children with reading difficulties. The reading specialist may help the classroom teacher detect children needing extra reading help, diagnose their reading difficulties, and provide appropriate materials and techniques. Occasionally, a child with severe learning disabilities is detected. This child cannot be treated adequately within the classroom setting. School systems provide for such children when they establish a central reading clinic staffed with remedial reading specialists who are prepared for the diagnosis and treatment of handicapped readers. Referral to a learning disability center will provide the additional services of specialists in the fields of vision, hearing, speech, psychology and psychiatry, pediatrics, and neurology. Thus a professional multidiscipline team approach to learning problems can be initiated.

The teaching of reading is a complex process. Assuring reading competence for all children is a monumental task. New teachers need all of the help they can get from various sources—their college reading courses and attendant textbooks and reference sources; the manuals of the basal readers; materials from publishers of reading textbooks and workbooks; in-service programs devoted to reading; and school personnel such as reading consultants, supervisors, principals, and experienced colleagues. Specifically, new teachers need to understand the sequential development of such basic skills as vocabulary, comprehension, and study skills. (See Chapters 4, 5, and 6). They need to be able to locate materials that will provide practice at any point in each of these skills areas. (See Chapters 9–11.) They must be able to appraise an individual's current status in level of reading achievement. (See Chapter 13.) They should be able to challenge every child in their classes, whether slow or gifted, average, retarded, reluctant, or disadvantaged. (See Chapter 14.)

CURRICULUM PLANNING FOR READING

Curriculum planning has sometimes been the province of the school administrator. Because he may not have the know-what to actually provide the know-how, he sometimes leaves this task to the individual teacher. When the administrator builds the curriculum it often results in an autocratic, rigid curriculum that does not adequately meet the needs of the children, and when the teacher does it, it often results in a rambling, meandering, disconnected series of experiences that leaves to chance the opportunity of the children to become good readers. The solution lies in an appointed systemwide reading committee with the responsibility for upgrading the reading instruction and program. The membership of this committee should contain both generalists and specialists. Its composition might be (1) a capable classroom teacher from each grade, (2) the reading specialist, and (3) a representative from the administration—usually a principal or two.

The reading committee's first function is to identify the goals of their reading program. Next, all kinds of reference materials must be studied to assure a strong background of modern theory and practice in reading instruction. Then the committee can get down to the business at hand: (1) assessing the current status of the program by examining the overall testing results and identifying strengths and weaknesses, using the school's needs assessment and the planning procedures of Right-To-Read; (2) evaluating current materials in use—books, A-V aids, other supplementary materials; (3) studying organizational patterns for instruction; (4) examining innovations or their absence; (5) assessing parent reactions; (6) developing regular criteria for evaluating materials and procedures; and (7) developing a course of action and recommendations—one course of action must be the committee's liaison with both teachers and top administration. The committee can be most successful if it obtains released time for its work (preferably 9:00 A.M. to noon) so that its sessions do not have to be at the tired end of a teacher's or administrator's busy day. It is also reasonable to expect secretarial help to compile its findings and disseminate its reports.

After the committee reports its findings, the next logical step may be the development of a reading guide or course of study. At this point, true curriculum planning is undertaken and the committee requires the help of subcommittees and *ad hoc* committees for two reasons: (1) to spread the work among the various strengths and specialties of various personnel, and (2) to encourage the involvement of as many of the personnel as possible. Of course, the major goal of the guide is to provide a ready reference for all teachers, not as a standardization of the reading curriculum, but as a true guide with clear goals, helpful suggestions, creative approaches, and a variety of suggested materials so that the needs of every child may be appropriately and adequately met.

A good course of study or reading guide would contain all of the characteristics mentioned in this book. It usually contains an introduction delineating the community and school setting in which reading takes place. It outlines the reading program grade by grade or level by level. It lists materials and methods of instruction, current and suggested. It outlines organization, administration, and personnel roles. Ordinarily, it outlines some innovative plans that might be tried. It usually has an appendix listing supplementary materials that may be used for enrichment purposes. It outlines evaluative procedures including special diagnostic instruments to be used for special purposes. Regular testing programs are outlined. Cumulative records and reporting to parents are shown.

When teachers objectively evaluate the reading guide, they look for continuity in the sequence of reading development from the readiness stage to beginning reading to the initial independent reading to the transition and fluency stage to the intermediate and interpretive skills to the advanced skill stage. They look for the articulation between levels and the provisions for turnover and mobility and promotion and grouping. They look for evidence of the objectives in the program and procedures of meeting the objectives that were initially set forth. They look at the scope of the program —special help for reluctant readers, enrichment, relating reading to the content areas, storytelling, literature, library usage, and so on. They look at the evaluative procedures to see if they influence instruction and keep everyone, including the child, informed of progress. They look at the content—its range and validity for the children involved. And they look at all the materials—their range and validity. Finally, they may be able to judge how adequately this reading program meets the needs of this community of children.

Planning must be a continuous process, not resting on the laurels of a job completed. Its potential for success depends upon three separate aspects: (1) a strong, balanced reading program, (2) a strong teacher of reading, and (3) the adaptation or individualization of instruction for the particular child. The latter two really mean an unbalancing of the program for a given child, for the discerning teacher knows that there are different ways of presenting sequences and some children can be allowed to skip parts whereas others have to work slowly through those parts. The teacher has to build diversity along the many tracks leading to the same general goals, we are told by experimenters such as Jerome Bruner of Harvard University. This may be the reason an innovative procedure is often successful—both the teacher and the pupil(s) catch fire from their intensive work with the new method. So planning must always allow the flexibility of innovation and its assessment. Planning must be continuing.

THE TEACHER'S PLANNING

Long-Range Program for the Year

The reading program for the year will not necessarily be the standard of the grade level. Its gradients will be those of the particular children in the class. This is the reason the teacher must individually plan his program. Naturally, the first step is to identify the beginning abilities, learning rates, and status (reading levels) of the children. The next step is to discover their needs in terms of progress toward mastery of the skills. The third step is that of selecting the materials that will be necessary to help them achieve mastery. The fourth step is to plan the sequence of presentation of the materials and instruction. The fifth step is the organization of children and materials for learning. Although it seems foolish, the teacher often does this fifth step without carefully going through the previous four steps. As a matter of fact, this fifth step is often mandated by the administrators of the school system on the basis of normative data and traditional procedures.

Inexperienced teachers have a tendency to follow the reading guide of the system and/or the teacher's guide to the basal readers rather closely. This, in fact, may be their best approach because experienced people have built these guides. But again, this is a normative approach that may have to be altered and adjusted to fit the teacher and the children. With experience accumulated through the study of the children and the use of the material, teachers know where to depart from the guide, where to supplement, where to speed up or slow down, where to be selective in its use, and where to suggest actually revising the guide itself.

At this point it would be repetitious to list all the areas, approaches, and materials that should be a part of the yearly plan. A word of warning is necessary though—the plan must be considered as a tentative, flexible guide to keep the program goals in sight. The unit, the weekly plan, the daily lesson plans, the diagnostic and follow-up activities are crucial to success in instruction. Flexibility, then, becomes the key to continued success, but not the kind that occurs in purposeless whims or jumping on every bandwagon that comes along. Teachers need to be creative and experiment with approaches and new ideas but can do so in a controlled atmosphere where evaluation of the relative success will prove the degree of usefulness. They can discard quickly those approaches that are not working successfully, persist with those that show discernible results.

Unit Planning

The reading unit is a portion of the reading program with very limited, specific goals. When the teacher decides that a given unit would help meet those goals, there are several things to be done: (1) gather interesting material at the appropriate readability levels of the children, (2) find ways to relate the unit to previous learnings and to project into future learnings to fit the unit into the scope and sequence of the program, and (3) plan the best procedure for instruction. At the early primary level the unit is rather short; it may be a three- or four-page story. In progression through the grades the units become longer; middle and upper grade units may consume three to six weeks of class time. Thus the unit becomes an intermediate plan between the yearly plan and the daily lesson plan. The teacher prepares for the unit first; then the children have to be prepared for it. We usually call this step *developing readiness*. In the class the next step is teacher-pupil planning; this continues from time to time as the work progresses. It is followed by individual reading, cooperative reading, discussion, assignment of tasks, reporting, and much discussion. Some form of culminating experience brings the major learnings together, and, finally, the experience is evaluated. One very important aspect of unit teaching is the quality and preciseness of questions that are raised. Usually, children begin with very general questions, and these have to be focused, often with the teacher's questions, to provide direction for reading.

Daily Lesson Planning

It is necessary to plan daily lessons within the framework of the overall planning because groups and individuals vary so much in their daily accomplishments and in their emerging needs as assessed through diagnostic teaching. The teacher must be prepared to meet their needs with appropriate materials and procedures. Daily plans provide the little detours that are necessary for groups or individuals in their learning and practice. Thus daily planning includes the follow-up activities for the reinforcement or correction of skills.

The beginning teacher profits from detailed written plans; the experienced teacher recalls details that have worked before and may need only skeleton planning. After thirty-plus years of teaching your authors still do daily planning (in writing) for their classes. In a sense, this is a quick run-through of the lesson to (1) be fully prepared in informational background and (2) the collection of materials that may be needed, (3) to get a feeling for the timing of the lesson, and (4) to be sure the lesson meets the sequential learning needs of the students.

The teacher's plan contains several steps that do not appear on the surface if one were observing the directed reading lesson in session. First, there is the teacher's careful selection of the story, or reading selection, that will be the vehicle for accomplishing the desired aims of this lesson. Second, there are the characteristics of this story to help meet those aims —be they content through story plot or characters and/or skill aims, social aims and/or worksheet or other types of follow-up. Third, there is the planned methodology of preparation of the children for the lesson—the interest and curiosity and pictures and vocabulary and background of experience that must relate the new learnings to previous learning. This third may determine the way previously learned sight words can be utilized to help in learning the new vocabulary of the lesson. Fourth, there is the gathering of the materials for the lesson or the placement of the projector for use or the placing of material on the bulletin board or chalkboard or the arrangement of the realia in position on the table or the placement of a poem or additional books within quick grasp of the setting for the lesson.

The steps in the daily lesson with a group of children might be as follows:

1. Build readiness for reading. Arouse the children's interest in the selection through pictures, words on the chalkboard, the bulletin board, discussion, realia, extension of previous learnings, and so on. This should be brief, but it should set the purpose for reading.
2. Introduce new vocabulary. Use word cards or the chalkboard to relate new vocabulary to that previously learned.
3. Guide the silent reading. Ask thought-provoking question(s); factual, inferential, motivating questions. Give help at once where needed. Emphasize comprehension.
4. Interpret and discuss. Evaluation of the story and title and relation to life and other factors take place at this point. Further questions may arise from discussion.
5. Reread. Rereading is always done for a specific purpose—why, what, when, where, enrichment, fluency. Oral reading could be done here if appropriate.
6. Skill-building process. Practice forms of expression, word drills, word analysis techniques. Lead into other activities—chalkboard, workbooks, duplicated material.
7. Evaluate the lesson. Discuss with children the facts learned, experiences enjoyed, interests, skills, habits, and so on.
8. Extend and enrich concepts and skills. Individual reading with challenging experiences for independent work—building attitudes, organizing ideas, perceiving relationships, improving study techniques. Encouraging creative activities (dramatization, art, music, literature) may help to extend the experiences of the lesson. The one major purpose of this step is to give children the opportunity for practice on their independent reading level, which will enhance their ability to the point where they will desire to read and will read on their own.
9. Finally, the teacher makes sure that the lesson and its follow-up activity properly fit into the reading unit and do not take a disproportionate amount of time and energy in terms of their value.

Figure 11 may help the teacher in planning for the differential abilities of poor, average, and good readers in the classroom. Notice the differences in types of questions, quantity of reading, and concreteness versus abstractness.

Planning for individualized reading where this is the modal approach in the classroom is first geared to the ability of each individual child. Where grouping is arranged to meet some common need, then the steps of the lesson plan shown previously should be followed. Many suggestions could be made for planning for independent reading activities. The creative teacher finds ways simultaneously to routinize, glamorize, and efficiently have available at all times procedures whereby children can go to tasks on their own. A daily chalkboard agenda is one teacher's answer; a programed materials corner, a corner with a record player or tape recorder with individual earphones, a "help yourself" box, a task agreement, outlining sequential procedures, a free reading library table are others that teachers have found successful. An individual, carefully planned lesson can be only as strong as its follow-up activities for reinforcement. Learning and skills need reinforcement.

Teacher-Pupil Planning in Class

Daily planning results in the teacher's knowing the material thoroughly and having thought through procedures so that work with the children can be of a spontaneous nature. Plans are discussed with the children, and records are kept by both teacher and children. In this way, children are constantly aware of their successes and their changing needs. They can make their own decisions about who will be doing which tasks. When school starts in the fall, they begin developing a self-reliance for independent work and group work with full knowledge of (1) what they are doing, (2) why they are doing it, (3) the timing or scheduling of work, and (4) their progress to date. This kind of planning with children allows the teacher to hold some individual conferences, to plan between group sessions for materials and goals, to work with a group for a while, to move from one group to another, and to record progress and needs as the children proceed with their activities. To give the children a sense of timing, a sign-up sheet could be available, and they could sign for the time when they are ready for a conference; the teacher watches to make sure conferences are held with every child at least once a week. Some will need more frequent conference time than others; but all should have a conference at least once a week. If responsibility for preparation is placed on each child, he or she will gradually learn to assume and meet his or her obligations.

Corrective work in the classroom on the children's difficulties should be handled this same way. After evaluation of their learning and skill development, flexible regroupings to add kinesthetic, audiovisual, or tactile

Figure 11. *Planning Lessons to Help All Readers*

	POOR READERS	AVERAGE READERS	GOOD READERS
I. Motivation Arouse interest, curiosity Build background of meanings, concepts	Through bulletin boards, pictures, films, filmstrips, transparencies		
	Anticipate difficult vocabulary; discussion; dictionary		
II. Guided Reading To read for a purpose To think about the reading	Ask a question— Students read *one* paragraph to find answer; continue	ASK A MAJOR MOTIVATING QUESTION	
		Students read page or entire section silently to find answer.	
		List additional questions to be answered	
III. Group Interpretation Written expression	WORKSHEET: Concrete, easily found answers	WORKSHEET: Concrete and abstract thinking required	WORKSHEET: Answers requiring inference, comparison, critical and creative thinking
	ORAL DISCUSSION: 1) instead of worksheet 2) to follow worksheet	ORAL DISCUSSION: 1) instead of worksheet 2) to follow worksheet	ORAL DISCUSSION: to stimulate further thinking and reading
Discussion with peers Personal experience Personal reactions Self-expression, listening experience			
IV. Skills-building Practice Vocabulary Comprehension Fluency Rate	Word analysis as needed Phrase reading as needed Rereading as needed Comprehension checks	Word analysis as needed Phrase reading as needed Rereading as needed Comprehension checks	Common roots, affixes (Greek, Latin) Picturesque word meanings Time reading to increase rate of comprehension
V. Extension and Enrichment	Newspapers, magazines, library books, encyclopedias, interviews *In* classroom; outside assignment		

approaches to their problems are scheduled in short, frequent, intensive sessions. All through this procedure, the children are aware of their needs, and their goal is improvement in their work with full knowledge of their progress. Reinforcement should be scheduled frequently to maintain their skills. The teacher does this *with* the children, not *to* them.

SOURCES OF HELP FOR THE TEACHER

There are many sources to which the teacher may turn for help in planning the reading program and the daily activities. *The First R* [2] reports that the Harvard-Carnegie study showed that the most frequently used source was the workshop to introduce new materials, to develop instructional aids, to demonstrate new techniques, and to report research findings. This was followed by preschool orientation or institutes, demonstrations, visits to classrooms or other schools, faculty meetings, grade level meetings, and area meetings. Less frequently mentioned by the schools were individual conferences, observations with follow-up interviews, experimentation, and research projects. The frequency of these was identified as "as often as needed," "when the occasion arises," "occasionally," or "now and then." Obviously, these procedures are not typically regular, ongoing activities aimed at consistent improvement of instruction.

Personnel

The administrator is in a position to be a major resource to the teacher in planning. The provision of materials, time for planning, the setting in which planning can take place, and budgetary support are but a few of the administrator's responsibilities. Bulletins in which excerpts are reported from the wealth of literature crossing his desk can be a great help to teachers. Providing supervisory help is another of their responsibilities—especially for the new teacher, but also for experienced teachers. Their arrangements for utilizing the services of other experienced teachers, publishers' representatives, and the effective use of all personnel influence their impact on the planning that is done.

The reading specialist or supervisor is a ready source of help in planning and normally plays a leadership role in the instructional process, helping teachers get the right materials, organize instruction, and meet whatever special needs of children they encounter.

All administrative and supervisory personnel are constantly alert to excellence in instruction, and they should encourage good teachers to share

[2] Mary C. Austin and Coleman Morrison, *The First R* (New York: Macmillan Publishing Co., Inc., 1963), p. 170.

their newly acquired knowledge and to demonstrate successful activities and skills for their fellow teachers. They should thus encourage cooperation among the faculty rather than competition. This is a great impetus to planning.

Materials

Many attempts are made to bring teachers and materials together so that wise choices of appropriate materials will be made to suit the youngsters and the program rather than adjusting to whatever materials are at hand. Teachers learn of the materials through professional books and journals, through contact with publishers' literature and representatives, textbooks, manuals, and many other services. The library is a good source for this help, too; the school, the public, and college libraries are rich in resource material. An example is the *Educator's Guide to Free Curriculum Materials.* Yearbooks of associations and conference reports are helpful. Some special sources your authors have found helpful may serve as further examples:

BOOKS

HAFNER, LAWRENCE E., and HAYDEN B. JOLLY. *Patterns of Teaching Reading in the Elementary School.* New York: Macmillan Publishing Co., Inc., 1972.

HARRIS, ALBERT J., and EDWARD R. SIPAY. *Effective Teaching of Reading,* 2d ed. New York: David McKay Company, Inc., 1971.

HEILMAN, ARTHUR W. *Principles and Practices of Teaching Reading,* 4th ed. Columbus, OH: Charles E. Merrill Publishing Company, 1977.

SPACHE, GEORGE D., and EVELYN SPACHE. *Reading in the Elementary School,* 4th ed. Boston: Allyn & Bacon, Inc., 1977.

BOOKLISTS AND SOURCES

Best Books for Children, R. R. Bowker Company
Basic Book Collection for Elementary Grades, American Library Association
Association for Childhood Education
The Horn Book Magazine
The Instructor
A Multimedia Approach to Children's Literature, American Library Association
National Council of Teachers of English Lists
Textbooks in Print: El-Hi Textbooks in Print; Children's Books in Print—R. R. Bowker Company
H. W. Wilson *Children's Catalogue*

OTHERS

American Guidance Service (instructional programs, educational
materials), Publishers Building Circle Pines, MN 55014
Garrard Publishing Company (book and teaching aids catalogs),
Champaign, IL 61820
Media Materials Inc. (individualized cassette learning packages), 2936
Remington Avenue, Baltimore, MD 21211
The Viking Press (Audio Visual Catalogue), 625 Madison Avenue, New
York, N.Y. 10022
"New Materials on the Market," *The Reading Teacher*, 31,5:532–56
(Feb. 1978) (latest).

Even the newspapers contain frequent book reviews and articles that
are helpful to the teacher. They may also contain another source for the
alert teacher—community resources and people to enrich the reading program as well as social studies and other curriculum areas. In particular, the
museums, city publications, historical landmarks, and airports are rich in
resource material.

Complete sets of new basal series and many trade books are an absolute
necessity; they may be compiled and reported to teachers by the reading
specialist, the librarian, and/or the administrator. They should also be
readily available for perusal.

Courses of Study

As previously mentioned, courses of study can be of considerable help to
the teacher as sources of information, as sources of materials, and as guides
to the program that was developed locally. Some school systems have also
gathered some courses of study from other cities and placed them in the curriculum library or materials center in order to give teachers the opportunity
to compare their own program with those of other school systems. Discussing the pros and cons of other programs may be a good approach to the
insights necessary for thinking of the long-range planning of their own
program.

In-Service Programs

The Torchlighters and *The Torchlighters Revisited*[3] have made many
school systems aware of the great need for strong in-service programs in
reading. Most teachers in elementary schools begin teaching reading with a
very minimum course background—one course in reading or one course in

[3] Mary C. Austin and Coleman Morrison, *The Torchlighters: Tomorrow's Teachers
of Reading* (Cambridge, MA: Harvard University Press, 1961); Coleman Morrison and Mary C. Austin, *The Torchlighters Revisited* (Newark, DE: International
Reading Association, 1977).

language arts. A continuous, strong in-service program can help these teachers. The purposes, then, of such programs are (1) to help teachers meet the needs they identify in their instruction; (2) to extend their knowledge; (3) to improve their skills in methodology; (4) to give them the opportunity to examine new materials and see them in use; (5) to help teachers organize their instruction; (6) to change teachers; (7) to broaden their perspective of reading instruction; (8) to help them understand their children, diagnose needs, vary procedures; (9) to apply reading to the act of learning in content areas; (10) to assess their own needs; and finally (11) to add professional stimulation to their efforts.

Preparation for in-service programs involves several important steps. The initiation of a specific program usually comes from the administrator; but the spark that ignites the move may come from a teacher who has attended summer school and been inspired to attack the problems encountered in a broader setting; or it may come from a recognized need from teacher discussions, a faculty meeting, or a supervisor's observations. Parents' criticism or a series of criticisms may be the motivating force. At any rate, a need is identified and focused so that the purpose of the program is clear. The in-service program is set up to meet the needs of a single school or school system. Participants are identified, and these include teachers, at least one administrator, a parent or two from the PTA, related personnel from special services, and possibly some experts. The latter might include consultant(s) from a nearby college or university or another school system, the state department of education, or from the IRA or a similar professional reading organization. The administrator must plan for funds for the program —board support with complete funding is best, although federal or state or industry grants may be obtained. The question of college credit is one that should be given some attention, for many teachers could profit from this in their advanced degree work and have the professional desire to improve themselves in this manner. A correct setting for the work must be planned—a room that is just right in size and convenience and with tables so that actual work can be done. Parents should be notified about the program for their support, and cooperation is usually needed at some stage of progress. Materials have to be obtained to make the program a success— more about this later.

Leadership for the in-service work is an extremely important feature. A lead teacher, resource teacher, reading specialist or other qualified individual could provide the expertise for program change and improvement, through interactive forms of in-service functioning. The expert or consultant should be one who knows how to motivate people. He or she must realize that lectures must be kept to a very minimum if true involvement is to occur. He or she must be skilled in the timing and procedure of (1) exerting inspiring leadership in the planning and beginning stage, (2) reducing his or her role to that of helper, (3) applying just the right amount of pressure to create change, (4) instigating change where necessary, (5) being sure that responsibilities are delegated to individual participants, and (6) observing and instituting the principles of continuous evaluation.

The major procedure in an in-service program should be extensive reading and study. Other procedures include observations of good instructional practices, the sharing of ideas, discussion, the examination of materials directly, and the observation of various interpretations of theory and various organizational practices.

Materials that are used should be varied. Television, especially planned programs on closed-circuit TV, is effective. Case studies provide a valuable basis for discussion. Research reportings, theory books and articles, teaching materials, and professional and nonprofessional books may be excellent motivation. Weiss [4] states, "I do not use just books on how to teach reading. I will include such books as Sylvia Ashton-Warner's *Teacher,* John W. Gardner's *Self-renewal,* Nancy Larrick's *A Parent's Guide to Children's Reading,* and John Holt's *How Children Fail."* Units, courses of study, articles on theory and issues, curriculum documents, lesson plans, typical assignments, films, advertising literature, and many other materials should be collected and made available for study. Specialists who are proponents of a specific organizational pattern, an approach to beginning reading, or an emphasis in instruction should be consulted and, if found desirable, should be invited to a session to present their viewpoint and the assessment of their own program. The leadership should determine the balance in this approach. The evaluation of such programs and materials is a continuous process.

Intense work on the teacher's own professional problems in the school setting is the most likely form of experience to create change and improvement. As long as continuous evaluation accompanies this process, the school's programs in reading, the individual children's learning, and the professional stimulation of the teacher will benefit. The teacher's confidence increases with growth and change; this is the way he or she feels secure in approaching the daily task of instruction. In-service education can accomplish more in a given amount of time and with a given amount of effort than can preservice courses in reading.

One final note of warning, though, is in order. The board of education must realize that no in-service program can be a final answer to their problems in the reading program. Recommendations and results must have follow-up activities, and this leads into further in-service programs. They should be continuous.

Professional Associations and Conferences

Your authors have never been sorry that they budgeted for and joined any professional organization. The rewards far surpass the value of the monetary

[4] M. Jerry Weiss, "Developing a Dynamic In-Service Teacher Training Program," *The Journal of the Reading Specialist,* 5,4:149 (May 1966).

investment. The major value of membership in the organization is its official organ of publication, with articles of interest and challenge in education. The teacher of reading who wishes to keep abreast of the changes, the current thinking, the research, and the innovative ideas and procedures and who wishes inspirational replenishing of the psyche must read the literature of his or her professional organizations. In order of priority, for the reading specialist, these are

1. The International Reading Association (IRA).
2. The state and local IRA councils.
3. The College Reading Association (CRA).
4. The National Reading Conference.

Other professional organizations include

1. The National Education Association (NEA).
2. The state and your local association.
3. American Educational Research Association (AERA).
4. Association for Supervision and Curriculum Development (ASCD).
5. National Society for the Study of Education (NSSE).
6. Association for Childhood Educational International (ACEI).
7. An association in your academic field if you choose, such as the National Council for the Social Studies (NCSS) or the National Council for the Teachers of English (NCTE).

All teachers have to decide what they can afford by way of association membership and a priority listing, then join all possible. Besides publications there is great value in attendance at their annual conventions and participation actively as an officer in one or two of one's major associations. The contacts with other members of the profession and the exchange of ideas and the publishers' exhibits can be very rewarding. There is no reasonable substitute for these activities to keep one inspired in his work and knowledgeable about current developments. Conference attendance allows teachers to be challenged and to exchange ideas and find some possible answers to their recurring questions.

Authorities in the Field

There are many very fine contributors to the field of reading who are available for consultant service to school systems. There are four methods of identifying these people: (1) consult the authors of reading and related books in the appendix of this book; (2) consult the contributors to the IRA and similar publications, especially those who appear on the platform of the IRA conventions reporting on their research and experimental programs and appear in the *Proceedings;* (3) consult the nearby universities and colleges and the state education department; (4) attend conferences and get acquainted with people in your field who might make a contribution to your reading program. Be especially alert to individuals who might contribute insight into a related field, such as linguistics, educational psychology, child development, medicine, optometry, and others. Be sure that they have recognized competence in their own field so that the information they bring can then be applied to the instructional process in reading by those who are competent in the educational program. Every reading teacher should be familiar with the role of the specialist in reading. A good beginning would be to read in the March 1967 issue of *The Reading Teacher* such articles as "The Reading Consultant of the Past, Present, and Possible Future," pages 475–82; "Standards and Qualifications for Reading Specialists," pages 483–86; "The Role of a State Reading Consultant," pages 487–93; "A County Consultant," pages 494–99; and "A Reading Consultant in a Private School," pages 505–08; and selected other articles. In essence, these articles outline what kinds of activities can be expected from the consultant. Authorities in reading make the greatest contributions to the local program when their role is clearly identified, when they spend enough time in the school to recognize its needs, and when they play a soft leadership role of supporting the efforts of the local personnel rather than telling them what to do.

Special Services

The school system has children who need the help of personnel beyond that of the classroom teacher. The gifted children need a program that is enriched far beyond what the normal classroom can offer them. In planning such a program, special services can help identify those children, can help coordinate their learning and facilities with the regular program, and can help in advisement as far as their special needs are concerned. The same is true where those children who encounter learning difficulties are concerned. The kinds of problems can be identified through the diagnostic work of special services. Advice can be offered to the classroom teacher regarding children's special needs in learning, in social problems, in physical problems, in intellectual deficiencies, and in psychological or behavior problems. Obviously, special services must be represented in all areas of planning whether it be schoolwide or classroom.

Summary

This section on planning has presented the task as the responsibility of all the personnel of the school system and includes the desirability of enlisting the help of some individuals outside the school system—some parents, some consultant service, some organizations. It emphasizes the need for careful, consistent day-to-day planning and overall planning to ensure a strong program that will make every child one who is interested in reading, one who can read, and one who does read.

THE WAYS IN WHICH EFFECTIVE READING PROGRAMS GROW

Introduction

Education has come a long way from the day when it could be described as "The teacher on one end of a log and the pupil on the other." This is a reference to President Garfield's well-known characterization of Mark Hopkins as a great teacher: "Give me a log hut, with only a simple bench, Mark Hopkins at one end and I at the other, and you may have all the buildings, apparatus, and library without him." Preventing the possibility of any simple description today are such complications as the population explosion, the current knowledge explosion, advances in technology, demands of a changing society, and numerous innovations such as the hardware and software proposed by some as cures for educational ills.

Those who pause long enough to consider an appraisal of the current scene with a view toward improvement must look backward before looking forward. Currently, they see growing dissatisfaction with phases of the nation's reading programs. In the previous decade from 1960 to 1970 educators' dissatisfaction with the *status quo* was reflected in such projects as (1) the First Grade Reading studies sponsored by the United States Office of Education; (2) new alphabets, such as i.t.a., to replace traditional orthography for beginning readers; (3) Durkin's reports of children who read before entering school; (4) innovative organizational plans, such as modified Joplin and team teaching; (5) changing approaches to reading instruction, as noted in emphases upon individualized reading, language-experience, words-in-color, the contributions of linguistics to reading, and (6) urgent demands for more functional reading research.

In another look backward, educators might review the progress made in the first six decades of this century and ask why more progress toward wholly effective reading programs did not materialize. Possibly, the word *apathy* will give as good a clue as any to the answer. They will find evidence of apathy on the part of the educator and the college that trained him or her, the parent and other members of the community, professional organizations, and even the publishing companies.

The great knowledge explosion of the past quarter of a century emphasized subject areas in schools and colleges. Somehow the majority of educators ignored any suggestions that adequate *reading* skills would be important to students' acquisition of knowledge. Colleges sent into elementary and secondary classrooms teachers who were prepared to teach content area subject matter but were often unprepared to teach the efficient *reading* of that content. Parents were dismayed when some children were poor readers; employers were appalled by the poor communication skills (reading, writing, and spelling) of some graduates of the schools. Yet neither parents nor employers showed a willingness for commitment to support the improved programs that better facilities, instructional materials, and teacher-in-service programs would provide. Professional organizations, such as state and national teacher groups, were expanding in too many directions. They were not immediately alert to a basic deficit in education—the *reading* skills of the children.

Improvements in the future will depend upon the development of a more knowledgeable public and profession. Results of previous research will need to be disseminated. A better understanding of educational objectives would result in more reasonable demands upon the school. An enlightened look at the end product—the informed citizen who reads willingly—should facilitate the formulating of functional educational objectives and should lead each community to a study of a very basic question: How can we achieve the type of reading program that will produce effective readers for our changing society?

The elementary teacher who is presently concerned about his or her role in providing effective reading instruction for all of the children entrusted to his or her care will profit from analyzing the implications in such questions as "Why should *I* be concerned with the development of effective reading programs? What is the teacher's responsibility?" "What is an effective reading program?" and "How do effective reading programs develop?"

The Teacher's Responsibility

Both the experienced teacher and the neophyte are on the firing line. Daily they see in their classes children who *are* reading, and reading well. They see others who do not read as well as expected. They note the reluctant readers and the nonreaders. They face the criticisms voiced by the public in such questions as "Why can't my son read?" "Why doesn't Miss Smith give my child individual attention?" "Why doesn't the kindergarten teacher teach reading?" "How come our schools aren't using those reading materials (or methods) the neighboring town is using?" "Why aren't (or, why are) they teaching reading in the junior high?" "Why does the school superintendent want to hire a *reading* specialist?"

Certainly, the classroom teacher, along with the school principal, is in a key position to give responsible leadership for effective reading programs.

Alert to the public critics yet aware of problems faced by the educational system, these educators can become directors for positive action in their community. They can keep a finger on the pulse of the community. They can make the community aware of their professional competence by showing their affiliation with local, state, and national educational and reading associations. They are active participants when they attend reading conferences, prepare papers, and report their own classroom activities. From their college reading courses and professional journals they have at hand a background of knowledge concerning professional literature and reports of reading research. They can use research findings to initiate changes in their programs. They can continue to participate in the action research that might well become the Open-sesame to improved programs. Teachers and principals are the best people to answer such criticisms as implied in the questions raised by the public in the preceding paragraph. They can provide a type of group parent conference—a regularly scheduled dialogue between parents and the school. For example, the kindergarten teacher and the primary teachers, reinforced by the principal and the reading specialist, can explain their sequentially developed reading programs in relation to the best research concerning child development and the ways children learn. When questions are raised showing parent dissatisfaction or concern, explanations can be forthcoming, and possibilities for improvement can be investigated. Thus, criticisms will not be discussed in a vacuum—or in a state of shared ignorance: competent, professional guidance can give direction toward responsible action. Forward-looking educational personnel are constantly alert to the forces shaping society. They stand ready to investigate the possibility of developing a reading program more effective for *all* children than the one currently in progress. Today's emphasis on accountability indicates that through legislation and court action those teachers and school systems which do not meet children's current needs, will be in trouble. The way to prevent this problem is the exercise of teacher and administrator responsibility to the educational endeavor all along the line.

An Effective Reading Program

A Functional Definition. Basic to educators' investigations of an effective reading program is a functional definition. A dynamic reading program for any school system is one that has been established to meet the educational objectives of the specific community. To be effective it must include (1) a strong developmental program that provides for systematic and sequential reading instruction geared to each pupil's current achievement levels, from prereading through secondary and junior college; (2) a reading improvement program that provides for the 10 to 15 per cent of pupils whose reading difficulties require more specialized or an intensive corrective or remedial instruction; (3) a wide-reading program that provides every pupil with the incentive for reading practice, appealing to pupils' innate curiosity and awakening interests.

Within this threefold framework when varied materials are available, skillful teachers can use diversified approaches and techniques to make reading instruction effective for everyone. When new materials and techniques appear, they can be given a trial in a carefully controlled situation so that fair comparisons would result for the ultimate good of the children involved. Teachers use every opportunity for extending reading experiences beyond the classroom, to make reading functional for all students.

Thus, an effective reading program can further be identified as one under a constant state of revision—with everyone concerned alert to ways and means of improving and making functional every segment of the developmental, remedial, and recreational aspects of the learning environment.

The Development of an Effective Reading Program

When school personnel and the community explore their aims and objectives they find that they have certain goals in common. They want to provide an on-going program that will meet each child's current and future needs, a dynamic program related to his abilities and interests. They want to prepare him to become a functioning citizen in the world, so that he can take his place in a rapidly changing society. They discover that they want to know how they personally can contribute to the ultimate attainment of these goals.

Dialogue Between Parents and the Schools. In the regularly scheduled sessions previously suggested, the dialogue between parents and the school, the roles of everyone who can influence the school's reading program can be clarified. Group conferences oriented to task analysis will bring into proper focus the specific ways in which the following contribute to the success of the school's reading program: the parents, teachers, librarians, adjunct personnel, administrators, and school board members.

Parents. Parents help their children toward ultimate reading success in a number of ways, indirectly and directly. They set a good example in the home when they read and discuss newspaper items, magazine articles, and books they enjoy. They begin reading children's stories to their offspring when boys and girls are too young to read to themselves. They buy picture books and magazines when a child is very young. Later they get him books he can read so that he will read for fun and to find out things he wants to know. They take him to the library and make sure that he gets a library card as soon as he is ready. They encourage him to read his library books in quiet moments in a comfortable setting. They show an interest in his reactions to the books and stories he has read. When the toddler asks, "What's that?" or "What's that word?" they provide answers like "That means doctor's office" or "That sign says, 'Stop.' " Thus parents provide the teaching technique of associating the symbol with the oral explanation when the child expresses an interest.

Parents show their interest in other ways. They attend Parent-Teacher Association meetings in which they work for the support of adequate libraries. They sponsor book fairs and out-of-school clubs or societies for children. They attend the school-sponsored meetings that acquaint parents with the school's programs and procedures. They have been introduced to professional literature about reading written especially for parents. As they become better informed about the various aspects of education, they see the need for hiring such qualified personnel as competent reading teachers and specialists and for purchasing varied materials and equipment. They show the school board that they favor spending money for quality education—such as improved reading programs.

Teachers. Classroom teachers need to reach and teach all youngsters in the classroom. Their professional preparation, preservice and in-service, has been designed to acquaint them with the nature of children, learning theories, the curriculum, instructional materials, and methodology.

As they enter classrooms in the cities, suburbia, and rural areas, teachers find a variety of classroom organizational plans, innovative experiments with curricula, materials, and initial approaches to reading instruction. When they have been well prepared in their college years, they will have a feeling of security in any teaching situation, traditional, progressive, or experimental. Such preparation would include a variety of experiences—in the *cognitive* domain, learning about types of programs from books and from college lectures; *affective* domain, acquiring attitudes, values, relationships; *manipulative* or *psychomotor,* acquiring familiarity with, and using, the materials of instruction available for teaching reading through observation and practice in real teaching situations.

Forward-looking teachers will teach reading in a total educational environment. To be effective teachers of reading, they will call upon their knowledge of psychology, the nature of children, and the nature of learning; they will put reading into its proper perspective in the language arts or communication arts; and they will utilize the best of methodology concerning the nature of effective teaching. They will use formative and summative types of appraisal, in order to do the diagnostic teaching and long-range evaluation delineated in previous chapters.

When teachers recognize the importance of teaching the reading skills necessary for reading the textbooks and supplementary material of the content areas, they are giving the child an opportunity to use in very practical ways his or her newly found skills. When teachers encourage the reading of trade books, magazines, and newspapers as part of the daily classroom assignments, they are developing lifetime reading habits.

Although many factors influence the development of a good reading program, none is as important as the classroom teacher. The successful classroom teacher sincerely wants to help children learn, and somehow he conveys this attitude to his pupils. He is interested in them as individuals, exhibiting an understanding of their interests and needs. With patience and good humor he shows students that he likes them and likes to teach them. The title of such a teacher might well become descriptively "Director of Learning."

Librarians. The librarian's role in the elementary school is emerging as increasingly important to an effective reading program. Children's reading skills will not operate in a vacuum. In fact, even their well-drilled classroom skills may deteriorate completely when they have no opportunities to use them successfully.

One way that schools may measure the success of their reading program is to gauge the use of the library. Children who are guided into meaningful projects and units will use the library resources to go beyond the textbook assignments. Teachers who organize their unit teaching in content areas will find opportunities to direct children's attention to articles, stories, biographies, novels, and other appropriate materials in the library.

The librarian is a key figure in locating multilevel reading material for the levels of reading ability detected in any one classroom. Thus children will experience the satisfaction of being able to read interesting material, at their present reading level, whether for classroom information or for recreation.

When the library is an integral part of the elementary school, the librarian can guide the children's use of reference materials. He can devote part of his time to teaching locational or library skills, such as the card catalog, guides to periodicals, fiction, and reference materials, and the Dewey decimal system and the Library of Congress System. He can be available during the school day when groups of children come in to browse. He can also provide guidance for the individual who is released from the classroom at the moment when he wants to locate material for his personal information or for his part in a class project. In fact, this type of library functioning leads us in the direction of the modern concept of the library as an instructional resource center.

Another service that the librarian is called upon to supply is the selection of books for a classroom library. Such books, of various grades of difficulty, are selected with the help of the teacher. They may remain for a semester or a shorter length of time, to be replaced periodically with others.

The enthusiastic librarian can help develop in children a love of reading and books by setting up attractive book displays and bulletin boards and by expressing an interest in children's book selections.

Administrators. Broadly defined, the administration of the elementary school may include the superintendent, the assistant superintendent, the elementary supervisors, and the principals. They implement the school system's philosophy of education and its basic reading philosophy. They are in a key position to see that there is a coordination of effort in the developmental reading program in the primary, intermediate, and secondary levels of the schools.

Within the administration lies the authority for action. When any segment of the school system desires change—whether in curriculum, organization, materials, or techniques—the administrator can be receptive to suggestions, opening doors for research and study.

The administrator's responsibilities for the reading program are manifold.[5] Provision of an adequate school plant produces a good school environment for the teaching of reading. His attention to supplying a wide variety of instructional materials helps teachers meet the reading needs of a diversified school population. His open-mindedness in matters of research and experimentation encourages teachers' efforts to improve reading instruction. When the administrator provides flexible plans of school organization he opens the way for teachers to offer appropriate instruction for all types of students, from the slowest to the gifted.

The administrator can implement in-service programs for teachers. He will need to plan meetings for the orientation of new teachers to the philosophy, curricula, and requirements of the system. He can be alert to special needs in reading, occasioned by the adoption of new textbooks, the opening of a school library, the initiation of a new plan of organization, such as nongraded primary classrooms, or requests of teachers for professional workshops in specific areas of reading. In other meetings he can help orient the public to the aims of the school's reading program.

The knowledgeable administrator is alert to acquiring new personnel trained for the most important task of their daily assignment—teaching the reading skills their pupils need. He will need to put money for reading needs—personnel, space, and supplies—into his budget. His leadership in all aspects of the educational program is essential, but never more so than in his awareness of the importance of the development of an efficient reading program.

Reading Consultants and Specialists. The one individual with the broadest preparation and background for reading instruction in most school systems is the reading consultant. Having specialized in his field, he may be called upon to provide help in the improvement of reading programs.

---

[5] Mary C. Austin, Clifford L. Bush, and Mildred H. Huebner, *Reading Evaluation* (New York: The Ronald Press Company, 1961), pp. 109–10; Thorsten R. Carlson, ed. *Administrators and Reading* (New York: Harcourt Brace Jovanovich, Inc., 1972).

Consultants can help the new classroom teacher in evaluating the reading levels of the children, in forming instructional groups, in providing appropriate materials of instruction. They can identify the retarded reader and give him or her special reading instruction. They can guide the teacher to plan for the pupil's improvement within the classroom by suggesting appropriate materials and methods. They can help teachers with demonstration lessons when requested or when new procedures are being initiated.

They can plan in-service programs and reading workshops, helping teachers to keep up-to-date in matters related to the teaching of reading. They can assist teachers who wish to do research or to experiment with new approaches or materials.

Although reading specialists or consultants have often been limited to activities within the remedial reading part of the program, they can give invaluable assistance to the developmental reading program. They are in a better position than is the classroom teacher to make the professional contacts so necessary for an overall view of a program. Because they get into classrooms at all levels, they can observe strengths and weaknesses. They can see the implementation of the curriculum as a whole, and the relationship of reading to the total curriculum. They can suggest the periodical evaluations necessary for learning whether objectives are being achieved. They can help interpret test results to classroom teachers, with the aim of translating needs into action. They can establish and supervise experimental designs, conduct controlled experimentation, and see that accomplishments are noted in the professional literature, to help their own and other school systems. Thus improved developmental and remedial reading programs can be fostered.

The specific roles of the reading consultant have been outlined by Robinson and Rauch [6] as the resource person, adviser, in-service leader, investigator, diagnostician, instructor, and evaluator. The reading consultant of the future can play an important part in organizing and coordinating the varied facets of a good reading program.

There are other groups of specialists who at any given time may wield an extensive influence on the reading program. One example is a basic research-on-reading group directed by Dr. William J. Gephart and sponsored by the United States Office of Education, which is attempting to define reading and develop basic knowledge about how people read. This group will attempt to tie together in a unified theory the factors—physical, psychological, and so on—that effect reading. Their objective is to produce a plan that shows an orderly step-by-step procedure for research tasks needed to be undertaken to arrive at a clear understanding of the nature of reading.

[6] H. Alan Robinson and Sidney J. Rauch, *Guiding the Reading Program* (Chicago: Science Research Associates, Inc., 1965), pp. 1–3.

Adult Influences on the Program

Although adult influences on the child's reading were discussed earlier as part of his or her environment, they need reviewing here in order to gain perspective as to their influence on the school's reading program. Sometimes their influence is desirable and helps to build good strong programs. Sometimes their influence is negative, and we find the proverbial tail wagging the dog. They are thus reviewed briefly to encourage their positive favorable use.

Professional Influences. RESEARCH IN CHILD DEVELOPMENT—The research of Olson, Bruner, and Ilg and Ames has been influential in the placement of material in reading programs and in the pacing of the programs. Experimentation is done with children; it is interpreted and reported in the professional literature, and gradually programs are changed in the light of the interpretations. Often experimentation is conducted in the classroom with different children to apply the findings of reported research before changes are made. This is healthy. An example of the latter would be the application of the theory of Piaget, discussed briefly in Chapter 2.

PUBLICATIONS OF ASSOCIATIONS—Teachers read the research, theories, and discussions presented in their professional journals, such as those of the International Reading Association, the National Council of the Teachers of English, and the National Education Association affiliates (American Association of School Administrators, National Elementary School Principals Association, and so on). In a sense, these represent adult professionals talking to professionals in their own language. They say, "This is what I think" or "This is what I have found to be successful." Teachers read the article and relate it to their own situation. They may try out the suggestions, follow the guidelines set up in the article, or repeat the experiment with their own students. Thus they apply the results of their own reading to the reading program in their school setting.

COLLEGE CONTRIBUTIONS—Colleges contribute to local school programs in several ways. They offer reading courses to develop teachers' knowledge and skills in the form of specific campus courses, in-service courses, workshops, institutes, and conferences. They also provide the setting for association meetings and publishers' displays. Their professors participate in public school preschool teacher orientation, school surveys, evaluation sessions, and consultant services. Professors are consumers and practitioners of research in reading to help schools develop their reading programs— sometimes directly, sometimes indirectly.

SCHOOL STUDY COUNCILS—Many school systems belong to a regional school study council, which sponsors research and disseminates information to help them with their programs. This is usually a helpful activity because the schools focus their attention on their own program; but they receive the benefit of the work of other nearby systems and a wealth of help in personnel from schools and a university. Thus they have help in setting up an experimental design and the step-by-step follow-through to the completion and application of the study.

Community Influences. PUBLIC CRITICS—It is not unusual for a popular magazine or a newspaper to carry an article critical of the reading programs of the schools or a report of a new-found panacea for children's reading problems. School personnel have several alternatives: (1) they can lie low until the storm blows over—though this is not recommended; (2) they can provide statistics that belie the criticism; or (3) they can reexamine their program in the light of the criticism and determine how much of it is applicable or to what degree it is justified and then move to correct it. The best procedure is a constructive approach to the problem, either solution (2) or (3), coupled with the attempt to educate the community regarding the local program. If the latter is done continuously, the task is easier when criticisms do appear. If the parents are really interested, such criticisms and questions will appear frequently. Perhaps we educators need them to keep us on our toes.

OTHER COMMUNITY INFLUENCES—The program can also be influenced by other aspects of the community, such as the availability of books in paperback form in the drug stores and books from the community libraries. These can enhance the program by giving children plenty of opportunity to use their skills. The ready availability of reading matter is recognized as a very strong factor in independent reading. The school can build into its program ways to encourage outside reading—book fairs, story hours, and parental encouragement to obtain books.

Financial Support by the United States Office of Education

The United States Office of Education has recently been influential in local reading programs through its funding of projects. Some states, using these moneys, have established minigrants to school personnel for research projects. Federal grants for preschool programs, for programs for the disadvantaged, and for the purchase of materials have helped many schools strengthen their programs.

Summary—Adult Influences

When all these adult influences are brought into focus, their importance to school reading programs has been considerable, and it is expected that they will continue to upgrade teaching, add good reading materials, and strengthen overall programs. It is up to us, the professionals, to see that they remain constructive influences.

SUMMARY

Strategies that can shape the emerging effective reading programs of the future involve the cooperative efforts of teachers, reading specialists, librarians, school administrators, the colleges, and the community. Together they can explore the philosophy and objectives of a good reading program. They can examine their own responsibilities for the development of the program. Thus apathy can be overcome. All teachers from kindergarten through grade twelve will be teachers of some aspect of reading. They will be knowledgeable as to reading, methods and materials. They will have studied reading, at both undergraduate and graduate levels, viewing reading instruction as the most important contribution they can make in their teaching. Colleges will provide adequate training for prospective teachers, with several undergraduate reading courses. They will also provide advanced graduate study in reading as well as leadership for in-service programs in reading at the grass roots level. All segments of the community will be interested enough to be willing to pay for quality education, for excellent teachers, schools, libraries, and instructional materials.

SELECTED READINGS

Burg, Leslie A.; Maurice Kaufman; Blanche Korngold; and Albert Kovner. *The Complete Reading Supervisor.* Columbus, OH: Charles E. Merrill Publishing Company, 1978.

Carlson, Thorsten R., ed. *Administrators and Reading.* New York: Harcourt Brace Jovanovich, Inc., 1972.

Fay, Leo. *Organization and Administration of School Reading Programs.* Reading Research Profiles Bibliography. Newark, DE: International Reading Association, 1971.

Ford, David H., and Mildred A. Fitzgerald. *Contingency Management and Reading.* Newark, DE: International Reading Association, 1973.

Latham, William, ed. *The Road to Effective Reading,* Selected United Kingdom Reading Association papers. Newark, DE: International Reading Association, 1975.

Merritt, John, ed. *Reading and the Curriculum.* Newark, DE: International Reading Association, 1971.

Morrison, Coleman, and Mary C. Austin. *The Torchlighters Revisited.* Newark, DE: International Reading Association, 1977.

Otto, Wayne and Richard Smith. *Administering the School Reading Program.* Boston: Houghton Mifflin Company, 1970.

Chapter 10

Reading Programs: Structure

OBJECTIVES

To know the structure of beginning reading
programs

To know the scope and sequence of middle
and upper grade reading programs

To know the strengths and weaknesses of
elementary school reading programs

To know the steps necessary in changing
a system's program

To be acquainted with the sources for help
in strengthening an existing reading program

To learn the strategies for choosing the right
prescriptive program for each child

INTRODUCTION

Chapter 10 is an introduction to specific elementary reading programs. Its overall purpose is to present a brief analysis of current representative programs. A teacher does not need to be thoroughly knowledgeable about all of them. However, the teacher does need to know a few programs really well and have access to descriptive material on many programs and/or personnel such as the reading specialist, who knows all programs and their strengths, weaknesses, and appropriateness for specified children. The teacher should know the children very well: reading levels, interests, backgrounds, specific skills, status, and so on; and he or she should have a philosophy of reading instruction that would help him or her recognize the basic assumptions behind each program and thus know immediately whether its structure is appropriate to his or her philosophy of education. For example, one philosophical position would be that children must first learn the association of sound and letters, thus meaning is not important whereas another position would be that English has poor letter-sound correspondence, so that correspondence is *not* emphasized and the start should be with meaningful units.[1]

PREREADING AND EARLY READING PROGRAMS

The Montessori Method

The Montessori method for early childhood provides a prepared environment with specially constructed materials. In reading, these include a three-dimensional alphabet and sandpaper letters, which in their use emphasize the tactile approach. Mental concepts are built by constructing experiences that lead gradually from the concrete to the abstract. Disadvantaged children seem to profit especially well from the sensory stimulation afforded by their manipulation of blocks, bells, sandpaper letters, buttons and ties on clothing and by other opportunities to develop perceptual abilities. In this prepared environment teachers direct children in the correct use of didactic materials (such as color tablets, cubes, and so on). The teachers also place great emphasis on oral language experiences.

Teachers need special preparation to teach in the Montessori method. They must present the graded materials such as cubes, rods, and prisms in the correct sequence. Every experience of the child is guided by the teacher so that he or she will start with concrete objects and proceed to the development of abstract mental concepts. Nothing extraneous must be allowed to interfere with the child's directed learning. By being alert to a child's interest in exploring and experimenting, the teacher can direct his or her energies into self-creative experiences.

The Montessori method is not a new one. It was described by Maria Montessori as early as 1912, when she had applied her theories first to the education of slow-learning children in Rome and later to typical children between the ages of three and six. In a revival of her techniques, the Whitby School of Greenwich, Connecticut, became the first "pure" Montessori school in the United States. Adaptations of the method have been used recently to teach beginning reading where teachers emphasize (1) the tactile approach through the manipulation of three-dimensional letters and the tracing of sandpaper letters, and (2) the oral language approach through class discussion and oral reading to the children.[2]

---

[1] Arlene Marturano, "Commentary: A Procedure for Continuing 'The Great Debate,'" *The Reading Teacher,* 30:852–854 (**May** 1977).
[2] E. Mortimer Standing, *The Montessori Method* (Fresno, CA: Academy Library Guide, 1962).

The Language-Experience Approach

The language-experience approach to the teaching of reading emphasizes the communication skills of speaking, listening, and writing, along with reading.[3] This approach is initiated at the kindergarten levels, where children are encouraged to tell a story, which is recorded by the teacher. He or she reads the stories to the children. Children also dictate to the teacher in the first grade, where they begin to learn the symbols for sounds. Children begin independent writing in this grade and share with others what they have written.

Teachers provide many opportunities for young children to use language, as explained in the section on readiness for vocabulary development in Chapter 4. Children are encouraged to talk about anything interesting to them—what they did, what they saw, what they received, what they lost, and so on. They gain familiarity with oral language as they use it and as they listen to others. The teacher records their expressions as short sentences on the chalkboard and later on a large chart. Thus the group experience chart becomes a cooperative endeavor, with several children telling "what we saw" or "what we did" on a group trip, for example. Children "read back" their descriptions in their own words, gradually associating written symbols with their own oral language. Copying a chart story later on their own paper, they learn their next tool for communication—writing the symbol for the sound. After many such experiences associating sight with sound, children begin to read. A basic tenet of this approach is that children who can *listen* and *talk* can learn to *write* and finally to *read* what they have expressed orally. Decoding others' words in print follows in logical sequence because of the insights children have gained concerning the meaning of reading. Initial instruction in reading closely parallels their own language patterns, a natural and logical approach.

In the initial stages when children dictate their own stories, the teacher as recorder points out letters that stand for sounds, good words the children have used to express their ideas, and sentence structure. He or she helps the child note similarities in beginning and ending of some words and helps the children build a basic stock of sight vocabulary useful in their reading and writing.

Meaningful experiences with clay, paint, and other materials provide opportunities for further self-expression. As children spontaneously talk about their activities, they are encouraged to write their own stories. They write again in content areas as they record information on topics of interest, contributing to class newspapers or class books. The teacher encourages

[3] Dorris M. Lee and R. V. Allen, *Learning to Read Through Experience* (New York: Appleton-Century-Crofts, 1963).

Monitoring the lesson

self-expression and helps children as they ask for spelling, punctuation marks, and other aids to writing. Reading practice is obtained as children read their own writing, each other's, and, finally, the adult writing in published material.

Older nonreaders have been taught to read when remedial reading teachers have used the language-experience approach. Unable or unwilling to tackle typical beginning reading materials, the older child can tell of his own experiences. His words are written or typed, and he is encouraged to read them. Often he can supply seemingly unfamiliar words or phrases in such text, because they were words he himself used, his own language. Soon he has met with some frequency certain tool words such as *and, this, me, my, was, am, have*. He finds that he really knows these words in print. Now he wants to learn more words so he can read *books*. The teacher builds upon the initial success experience involved in reading his own "talk written down" by teaching him the word attack skills he will need to be a successful independent reader.

The language-experience approach has been tried with urban children whose language patterns are not typical. They exhibit brevity of speech, dialects, "street" language, and so on. Their means of communication are quite unlike the language patterns found in most books in print. When these children appear in classrooms, teachers may be at a loss when they try to find appropriate material for teaching reading and writing skills. They can initiate their instruction by encouraging these children to express themselves *in their own type of language.* Even though their words are not "Standard English," they can be praised for their own creative efforts. Thus they experience success and can advance in reading on an individual basis. With this technique they are not penalized by the stereotype of a single standard for all.

For any of these children, the strategy of the language experience approach can be followed by a plan of individualized instruction or by one of the various grouping plans. Albert J. Harris in a pilot study in New York with teachers of disadvantaged beginning readers underscored the advantages of using language-experience charts as a basis for beginning reading for the disadvantaged. Direct teaching of skills needed for independent reading can follow, as the teacher guides the disadvantaged student toward the goal of becoming an effective reading citizen.

Whereas the preceding discussion has pointed out many advantages of this type of approach to the teaching of reading, some disadvantages have been noted. One is the danger that real learning may be so incidental that there are large gaps which impede reading progress and are not detected by the teacher. Another is the danger that no effective evaluating techniques will be employed to give the teacher a continuous picture of a pupil's progress. Despite these possibilities on the part of an unskilled teacher, the language-experience approach is one of the most promising of the current reading practices for initiating reading instruction.

For beginning reading, the language must fit the children's current language and life experiences. If the primers and beginning readers that are available do not fit the children and if your school will not buy you more suitable ones, then you can do as Zina Steinberg did [4]—from short field trips use discussion, and do experience charts from the children's dictated reactions, and compile your own (the children's own) books. This could take the form of a class newspaper if so desired. The general reaction of teachers who use the language-experience approach is that they get good results. In the hands of a good teacher, this evidently is a successful way for children to approach the many-faceted reading task in school. It can be used alone at the very beginning, or it can be part of an eclectic program.

Other Instructional Media

Countless trade books, multilevel programed kits, multilevel literature programs in paperback form, programed material for various hardware or machines, films, filmstrips, varied phonic programs, and phonic adaptations such as i.t.a. and Words in Color are among the numerous instructional materials that teachers may encounter in schools today. Some purport to be

[4] Zina Steinberg, "Batman Books: Homemade First Readers," *The Reading Teacher,* **29,**7:676–82 (April, 1976).

reading programs in themselves; others are advertised to be used as supplementary to existing reading programs.

Initial Teaching Alphabet. Some children in Great Britain [5] and parts of the United States (notably Bethlehem, Pennsylvania) have been taught to read initially with the augmented Roman alphabet. Currently known as the Initial Teaching Alphabet (i.t.a.), it was designed by Sir James Pitman. His purpose was to develop an alphabet with a consistent pattern of sound-symbol relationships. He devised an alphabet of forty-four symbols, twenty-four letters of the traditional alphabet and twenty new symbols. Examples of the new letters are æ and œ for the long a and the long o sounds regardless of their spelling in any words. Thus one symbol, æ, would represent the *a* in ate and the *eigh* in eight.

Children at the beginning reading stage are taught by a look-say and phonics approach. They practice their skills in books printed with i.t.a. symbols. They write their own stories, using the new alphabet. Some schools have made available a variety of i.t.a. trade books and other reading materials in the schoolroom so that children can read widely in i.t.a. at early stages. The transition to traditional orthography (TO) is made as children encounter easy-to-read materials either in the second or third year of the program.

Advantages have been reported as early understanding of sound-symbol relationships, ease of self-expression in creative writing, and a feeling of self-confidence at an early reading stage. Disadvantages have been reported as lack of good material for children to read in i.t.a., their concurrent exposure to TO in most of their "outside" experiences, and difficulty in the transitional period as children transfer from their i.t.a. reading to the typical orthography in the regular textbooks, beyond the initial learning-to-read stage.

Words in Color. Attempts to make the reading of English words easier for beginning reading have been many. The i.t.a. system aimed for this goal by changing the spelling of words to a consistent pattern. A method of presenting words in color, or color coding, was devised by Caleb Gattegno.[6] His purpose was to present the phonetic nuances among varied spellings of a single sound, without changing the spelling of any word. In his approach he developed the printing of twenty vowel "sounds" and twenty-seven consonant "sounds" in different colors. For example, his short *o* is colored orange, the short *i* is red. When several spellings occur in regular English for a single sound, only one color is used. There are twenty-one color charts for beginning instruction. Short vowel sounds and several consonant sounds are first introduced. Children are thus taught many syllable sounds through the blending of color sounds in various combina-

[5] John Downing, *Initial Teaching Alphabet* (New York: Macmillan Publishing Co., Inc., 1964).

[6] Caleb Gattegno, *Words in Color* (Chicago: Learning Materials, Inc., 1962).

tions, called *visual dictation.* When such combinations produce a sound recognized as part of a real English word, children "discover" words. Later sentences and paragraphs are introduced. The technique used in the Words in Color approach emphasizes the sound-sign relationship as children form mental images through the use of color. For children who are color-blind, this approach can *not* be successful.

Linguistic Concepts

Linguists have made a significant contribution to the field of reading. They have also created some confusion in reading instruction. Because linguistics is the scientific study of the origin and structure of language, it seems natural that some linguists would become interested in the relationships between their field and reading.

Leonard Bloomfield and Clarence Barnhart [7] developed a beginning reading program that stressed learning to recognize word families, or regularly spelled words, that is, *fat, sat, cat, mat,* and so on. Fries [8] took a similar position, emphasizing the sound-symbol correspondence and leaving meaning to later development.

Since those early attempts, there have been many changes in reading programs and the influence of linguists and psycholinguists on those programs. Ronald Wardhaugh, Carl LeFevre, Kenneth Goodman, and Robert Ruddell [9] are some of the linguists who have spoken out and written about the incorrectness of those early linguistic attempts to teach reading. As teachers become more knowledgeable in linguistics, they are adapting programs and developing new programs, using the principles discovered and promoted by the linguists. The latter have become interested in the problems of children from another language background or a different dialect in learning to read in standard English. Thus we have the child's psycholinguistics and sociolinguistics influencing reading materials and instruction. Some linguistic reading series currently being used in our schools are

> *The Merrill Linguistic Readers*—Smith, et al.
> *The Sounds and Letters Series*—Hall
> *The Miami Linguistic Readers*
> *The Structural Reading Series*—Stern

[7] Leonard Bloomfield and Clarence Barnhart, *Let's Read: A Linguistic Approach* (Detroit: Wayne State University Press, 1961).
[8] Charles Fries. *Linguistics and Reading* (New York: Holt, Rinehart and Winston, 1963).
[9] Ronald Wardhaugh, *Reading, a Linguistic Perspective* (New York: Harcourt Brace Jovanovich, 1969); Carl LeFevre, *Linguistics and the Teaching of Reading* (New York: McGraw-Hill Book Company, 1964); Kenneth Goodman, "A Linguistic Study of Cues and Miscues in Reading," *Elementary English,* 42:639–42 (Oct. 1965); Robert Ruddell, *Reading-Language Instruction: Innovative Practices* (Englewood Cliffs, NJ: Prentice-Hall, Inc., 1974).

Gibson and Levin [10] call attention to some important linguistic parallels between hearing-speaking and reading-writing. They then go on to discuss the research that has developed linguistic concepts and, in later chapters, relate them to reading instruction with a couple of illustrative new programs that were developed solely from those concepts. It behooves every teacher to become familiar with the linguists' phonology, morphology, syntax, grammar, and suprasegmental features applications to reading.

Individualized Reading

Effective reading instruction has been initiated in some classes with the development of the individualized approach. Because individuals do vary in many ways from each other, grouping them may not be to the best advantage of everyone in a particular section. An individual's interests and level of reading achievement may be useful determinants for his reading material—a book of his own selection that he can read at his own pace. Not limited by group standards or frustrated by peer competition, the individual may progress as his own growth pattern permits.

Each child who takes part in this program has a session each day when he reads part of a book he or she has selected because of its special interest to him. While the child and others are reading, the teacher has an individual conference with one of the other children. The teacher listens to the pupil as he reads some of the book. The teacher asks questions and helps with any problems the student has, such as unlocking new words. The teacher also keeps records of the student's status. If several children need help on a reading skill, such as beginning consonants, the teacher organizes them into a temporary group for instruction in this skill. The teacher is limited by time as to how many children will be met in individual conference. The children have other meaningful tasks to perform when they finish their silent independent reading, such as writing a report of their reading, preparing a dramatization, finding material for a content-area project, using the dictionary or reference books, and so on.

The teacher organizes for individualized reading instruction by

1. Assessing the individual's reading levels—instructional, independent, and capacity.
2. Ascertaining interests by taking an interest inventory (see Chapter 8).
3. Gathering a large selection of reading materials appropriate for the range of reading abilities and interests thus assessed.
4. Preparing suitable skill-building materials for independent use.

[10] Eleanor Gibson and Harry Levin, *The Psychology of Reading* (Cambridge, MA: The M.I.T. Press, 1975), p. 88.

5. Preparing library tables and work centers with records, films, and filmstrips.
6. Allotting time for individual conferences.
7. Planning small-group skills lessons as needed.
8. Planning time for the sharing of books read, information gleaned, and so on.
9. Keeping records of individual achievement, activities, and progress.
10. Personally reading as many of the children's books as time permits.

The students' role in individualized reading programs may be summarized: They must be self-motivated to select and read available books. They must be able to unlock unfamiliar words. They must be able to follow the author's pattern of thought. They must be able to work independently on other tasks while the teacher holds individual conferences with other children.

Several advantages have been noted. Children may encounter a wide variety of reading material. Children's interests may be stimulated to *more* reading and a continuing interest in reading in the future. Children may read independently, not waiting for others in a group and not bored by others' errors. Individual children may progress at their own rate under expert teacher-guidance. Children's self-confidence and interest in reading is often increased.

There are some problems with individualized reading that beginning teachers and even some experienced teachers face. Building an adequate available supply of reading sources—basals, trade books, newspapers, magazines, paperbacks—at the range of readability levels necessary for a total class can be difficult. A primary class needs one hundred to two hundred sources for a year, and the middle grades need four hundred to five hundred per class. The grade level books are often easier to get than the adequate supply for the best and poorest readers. In some schools this is accomplished by exchange of a portion of the sources at midyear. This exchange requires some record keeping and planning of lessons for the new sources—though some teachers have worked out a system of exchange of teaching plans with the exchange of the sources—thought questions on the material, skills items checklist, and skills development exercises.

A second problem can be the management techniques to arrange appropriate time for individual conferences, small flexible shifting skill and/or special interest groups, teacher's record keeping (there is no more obvious need for *continuous* evaluation) of a skills checklist, entire group sessions, and so on. One simple answer to this problem is to build a plan of scheduling over a greater period of time. The teacher does not have to have a conference with every child every day. Instead of daily plans, construct the plan over a week or even ten days if necessary. This usually eases the harried feeling of the teacher. The child does better, and the teacher feels better if the program has an air of leisurely industriousness.

A third problem arises where the teacher loses sight of one of the purposes of the program—to motivate and build initiative, persistence, and independence. The child should gradually take over the responsibility for selection, pacing, self-evaluating, scheduling extra help, time to share with others, and helping others (peers). When the child does these, the teacher is succeeding in the supervision of learning. Individualized reading is a really great vehicle for this independent learning.

A fourth and probably basic problem may be the correct timing for the introduction and the speed of introducing individualized reading. Some children should be introduced to it by the end of first grade. Others have not developed a sight vocabulary and maturity to work independently until late second or early third grade. Some children must move toward individualized reading slowly to build confidence and self-concept as they go along.

Now for a look at the overall picture. Teachers who have never taught the individualized reading approach need some training and preparation for it. When it is handled skillfully, materials are sufficient, children are ready, and the administration supports it, the individualized reading approach is an excellent one.

Basal Readers

From the time of the introduction of the McGuffey Readers in 1840 to the present, the most common reading program has been the basal series. A quick survey of the teachers in the immediate area of your authors indicates that the basal reader series is still the most frequently used. It may not be *the* basic program; it may be used in conjunction with another approach. As stated before, programs seem to be eclectic in an increasing number of school systems.

The basal reading program usually consists of a preprimer (pronounced prē-prĭm-er), a primer, and from one to three other books for each grade level. The books are supposed to be in ascending order of difficulty from front-to-back and from book-to-book. In general, this is true, although there do seem to be exceptions, due in part probably to the readability measure utilized and the particular areas of weakness of and strengths of the reader (child). Most basal series also have accompanying workbooks that serve to give the child additional application of the skills encountered in the basal book. The basals invariably have a teacher's manual suggesting teaching procedure, a variety of questions, and activities to accompany the stories in the book. A fairly recent development is the inclusion of criterion-referenced tests to accompany each unit. The publishing company provides a chart showing the scope of the program level-by-level and the sequence of introduction of new learnings. A careful study of the chart indicates where in the program a particular phoneme is presented and what preceded and what follows it, where getting the main idea of a paragraph is introduced and where the concept of summarizing dispersed ideas is presented. The chart is sort of a bird's-eye view of the total program.

The best way for the student of methodology to learn about basal programs is to (1) study the publisher's flowchart of the program, (2) go to the curriculum library and read the basal series with the flowchart in front of him or her, and (3) observe at several different levels the basal reader instruction in the classroom. When the reading committee is considering the use of a basal series in their school system, the members should also ask the company representative to set a demonstration of the basal by one of the company's teachers, go and observe the program in action in nearby school(s), and get the manuals and any technical reports (from the publisher) and study them in comparison to the strengths and weaknesses of their own students' achievement records. In other words, the committee should be trying on the basal program for fit of their *own* students. Most publishers will run a training program for teachers where the basal program is going to be introduced to their school system.

There is great variation among basal programs in their philosophies as represented by order of presentation of consonants, glides, vowels, linguistic emphasis on regular words, sight words, phonic emphasis (separately or within the framework of the stories), the steepness of the introduction of new words, and the frequency of repetition of words. In their attempt to cover the complete range of skill development, motivation, interests, habits, and attitudes, most basal series utilize a vocabulary control process in the beginning books and move to very extensive vocabulary in the upper grade books. In teaching the lesson, the teacher consults the manual and determines groups of appropriate size for that lesson. Then (1) the children are prepared for the lesson by introducing discussion of the main idea and introduction of new words; (2) the directed reading lesson goes through the stages of a planned presentation (objectives, preparation, silent reading, questions, answers and oral reading of specific justification for answers, discussion, follow-up activity, evaluation); (3) periodic review of concepts, words, and specific skills may be necessary; (4) periodic or criterion testing to determine progress and retention may be necessary; (5) application of skills to other settings (workbook, social studies, science, free reading, and so on) may also be necessary.

One obvious advantage of the basal program is that it is easy for teachers to relate parents to the program. Most parents had a basal reader introduction themselves. The book, if taken home for reading, is something tangible the parents identify with. They can hear the children read aloud to them and can get a pretty accurate understanding of how well the child reads in *that* book. Parents can be helpful in the child's reading development; some have to be told to decrease pressure on the child. Some publishers have cassettes or mimeomasters that can provide parents with material to help the child. If the teacher knows the parents through parent-teacher conferences, it is easy to judge what reliance should be placed on the parent for help and home supervision of study.

Children should be allowed to move through basal levels at their own rate. This means that grouping for instruction must be extremely flexible— even allowing at times for a group of two—or even a single reader for certain reading experiences. Enrichment is usually preferred to acceleration, but there are times when the latter is needed to challenge the really gifted reader to maintain his or her interest in learning.

Basal series reflect the concerns of educators and change according to the authors' perception of the unmet needs. The *Bank Street Readers* series was published by Macmillan to meet a multiethnic concern, as was Webster's *Skyline Series*. Scott Foresman published *Reading Systems,* with shorter units and more linguistically oriented stories. The *Chicago Dialect Readers* [11] series has two books, one in dialect and a comparable one in standard English. The newer the basal series edition, the more consciously it reflects ethnic influences, linguistic influences, and television influences in word recognition. Some programs have been introduced only to provide the foundation for later reading instruction: Phonovisual Method, i.t.a., Lets' Read, Palo Alto Program, Distar, Words in Color. Current basals seem to be returning to their traditional format with high interest, varied cultural stories; this is more or less in line with the movement popularly called "Back to Basics."

PROGRAMED AND SYSTEMS APPROACHES

Introduction

Until the 1960s the major media of instruction in the schools were the book, the workbook, the chalkboard, the film, and various classroom materials such as games, cards, and numerous teacher-made devices. During the 1960s a great deal of experimentation has taken place with a variety of audiovisual materials, with teaching machines, with the various aspects of programed learning. The impetus for this experimentation has come from a number of sources: (1) funds from the federal government; (2) funds from state governments; (3) funds from foundations; and (4) aid, ma-

[11] *Dialect Readers,* A Psycholinguistic Reading Series (Chicago: Board of Education).

terials, and encouragement from publishers and industry. One other factor has made possible the research and experimentation in the public schools —the growth of school systems to meet an expanding population has created the settings in newly built schools for different organizational patterns wherein new instructional media may be tried.

Previous chapters have cited illustrations and described the standard media of instruction. No discussion of the teaching of reading would be complete without the inclusion of teaching machines and programed learning, for these are among the newer media being tried in the classroom with children of different abilities, at different levels of learning, and with different specific needs in the learning process. If the machine and programed materials can help the teacher individualize instruction, then we are justified in examining the potentialities of these media rather closely.

Description of Programed Materials

Programed instruction is a kind of learning experience in which a program takes the role of the teacher or tutor for the students and leads them through a set of specifically designed and sequenced behaviors so that they learn that which the program is designed to teach. The program is the important thing, whether it is housed in a machine, a book, or a workbook. It is characterized by

1. A series of small, sequential steps or frames.
2. A student response to each step—writing a word, placing a check mark, pushing a button, turning to a specific page.
3. Immediate knowledge of the correctness of the response—feedback.
4. Self-pacing by the student.
5. Results recorded for evaluation by the teacher—a permanent record of the student's behavior performance.
6. A thoroughly tested program through successive tryouts with students of a given ability level and beginning knowledges and skills, with this information made available to the teacher who may be selecting it for a given student.

The process through which the student goes is read-write-check-advance. This constructed response is linear programing where each item requires an overt response, which the student checks and then moves on to the next item.

Branching is an intrinsic programing where, if the student misses the test question, he branches to review the section and his error is explained to him, then he continues. In a scrambled test, the student is told to turn to a certain page to continue.

Computer-assisted instruction (CAI) is being tried in a number of school systems. A student sits at a console or station and may receive audio information through earphones or a speaker and visual information through a television screen. He or she may respond through a typewriter keyboard or by touching a light pen to a cathode ray tube or by pushing the appropriate button or by standard writing. The console is connected by telephone line to a central computer, from which the programed material emanates. Programs for CAI are of three types or systems: (1) individualized drill and practice, (2) tutorial, and (3) dialogue systems. The first one is self-explanatory and has been quite successful in practice. The second, tutorial, is a deeper level of interaction between student and computer for presenting a concept and skill in its use. When the student displays a mastery through practice exercises he moves on to the next concept. The third type, dialogue systems, has yet to be successfully developed because of the technical problems encountered, such as the computer's recognizing the spoken speech of the young child. Parts of language arts and reading programs have been tried mainly in the first two systems. A large, centrally located computer could be the source of a number of programs of different levels and multiple classrooms of a school system simultaneously. In the experimentation to date, the student makes selective use of CAI as a small portion of the daily program. CAI meets all six criteria of a program listed at the beginning of this section.

Gibson and Levin [12] have reviewed the Stanford Computer Assisted Instructional Reading Program. It uses the branching technique when the student makes an error. In this program the child is at the computer for about twelve minutes per day; an adult is present to help where needed. On the *Stanford Achievement Test* and the *California Cooperative Primary Test* and the *CAI Reading Project Test,* the CAI students were definitely superior in nearly every subtest to the control students. "The computer-instructed children averaged from .4 to .7 years superiority in grade placement after only 5½ months of CAI." [13] The program uses the syllable as the basic instructional unit. Orthographic patterns are presented; but Gibson and Levin question this learning technique's value for inducing children optimally to learn the rule-governed structure of English orthography.

Effective Use of Programs and Machines in Learning

In the allocation of the student's portion of classroom time to programed learning, several important factors must be considered. In regular classroom instruction, the teacher does the programing and instruction together. When programed materials are used, the teacher selects the right program for the right student, and the teacher's role changes to that of adviser, guide, and motivator. This assumes that the programed material is supplementing

[12] Gibson and Levin, op. cit., pp. 316–22.
[13] Ibid., p. 321.

classroom instruction with the aids that will help the student most and that such material is integrated with the total curriculum. The teacher would naturally have to try the program with some students before adopting it as a regular supplementary tool. Thus a single preparation of a lesson (program), based on (1) sound techniques of programing, (2) knowledge of subject matter and how children learn it, and (3) knowledge of problem areas, may save valuable time for both the teacher and the student. The change of pace, the individualized pacing, and the immediate knowledge of results provide valuable psychological stimulation to students for their learning. Also, the teacher is freed to work predominantly with other students.

Programed Learning Materials in Reading

The very best way for the teacher to become familiar with available programed materials is to get them and work through the program just as the student would do. Because available programs are constantly changing, representative samples are mentioned here as a beginning or starting point for the teacher.

FOR BASIC SKILLS

Lessons for Self-Instruction in Basic Skills. California Test Bureau, Monterey, CA. Sections include vocabulary, following directions, reference skills, interpretation—grades 3–9.

FOR DICTIONARY SKILLS

David Discovers the Dictionary. Coronet Instructional Films, Chicago. A programed text for grade 4.
How to Use the Dictionary. Macmillan Publishing Co., Inc. New York. For the intermediate grades.

FOR SPELLING

Goals in Spelling, McGraw-Hill Text Film Department, New York. For grades 2–5.

FOR PHONICS, VOCABULARY SKILLS

Beginning Sight Vocabulary. E-Z Sort Systems, San Francisco. For primary grades; requires teaching machine.
Basal Progressive Choice Reading Program. Institute of Educational Research, Washington, DC. Contains sections of letter forms, sounds, and words; for primary grades.
Phonetic Analysis and Structural Analysis. Center for Programed Instruction, New York. For primary grades and remedial work.

Spectrum of Skills. Macmillan Publishing Co., Inc. New York. For vocabulary and word attack skills; intermediate grades.

Synonyms, Antonyms, Homonyns. Learning, Inc., Tempe, AZ. For intermediate grades.

Vocabulary Building I. Cenco Center, Chicago. For elementary school; requires a machine.

FOR AN ELEMENTARY READING PROGRAM

Programed Reading. Cynthia Buchanan and Sullivan Associates, Webster-McGraw-Hill Company, St. Louis. For beginning reading through Book 2. Includes sight vocabulary, word attack, comprehension, linguistically oriented programed text, and workbooks.

FOR OTHER PURPOSES

There are numerous programed materials for tachistoscopes, pacers, and controlled readers for speeding up the use of reading skills once they have been learned.

Multilevel and multimedia materials to individualize instruction include *Tachisto-Filmstrips,* Learning Through Seeing, Inc. Sunland, CA; *Language Master,* Bell and Howell Company, Chicago; and *Listen and Think Program,* Educational Development Laboratories, Huntington, NY.

Computer Assisted Instruction (CAI). Stanford University, and others. New York City Center, 229 E. 42 Street, New York. (A million dollars worth of advanced electronic equipment; can handle 192 children simultaneously. Visitors may participate for the experience.)

Automata 450. Automata Corporation of Richland, WA. A scoring system for inventory evaluation of up-to-300-pupil school, every day if desired. Teacher can build personal profile of students.

Programed Word Attack for Teachers, Robert Wilson and Maryanne Hall. Charles E. Merrill Books, Inc., Columbus, OH.

Fountain Valley Teacher Support System for grades 1–6. Tests are included for mastery of skills and needs are indicated from these results; list of basal and supplementary materials is recommended. Richard Zweig Associates.

Prescriptive Reading Inventory for grades 1–6. Color-coded tests are computer-scored by the company, and the profile of results is returned to the school. Program Reference Guides list the textbooks and other instructional sources to use for each area of the tests. The skills cover the objectives obtained from a survey of basal reader programs. CTB/McGraw-Hill, Monterey, CA 93940.

Wisconsin Design for Reading Skill, Kindergarten through six. Identifies reading objectives and skills; provides tests, analysis, and teacher guides to sources for instruction and techniques. Interpretive Scoring Systems.

Research studies have produced a number of generalizations that would regulate the use of materials such as those previously listed. The most striking one is the "Ruleg *vs* Egrule," [14] where the *rule* plus the *e.g.* (for example) is a deductive process, and the *Egrule* is the inductive process. Which one is used in developing the programed lesson is dependent upon the target population. If the program is to be an easy one, it should be *Ruleg*. The *Egrule* approach is more difficult.

Another result of research studies is that some areas of reading are much more amenable to programing than others, and these areas might, therefore, be the ones where programing would form the best supplement to the classroom reading program. Word-attack skills fall in this category.

One final interpretation of recent research is that no one single approach to reading instruction is definitely superior to all others. Up to the present time, programed reading fits this interpretation. Consequently, it is necessary for each instructor to determine the appropriate role programed reading might play in the classroom.

Implications of Programed Reading

The proponents of programed materials have some very good supporting arguments, such as (1) the lessons of master teachers and plans can be available to anyone, anywhere; (2) each student can learn at his or her own pace; (3) reinforcement and feedback are available at every step of the learning process; (4) the classroom teacher would be free of drill work and correcting it so that he or she could devote this time to other aspects of the curriculum and to individuals; (5) a continuous, cumulative evaluation of the student's progress is instantly available; (6) the student has an individual tutor; (7) material is presented to the student in a logical, organized sequence; and (8) Crowder-type (branching) programs adjust to the individual in learning sequence, depth and mode of material, and rate of progress. Bruner [15] states that it is not likely that machines will have the effect of dehumanizing learning any more than books do, for a program can be as personal as a book, laced with humor or grimly dull; it can be either a playful activity or tediously like a close-order drill.

There are some deficiencies in programed materials: (1) students are not encouraged to invent questions as well as answer them; (2) they do not receive the guidance and example of the teacher (human) except incidentally; (3) conversation among group members is not encouraged; (4) not all programs fit all machines; (5) dramatization could not be

[14] William Clark Trow, *Teacher and Technology, New Designs for Learning* (New York: Appleton-Century-Crofts, 1963), pp. 110–11.
[15] Jerome S. Bruner, *The Process of Education* (Cambridge, MA: Harvard University Press, 1960), p. 84.

spontaneous in working with a program and a machine; (6) programs are written by adults and have to be tried and rewritten (essentially by the students in their trial runs); (7) programs and machines are expensive (but if used appropriately and sufficiently, they would become very inexpensive comparatively); (8) these are partial, supplemental, supportive materials, and should not be considered comprehensive reading programs.

As the pros and cons are examined, it appears that the overall picture is favorable. When programed materials are compared with lectures, large-group teaching, traditional workbooks, unadjustable (to fit the students) textbooks, errors that go undetected, the passive participation of children in groups, and the inflexible rates in television and films-programed material, programed material seems to be a boon to educational instruction. Then, by comparison with the impatient teacher who abhors drill or the inflexible teacher or the poorly informed teacher who does not adjust the classroom program to the abilities of the individuals, programed reading is pedagogically much more sound. Two big questions have not as yet been answered: (1) Will teachers adopt or adapt programed instruction? (2) Will technologists and educators work together to develop the educational use of computers, other electronic devices, and programed materials?

These questions deserve our careful and full attention. Good strong programs must be developed; many are in process right now. Costs must be brought down to the level where all school systems can easily afford them. We must reiterate—small-scale experimentation should precede the fitting of any program into the curriculum of the school. Any programed material, large or small, must fit its target population.

SUMMARY

One aspect of many of the aforementioned programs that stands out as they are studied is that the chief and, in some cases, *only* major objective is the development of *skills*. Many are labeled—skill-development program. They emphasize the outcome that the child, upon completing the program, *can* read. Actually, that is one step in the educational process, but it is far short of our educational goals. The real goal is that the child *does* read, that the teen-ager *does* read, that the adult *does* read. For pleasure, for personal business, interests, professional business, as a leisure-time activity (habit), these are purposes of readers who have learned the full richness of reading. This being true, the teacher must be responsible for building the will to read, now and continuing. If the adopted program is narrow, the teacher must broaden it through opportunities for literature, writing, application to content area subjects, exploration of total environment, and contact with experts who excel at their craft.[16] If reading were only a subject taught in school, then when school is over, reading is recessed, too. As previously stated, some programs are designed to build the bridge between learning skills and habitually practicing and improving performance. It is up to the classroom teacher to broaden those programs or go beyond those programs that only do part of the job.

SELECTED READINGS

Aukerman, Robert C. *Approaches To Beginning Reading.* New York: John Wiley & Sons, Inc., 1971.

Calfee, R. C. *Diagnostic Evaluation of Visual, Auditory and General Language Factors in Pre-Readers.* Paper presented at American Psychological Association, Honolulu, 1972.

Chomsky, Noam. "Phonology and Reading." *Basic Studies on Reading.* Ed. H. Levin and J. P. Williams. New York: Basic Books, Inc., Publishers, 1970, pp. 1–18.

DeStefano, J. S. "Social Variation in Language: Implications for Teaching Reading to Black Ghetto Children." *Better Reading in Urban Schools.* Ed. J. A. Figurel. Newark, DE: International Reading Association, 1972, pp. 18–24.

EPIE Materials Report: Numbers 82M and 83M EPIE Institute, 475 Riverside Drive, New York, NY 10027.

Gibson, Eleanor J., and Harry Levin. *The Psychology of Reading.* Cambridge, MA: The M.I.T. Press, 1975.

Goodman, Yetta M., and Kenneth S. Goodman. *Linguistics, Psycholinguistics, and the Teaching of Reading.* Newark, DE: International Reading Association, 1971. Annotated Bibliography.

Hafner, Lawrence E., and Hayden B. Jolly. *Patterns of Teaching Reading in the Elementary School.* New York: Macmillan Publishing Co., Inc., 1972.

Hunt, Lyman C. *The Individualized Reading Program: A Guide for Classroom Teaching.* Vol. 11, Part 3. Proceedings of the Eleventh Annual Convention International Reading Association. Newark, DE: International Reading Association, 1967.

Ruddell, Robert B. *Reading-Language Instruction: Innovative Practices.* Englewood Cliffs, NJ: Prentice-Hall, Inc., 1974.

Sartain, Harry W. *Individualized Reading.* Newark, DE: International Reading Association, 1970. Annotated Bibliography of program descriptions booklists, research, and experimental studies.

Smith, James A. *Creative Teaching of Reading in the Elementary School,* 2d ed. Boston: Allyn and Bacon, Inc., 1976.

[16] Edith Billig, "Children's Literature as a Springboard to Content Areas," *The Reading Teacher,* 30:855–59 (May 1977).

Venezky, Richard L. *The Structure of English Orthography.* The Hague: Mouton, 1970.

———. "Regularity in Reading and Spelling." *Basic Studies on Reading.* Ed. H. Levin and J. Williams. New York: Basic Books, Inc., Publishers, 1970, pp. 30–42.

Wilson, Richard, and Helen James. *Individualized Reading: A Practical Approach.* Dubuque, IA: Kendall-Hunt Publishing Company, 1972.

Chapter 11

Sources of Reading Materials

OBJECTIVES

To become familiar with the range of
materials of instruction currently available

To become familiar with the use of varied
instructional materials

To understand how the provision of
carefully chosen materials may help instill in
children effective reading habits that persist
into adulthood

INTRODUCTION

The concept of reading as a functional tool for many purposes will be found deeply ingrained in the philosophy and objectives of the forward-looking school. Teachers with this concept view reading instruction in its proper perspective. At any step, from early primary level through the secondary school, a teacher may ask himself or herself such questions as *"When* and *why* do children really read?" and *"What* do children read?" In the answers to these questions are found teachers' purposes for teaching reading. Children read when they discover that they *can* read, that reading is fun, that they can find answers to their own questions, that they can satisfy their curiosity about many things, and that they can enjoy many varied experiences vicariously through reading. Children who can read will be found at any age perusing written material in their environment—box tops, television by-lines, road signs, billboards, picture captions, newspaper headlines and articles, comics, magazines, trade books, games, directions for assembling toys and games, as well as the various textbooks, workbooks, and other study materials in their classrooms.

Because children's abilities, interests, and achievement levels differ, the quantity and quality of their reading will also differ. Some children have learned how to read before they come to school. Others on entering school are not even aware of letter combinations as words that convey meaning. In the upper grades some pupils read prodigiously, exhausting every source in their zeal to satisfy their curiosity on a topic of interest. At the other extreme are the children who have never displayed any independence in finding answers in print; they are either indifferent or poor readers. Certain children at any age do a surface type of reading. They see reading in black and white rather than in technicolor. They do not make association between real life and an author's words in print.

The classroom teacher is challenged daily to meet the reading needs of the child who is progressing normally and also to meet the very different needs of some of the children who are like those previously mentioned. Motivating every pupil to be one who reads is the most important task the teachers of reading face. They help children become good readers by guiding their reading skills development. They help improve the quality of children's reading performance when they provide appropriate, stimulating reading material for all areas of the curriculum. They help improve the quantity of reading as they motivate children to read for many purposes both in and out of school. Thus they guide the learner to be a good reader who, in the final analysis, has become a good reader because he or she has done a great deal of reading!

The most effective teacher at any level will be providing reading instruction at the point needed by each pupil in his or her sequential development. This instruction will be of greatest consequence when it helps the pupils read not only their basal reader but also any of the other reading material they may encounter daily. Therefore, it is important for the teacher to be very well acquainted with the varied sources of reading matter appropriate for each age level, as well as the skills necessary for effective comprehension in each type of material.

It is possible for a teacher to become "a 1980 teacher" or for a classroom to become "a 1980 classroom," simply because the teacher after graduation no longer investigated new instructional material, and/or the classroom retained materials purchased at some previous date, with nothing new added thereafter. How can a new teacher make certain that his or her classroom materials are both effective and up-to-date, reflecting the "tried and true" as well as current research-oriented concepts? Publishers continue to advertise new products in professional journals such as *The Reading Teacher, The Journal of Reading, Language Arts,* and *The Instructor,* to name a few that may be in the school's professional library or available through the teacher's subscription. *The Reading Teacher,* in its issues for February in 1975, 1976, 1977, and 1978, has supplied its readers with sources of such types of currently published reading materials as basal and supplementary readers, audio and visual aids, boxed materials, as well as teaching machines and devices.[1] The articles provide information concerning the reading difficulty, reading interest, and the skills developed; but they do not provide an evaluation of the materials. Such evaluation must be made by the educator as user, who must first consider the needs of specific pupils as well as the purposes suggested for the product. He or she may then suggest that a sample of the product be purchased in order to (1) learn whether or not the product fulfills its stated purpose, (2) decide which children would benefit from its use, and (3) determine whether its best use would be as basal or supplementary to the existing reading program.

TYPES OF MATERIALS

The well-equipped classroom will have an adequate supply of basal readers, supplementary readers, workbooks, dictionaries, reference materials, children's magazines and newspapers, content area textbooks and supplementary reading aids, trade books (library books), charts, graphs, maps, films, filmstrips, multilevel kits of reading and study aids, various programed materials, and teacher-made materials. Some of these materials will be used in instructional groups, others as supplementary material to be read independently, and still others for browsing. The classroom that is organized for individualized reading will need all of these varied materials with a special emphasis on the acquisition of a wide supply of multilevel trade books and supplementary reading materials.

In their daily planning for each pupil's continuous development, teachers ask themselves a basic question, "What can I do for Tom now?" Armed with an up-to-date appraisal of Tom's achievement level and needs, his teacher is ready to select some materials that will introduce a new skill, reinforce skills already initiated, provide wide reading practice, and/or motivate Tom to do further reading on his own.

The materials to be examined for such fundamental purposes may be categorized in three broad types: (1) *basal*—readers, accompanying workbooks, content area textbooks, and workbooks; (2) *supplementary*—readers, workbooks, multilevel kits, games, reference and supplementary materials in content areas, films, filmstrips, and programed materials; and (3) *literature*—trade books, magazines, newspapers.

---

[1] "New Materials on the Market," *The Reading Teacher,* 28,5:478–487 (1975); 29,5:474–485 (1976); 30,5:518–535 (1977); and 31,5:532–550 (1978).

Silent reading for information

Basal Materials

Basal Readers. Basal reading series represent a comprehensive program for developing children's reading skills in a sequential pattern. Typically, their content has been geared to current knowledge of the nature of the interests and abilities of the child at various stages of development. Special exercises that give children extra practice in new skills are usually included in the workbooks accompanying each level of reader in a series. Teachers' manuals provide lesson plans that suggest readiness exercises, directions for the teacher to build vocabulary knowledge and heighten comprehension, and further activities for practice, extension, and enrichment. There are usually one or more textbooks at each level, thus providing a careful gradation in difficulty of vocabulary, sentence structure, and concept formation.

The psychological principle of proceeding from the known or familiar to the unknown or more abstract has been incorporated as a basic feature in many of the series published to date. Thus, in the preprimers, primers, and early primary readers, children find stories about other children, pets, family members, home life, and community helpers and resources before they encounter in print the more difficult time and space concepts of history and science. Some basal series differ from this traditional pattern by introducing multiethnic or urban characters and situations rather than those of suburbia. Others differ in format, style, or approach to instruction. Schools can obtain series that have been published with no pictures, with color coding of words in chart form, with a new orthography, with an emphasis on the sounds of words, or with an emphasis on a linguistic approach. Some series have been put on the market frankly to be cobasal or supplementary to another publisher's basal series.

Above the primary grades the books in many of the basal series have been written with an attempt to provide for more varied types of reading practice. They often include units on biography, history, science, folklore, poetry, and so on. Mainly, however, they provide more experience in literature-type reading, rather than emphasizing the reading skills required in content fields of the curriculum.

Textbooks in Content Areas

Content area textbooks and workbooks, such as series in social studies, science, health, and so on, are usually designated by grade level. The older series, still to be found in many schools, bore the publisher's gradation, which often did not fit the reading levels of many of the children in the classroom. More recently, content area series have been more carefully graded in terms of vocabulary and concept introduction, sentence length, and style of writing. In their selection of basic content textbooks, teachers need to consider the reading levels of the children, in order to provide them with books they will be able to handle. Certainly, when the teacher is guiding the lesson step-by-step, the content textbook can be at the student's instructional level. For reading level definitions see Chapter 13. When the pupil's assignment is to read in the textbook at home or on his own in school, the textbook will need to be chosen at the student's independent reading level. Each content area, however, presents some difficulty for the reader because of new vocabulary terms, the author's form of presentation, the reader's background for the subject, and so on. Guiding the pupil in his or her reading of textbooks requires on the part of the teacher a good grasp of the reading skills involved. (See content areas in Chapter 6.) The fact that Tom's reading score on a standardized test is above third grade will not guarantee his efficient reading of a map or graph in the fourth grade social studies book if he has not been taught how to read either one.

The basic textbooks and workbooks in reading and the content fields provide the classroom material that will help the individual learn new skills and practice those already learned. With the teacher's guidance, they may also motivate the pupil to do further reading on his own because of some interesting content he encountered.

Teachers' Manuals

Manuals provide some insurance that children will receive a balanced program of reading instruction, that a sequential pattern will be developed for the acquisition of skills such as concept development, vocabulary building, reading comprehension, critical reading, literature appreciation, and so on. Teachers find that the next lesson in a sequence has already been analyzed for its new vocabulary, the need to use structural or phonetic analysis for word recognition, and the possibilities of building interpretation skills. Questions have been raised to motivate the pupil to read and to sharpen his comprehension. Techniques for appraising his or her progress have been detailed. Further reading in supplementary material has been outlined; reinforcing practice in workbook pages or in material suggested for teacher preparation has been carefully presented.

Effective Use. To the extent that the teacher suits the plans in the manual to the needs of groups and individuals in the classroom, the manual can be a valuable tool. As new teachers gain experience in developing lesson plans similar to those for the daily lesson suggested in the reading manuals, they are preparing themselves for the task of making good *reading* lesson plans in the content areas, the segments of the curriculum where such plans are frequently missing. The habit of presenting new vocabulary for class discussion, of raising questions to direct the reader's attention, and of motivating the reader to further learning in content areas—all should be part of every teacher's repertoire of techniques to ensure adequate reading comprehension in content fields.

Misuse. Occasionally, experienced teachers have become slaves to habit. They have used the manual so compulsively that it becomes the tail wagging the dog. Their own creativity and that of the children are overlooked in their dependence upon a tool that for them has become a crutch. At best, the manual has been designed to suggest a variety of activities that will be needed by some of the children, yet seldom by all of the children who study the textbook.

Sometimes teachers consistently skip or ignore one or more of the practice exercises suggested in the manual, either because they fail to understand the rationale for the use of that type of practice, or because they lack personal (adult) interest or enthusiasm for an exercise. Thus they may never give their pupils practice lessons in which they use context clues to meaning, or they may not bother to provide time for the informal class discussion suggested as preparation for certain lessons. This does not mean that when a child knows some concept or can perform a skill, the teacher must teach it anyway because it is in the manual.

TEXTBOOK SELECTION

There are numerous basal series in reading and in content areas available from various publishing companies. Publishers spend large sums to assure

Figure 12. Checklist for a Basal Reading Series

SERIES_____: ____GOOD ____FAIR ____INADEQUATE

Content

  Appropriate to age
  Interesting to children
  Relevant
  Varied
  Lacking bias
    Ethnic
    Racial
    Sex stereotypes
    Urban-suburban
    Other

Program of Skills

  Readiness
  Vocabulary
    Word recognition
    Word meaning
    Word analysis
  Comprehension skills
  Work-study skills

Special Approaches

  Analytic/synthetic
  Linguistic
  Phonic-linguistic
  New orthography
  Other

Readability

  Appropriate to levels of
    reading achievement

Authorship

  Expertise in reading

Manuals

  Detailed lesson plans
  Motivational suggestions
  Provisions for reinforcement
  Record-keeping aids

Workbooks

  Attractive
  Worthwhile activities
  Independent reading level

Tests

  Readiness for new materials
  Informal reading inventories
  Criterion-referenced
    evaluation of progress

Format

  Paper quality
  Size of print
  Art

Other Materials

  Cassettes
  Filmstrips
  Records
  Other audiovisual aids

Cost of Total Program

Potentiality

  Basal program
  Cobasal
  Multibasal
  Supplementary

the relatively high level of sophistication reached in today's publications.[2] The completed textbook typically represents the combined competencies of subject matter specialists, child psychologists, linguists, artists, and photographers, to name a few. Variations among reading textbooks occur when

[2] Mike Bowler, "Textbook Publishers Try to Please All," *The Reading Teacher,* 31,5:514–18 (Feb. 1978).

certain writers reflect a basic philosophy or a certain approach that might differ from others. Examples would be the inclusion of multiethnic stories and pictures, an emphasis on either an analytic or a synthetic approach, or a presentation of stories written in a different alphabet such as i.t.a.

Textbook Committees

School systems may adopt a single textbook in a curriculum area. Sometimes they have a multiple adoption plan, with either a cobasal series or several basal series in elementary grades. Usually, committees of experienced teachers and administrators make textbook recommendations based upon their study of the various series. From time to time they make comparisons with newly published material before recommending new adoptions. Members of the committees studying textbooks set up criteria for analyzing the material. In subject areas, such as social studies and science, they consider the content in relation to their curriculum. In reading they examine the content and note the appropriateness of the story content to the age and interests of the children. They study the manuals to make certain that they include a carefully planned gradation of presentation, a sequential skills development organization. They look for workbooks that will provide children with meaningful practice of the skills initiated in the basal program. Their aim is to make selections that will give children the foundations in content and the skills compatible with previously determined objectives of education.

Beginning Teacher

The beginning teacher will, therefore, find that textbook selections have been made before he arrived on the scene. He will be most effective when he analyzes the reading and subject matter textbooks, and the accompanying workbooks and teacher's manual, assigned to his classroom. He will need to be aware of their place in the pattern of continuous and sequential skills development necessary for each pupil. In the classroom he or she will need to understand each pupil's strengths and weaknesses so that he or she can supplement the basal program with sufficient and relevant practice material.

SUPPLEMENTARY MATERIAL

The range of reading abilities and interests within any one classroom presents a special problem when materials are being considered. There must be material available to challenge the gifted reader as well as material easy enough to give some self-satisfaction to the poorest reader. A wide span of interests makes necessary a wide selection of topics. Multilevel kits, such as the *SRA Reading Laboratories,* have helped classroom teachers to have more than a single level of reading material at hand to meet individual needs. Programed materials supply practice in sequence of skill learnings as well as additional supplementary reading. (See Chapter 10.) Another provision for skills practice is the table with games and reading devices that many classrooms have developed. Pairs of children and small groups can gain reinforcement of their reading skills. Children can satisfy their curiosity about new topics and new words by turning to the reference books, encyclopedias, and dictionaries in the classroom and the school library. Filmstrips supply pictures and text that can be viewed or reviewed at a pupil's individual pace. Some filmstrips reinforce literature learnings. Some present other phases of the language arts, such as spelling and word analysis.

Teachers will find it useful to build a classroom file of practice materials arranged by such topics as vocabulary meaning, phonetic and structural analysis, and the various comprehension skills. They can cut apart workbook pages so that numerous practice pages are available when a certain skill needs reinforcement. They can build picture files. They can make notations concerning filmstrips after viewing them. The following lists have been compiled to point out the wide variety of materials available, and more appear on the market yearly.

Selected Workbooks

Ann Arbor Publishers, Worthington, OH. *Critical Reading, Workbooks A, B, C, D.*

Barnell Loft, Ltd., Rockville Center, NY: grades 1–6; *Following Directions, Getting the Facts, Using the Context, Locating the Answer, Working with Sounds.*

Columbia University, Bureau of Publications, New York: *Gates-Peardon Practice Exercises,* grades 3–6; *McCall-Crabbs Standard Test Lessons in Reading,* grades 2–7.

Educators Publishing Service, Inc., Cambridge, MA: *Reading Comprehension in Varied Subject Matter: Independent Reading.*

Lyons & Carnahan, Chicago: *Phonics We Use,* primer–grade 6.

McCormick Mathers Company, Wichita, KA: *Building Reading Skills,* phonics series, grades 1–6.

Charles E. Merrill Books, Inc., Columbus, OH: *New Phonics Skilltexts,* grades 1–6; *New Reading Skilltexts Series,* revised, grades 4–6; *Reading Adventures; Using the Library Skilltext,* grades 4–8.

Prentice-Hall, Inc., Englewood Cliffs, NJ: *Be a Better Reader,* Books A, B, C, grades 4–6.

Science Research Associates, Chicago: *SRA Better Reading, Books* 1, 2.

Webster, McGraw-Hill Company, St. Louis: *Eye and Ear Fun,* Books 1–4; *Conquests in Reading,* grades 2–6.

Programed Materials and Kits

Bell and Howell, Evanston, IL: *Language Master System III.*

California Test Bureau, Monterey, CA: *Lessons for Self-instruction in Basic Skills,* grades 3–9.

Center for Programed Instruction, New York: *Phonetic Analysis,* primary or remedial; *Structural Analysis,* primary or remedial; *Contextual Clues,* primary or remedial.

Chester Electronics Laboratories, Chester, CT: *Dialog I,* programed *phonics,* grade 1 or remedial.

Continental Press, Inc., Elizabethtown, PA: *AIMS: Initial Consonants Kit, Initial Vowels Kit, Comprehension Kit.*

Croft Educational Services, New London, CT: *Phonics for Pupils,* programed text in two parts, elementary.

Curriculum Associates, Inc., Newtown, MA: *Add-a-Word, Build-a-Word, Reading Skills Practice Kit.*

Educational Developmental Laboratories, Division of McGraw-Hill Book Company: *EDL Study Skills Libraries,* science, social studies, library skills, grades 3–9.

General Education, Inc., Cambridge, MA: *Phonics* with Studentutor machine, primary.

Harcourt Brace Jovanovich, New York: *Palo Alto Reading Program; Speech-to-Print Phonics Kit.*

Honors Products, Cambridge, MA: *Word Clues: Be a Word Detective,* intermediate; *Fun with Words: Homonyms,* intermediate; teaching machine needed.

Houghton Mifflin Company, Boston: *Listen and Do,* kit with sixteen records; duplicating masters for worksheets.

Macmillan Publishing Co., Inc., New York: *Reading Spectrum,* grades 1–6.

Science Research Associates, Chicago: *Reading Laboratories,* grades 1–college; *Graph and Picture Study Skills; Map and Globe Skills; Organizing and Reporting Skills; Reading for Understanding; Pilot Libraries; Literature Sampler; Sampler Library* (paperbacks); *Classroom Library Books.*

Society for Visual Education, Inc., Chicago, IL: *American Story Kits.*

Steck Company, Austin, TX: *Steck Teaching Aids,* boxes of cards for word analysis.

Teaching Machines, Inc., Grolier Incorporated, Danbury, CT: *Modern English Series—Remedial Reading,* primary; *Modern English Series— Spelling,* grade 3 up.

Webster, McGraw-Hill Company, St. Louis: *Classroom Reading Clinic,* kit; *Programed Reading,* grades 1–6.

Games and Other Devices

Adhere-O-Learning Aids, Wilmette, IL: *Adhere-O-Learning Aids,* phonics cutouts for flannel board.

Educational Development Laboratories, Division of McGraw Hill Book
  Company: *Flash-X,* individual tachistoscope; *Controlled Reader,*
  elementary stories on filmstrips; *Tach-X,* filmstrips in a tachistocope.
Garrard Publishing Company, Champaign, IL: *Dolch Basic Sight Cards;*
  Dolch Basic Phrase Cards; Consonant Lotto; Vowel Lotto; Group
  Sounding Game; Sight Syllable Solitaire; Take.
Harcourt Brace Jovanovich, Inc., New York: *Word Analysis Practice*
  Cards, grades 4–6.
Keystone View Company, Meadville, PA: *Tachistoscopic Training Series,*
  slides with words and phrases.
Little Brown Bear Learning Associates, Miami, FL: *Hobo Joe, Mousetrap,*
  Play 'n Read.
Milton Bradley Company, Springfield, MA: *See and Say Consonant Game.*
F. Owen Publishing Company, Dansville, NY: *Everyday Language Skills,*
  sets of graded charts, grades 1–6.
PhonoVisual Products, Washington, DC: *PhonoVisual Method,* charts and
  other aids.
Remedial Education Center, Washington, DC: *Go Fish; Short Vowel*
  Drill; Vowel Dominoes.
Science Research Associates, Inc., Chicago: *Phonics Kits: The Phonics*
  Express, Phonics Explorer.
Scott, Foresman and Company, Chicago: *Linguistic Blocks* series, primary.
Spin-a-Test Company, Pleasanton, CA: *Game Power for Phonics,* 1280
  Phonics Games.
Trend Enterprises, Inc., New Brighton, MN: *Parts of Speech Bingo.*
Webster, McGraw-Hill, St. Louis: *Word Wheels.*
Woodcrafters Guild, St. Albans School, Washington, DC: *Syllabascope,*
  with cards for word analysis.

Films and Filmstrips

The films and filmstrips that have been made for children are both recreational and informative. They have been found very useful in stimulating
reading interests. Some help clarify or reinforce basic reading skill instruction. Filmstrips may be studied one frame at a time by a group or by an individual. Good class discussions can be directed by the teacher in conjunction
with the showing of a film or filmstrip that correlates with the unit or lesson
of the day.

Catalogs of the films, cassettes,[3] and filmstrips [4] available to elementary
schools can be obtained by teachers and librarians. Because there are too
many for inclusion here, a sampling of the variety follows:

Coronet Films: *Look It Up; We Discover the Dictionary; Who Makes*
  Words?

[3] Coronet Instructional Films, 65 E. South Water Street, Chicago.
[4] *Filmstrip Guide.* H. W. Wilson Company, 950 University Avenue, New York
10452.

Encyclopaedia Britannica Films, Inc.: *Marine Life; Thumbelina.*
McGraw-Hill Filmstrips: *How to Use an Encyclopedia; Some Words Mean Two Things.*
Society for Visual Education: *Basic Primary Phonics.*
Weston Woods Studio: *Andy and the Lion.*
Ginn and Company, Columbus, OH: *Ginn Decoding Sound Filmstrips; A Holiday Festival,* Set II, Walt Disney Educational Media Company, Burbank, CA.
Jabberwocky, San Francisco, CA: Cassette Classics *Library V—Pied Piper of Hamlin,* and others.
Learning Tree Filmstrips, Boulder, CO: *Let's Read Series.*
Media Five/Film Distributors, Hollywood, CA: *The American Dinosaur.*
Media Materials, Inc., Baltimore, MD: *Cassette Learning Packages: Primary Reading Comprehension.*
Miller Brody Productions, New York: *Newbery Award Sound Filmstrip Library.*

Reference Materials

Once in a while we are dismayed to learn that we have overwhelmed a child in response to one of his continual questions, "Why? What? How?" We may have put into his hands a whole book on the topic he has questioned, only to find that he has returned the book without completing it. He just did not want to know that much about the subject!

Yet, they were interested enough to ask the question or to look up the answer to their question. For many children an immediate answer is of paramount importance. For these children a handy reference source, immediately available, provides information in at least a basic form. Children are naturally curious about many things at home and in school. One topic under study may suggest several avenues of investigation. Encyclopedias, almanacs, dictionaries, and other reference materials are the ready-made sources of answers to children's immediate problems. When they want more information, they will be ready to ask for further sources, for whole books on that topic of high interest to them.

Several encyclopedias have become popular with children in schools, libraries, and homes. These include the *Britannica Junior* and the *World Book Encyclopedia.* These are reference sets that have been written especially for children. Their topics have been broadly chosen and are presented in the alphabetical arrangement that children find easy to use. The sets have been kept up-to-date through frequent revisions. The editors have been conscientious in preparing articles that are readable by the children for whom they are intended. They have simplified the vocabulary and sentence structure and have clarified concepts with readable definitions and excellent illustrations.

Other popular encyclopedia sets include Grolier's *Book of Knowledge* with classified arrangement and the easy-to-read *Golden Book Encyclopedia.*

Herbert Zim, who has written numerous science books for children, has edited an eighteen-volume encyclopedia entitled *Our Wonderful World.* The older boy who reads *Popular Science* with his father will enjoy Grolier's recent set of ten volumes, *Book of Popular Science.*

Several single-volume encyclopedias have appeared in the last few years. The *Columbia Encyclopedia* has been a favorite because of the amount of information found within its covers. Topics in social studies may be investigated in such single-volume books as Rand McNally's *Book of Nations,* the *Concise Encyclopedia of World History,* the *Encyclopedia of American Facts and Dates,* and the *Worldmark Encyclopedia of the Nations.* These books provide students with a survey of many countries, including their own, and with a basis for understanding international relationships.

When children have a real purpose for doing research, as part of a school-initiated unit of study or as a matter of personal curiosity, they can begin with an investigation of the kinds of information contained in encyclopedias and other available reference books. A good source for teachers is *Encyclopedia Buying Guide* (1975–76), a Consumer Guide to general encyclopedias in print. (R. R. Bowker Co.).

SELECTED ENCYCLOPEDIAS

The New Book of Knowledge. Grolier Incorporated, 1975. 20 volumes. Alphabetical arrangement, for children ages 7 through elementary grades.

Book of Popular Science, American People's Yearbook. Grolier Incorporated, 1962. 10 volumes. Articles written at about same level as *Popular Science.*

Britannica Junior. Encyclopaedia Britannica, Inc. Revised annually. 15 volumes. Alphabetical arrangement of topics; written to provide the elementary school child with a reference source easily read and understood.

Childcraft: The How and Why Library, 1975. 15 volumes.

Compton's Precyclopedia, F. E. Compton and Company, 1973. 16 volumes. Excellent reference source for elementary and junior high students; indexed, and well illustrated.

Golden Book Encyclopedia. Golden Press, 1970. 16 volumes. With illustrations in color on every page, the articles are readable for the elementary grades 3–6.

Harvey Junior World Encyclopedia, 1972. 16 volumes.

Young Students Encyclopedia, 1973. 20 volumes.

World Book Encyclopedia. Field Enterprises, Inc., Annual Yearbook, 22 volumes with *Reading and Study Guide.* Authentic, comprehensive articles with varied illustrations—pictures and maps in color, photographs, pictorial diagrams, and other visual aids.

ONE- AND TWO-VOLUME ENCYCLOPEDIAS

Book of Nations. Rand McNally & Company, 1960. One volume. Arranged
by countries within each continent.

The New Columbia Encyclopedia. W. Bridgwater and E. Sherwood, eds.,
Columbia University Press, 1975. No illustrations, yet valuable for
the variety of information included in one volume. For older students.

The Worldmark Encyclopedia of the Nations. Worldmark Press Inc.,
Harper and Row, 1960. One volume. Arranged by countries, with
brief treatment of the geography, history, politics, and social and
economic status of each.

LIBRARY-MEDIA CENTER

Reading skills will not operate in a vacuum. In fact, they may die from disuse when children do not have personal reasons for reading. Part of the
school day can profitably be spent in literature reading—library books and
children's magazines and newspapers. Reading habits fostered through such
reading in school will usually persist beyond the school day and the school
years. Thus a major objective of education is accomplished, when schools
produce citizens who have the habit of reading newspapers, magazines, and
books.

A classroom library and the school's media center will help acquaint
children with the pleasures of good literature, the accumulated knowledge
of the past, and the current knowledge explosion. Even the very young child
can be introduced to the pleasures of good books as he or she listens to fascinating stories in a storytelling period or turns the pages of a picture book.
Many children first read independently the stories they have heard read over
and over again. As their skills improve, they branch out according to their
interests—animals, stars, cowboys, fairy tales—books become a world of
entertainment. Some children have become omnivorous readers because of
their impatience to get some answers, to satisfy their personal curiosity. They
read not only for recreation, but also for information. Books with factual
information on history, science, biography, and the space age seem to hold
special interest for children currently, possibly because the elements of action
and suspense parallel their usual or current preoccupation with television.
The abstract concepts of time and space take on significance when they form
a background in narrative literature.

Some children gain insights into their own character or their own problems as they read. A boy may see something of himself in the character of a
story. Another boy learns that other children may have problems similar to
his own. Children may learn a great deal about children in other lands and

of other races and in the process gain insight concerning the "one world" concept.

Bresnahan [5] emphasized the need for racial understanding. She pointed out that both black and white children need to read about blacks as well as whites. She listed books for young children for the purpose of promoting better understanding among all children. Among the books she listed were the following:

> Graham, Lorenz. *David—He No Fear*. Ill. by Ann Grifalconi. New York: Thomas Y. Crowell Company, 1971.
> Katz, Bobbi. *I'll Build My Friend a Mountain*. Ill. by Estel Von Storp. New York: Scholastic, 1972.
> Van Leeuwen, Jean. *Timothy's Flowers*. Ill. by Moneta Barnett. New York: Random House, Inc., 1976.

Spache [6] has listed and annotated many books that have been written about minority groups in America. Through their reading of books from this list, children can learn about each nationality's roots, its problems, and its dreams.

The new teacher first gets acquainted with any reading materials assigned to his or her classroom. He or she needs to be constantly alert for any additional suggestions for securing pertinent materials to be placed on the reading table or shelves in the classroom for easy access as projects are developed and new units are studied. Some of the suggestions are found in the teacher's manuals and in certain content area textbooks. Numerous booklists are available to help teachers choose appropriate titles. Further suggestions can be made by the school's librarian once he or she has been alerted to the upcoming projects. Children may be directed to the classroom's library corner or to the school's library to locate books, magazines, and newspapers of current import.

SOURCES FOR TEACHERS

Several sources teachers can use to become acquainted with children's books follow:

> "Classroom Choices for 1977: Books Chosen by Children." *The Reading Teacher*, 31, 1:6–23 (Oct. 1977).
> "Classroom Choices: Children's Trade Books, 1975." *The Reading Teacher*, 30, 1:50–63 (Oct. 1976).

[5] Mary Bresnahan, "Selecting Sensitive and Sensible Books About Blacks," *The Reading Teacher*, 30,1:16–20 (Oct. 1976).
[6] George D. Spache, *Good Reading for the Disadvantaged Reader* (Champaign, IL: Garrard Publishing Company, 1975).

"Classroom Choices: Children's Trade Books, 1974." *The Reading Teacher,* 29, 2:122–132 (Nov. 1975).

1977 Children's Book Showcase Catalog. The Children's Book Council, Inc., New York.

Notable Children's Trade Books in the Field of Social Studies, 1976. The Children's Book Council, New York.

Outstanding Science Trade Books for Children in 1976. The Children's Book Council, New York.

Teachers and children can become acquainted with the juvenile books that have won annual awards of which the principal ones are the Newbery, awarded since 1922, and the Caldecott, awarded since 1938.

The school librarian can teach children the locational skills of using the card file and cross-reference techniques. He or she helps children become independent in the library when he or she explains the *Reader's Guide to Periodical Literature,* the *Subject Index to Poetry,* the *World Almanac,* and other specific reference materials, such as children's encyclopedias and dictionaries.

Many trade books are available today in paperback form, attractive to children and easy on the school budget. Some books of the high interest, low difficulty variety may prove interesting and informative to the pupil who has trouble assimilating the content of the regular textbook. In easy-to-read supplementary material a pupil might follow up a topic to which he or she was introduced in his or her science or history book.

INTEREST IN READING

American Book Co., Cincinnati: *Reading Round Table,* classroom libraries (grades 1–6).

Beckley-Cardy: *Cowboy Sam Series* (primer–grade 3).

Benefic Press, Chicago: *World of Adventure,* series ranging from grades 2 through 6 in difficulty.

Children's Press, Chicago: *America and Its Indians* (grade 4 reading level); *Discovering Science on Your Own* (grade 4 reading level); *Enchantment of America Series* (grade 4 reading level); *Frontiers of America Series* (junior high interest, grade 3 reading level); *Let's Travel Series; True Book Series.*

Garrard Press, Champaign, IL: *Discovery Books; Junior Science Books; Rivers of the World Books; Indian Books; Sports Library*

Grosset & Dunlap, Inc., New York: *We Were There Books.*

Harr Wagner Publishing Co., San Francisco: *Deep Sea Adventure Series* junior high, reading levels 1.8–5.1; *Morgan Bay Mysteries* elementary and junior high, reading levels 2.3–3.5; *Wild Life Adventure Series* elementary, grade 4 reading level; *Jim Forest Reader* elementary,

reading levels 1.7–3.1; *Reading Motivated Series* junior high, grade 4
reading level; *Time Machine Series* primary, reading levels PP–2.0.

Holt, Rinehart and Winston, New York: *Little Owls, Young Owls, and
Wise Owls* collection of elementary books for supplementary reading
in literature, science, social studies, and arithmetic.

Houghton Mifflin Company, New York: *North Star Series.*

Macmillan Publishing Co., Inc., New York: *Aviation Series.*

Random House, Inc., New York: *All About Books; Landmark Books;
Signature Book Series.*

Reader's Digest Educational Division, Pleasantville, NY: *Reader's Digest
Skill Builders* grades 1–16; *Reader's Digest Science Readers.*

Scholastic's *Readers' Choice,* Englewood Cliffs, NJ: Readers' Choice
Paperbacks.

Scott, Foresman and Company, Chicago: *Invitations to Personal Reading*
grades 1, 2, 3, three sets of 25 books each geared for slow readers,
middle group, and accelerated readers; *Easy Reading Books,* third
grade vocabulary in adventure and mystery stories.

L. W. Singer Company, Syracuse, NY: *Prose and Poetry Series* PP–6,
literature series.

Franklin Watts, Inc., San Francisco: *First Books.*

Webster Division, McGraw-Hill, St. Louis: *Read for Fun,* independent
reading books for primary grades.

ASSIGNING APPROPRIATE READING MATERIALS

Many types of reading materials, written at various levels of difficulty,
are available to the children in the modern schoolroom. Such materials
present a challenge and a responsibility to classroom teachers. They will
need to choose basal instructional materials in curriculum areas, supplementary reading materials, workbooks, games and trade books, all of which must
be readable for some of the pupils in the class. Challenged to fit the right
book to the right child, they must have adequate knowledge of each child's
reading level.

In some cases, the classroom teacher at the beginning of a school year
will need to rely upon standardized test scores for an immediate indication
of the pupils' reading achievement level. When he interprets these scores as
frustrational level, he will realize that he cannot hand reading material of
this level to his pupils, either for purposes of instruction or recreation. He
must assign reading materials one or more grades below those indicated by
standardized test scores for effective instruction.

When teachers take time to administer the informal reading inventory
they can appraise the pupils' instructional and independent reading levels.
They are then in a good position to make assignments in appropriate reading materials. See Figure 13. They may discover that for their fifth grade

Figure 13. Assigning Reading Material

PUPILS' READING ACHIEVEMENT LEVEL (STANDARDIZED TEST SCORE)	PUPILS' APPRAISED INSTRUCTIONAL READING LEVEL (IRI)	BASAL READERS PROGRAMED MATERIALS	SUPPLEMENTARY MATERIALS, LIBRARY BOOKS, AND CONTENT AREA TEXTBOOKS
Derived Grade Levels		*Labeled Grade Levels*	
3	1	PP, P, 1	Picture–Primer
4	2	2	1
5	3	3	1, 2
6	4	4	2, 3
7	5	5	3, 4
8	6	6	4, 5
9	7	7	5, 6
10	8	8	6, 7
11	9	9	7, 8

class they need textbooks graded from third to fifth grade, whereas library books will be needed covering a range from first to fourth grade in difficulty. In upper grades where even wider levels of reading achievement appear, a broader range of readable materials will be required.

Figure 13 for assigning reading material indicates levels of materials that can be provided within an elementary classroom when children's instructional reading levels are known. If the teacher plans to put a child into a fourth grade basal reader, for example, other materials would be assigned at lower readability levels. Thus, content area textbooks with their heavy load of new concepts and vocabulary, as well as often unfamiliar subject matter, will prove a sufficient burden without difficult readability levels. The extent to which content area textbooks should be lower than the child's instructional level would depend upon the teaching techniques used by the teacher. The textbook that is assigned for seatwork or homework should be at the student's independent reading level, so that he or she can concentrate on the content rather than on unlocking many unfamiliar words. Library books will be read and savored if he or she can read them. Otherwise, as many librarians have learned, the book with the captivating title is returned unread because the child could not wade through the author's difficult style of writing. Programed materials, filmstrips, and games also need to be analyzed for their difficulty levels before assignment to a pupil or group.

Materials for an Intermediate Classroom

When the instructional reading levels of the children in the classroom range from second to sixth grade, a variety of graded materials will be needed.

Figure 14. *Reading Materials—Six-year-olds*

AN ENTERING CLASS OF SIX-YEAR-OLDS	BASAL *	SUPPLEMENTARY †	LITERATURE ‡	MISCELLANEOUS (GAMES, ACTIVITIES)
Average	Readiness to preprimer	Readiness	Picture books, pre-primer	Picture dictionary, games, filmstrips
Superior, gifted	Readiness to grade 4	Readiness to primers	Preprimer to grade 1	Picture dictionary, games, filmstrips
Slow, reluctant	Readiness	Readiness	Readiness, picture books	Games
Disadvantaged	Preschool activities, readiness	Readiness	Readiness, picture books	Games
Full range ‡	Preschool to grade 4	Readiness to primers	Picture books to grade 1	Games, and so on, preprimer to grade 1

* Based upon instructional reading levels assessed through informal reading inventory.
† Based upon independent reading levels assessed through informal reading inventory.
‡ Content reading levels determined through readability formulas and judgment of librarians and teachers.

Figure 15. *Reading Materials—Seven-year-olds*

A CLASSROOM OF SEVEN-YEAR-OLDS	BASAL.*	SUPPLEMENTARY † AND CONTENT AREAS ‡	† AND ‡ LITERATURE	MISCELLANEOUS, REFERENCE, RESEARCH, REINFORCEMENT
Average	Grade 2	Grade 1	Grades 1, 2	Primary dictionary, Reading games
Superior, gifted	Grades 2–4+	Grades 1–3	Grades 1–3	*SRA Reading Laboratory I*, Ia, Ib, and so on, films, filmstrips, resource materials, encyclopedias
Slow, reluctant	Readiness, preprimer, primer, grade 1	Picture through grade 1	Picture books, easy-reading books	Reading games, certain programed materials, picture dictionary
Disadvantaged	Readiness to grade 1	Readiness, preprimers	Picture books, pre-primer level	Picture dictionary, some games, certain programed material
Full range of materials ‡	Readiness through grade 4+	Readiness and pictures through grade 3	Picture books through grade 3	Games to research (reference books)

* Based upon instructional reading levels assessed through informal reading inventory.
† Based upon independent reading levels assessed through informal reading inventory.
‡ Content reading levels determined through readability formulas and judgment of librarians and teachers.

Figure 16. *Reading Materials—Eight-year-olds*

A CLASSROOM OF EIGHT-YEAR-OLDS	BASAL *	SUPPLEMENTARY,† AND CONTENT AREAS ‡	† AND ‡ LITERATURE	MISCELLANEOUS, REFERENCE, RESEARCH, REINFORCEMENT
Average	Grade 3	Grade 2	Grades 1–2+	Primary dictionary, reading games
Superior, gifted	Grades 3–5+	Grades 3–5	Grades 3–5	*SRA Reading Laboratory,* films, filmstrips, resource materials, encyclopedias
Slow, reluctant	Grades 1–2	Preprimer to grade 1	Picture books, easy-reading books	Reading games (as Dolch)
Disadvantaged	Grades 1–3	Preprimer to grade 1	Picture books to grade 1	Picture dictionary, easy games, programmed material
Full range of materials †	Grades 1–5Æ	Preprimer to grade 5	Picture books through grade 5	Games to research (reference books)

* Based upon instructional reading levels assessed through informal reading inventory.
† Based upon independent reading levels assessed through informal reading inventory.
‡ Content reading levels determined through readability formulas and judgment of librarians and teachers.

Figure 17. Reading Materials—Nine-year-olds

A CLASSROOM OF NINE-YEAR-OLDS	BASAL *	SUPPLEMENTARY † AND CONTENT AREAS ‡	LITERATURE † ‡	MISCELLANEOUS, REFERENCE, RESEARCH, REINFORCEMENT
Average	Grade 4	Grades 2, 3	Grades 2, 3	Dictionary
Superior, gifted	Grades 4–7+	Grades 4–6	Grades 3–6+	Encyclopedias, reference
Slow, reluctant	Grades 1–3	Primer to grade 2	Pictures to grade 2	Primary dictionary, reading games
Disadvantaged	Grades 1–4	Primer to grade 2	Pictures to grade 2	Primary dictionary, reading games
Full range of materials ‡	Grades 1–7+	Primer to grade 5	Picture books to grade 6+	Primary dictionary to encyclopedias

* Based upon instructional reading levels assessed through informal reading inventory.
† Based upon independent reading levels assessed through informal reading inventory.
‡ Content reading levels determined through readability formulas and judgment of librarians and teachers.

Figure 18. *Reading Materials—Ten-year-olds*

A CLASSROOM OF TEN-YEAR-OLDS	BASAL *	SUPPLEMENTARY † AND CONTENT AREAS ‡	† AND ‡ LITERATURE	MISCELLANEOUS, REFERENCE, RESEARCH, REINFORCEMENT
Average	Grade 5	Grades 3–4	Grades 3–4	Elementary dictionary, elementary *SRA Laboratory*, *films*, *filmstrips*
Superior, gifted	Grades 5–8	Grades 5–6	Grades 4–7	Encyclopedias, study kits, films, filmstrips
Slow, reluctant	Grades 1–3+	Grades 1–2	Grades 1–3, easy-reading trade books	Reading games, primary *SRA Reading Laboratories*
Disadvantaged	Grades 2–4	Grades 1–2	Grades 1–3, easy-reading relevant trade books	Reading games, relevant programed materials
Full range of materials †	Grades 1–8	Grades 1–6	Grades 1–7	Grade 1 materials through grade 7

* Based upon instructional reading levels assessed through informal reading inventory.
† Based upon independent reading levels assessed through informal reading inventory.
‡ Content reading levels determined through readability formulas and judgment of librarians and teachers.

Figure 19. *Reading Materials—Eleven-year-olds*

A CLASSROOM OF ELEVEN-YEAR-OLDS	BASAL *	SUPPLEMENTARY † AND CONTENT AREAS ‡	† AND ‡ LITERATURE	MISCELLANEOUS, REFERENCE, RESEARCH, REINFORCEMENT
Average	Grade 6	Grades 4, 5	Grades 4, 5	*SRA Reading Laboratory*, films, filmstrips
Superior, gifted	Grades 6–9	Grades 5–7	Full range literary areas	Reference, research reading, study kits, films, filmstrips
Slow, reluctant	Grades 2–4+	Grades 1–3	Easy-reading trade books, reading series, *Reader's Digest Skill Builders*	Reading games, programed materials, workbooks
Disadvantaged	Grades 2–5+	Grades 1–3	Easy-reading trade books, reading series, *Reader's Digest Skill Builders*	Programed materials, workbooks
Full range of materials ‡	Grades 2–9	Grades 1–7	Easy-reading (grade 2) to full-range library	Grade 2 materials through grade 9

* Based upon instructional reading levels assessed through informal reading inventory.
† Based upon independent reading levels assessed through informal reading inventory.
‡ Content reading levels determined through readability formulas and judgment of librarians and teachers.

For those at second and third grade reading levels, many of the Dolch games would be useful because they include the primary grade skills of sight words, phrase reading, and the sounding of vowels and consonants in easy combinations. Practice in word analysis for those with middle grade reading levels would be provided with Webster Word Wheels and Durrell's Word Analysis Practice Cards.

Upper grade children who need practice on left-to-right sequence, a steady reading pace with no opportunities for regressive eye movements, and an immediate check on rate of comprehension will find the Controlled Reader useful. It shows elementary stories on filmstrips at a pace set by the instructor. Each story is followed by a set of questions. Children can watch their own progress as they learn to concentrate on the *who, what, where, when,* and *why* of short, interesting selections.

Programed materials and kits may be used by some children in this classroom. An example would be the teaching machine provided with two sets of lessons for middle grade readers.[7] Although lessons on homonyms can be found in workbooks, teachers' guides to basal readers, and in language arts textbooks, they have more appeal for certain children when encountered in a machine.

In addition to the library books selected from grades one to five lists for this particular classroom, other high interest collections might be placed on the shelves of the classroom library. Wide reading in easy-to-read books at each stage of the child's reading development helps to ensure mastery of reading skills. At the same time the reader is developing a very important asset—the habit of reading for information and enjoyment.

The librarian can direct some of the children to more challenging books, magazines, and reference materials when they visit the school library. In discussion periods, all can share their enjoyment of their books, because everyone had been led to books they could read.

Teachers will find that every type of reader will upon occasion appear in their classrooms. They may find a few of the extremes—highly gifted readers and the very poor or nonreaders. They will find several children who are slow but achieving at their own pace. They will find a majority achieving at a regular or expected rate. They will find a few who far exceed the expectations for children their age and grade level—the gifted readers. They will occasionally find children whose achievement is below their assessed abilities—retarded in reading, whether of average, high, or low mental ability. They will find children whose background—socially, emotionally, culturally, and so on—has not prepared them for our typical formal education. These are the disadvantaged children who (1) may be a part of a highly mobile section of our population, (2) may be restricted or limited in terms of con-

---

[7] Honors Products. Cambridge, Mass. Word Clues: Be a Word Detective; Fun with Words: Homonyms.

tacts with other segments of the population, (3) may be reacting emotion-ally to the frustrations of a limited environment, or (4) may have learned to speak in another language, yet must read in English.

Figures 14 through 19 indicate the range of reading materials teachers will find useful when they have studied the abilities and backgrounds of the children assigned to them for the school year. Thus, a group of six-year-old youngsters may require materials ranging from preschool activities for the immature and the disadvantaged to some material as high as grade four for the gifted or the few who were already reading when they entered school. A group of nine-year-olds may require a range of materials from first grade level, for the slow, the reluctant, and the disadvantaged, to the seventh grade level for the superior and gifted readers. Teachers can use these charts as guides for matching children and reading materials in classrooms where children are grouped for instruction as well as in the individualized pattern of organization.

SUMMARY

Teachers face the challenge of preparing children for many varied reading tasks. They need to locate material that is appropriate to the developmental level and interests of all pupils in the classroom. In their daily planning they provide a range of experiences, activities, and skills practice, so that all children will eventually become independent in their reading.

Basal readers, subject textbooks, reference materials, and trade books become the media through which children practice their reading skills. As children experience success in their day-by-day reading, they establish the habits that will make them lifetime readers.

SELECTED READINGS

Bettelheim, Bruno. *The Uses of Enchantment.* New York: Alfred A. Knopf, Inc., 1976.

Blue Book of Audiovisual Materials. Educational Screen and Audiovisual Guide. Chicago. (Annual.)

Brown, James; Richard B. Lewis; and Fred Harcleroad. *AV Instruction Media and Methods.* New York: McGraw-Hill Book Company, 1969.

Duffy, Gerald G., and George Sherman. *Systematic Reading Instruction.* New York: Harper & Row, Publishers, 1972.

Educational Media Index. McGraw-Hill Book Company.

El-Hi Books in Print. 8th ed. New York: R. R. Bowker Company, 1977.

Erickson, Carlton W., and David H. Curl. *Fundamentals of Teaching With Au-*

diovisual Technology. 2nd ed. New York: Macmillan Publishing Co., Inc., 1972.

Painter, Helen W. *Reaching Children and Young People Through Literature.* Newark, DE: International Reading Association, 1971.

Rufsvold, Margaret I., and Carolyn Guss. *Guides to Educational Media.* 3d ed. Chicago, IL: American Library Association, 1971.

Spache, George D. *Good Reading for Poor Readers.* 9th ed. Champaign, IL: Garrard Publishing Company, 1974.

————. *Good Reading for the Disadvantaged Reader.* Champaign, IL: Garrard Publishing Company, 1975.

Chapter 12

Organization of Instruction: Administrative

OBJECTIVES

To know the structure and function of the school's reading committee

To be familiar with various media and their use to support reading instruction

To learn the strategies of transferring reading skills and understandings to the study of the content area subjects

To learn how to use peer and cross-age tutoring to help both tutors and tutees

To learn the appropriate use of aides and paraprofessionals in the reading program

To know the various types of classroom and program structures, how to organize them, and their strengths and weaknesses

To learn the role of the administrator in strong reading programs

INTRODUCTION

The organization of the school makes a difference in the learning program. The organization of the classroom makes a difference in the learning that transpires there. For example, the Joplin plan requires that the reading program start and stop by the clock, that students move to a special designated place for reading. If transfer of the learning in reading class is to take place, it is up to the teachers and pupils to arrange for it purposefully. If they do not, then reading becomes an isolated subject and thus not very effective.

Another example, in the classroom, is that of the traditional basal reader teacher who is suddenly plunged into a newly organized individualized reading program. Can the teacher continue to function in this new organization as in the old? The teacher is apt to be overwhelmed by the myriad tasks, shortage of time for each pupil every day, shortage of appropriate materials, and the record-keeping tasks?

A change in organization and program calls for a change in teaching techniques, new strategies of behavior, new temporal arrangements, adequate new materials. These call for administrative support, supervisory guidance, visitation to successful comparable programs, in-service training, demonstration lessons, and other strategies. We now look at instruction in reading through the medium of different organizational structures and administrative strategies.

THE READING COMMITTEE

The school's reading committee is usually composed of the reading specialist (chairing), the administrator, representatives of grade levels and buildings, a parent representative, representatives of special areas—library, speech, learning disabilities, the school psychologist. The committee's first task is to assess the current reading program—the strengths and weaknesses. A new assessment would cover objectives, redevelopment; practices and structure that should be continued as they are; changes that would improve the effectiveness of the program; strategies that would enhance and enrich the instructional program.

If the tasks are outlined by the committee and found to be too cumbersome for the total group, the committee should break into smaller groups with specific tasks for each to explore and report back. The total committee should review the proposals of the subgroup and then present the recommendations to the total faculty and administration. A word of caution—an administrator should be a member of the committee, and there should be full assurance of his or her backing before the recommendations are made to the faculty and administration.

What starts as a desire on the part of a few faculty to improve the reading program often turns out to be a bonanza (serendipity) because enthusiasm grows as teachers exchange ideas, enlarge their professional reading, and get a chance to interreact, visit other schools and programs, talk with teachers from other systems, and develop a running dialogue on structure and strategies in reading.

MEDIA USE

Media, as used here, refers to those instructional materials that support and enhance the teaching program. The word is used commonly as a collective noun in education in spite of the lexicographers' objections. In a dynamic school library program, the library media specialist contributes to instruction as a resource person working with other teachers and as a counselor providing individual guidance to students, helping them select and use learning materials and explore interests that go beyond the individual's classroom. Media are organized and stored so that everything is available to the classroom (reading) teacher. Cooperation of the administrator, reading specialist, librarian, and classroom teacher is the key to regular and effective use of media for instruction.

The American Association of School Librarians and the NEA Department of Audiovisual Instruction have combined to establish standards for school learning resources. They believe each school should have a unified media program, including printed and audiovisual materials and related equipment under a single media director (see materials listings in Chapter 11). The standards recommend that schools with 250 or more students should have at least 6,000 to 10,000 titles representing 10,000 volumes or twenty volumes per student. The standards propose similarly augmented collections of periodicals and newspapers and of professional materials for teachers. Quantitative standards for filmstrips, films, recordings, art prints, maps, globes, and transparencies are also specific and cover the range of the curriculum; that is, each school should have 500 to 1,000 filmstrip titles representing 1,500 prints or three prints per student and should also have 1,000 to 2,000 tape and disk recording titles representing 3,000 recordings, or six per student.[1] In addition, the standards recommend one professional media specialist (librarian or A-V specialist) for every 250 students and two media aides or technicians for each professional.

These guidelines express the philosophy that instruction should be greatly enhanced by an adequate supply of instructional media. It is up to the teacher to see the need for media and to use media correctly and in a timely setting. If so done, media supports and improves instruction—it can never take the place of the teacher and his or her instructional strategies.

READING IN CONTENT AREAS

One of the purposes of learning to read is to develop the ability to read content area material with understanding and be able to use that material in

---

[1] Richard Darling, *Teams For Better Education—The Teacher and the Librarian* (Champaign, IL: Garrard Publishing Company, 1972).

further study all the rest of one's life. Why not, then, begin making the application as the child learns the reading skill? We do! Why, then, do content area teachers complain that their students cannot read their subject profitably? One logical answer lies in the fact that many students can; but in a class of thirty students there will be a range of abilities in basic reasoning, cognitive abilities: part-whole analysis, invariant time sequence, major-subordinate relationships, cause-effect, and comparison and contrast of ideas. These areas of reasoning must be *exercised* in the classroom under guidance of the teacher.[2] Content area material in science, math, and history can be used to do this.

The reading teacher must be continuously aware of the need for special skills in the academic areas of study. There are some skills that are basic to reading in all the content areas. The first one is the skill of getting an overview of the material, sometimes referred to as previewing. Teachers should have a clear picture of the structure of the material—a "clear picture of the forest before getting in among the trees." This orientation is necessary to read efficiently. As soon as teachers know the structure of the total reading selection, *skimming* and/or *scanning* may effectively take place. Skimming is the process of quickly going over the selection to get the main idea (and the experienced reader picks up other supportive facts). This skimming technique has to be learned and, in many cases, taught. *Scanning* is the process of quickly locating specific information in the material without reading the whole selection. Practice, under guidance and with immediate feedback, makes students proficient in their use in any content area. They soon learn to look for clues that help in the process: listing by numbers, italicized words, the words *especially, also, but, causes, results, all*. First, second, and third order headings are recognized as representing the author's structure of his or her presentation. Then there is the special (technical) vocabulary and group of concepts that are peculiar to that content area. These preferably are the concern, or should be, of the content area teacher. In departmentalized programs, where the content area teacher is not the reading or language arts teacher, the student has to recognize the transfer of skills. If he or she does not, the content area teacher must bridge the gap with specific vocabulary and conceptual background study and assignment. Too many content area teachers in the past have "cursed the darkness instead of lighting the one small candle."

Many content area textbooks have a heavy concept load and a heavy technical vocabulary load. By the middle grades, students begin encountering this problem. *Every teacher* should, therefore, prepare the students for both of these *before* assigning reading in the textbooks. The experienced teachers can recognize these by reading over the material and preparing brief exer-

[2] Beatrice Kachuck and Albert Marcus, "Thinking Strategies and Reading," *The Reading Teacher*, 30:157–61 (Nov. 1976).

cises for chalkboard presentation, discussion, and Socratic questionning in class. Duffy and Sherman [3] have some interesting practice exercises for the new teacher in teaching reading in the content areas.

USE OF PUPILS AS TUTORS

A great deal of success has been reported in the research literature for tutoring of their own classmates by students. The improvements have been reported not only in reading achievement, but also in attitudes, interests, and enthusiasm for reading. One typical example is reported by Boraks and Allen.[4]

Cross-Age Tutoring

Cross-age tutoring is the term describing the use of older students to tutor younger students. It, too, has been proved helpful to both the tutors and tutees. There are many possibilities for this arrangement to be employed. Upper graders in an elementary school can go into the second and third grades to work with the children there—listening to them read, helping them with words, reading to them, organizing and supervising reading games, and so on. A shy sixth grade girl might enjoy working with a second grade girl who is having difficulty with her reading. In some school systems, high school students go into the elementary school to work with the young children. Typing students can take dictated stories by children who are ready for this and put them in booklets of typed stories. Music students can talk to young children about the instrument they play.[5] Powell [6] discussed a successful procedure to be employed in this procedure.

One fascinating study was conducted at Maimonides Community Mental Health Center in Brooklyn,[7] where disruptive students who were reading below grade level were trained to work with poor readers and nonreaders of third and fourth grades. They were supervised in their sessions throughout the program. After establishing rapport with the older students, the staff

[3] Gerald Duffy and George Sherman, *How To Teach Reading Systematically* (New York: Harper & Row, Publishers, 1970), pp. 242–50.
[4] Nancy Boraks and Amy Allen, "A Program To Enhance Peer Tutoring," *The Reading Teacher,* 30:479–84 (Feb. 1977).
[5] *Reading Ideas: A Newsletter for Teachers of All Levels,* Vol. 1, No. 3 (Nov. 1975). Reading Ideas, Box 1524, San Jose, CA 95109.
[6] Barbara Powell, *Children as Teachers: Stages in Cross-Age Tutoring.* Paper presented at the AERA Annual Meeting, April 1975.
[7] Patrick Lane, Cecelia Pollack, and Norman Sher, "Learning By Teaching: A Study in Re-Motivation of Disruptive Adolescents," *The Reading Instruction Journal,* 15:47–48,64–65 (March and June 1972).

trained them in the reading work *and* in role-playing and modeling as well. Rap sessions were held periodically. The staff began to notice achievement and changes in behavior, pride in successes, growth in the adolescents' knowledge and abilities in reading, pride in the growth of the younger children. There was an evaluation that indicated in the year's program a mean growth of fourteen months of the younger children and a mean gain of nineteen months for the tutors. The character and attitude changes were marked. This laboratory-type experiment indicates that the regular public schools could do much the same thing with some careful attention to individuals and some precise training of the tutors.[8]

USE OF AIDES—PARAPROFESSIONALS

As in other professions, such as medicine, administrators and boards of education have been moving in the direction of the employment of paraprofessionals to perform nonteaching duties in the classroom and school as a whole. Teaching can be more efficient and effective if teachers can spend their time in teaching pupils entirely and turn over some of the routine nonteaching tasks to others. Paraprofessionals, or aides, are recruited from parents and local citizens, many of whom have strong clerical, technical, and experiential backgrounds that are superior to those of the teacher.

One of the most important aspects of the program using teacher aides is the working relationship between teacher and aide, the understanding of ways of working together so that the learning of the children is enhanced. A workshop may be in order—where both teachers and aides explore the ways they will work following initial aide training. In some states the board has set up rules and regulations and recommendations governing the role of aides. They suggested *clerical* tasks for the aides—recording book lists and books children have read, typing, duplicating, updating pupils' folders, and so on; *noninstructional* tasks—gathering supplementary books, preparing reading games; *A-V assistance*—ordering, getting, and returning films and equipment and setting up equipment; *semi-instructional*—correcting standardized tests and recording results, preparing instructional materials (flashcards, charts, transparencies), tutoring individual child, storytelling, assisting in drill work, and so on.

In some situations aides are paid, and in others they are volunteers. Where volunteers are used, they are usually in the classroom a portion of the day, or they may be used just one afternoon a week. Almost any kind of arrangement for time has been explored in urban and suburban schools

[8] Ralph Malaregna, as cited in "Has Older Students Tutoring Younger Students Proved to be Effective?" *Today's Education* 67:19–20 (Feb. 1978).

"I know how the story ends!"

where the volunteers are nearby and available and willing—some desiring to be useful for lack of something to do. Where the aide, whether paid or volunteer, is not working out well, he or she should be removed. He or she is there to improve the program, not to disrupt or harm it.

Research supports the use of parents and paraprofessionals in teaching pupils to read. The use of supervised tutorial programs by parents and aides is demonstrating increased gains for pupils.[9]

ORGANIZATION AND STRUCTURE

Ways of Organizing for Teaching

When patterns of organization for instruction are considered, changes often occur first at a single level, as in the primary or junior high school. Subsequently the change may be suggested for other levels. An example would be that of departmentalizing an elementary school in order to prepare pupils for the departmentalized pattern in the content areas of the secondary school.

Organizing for teaching has typically involved some consideration of such factors as the size of classes, grouping or nongrouping for teaching within the classroom, the individualization of instruction, the self-contained

[9] G. Della-Piana, et.al., "Parents and Reading Achievement: A Review of Research," *Elementary English.* 45:190–200 (1968); Michael and Lise Wallach, *Teaching All Children to Read* (Chicago: University of Chicago Press, 1976).

classroom versus departmentalized classrooms, the materials of instruction, the school plant, the homogeneity or heterogeneity of the pupils assigned to classrooms, competencies of teachers, sometimes the studied educational objectives, and even at times a strong desire to maintain the *status quo*.

An individual teacher, newly hired, may find himself within an organizational pattern that he thoroughly understands or in one for which he feels unprepared. Because the role of the teacher in the classroom is of paramount importance in the learning situation, it is imperative that a teacher understand and work efficiently within the framework of an existing organizational pattern. Research has shown that *all* of the preceding patterns, as well as others that were not delineated, have proved effective in some situations. Some teachers by temperament, bias, or training are better suited to certain patterns of organization than to others.

Possibly the best preparation a teacher can make to fit into a school's organizational pattern would be to attain the security that results from (1) an extensive knowledge of existing patterns of organization, and (2) a thorough grounding in effective techniques of teaching reading.

In this section a review of organizational patterns will be made for the purpose of showing the teacher how he can best fit reading into a specific instructional setting, once he has acquired the necessary techniques for teaching reading.

Self-Contained Classroom

The traditional pattern has been the self-contained classroom. Sometimes the teacher has instructed the class as a whole, on the assumption that his or hers was a homogeneous group. When individual differences within the classroom were recognized, the teacher divided the class into groups. Through the years the basis for grouping might be the results of reading tests that determine a single reading score, more flexible grouping based upon informally determined reading difficulties, reading interests, reading projects, or the level of a basal reader in which the pupil could be instructed. More recently, individualizing reading instruction has been interpreted as the self-selection of reading material followed with teacher conferences. The teacher in the self-contained classroom has occasionally combined several or all of these methods in order to teach effectively. When basal readers are used with groups of children, whole group instruction for the introduction of a needed skill would be occasionally the order of the day. When individualized reading is the main pattern, some teachers find it advisable and economical of time and effort to organize some groups for basic skill instruction as needs arise.

In discussing the influence of research upon the flexibility of organization for instruction in the elementary school, at the primary level, where the teacher's role often parallels that of the parent, the administrative pattern seems likely to remain that of the self-contained classroom, with a group working under the guidance of one teacher. The best size of the group with which the teacher may be working might be determined in relation to the lesson at hand. Certain skills might best be taught in small groups (three or four children) where teachers can supervise an individual's lessons. At another time the teacher may read a story to the whole class more efficiently and economically of the class time. Class size is a factor at any level when teachers are concerned about children's instructional needs in reading. In order to provide for continuous learning, the teacher needs to be familiar with each child's current achievement level, interests, abilities, and physical and social development—anything that will provide insights into his or her particular needs at any one time. Obviously, the teacher's attainment of this information can be complicated by the force of numbers. Following the path of least resistance, some teachers will open a textbook and "teach." Good teachers suit the textbooks to the children, knowing that no single textbook fits the achievement level of every member of a class.

In the self-contained classroom the most effective plan permits individualization of instruction, geared to individual abilities. Sometimes this is accomplished with flexible, small-group lessons. Sometimes this involves each child's moving along in reading at his or her own pace.

The typical lesson in a classroom with a group of children of relatively near reading abilities is as follows:

1. The teacher selects a story judged to be of high interest level.
2. On the chalkboard the teacher places, before the beginning work with the children, a title, author, words for study, and possibly a question or two as lead-ins or to lead up to a new concept.
3. Introduce the story theme and get the children talking about their own related experiences.
4. Introduce the new words *with* their use in sentences.
5. Children read the story silently.
6. Discuss the theme, plot, characters, setting.
7. Some oral reading to substantiate a point made by the teacher or pupils.
8. Follow-up: draw illustrations, paint, write, make a book, write own story, seatwork paper, and so on.

This directed lesson plan is good and should be practiced on occasion by every teacher. But to follow it slavishly day after day is a mistake. Probably many teachers do it, even after *The First R* [10] condemned the rigid practice, and children respond to this regimented approach with apathy after a time. In the pages to follow, your authors present many alternatives to this "lock-

[10] Mary C. Austin and Coleman Morrison, *The First R* (New York: Macmillan Publishing Co., Inc., 1963).

step" and variations of the alternatives. With the burgeoning development of methodologies and materials for reading instruction, there can be no excuse for today's modern teacher who fails to properly assess his or her students' needs and adapt the instructional program to meet their needs. The challenge is sometimes great, but the challenge can be met. We now turn to the different organizational structures to examine their strengths and weaknesses.

Grouping

How can new teachers organize their classrooms to assure reading competence for all children? As teachers in an elementary self-contained classroom, they will first need to know the reading levels of each child. On their own or with the help of the school's reading specialist they will determine the capacity and independent and instructional levels of each pupil. See Chapter 13 for a description of these levels. The teacher, after this diagnosis, may differentiate instruction by some form of intraclass grouping or by individualized instructional procedures. Teachers will use their knowledge of the children's instructional level to group them in basal readers and for reading any content area textbook in directed-lesson groups. They will use their knowledge of the children's independent reading level when sending them to supplementary reading books or content area textbooks they will read on their own. At times teachers will have a skills lesson for a group who exhibit a need for a new skill or a review of one previously taught. Some children will work together on a project related to a special interest or some phase of a topic developed in a social studies or science lesson. Reading material geared to their abilities will be needed for such group work and can be collected with the aid of the school librarian.

Teachers will use their knowledge of each child's probable capacity level to assure reading competence. Noting a discrepancy between Tom's capacity level and his current instructional level, his teacher can provide further instruction with appropriate materials. If the gap is too wide, the teacher may call upon the reading specialist to help correct Tom's reading deficiency or make a referral for special testing. Noting a gifted reader in his or her class, the teacher may make special provisions to challenge the child with provocative assignments, reading materials, and opportunities to use his or her special talent. Noting that another boy is capable but not comprehending his social studies assignments, the teacher may provide such study skills lessons as reading for main ideas, details, and sequence of events. When several pupils encounter difficulty with the science vocabulary, the teacher may group them for several lessons devoted to the development of meaningful scientific vocabularies.

Homogeneous vs. Heterogeneous. Within the classroom, reading lessons may be given to a group with nearly the same abilities. This is efficient as long as the assumption is true. If such groups are maintained without change throughout the year, it is not efficient, for if there are twenty different reading skills involved, there would (by the same assumption) have to be nineteen different groupings. Inflexible grouping, such as standard three-reading-groups to the classroom, is not effective a good share of the time. So if the philosophy is homogeneous in the classroom to meet particular skills or to accomplish a particular stage of reading development, it should be flexible, changing frequently. Is there a time for a heterogeneous reading class session? There are many such times. For example, the introduction to a new unit with its several new concepts would be taught the whole class and then followed up by differentiated work.

If the criteria for grouping are tied into the purposes or goals, grouping is apt to be a successful procedure. In and of itself, grouping is neither good nor bad. If grouping is to bring together those students currently reading with approximately the same ability, the group may have really challenging sessions, all students moving along at the relatively similar rate. If the purpose is to bring together those with similar current interests, the same successful results may prevail. If the purpose is to bring together those students who need help in some special skill, such as adding the inflectional ending *ed* to form the past tense, then some extra work with only these students may improve their performance considerably; and this would be a waste of time for the other students who are already proficient in this skill.

Another way to approach homogeneous grouping is to cut across grade lines for a reading period (cross-grade grouping or intraclass grouping) and bring together with the teacher those with similar abilities. One such plan is the Joplin plan. At a given time daily the two or three grades involved have the children move to another room for their own group for reading

"Let's try again."

and return to their own classroom after the session. The teaching of specific skills may be more easily done, but the application of those skills that is necessary for complete learning is lessened. The basis for the grouping is usually the reading assessment test. A different type of departmentalization is the Joplin plan, a redeployment for reading instruction. All teachers have a reading period under this plan. Children are assigned to a room according to their reading level. Thus the children for one period are homogeneously grouped by reading scores. How does the teacher prepare for the group that comes in for that hour daily? His or her difficulties in planning are due to the fact that a group, "homogeneous" on the basis of total reading scores, will have varied skills needs. Thus he or she cannot teach a single skills lesson that will meet the needs of everyone. The teacher will also be at a loss when trying to relate reading to other curriculum areas. His reading group is a cross-class sectioning. He will see only a few of them during the rest of the day when he becomes a content area teacher again. Such teachers could be more effective in their reading period if they diagnosed the reading levels and planned intraclass grouping for instruction. Experimental studies within the past decade have shown no significant benefits from the Joplin plan of grouping.

Heterogeneous grouping is the assignment of the students to classes randomly or by some criterion other than on the basis of scholastic or achievement testing. Some schools attempt this by age; some, alphabetically; some, geographically (children from the same small neighborhood, and so on). Some attempt to balance the number of boys and girls in the classes, to develop a mix ethnically, and so on. If there is more than one class per grade level in the school, some form of assignment criterion must be used. Probably the best method is a review of the situation by faculty and administrator jointly and having the determination made on the basis of what seems best for those local children. Inasmuch as the research literature is not clearly supportive of any one method and society changes periodically in its priorities, the current needs assessment and program objectives and programs should be the core criteria for the decisions on grouping.

INSTRUCTIONAL SYSTEMS

We are familiar with all kinds of systems. As an example, think of the water system in your home. Someone *deliberately designed* it for the home—with a *unified purpose, synthetic parts:* a pipe brings water to the house, through a meter for measuring, branching into and through the water softener, through the hot water heater, through pipes to radiators for heating the rooms; cold water pipes parallel hot water pipes into the kitchen sink for cooking, washing, drinking, through the dishwasher, through the refrigerator for ice cubes, to the bathroom for tubbing, showering, washing, and the toilet flusher, to an outside faucet for watering the lawn and washing the car, to a sprinkler system in case of fire, to a laundry tub and clothes washer —*interrelated and interacting components, which are employed to function in an integrated fashion to attain a predetermined purpose.*[11] Translated into a reading program, this would be a structure of organization of an orderly whole, which clearly shows the interrelations of the parts to each other and to the purposes of the whole. Some examples of reading management systems that use the systems approach are

> CAI Computer Assisted Instruction—Stamford University
> Project PLATO—University of Illinois
> Wisconsin Design—University of Wisconsin
> Fountain Valley Teacher Support System

Management support systems and the systems approach seem to be increasing in popularity in the educational field. Some specific sources that might be helpful to the uninitiated are

> Emery, F. E., ed. *Systems Thinking.* Baltimore: Penguin Books, 1972.
> Kling, Martin. "Background and Application of Systems Approaches to Reading," *Reading Management Systems,* ed. Jane Morse. Fall 1975. Reading Conference, Rutgers University.
> Wayne, Otto, and E. Askov. *The Wisconsin Design for Reading Skill Development Rationale and Guidelines.* Minneapolis, MN: National Computer Systems, 1972.
> Ruddell, Robert. *Reading-Language Instruction: Innovative Practice.* Englewood Cliffs, NJ: Prentice-Hall, Inc., 1974. See pp. 621–28, "Criteria for Evaluating Reading Systems."
> Sullivan, M. "What Is the Instructional System Approach to Reading?" *Educational Technology,* 13:15–18 (Sept. 1973).

If you are concerned about traditional emphases in the programs you have encountered and are willing to work at newer approaches and be innovative, then this concern can be channeled into new instructional design. A plan is presented by Kemp [12] and developed with explanations to accomplish this end. (See Figure 20 on p. 314.)

An example of a college move in this same direction is instruction of future teachers through the use of learning modules. See Duffy and Sherman.[13] Each component has modules within it. From the Table of Contents comes the following illustration:

[11] Bela H. Banathy, *Instructional Systems* (Palo Alto, CA: Fearon Publishers, 1968), pp. 2–3.
[12] Jerrold Kemp, *Instructional Design* (Belmont, CA: Lear Siegler, Inc. Education Division, 1971).
[13] Gerald Duffy and George Sherman, *How To Teach Reading Systematically* (New York: Harper & Row, Publishers, 1973).

COMPONENT ONE: DETERMINING THE NATURE AND
IMPORTANCE OF READING

Module 1   Stating What Reading Is
Module 2   Listing Reading Prerequisites
Outside Assignment, Evaluation of Basal Reading Sets [14]

The College Reading Association has prepared a booklet to help college reading professors develop modules to train teachers of reading.[15] *The Torch Lighters Revisited* [16] indicates that the modular approach in the redesign of teacher education is receiving considerable attention.

Figure 20. Design Plan

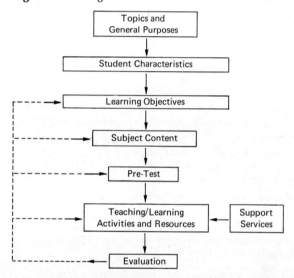

Cluster Grouping

Cluster grouping is a flexible arrangement very similar to the organization for team teaching. The difference seems to be mainly in the name by which it is labeled locally.

Team Teaching

In team teaching, a plan of cooperative teaching, several teachers, usually three to six, have joint responsibility for some twenty-five children per

[14] Ibid., p. vii.
[15] Carol O'Connell and Sandra McCormick, eds, *Preparing Learning Modules to Train Teachers of Reading* (York, PA: Strine Publishing Company, 1977).
[16] Coleman Morrison and Mary C. Austin, *The Torch Lighters Revisited.* (Newark, DE: International Reading Association, 1977).

teacher. Each teacher teaches all subjects in the curriculum. Each team includes several specialists who plan and do a major share of teaching in their specialty. Reading under this cooperative plan may be taught to several large groups while several smaller groups are receiving corrective instruction. The team meets weekly to note pupils' progress and to make plans for future lessons. New teachers have the advantage of working with experienced personnel in these aspects of planning, reviewing, and discussing objectives and progress to date.

Students experience such advantages as demonstrations by specially talented or trained team leaders, participation in frequent small-group discussion, and opportunities to express their own ideas or ask questions.

Problems have been encountered when any of the following occurred: insufficient provision for small-group instruction, insufficient time allotted for planning and evaluating progress, personality conflicts among team members, and inadequate provision of space for large and small groups.

A recent research report, covering fifteen years of team-teaching studies, indicates that academic performance is not enhanced by this organization. Nor does it indicate that this is a poorer structure.[17]

Open Classroom (School)

The open classroom is a relatively large space with bookshelves, desks, and files arranged as temporary dividers instead of solid walls separating "rooms," in which there is an ebb and flow of traffic as children work sometimes in a large group, in small groups, or singly. The children may shift from one activity to another on their own initiative; in philosophy they develop responsibility for their own learning, following their interests and the stimulation of the environment. This is a relatively unstructured learning environment. Reading turns out, usually, to be very similar in its composition to the individualized reading programs. There is some grouping for skills instruction in a flexible manner. There is a destructuring of the time schedule and also a partnership of children and teachers.[18] Many of the ideas for the open school came from England, where it has been an operating form for quite a few years. There has developed in American open schools a greater dependency on regular diagnostic information on the individual child and each task as opposed to standardized testing where the individual is compared to a norm (group). There is also a much greater use of community, colleagues, advisers, and a sort of interdisciplinary approach.[19] At

[17] David Armstrong, "Team-Teaching and Academic Achievement," *Review of Educational Research* 47:65–86 (Winter 1977).
[18] Alexander Frazier, *Open Schools For Children* (Washington, DC: Association for Supervision and Curriculum Development, 1972).
[19] Janette Rogers, "Reading Practices in Open Education," *The Reading Teacher*, 29:548–54 (March 1976).

the present time, much of the expository writing about open schools is favorable and encouraging; the research reports are typically either negative or neutral concerning cognitive learning after two or three years of open school education. Some are even negative about attitudes and self-concept.[20] Keep in mind that the goals may be different in the open school and, therefore, should be measured accordingly. The reorientation of the classroom teacher is absolutely necessary for successful performance in this flexible, unstructured setting; frequent meetings help for evaluation, planning, and interpreting. Probably some teachers are not adaptable to this kind of instruction. They, like some children, really feel more comfortable and can perform more effectively in the more structured classroom.

Team Learning

Pupils are paired as teacher-and-pupil for practice in certain skills. This technique can be an effective plan for organization in reading activities. These include word recognition, word analysis, using the dictionary, checking workbooks, oral reading, and storytelling. The teacher in this pattern of classroom organization needs to make a careful selection of materials and exercises and supervise the ensuing activities so that both teacher and pupil in each team share the reading experiences.

Learning Centers

Learning centers may refer to the learning stations or interest centers or resource centers that are a part of the classroom—relatively small areas devoted to individualized or small-group learning. They have resource materials that are geared to the level of the students and provide learning from that point—multilevel materials such as books, task cards, displays, cassettes and other A-V materials, kits, and so on. Characteristic of the center is a set of clear directions, clear objectives, choices for the student, answers, manipulative materials, and some evaluation means—preferably recording of learning. The characteristic that is most striking to casual observation is that the students are moving to the learning stations instead of staying seated at a desk all day. They take on the responsibility for their learning to a greater extent in so doing. They take some teacher-time to plan, organize, collect materials, and supervise; but they can save considerable time in the instructional process and enhance its success greatly. Some sources of information to help the teacher plan learning stations may be found in

---

[20] Robert Wright, "The Affective and Cognitive Consequences of an Open Education Elementary School," *American Education Research Journal,* 12:449–65 (Fall 1975).

Thelma R. Newman. "On Learning Centers." *NJEA Review,* **50**,8:26–28 (April 1977).

Aldon Skrypa. "A Learning Station Approach to Individualize Reading Instruction." *Reading Management Systems.* Rutgers University Reading Conference, (Fall 1975), pp. 6–9.

Louise Waynant and Robert Wilson. *Learning Centers, A Guide for Effective Use.* New York: McGraw-Hill, Book Company, 1974.

A related type of organization has resulted in regional teacher-learning centers being developed. The purpose of these centers is to be supportive of the instructional programs of the schools in their area. They collect a wide assortment of instructional materials, help teachers get materials, and show them how to use the materials. They also run in-service types of programs to bring the newer materials to the attention of teachers. They operate with a director and consultants, who work with teachers in their own school system setting. From the reactions of teachers who have used the centers' services, they are very helpful.

Departmentalization

Teachers have special interests and special capabilities. When they teach a content area, solely, they can become specialists in their subject. At the elementary school level, specialists first appeared in art, music, and physical education. Other subjects in the curriculum continued as part of the teacher's responsibility in his or her self-contained classroom. In a trend away from the child-centered curriculum toward a content-centered curriculum, other teacher-specialists appeared in such areas as mathematics, social studies, science, and even in reading. In this framework, reading was considered a content subject. One teacher taught reading for children in grades four, five, and six (sometimes seven and eight also). Thus a teacher met ninety or more students daily for their reading instruction. The rest of the day the students were in the rooms of other content teachers, who typically ignored the teaching of reading skills in the content area and taught their subject.

The reading teacher organized for instruction as best he could! The informal reading inventory to ascertain reading levels had to be discarded as impractical for such large numbers. A rough type of grouping in each class could be obtained as the result of a group test of reading, with those centering around the median in the average group, those above in the best group, and those below in the third group. The teacher who was well prepared in reading, if he could find the time, could do some diagnostic teaching in the third group, thus providing some corrective teaching for those below average. In the period allotted, usually forty to forty-five minutes, the teacher often confined his teaching to the basal reader. Less well-prepared teachers in this situation have sometimes taken the path of least resistance.

They have turned to the next story in the reader, called on the first person to read a paragraph, then called on the next and the next for a "barbershop" session, which may be considered worthless as a reading lesson. Analyzed at the end of the period, the lesson provided no vocabulary building, no directed attention to main ideas and details, no extension of skills to other assignments, and usually no attempt at enrichment or extending interests by pointing out further reading in related materials.

Reading needs in content areas were also ignored, except upon occasion, when a knowledgeable content area teacher pointed out the vocabulary of the new subject and gave directions on how to read the new textbook.

It may be pointed out that even a reading specialist, with a considerable knowledge of reading techniques and materials, could be at a loss in a situation where he or she was expected to meet nearly a hundred children each day, to ascertain their needs and interests, to provide effective teaching, and to produce competent readers at all levels. He or she would be further at a loss to help children read in content areas because he or she would not see the children in their subject classrooms to discover what reading difficulties each was encountering. In general, departmentalization is a less desirable plan than the others because of lack of transfer and application of skills.

Nongraded Classrooms

Like team teaching the nongraded plan [21] is another departure from the conventional system of organizing for instruction. Nongrading has as its main purposes

1. Continuous progress for each individual with no reference to any current grade level of accomplishment.
2. Differentiation of instruction so that each child will be challenged to learn at his or her own rate without competition with his or her peers.
3. A classroom organization that fosters individual and flexible small-group instruction.
4. The provision of a series of achievement levels or nongraded blocks of learnings to implement individual progress.

Although this type of school organization has been considered by some educators for both the elementary and secondary school, it has been attempted most frequently at the primary level. In the nongraded primary unit a child progresses toward a goal appropriate for him without the artificial barriers of a grade a year. The teacher plans for the reading (or arithmetic) lessons of the individual child. As the pupil progresses at his own

[21] John I. Goodlad and Robert H. Anderson, *The Nongraded Elementary School* (New York: Harcourt, Brace Jovanovich, Inc., 1963).

rate through a block of lessons designated for him, he does not compete with others whose abilities may be higher or lower than his. He experiences the personal satisfaction of successful achievement, whether he spends more or fewer years than the average in completing these achievement levels.

In this plan of organization teachers need a good background of knowledge concerning the sequential development of reading skills, methods, and materials of instruction. They need to understand fully the needs and current achievement levels of each child in order to provide appropriate instruction at a given time. In this plan, however, both teachers and pupils are freed from the artificial pressures sometimes accompanying the instruction in a conventional classroom. For the pupil these pressures are to complete a body of graded materials in a specified time or be penalized by retention and repetition of content. For the teacher the pressure has been a need to cover the assigned work for everyone within a time limit imposed by the grade-a-year concept. When it can be shown that pupils benefit from carefully planned curriculum sequences and periodic evaluations of their progress, the nongraded program can be recommended.

Some schools have been built especially for the purpose of nongrading instruction. Some recent examples are the Dixie and Lansdowne Elementary Schools in Lexington, Kentucky, and the Sherwood Elementary School in Greeley, Colorado. They have carpeted classrooms and movable walls, thus providing for such typical disadvantages as the higher noise level and the lack of numerous small areas that may be found in many existing elementary school buildings. They provide the possibility of flexible grouping, thus enabling children to work in different group levels in different subjects. Some traditional types of schools have been able to provide the flexibility needed for the nongrading concept even within the existing classroom structure.

Tewksbury [22] has reviewed three plans for implementing a nongraded program. In the first two plans, children are assigned to self-contained classrooms, either (1) on the basis of academic performance, according to age or (2) on the basis of performance levels with interclassroom achievement grouping. In the third plan children in mixed-age rooms are regrouped for interclassroom achievement grouping. The third plan thus involves a departmentalized or a team-teaching arrangement.

Composite Plans

The dual-progress plan was developed by Stoddard [23] for the elementary school. Its features are a combination of departmentalization, the Joplin

[22] John L. Tewksbury. *Nongrading the Elementary School* (Columbus, OH: Charles E. Merrill Books, Inc., 1967), pp. 62–99.
[23] George D. Stoddard, *The Dual Progress Plan* (Evanston, IL: Harper & Row, Publishers, 1961).

plan, and a core curriculum. Children are grouped on different bases in the morning and in the afternoon. They receive graded instruction in language arts and social studies in the mornings. In the afternoon they are instructed by subject matter specialists in mathematics, science, music, and art in achievement-level sections. Teachers can provide some individualization of instruction in the morning sessions as they become acquainted with individuals and their needs. Teachers in the afternoon are at a disadvantage in getting to know pupils well and in understanding their reading needs in content subjects.

The continuous-progress plan is a modification of nongrading. The program in effect in the Falk School,[24] a university laboratory school, has been described as a combination of nongrading, multiage heterogeneous sectioning, and modified team teaching. Its purpose is to provide differentiation through the flexible structuring of instruction. Sequential "develo-blocks" of increasing difficulty are prepared in each field of study in the curriculum. Readings are prepared at four levels: minimal, basal, horizontal enrichment, and vertical enrichment. Reading needs are met through the provision of basal reading and individual reading units. In the elementary section classes are primary, midgroup, and intermediate with an age range of two to four years each. Four to seven power groups are formed for reading in each room. Two homeroom teachers make up a team that plans class schedules and instructional procedures.

Modification Due to Method or Material

Through the last century there have been many attempts to break away from the traditional teacher-and-whole-class type of instructions. Shane outlined thirty-five plans that have been developed for the purpose of recognizing individual differences among children. In his list are the following: ungraded groups, primary-intermediate grouping, grade-level grouping, heterogeneous grouping, homogeneous grouping, XYZ grouping, intra-subject-field grouping, departmental grouping, Winnetka plan grouping, Dalton plan grouping, multiple-track grouping, platoon grouping, social maturity grouping, developmental grouping, organismic-age grouping, ungraded primary groups, intra- and inter-classroom grouping, self-selection grouping, and special grouping for the gifted and for the slow learning and the mentally retarded.[25] Even this abbreviated list will serve to point out that educators have long been concerned with discovering a workable structure in which individual differences could be considered. Some have been tried and discarded; others, absorbed in the organizational pattern of some schools.

[24] Sartain, op. cit., pp. 230–32.
[25] Harold G. Shane, "The School and Individual Differences," *Individualizing Instruction,* NSSE Yearbook, LXI, Part 1, (1962), p. 49.

Another plan for continuous progress through personalized teaching is the program of individually prescribed instruction at the Oakleaf School.[26] Sequences of lessons in reading, mathematics, and science have been designed for the first six years of school. A pupil finds his prescribed lessons in a folder four mornings each week. He studies independently, working at his own rate, and records his reactions to his lessons. These are studied by the teacher, who then prescribes his next series of lessons. On the fifth morning the pupil meets with his class for a seminar session or in small group sessions. Teachers prepare for this program by calling upon a large fund of resources—the numbered series of lessons, library books, tapes, recordings, and packets of materials assembled for integration with content subjects. A danger here is that the work of the teacher will become so mechanical that rapport and empathy with the learner will be sacrificed— certainly to the detriment of the pupil. This probability may or may not offset the advantage claimed for it in its development of an extensive inventory of self-managed instructional materials for individuals of varying abilities and competencies.

Alternative Schools

If we do not like the current program of the school system, we can experiment with new programs; we can get new materials of instruction and add them to our present ones; we can change the structure of the school and/or classroom to accommodate modified approaches; we can change the personnel or add reading specialist(s) to study the program and recommend changes. Or we can determine that the public school (or whatever school) is not meeting the needs of our children and go to a parochial, private, or alternative school. If the judgment was flawed in any way, this is tantamount to "jumping from the frying pan into the fire." If the decisions were based on a careful and appropriate assessment, the individual may find the change to the advantage of the child (children) involved. Probably no school can successfully meet the needs of *every* student better than any other school.

Your authors believe that the public schools are the very foundation of our democratic society and should be supported fully. Certainly, by the same thinking, there is a place in American society for those who want a different emphasis in education also to support alternative types of schools. We believe that our discussion of reading programs can be applied equally well to either setting. It is interesting to note that the so-called alternative schools, if they continue to operate over a period of time, approach nearer and nearer to the very public school programs that they rebelled against or whose value they questioned.

[26] C. M. Lindvall and J. O. Bolvin, "Programed Instruction in the Schools: An Application of Programing Principles in Individually Prescribed Instruction," *Programed Instruction,* NSSE Yearbook, LXVI, Part 2, (1967), pp. 217–54.

THE ADMINISTRATOR AND THE READING PROGRAM

The administrator is an important part of the reading program. What can the teacher expect from the administrator? First of all, the teacher can expect a clear definition of the role of all reading personnel, spelling out their obligations to the children and to the school as a whole. The role of the reading teacher, reading consultant or specialist, the reading supervisor —whatever the title—all individuals involved should know the obligations of that person, and any assessment of performance can then be based upon those duties. Second, the administrator should be good at his or her job of selection and recommendation of reading personnel. He or she should be able to assess the candidates' qualifications, demonstrate strong and precise interview techniques, and know what to look for in observing classroom reading lessons or the individual working with other teachers and should also demonstrate the ability to get the faculty to want to continue professional development. Third, the administrator should know how to evaluate and interpret the total reading program. Fourth, he or she has to know how to coordinate the efforts of the different personnel. Fifth, administrators should make their desire and commitment to full support of worthwhile experimentation in reading. Sixth, they should supervise a systematic review of programs and materials of reading instruction. Seventh, they should work with their personnel in the development of budget support year-round, not just sporadically. Where program budgets are involved, they should carefully weigh the priorities in assessing the programs from year to year. Finally, wherever they have a weakness in any of the preceding areas, they should seek the combined effort of those who *are* knowledgeable in the reading field, such as a reading specialist, to work with them on procedures of administration, supervision, instruction. Wherever it is found that an elementary school has a good program of reading, there is *always* a person (or persons) in the leadership role who has inspirationally gotten the teachers and the children to believe in their reading prowess.

Administrators as a group recognize the importance of reading as evidenced by the 1977 *Platform and Resolutions* of the American Association of School Administrators. Under Educational/Instructional Programs, item 25, Reading:

> The AASA, recognizing the increased levels of skill development required for full functional literacy, encourages Association members to continue to place the highest priority on reading with special emphasis on the needs of the individual.

One very simple procedure that seems to be effective is to build up a professional library on reading and reading instruction and make it readily accessible to the faculty. This latter point is important if the books are going to be read.

SUMMARY

Once again, it is the teacher-pupil contact that builds reading skills, love for reading, and interest in reading-related activities. The administrator's job is to see that the setting is maximized—space, professional skill, materials—for reading to take place. Whatever the organization, the teachers should be prepared to work up to their best functioning level. It takes a team to create success for a school system—parents, students, teachers, administrators, and supervisors.

SELECTED READINGS

Criscuolo, Nicholas. *Activities for Reading Enrichment.* New York: The Instructor Publication, Inc., 1975.

Emery, F. E., ed., *Systems Thinking.* Baltimore: Penguin Books, 1972.

Forgan, Harry, and Charles Mangrum II. *Teaching Content Area Reading Skills.* Columbus, OH: Charles E. Merrill Publishing Company, 1976.

Frazier, Alexander. *Open Schools For Children.* Washington, DC: Association for Supervision and Curriculum Development, 1972.

Howes, Virgil. *Individualization of Instruction: A Teaching Strategy.* New York: Macmillan Publishing Co., Inc., 1970.

Kemp, Jerrold. *Instructional Design.* Belmont, CA: Lear Siegler, Inc., Educational Division, 1971.

Lamme, Linda. "Self-Contained to Departmentalized: How Reading Habits Changed," *Elementary School Journal* 76 (January 1976), 208–18.

Morrison, Coleman, and Mary Austin. *The Torch Lighters Revisited.* Newark, DE: International Reading Association, 1977.

O'Connell, Carol, and Sandra McCormick, eds. *Preparing Learning Modules to Train Teachers of Reading.* College Reading Association, 1977.

Rauch, Sidney. "The Administrator and the Reading Program: Questions Administrators Ask . . . and Some Answers." *Reading World.* **XIV**,3 (March 1975), 198–200.

Ruddell, Robert. *Reading-Language Instruction: Innovative Practices.* Englewood Cliffs, NJ: Prentice-Hall, Inc., 1974.

Snow, Lawrence. *Using Teacher Aides.* Highland Park, NJ: Drier Educational Systems, 1972.

Strain, Lucille. *Accountability in Reading Instruction.* Columbus, OH: Charles E. Merrill Publishing Co., 1976.

Waynant, Louise, and Robert Wilson. *Learning Centers—A Guide for Effective Use.* New York: McGraw-Hill Book Company, 1974.

Part Four

Evaluation of Progress in Reading

(Accountability)

Chapter 13

Methods
of
Appraisal

OBJECTIVES

To explore the relationship between objectives and evaluation

To develop an awareness of the concept of accountability

To gain an acquaintance with a variety of appraisal strategies

To learn the use of informal classroom appraisal techniques

To learn the place of standardized tests in reading programs

To discover the importance of continuous evaluation

INTRODUCTION

Appraisal is the determination of the extent to which each child has attained the objectives of the reading program. This definition implies that there are clearly stated objectives for the reading program and that these objectives can be measured and attained. It also suggests that judgments can be made from the measurement data. The measurement may be made in a number of ways, among which are standardized tests, informal testing, informal reading inventories, the anecdotal recording of observations, questionnaires, and checklists. The total evaluation program is composed of the various appraisal techniques, which, in a sense, are intermittent samplings of children's behavior in reading situations, the assessment of materials and their use, and the overall picture of the program at any given time. Because a child's reading status is constantly changing, the classroom teacher should employ a continuous program of evaluation to make teaching effective.

The first step must be the statement of realistic objectives or goals for the children—attainable, measurable, specific, encompassing all skills necessary, and stated in behavioristic terms. Mager [1] identifies words such as *to know,* to *understand,* to *appreciate,* to *believe,* which are subject to varied interpretations and should, therefore, be avoided. Instead, those words should be used that have fewer interpretations, such as to *write,* to *recite,* to *construct,* to *list.* The latter words describe intended instructional outcomes rather than content. Terminal behavior describes the act(s) that will be accepted as evidence that the learner has achieved the objective. Objectives must not only be stated, but they must have a priority relationship or dimension.[2] They must also imply a philosophy and rationale, which have been so ably presented by Tyler,[3] as theoretical constructs for evaluation. The broader viewpoint is presented by Scriven [4] in a model with the formative evaluation procedures (day by day) in the development of curriculum and the summative (final post test) evaluation in selection among curricula. This he does by placing program-faculty-students in an intercorrelated relationship to the formative and summative dimensions. A slightly different and even broader perspective is shown in a model by Stake [5] as the generalizable content of a program that shows in juxtaposition the transactions that transform input (staff, students, media, facilities, administrative conditions) into outputs (enabling objectives, terminal objectives, and their interrelationships). Some classifications of objectives may be helpful to the teacher. Examples may be found in the following:

> Bloom, Benjamin S., ed. *Taxonomy of Educational Objectives, Handbook I: Cognitive Domain.* New York: David McKay Company, Inc., 1956.
> Krathwohl, David R.; Benjamin S. Bloom; and Bertram B. Masia. *Taxonomy of Educational Objectives, Handbook II: Affective Domain.* New York: David McKay Company, Inc., 1964.
> *The Barrett Taxonomy Cognitive and Affective Dimensions of Reading Comprehension,* in Clymer, Theodore, "What is Reading? Some Current Concepts," *Innovation and Change in Reading Instruction,* Sixty-seventh Yearbook of the NSSE, Part 2, ed. Helen Robinson. Chicago: The University of Chicago Press, 1968, pp. 19–23.

[1] Robert F. Mager, *Preparing Instructional Objectives,* 2d ed. (Belmont, CA: Fearon-Pitman Publishers, Inc., 1975).
[2] Robert E. Stake, "The Countenance of Educational Evaluation," *Teachers College Record,* **LXVIII**:523–40 (April 1967).
[3] Ralph W. Tyler, *Basic Principles of Curriculum and Instruction* (Chicago: The University of Chicago Press, 1967).
[4] Michael Scriven, "Methodology of Evaluation," American Educational Research Association Monograph Series on Curriculum Evaluation I (Chicago: Rand McNally & Company, 1967).
[5] Stake, op. cit.

Harrow, Anita J., *A Taxonomy of the Psychomotor Domain.* New York: David McKay Company, Inc., 1972.

Following the determination and statement of objectives, the teacher uses appraisal to determine the appropriate materials for instruction, to group children for instruction—developmental and remedial—to determine both strengths and weaknesses, to determine what further testing or investigation is needed, and to help the child set his or her own goals. The curriculum is determined as a result of appraisal, not in spite of it. *What* is taught depends upon the learning needs of the individual.

Suppose, for instance, among the stated objectives are (1) an interest in work that requires reading skill, (2) speed in completing reading assignments, (3) a desire to read independently, (4) taste in the choice of reading material, (5) a certain sight vocabulary, (6) phonic word-attack methods, and (7) good listening skills while others are reading orally. Picture the seven objectives this way:

1	2	3	4	5	6	7
				a	b	c

Objective 5 can be easily sampled by standardized word list *a.* Objective 6 can be tested by a teacher-made test *b.* Objective testing by a teacher-made test *c* can sample the child's ability in objective 7. What about the others? Careful observation, recording day-by-day behavior, and discussion may be the appropriate appraisal techniques for objectives 1 through 4. Each child's graph of performance or achievement will differ from the others. For instruction, those graphs that are similar can be grouped together. Some children may have to get individual instruction. The important point to keep in mind is the fact that some of the preceding techniques are one-shot appraisals whereas others are continuous. The one-shot appraisals must be supplemented with the teacher's daily addition of evidence, for they were only samplings at a given time in a given setting.

Most of the teacher's appraisal techniques do not measure causes of pupil behavior in reading. They point to symptoms or results. Like the iceberg that is only one tenth in view, the causes are often hidden in the child's slow development or psychological or sociological development. They may lurk in his or her poor health or frequent absences or immaturity. Inappropriate curriculum or poor teaching may be a causal factor. What is really important, then, is what the teacher does with the data after collecting all that are available. The appraisal process should be functional in its contribution to the reading program and broad enough so that it can relate to the child's total learning program. Teachers must be careful that they do not assign too much weight to minutiae that are relatively unimportant in the given setting. When a child is reading orally to transmit information or to relate a story, he or she should not be stopped for drill on a specific word ending. The teacher might make note of the need for this specific skill and place it in another lesson where it is important. It is better to get on with the task at hand than to deal with irrelevant minutiae at this point, thus retaining the emphasis on the major goal of the lesson.

INFORMAL CLASSROOM TECHNIQUES

Graded Word Lists

Basal reading series may be used when a teacher wishes to develop an informal vocabulary list. Samples of ten to fifteen words may be chosen from the vocabulary lists accompanying the preprimers, primers, and the books in grades one through six or eight, as provided in the series. The word recognition skills of pupils may be tested by having them say all the words in the list at each level until they miss more than one word. Their meaning vocabulary may be tested by pointing to the list in which they made one error and asking them to use the words in sentences of their own. This technique may be varied by asking them to define or explain a word, or to paraphrase a sentence the tester has devised to include the word. Samples may be chosen from the graded lists above and below the single level for further testing. See Figure 21.

At each level the teacher may select from the teacher's manual samples of the skills of structural analysis and phonetic analysis and make another list of graded items for each type. Thus in the primary grade lists of structural analysis, children would face words like *snowman, books, thanking,* and *unhappy.* In the upper grade lists they might attack such words as *improbable, instruction,* and *uninhabited.*

Graded samples of phonetic analysis might range from sets of words, such as *cap–rap, plant–play, not–note,* through the more difficult analysis of words like *advice–advise, placate–placid, necessary–necessity,* and so on.

Compiling a pupil's errors and noting the grade level at which he or she was most successful will help the teacher plan his or her skills program. Thus an upper grade pupil who misses polysyllabic words and has no technique for working them out may be helped to find root words, watch for common prefixes and suffixes, and learn how to divide words into syllables. He or she may even need help in sounding and blending in order to arrive at an eventual recognition of a word. Primary grade children who have trouble with *cap–rap, ran–tan,* or *shook–brook* may need further oral practice on rhyming endings, both in listening and in producing accurate sounds. Teachers who administer these informal tests obtain objective evidence of

Figure 21. *Meaning Vocabulary*

LEVEL			
PRIMER	FIRST	SECOND	THIRD
baby	fish	summer	spider
fall	dress	animal	cardboard
boat	street	candle	wander
cats	count	fast	insects
want	happy	hungry	machine
three	morning	grow	foolish
paint	last	table	studied
man	work	open	chuckled
please	brave	afraid	mountains
tried	cry	chain	dislike

FOURTH	FIFTH	SIXTH
laughing	prosperous	urgent
quickly	miniature	primitive
sloppy	requirements	hindrance
guarded	abundant	invincible
alley	emergency	unprovoked
stumbled	nostrils	pendulum
rehearse	trophy	uncertainty
sorrowful	suspense	perpetual
performing	persuade	specifically
	transport	ancient

specific lacks in skills achievement. They may then provide appropriately graded materials and instruction, individually or in small groups.

In addition to the lists that teachers may compile for themselves, word lists are available to teachers for an inventory of word recognition skills. Examples are the Dolch, Botel, San Diego, and Kucera-Francis word lists.

The Informal Reading Inventory

As a measure of attainment in reading ability the informal reading inventory is a practical technique for any type of classroom. It is invaluable in the hands of the teacher of an individualized classroom. In the nongraded school it might be considered as the *sine qua non*—that without which no teacher would consider teaching! In the traditional self-contained classroom it can be used to establish both reading groups and content area groups and to suggest the range of supplementary and library material that can be made available to the children. In schools organized under Joplin plans or other departmentalized plans, the informal reading inventory can guide teachers in their initial placement of pupils and in their continuous plan of guidance in reading.

Several informal reading inventories are available to teachers from various sources.[6] They may also be devised by a teacher or by a school system. The informal reading inventory consists of two selections chosen from each level of a graded series of books, basal readers, or content area textbooks, such as a social studies series. The length of the selections varies from forty or fifty words in primary grade books to one or two hundred words in upper grade selections. Questions are prepared to test the pupil's comprehension of both his or her oral and silent reading. The questions are mostly literal; but they may include some interpretive.

Elementary pupils will give evidence of their reading attainment in several ways. When they can read comfortably either orally or silently without encountering too difficult vocabulary or concepts and when they can understand the author's message, the pupils are on their own in their reading. The highest level at which they can read by themselves with adequate comprehension is known as their *independent reading level.* The teacher can ascertain the child's independent level by noting the grade level of the highest selection in which he or she reads with no less than 99 per cent accuracy in word recognition. At this level the student will be able to answer 90 per cent or more of the comprehension questions.

When students read material in which they encounter some difficult words and find that they have not thoroughly understood all that the author has written, they need the guidance of their teacher. At this point they have reached their instructional level. The teacher will note the grade level of the selection the pupil has read with at least 95 per cent accuracy in word recognition and 75 per cent or better in comprehension. This is the pupil's *instructional reading level,* where he or she will need the help of the teacher to develop reading skills further.

If students continue to a higher selection, they will meet many more unfamiliar words than previously. They may be puzzled by more complicated sentence structure and by concepts for which they have no background in personal experience. They may stumble over words, make many repetitions, point to words as if trying to keep their place, and at times lose the thread of thought. They will be successful in answering questions on less than half the material. At this point the pupil has reached his or her *frustration reading level.* The teacher needs to be aware of this level so that he or she will not assign textbooks or supplementary reading material that would be too difficult for the student.

These three reading levels—independent, instructional, and frustration

---

[6] Jerry L. Johns, *Basic Reading Inventory.* Dubuque, IO: Kendall/Hunt Publishing Company, 1978; Nicholas K. Silvaroli, *Classroom Reading Inventory,* 3rd Ed. Dubuque IO: William C. Brown Publishers, 1976.

—give the classroom teacher basic clues as to each pupil's level of attainment to date. For example, if Ted has an independent reading level of a third grader, his teacher knows that he has a mastery of such basic sight vocabulary as the Dolch 220 tool words comprising over 60 per cent of those he encounters in his reading at this level. The pupil can analyze certain words structurally and phonetically and understand the author's meaning in reading material no higher than third grade level. Ted will need his teacher's help as he gets into fourth grade readers and textbooks. Any material with a readability level higher than fourth grade will need to be avoided at this time, because it will present Ted with reading difficulties that would hinder his adequate comprehension of the subject matter.

Because of the many differences among pupils, teachers will need to know whether a particular pupil's present instructional level represents the best that can be expected of him or indicates less than that of which he is capable. Therefore, another level can be determined by the use of the informal reading inventory. The teacher may read to the pupil one or more selections above his instructional level. His *probable capacity level* is indicated when he can answer 75 per cent or more of the questions in one of the more difficult selections. The pupil who can understand materials at levels above his instructional reading level may profit from additional instruction to improve his or her reading skills. Thus, the gifted student may be guided to become a superior reader, and retarded readers may be detected and helped to improve through a remedial reading program geared to their needs.

Alert teachers today are well aware of the fact that individual differences among children's levels of achievement and performance exist. Just as they must be cognizant of the general and specific objectives underlying their instruction, they must also know how to guide all children appropriately. The informal reading inventory furnishes teachers with an evaluative procedure by which they can ensure for themselves and their pupils the attainment of instruction and materials effective for the individualization of learning.

Teacher Observations. Teachers observe children in natural reading situations daily. An anecdotal record should be kept of each child's responses in different kinds of situations, his or her attitudes, vigor, habits, and the skills he or she employs. The record keeping is an absolute necessity because teachers may forget previous behaviors as new ones appear (phychological factor of recency), they may misinterpret if they jump to conclusions with insufficient data, or they may let one situation analysis overshadow numerous others. Record keeping is also necessary to put strengths and weaknesses in their proper perspective—there is a tendency to notice successes and forget the failures. Both may be important. Observation is one very good way to supplement and corroborate other forms of measurement. The only proper way to appraise oral reading is with a checklist or marking

"You're doing fine!"

code in hand. This instant observation and recording requires some practice and skill on the part of the teacher. Teachers should memorize a marking code so that it will provide an accurate record of the child's oral reading. Many teachers generalize to the child's silent reading those errors they observe in oral reading. This should be avoided because many of the skills are different.

Another technique that helps children participate in their own appraisal of skills is the use of the videotape or tape recorder. Children read a selection, and then they can hear themselves and recognize their strengths and weaknesses with the help of the teacher. This has been found to be very effective. Repeated sampling of reading situation behaviors confirms or denies the ineffective habits that children are establishing, such as lip movements, using the finger as a guide, restlessness and fidgeting, incorrect posture, eye wandering, and inability to use certain study skills, such as the use of an index. The sampling must be adequate if a true appraisal is to be made. The teacher should be aware of the level so that determination can be made from observation whether the problem lies in the material itself (too difficult) or in the child's use of skills.

Individual Conference. If appraisal is to be made in the individual conference with the child, it should be planned carefully and structured so that the results can be used and interpreted. We recommend that a checklist be used in each of the areas to be measured—word-attack skills, comprehension, oral reading, appreciation—and that this checklist be supplemented with anecdotal records of behavior regularly in reading situations. This seems to be the best way the teacher can systematize learnings in the individualized approach to reading. Without this type of record keeping, the teacher is too dependent upon incidental learnings, memory, and haphazard measurement samples.

The Case Study. A thorough appraisal of a child's reading abilities together with background data may be compiled in a form called the *case study*. This is usually done preceding the establishment of a remedial program, where there is a serious problem relating to the child's achievement. The case study usually contains identification data of a personal nature, data regarding home environment, physical development, social development, educational history, mental abilities, any disabilities, and particularly standardized test results. A good compilation of case study data for developing skill in analyzing individual cases may be found in Putnam's book.[7] This technique is one procedure in remedial reading and reading clinic settings. Because the case study approach is time-consuming, it is typically used in the classroom only for those children with some special reading problems not easily diagnosed and quickly remedied.

Informal Tests. Teacher-made tests, the short tests that accompany children's newspapers, and many basal reader tests are discussed here because they are not standardized on a large cross-sectioning of students. Their purpose is to measure what has been learned from a particular unit or lesson. They are the same as criterion-reference tests only to the extent that the items measure what has just been taught. Objective items take the teacher a while to prepare, but they can be easily and quickly corrected and can readily be used over again on the same material. Objective items can measure nearly all of the skills of reading. They are made up of true-false, completion, matching, arranging in sequence or rank order, or alphabetizing items. They can measure memory, immediate recall, aided recall, unaided recall, following directions, in fact, most of the cognitive functions. They can also measure the affective domain, such as interests, attitudes, values, and appreciations, as these are expressed in overt behavioral manifestations. Besides using these measures, which relate to the decoding process, the teacher, by the use of carefully formed questions, measures the encoding process for which reading supplies the ammunition. Appraisals of the child's verbal performance in encoding may be made from the simple encoding task of preparing a caption for a drawing to the complex task of writing a story or a report on a trip to the zoo. These verbal expressions grow out of the child's actual experiences and vicarious reading experiences. A third type of informal classroom appraisal deals with the manipulative or motor-skill area. The child's ability to deal with spatial relationships is a part of

[7] Lillian Putnam, *Case Studies for Reading Teachers* (New York: American Press Publications, Inc., 1968).

Evaluating the seatwork

this, especially in reading readiness and beginning reading. The teacher who has not had a course in tests and measurements should read the booklets of the Educational Testing Service (Princeton, N J) or the brief publications on the development of good tests.[8]

Work Samples. One very good way for the children to observe their own growth is to save samples of their average work over a period of time. In this manner they can observe progress as well as discuss it with their teacher and parents. Samples of work in reading can be on tape for oral reading, answers to questions on comprehension, illustrative materials for creative efforts connected with stories or poems, and assignments that are written. They can keep records of their own reading accomplished, of check-lists on their own achievement in reading, of types of reading they have done, of books they have read from the library, of their reading rate on comparable selections, and of words they have learned and used. Card files or folder files kept by the children are especially effective in motivating them toward self-appraisal and improvement. Children may show a great deal of interest in a classroom log book of extraclass reading activities where there is a corner of the room set aside for independent reading and reading-related games. The children sign in and sign out and record their activity. If the teacher makes sure that there is an opportunity for *all* children to use

[8] William E. Blanton, Roger Farr, and J. J. Tuinman, *Measuring Reading Performance* (Newark, DE: The International Reading Association, 1974).

the corner and if there are appropriate materials there for everyone, all can benefit from this practice.

The Teacher's Self-Evaluation

Just as the teacher attempts to get the child involved in his own appraisal in order to capitalize on his knowledge of results, reinforcement, and need for self-actualization, so the teacher must do a self-appraisal to see if goals are being approached correctly. Specifically, here are some of the questions the teacher must ask and answer:

1. Am I collecting and systematically recording the *right* data for appraisal of progress toward our goals?
2. Do we both, the child and I, know his true status in each of the various skills, concepts, and understandings from day to day?
3. Do I better understand each child as each day passes?
4. Am I seeking causes of behavior rather than simply judging or misjudging from a few overt behavioral symptoms?
5. Am I capitalizing on my strengths and each child's strengths?
6. Am I regularly asking the full range of questions of the children to enhance their full cognitive growth (recall, inference, observation, criticism, example, classification, application, decision, comparison, contrast, and so on)?
7. Is my appraisal program of informal procedures in the classroom a balanced one that correctly supplements the standardized tests periodically administered?
8. Do the children in my classroom enjoy reading and meet frequent success and infrequent failure?

The Disadvantaged Child. Appraisal techniques in the classroom of the disadvantaged child do not differ in kind from those used in other classrooms. They have to be adjusted to the children and interpreted in the light of their backgrounds of experience. Teachers do have to examine their own selves, their attitudes, standards of behavior, and acceptance of verbal expression, in order to set realistic goals for these children. They may need to place greater emphasis on appraisal in the following areas: (1) the conceptual-informational background of the children, (2) receptive vocabulary, (3) auditory discrimination, (4) logic and reasoning, and (5) the related social-psychological needs (attitudes, aspirations, values, personal worth, self-actualization). When teachers attempt to place their classroom appraisal data in juxtaposition with standardized test norms, they encounter trouble, for those norms are based on a cross section of school populations. They do not adequately discriminate and measure the achievement progress of disadvantaged children. The teacher, therefore, has to rely primarily on informal classroom techniques of appraisal for a true picture of the children's achievement. The greatest challenge may be to help the child realistically appraise the child's own status and aspire to improvement through many means of encouragement.

This section on classroom techniques of appraisal has covered many devices, methods, and approaches for evaluating pupil status and pupil progress. They have all been classified informal techniques because of their lack of standardization. The next sections review standardized tests and other measuring instruments.

STANDARDIZED TESTS

Description

A standardized test is a published series of exercises or work samples that permit the individual to demonstrate skills so that his skills degree of success can be compared with the success of others. The standardization means that it has been administered to others, and the data have been used to establish norms for comparison. These tests are supposed to be secure in that they have not been used for instruction—only testing; they are sold only to teachers, administrators, or clinicians who keep them under wraps except when in use in testing situations.

In reading there are a number of classifications of standardized tests: (1) individual, (2) group, (3) oral, (4) essay, (5) objective, (6) speed, (7) power, (8) mastery, (9) verbal, (10) nonverbal, (11) performance, (12) survey, and (13) analytical or diagnostic. These terms describe the major characteristics of the test. Because the main concern here is the selection and use of the tests, some attributes of good tests are briefly mentioned as they must be considered:

1. Validity. Does the test measure content areas appropriate to the curriculum and objectives? This may be determined by inspection of the items (face validity) or by comparison with some other test or standard (criterion).
2. Reliability. Will the test consistently measure the individual's responses accurately and relative to others? The test-retest (temporal) factor indicates the stability of the measure, the scoring accuracy, and clear content. It is affected by the length of the test, the time it is administered, and the variability of the person himself.
3. Completeness of the manual. The manual should answer any question the teacher has about the test, such as those about the administration and scoring of the test, the time needed, the timing of sections, subtest scores, standardization procedures, the subjects used

in norm development, the adequacy and representativeness of its population sample, its validity and reliability evidence, its limitations, and how to interpret its results.

Purposes for Using Standardized Tests

There are two main groupings of the purposes for administering standardized tests. The first is a data-gathering process. These data (raw scores, standard scores, percentiles, or stanines) may be recorded on the permanent records so that school norms or system norms can be developed as soon as a sufficient quantity is on hand. They may be used by the teacher to help understand the pupils better, their abilities, needs, and growth. The growth may be determined from year to year or over a shorter period of time if there is experimental research being conducted. There may be evidence of learning difficulties in the data. From the data, the individuals may be selected who fit into a special category: (1) the remedial cases, (2) the specially talented, (3) the slow learners or underachievers, and (4) those who are making normal progress. Finally, the standardized test information may be used for reporting to parents, the board of education, the children themselves, or the general public.

The second major grouping of purposes is represented in the process whereby the test results are used with other information to project educational planning into the future. Children might be guided to plan their own goals with the help of the test data showing what they have accomplished to date. The degree of their readiness for more advanced instruction is implied by what they have accomplished. Similarly, test results may be used in planning curriculum changes for groups or for the whole school. The teacher also uses the data in further planning to improve teaching, to individualize instruction, to group tentatively according to present needs, and to select appropriate teaching materials. In a sense, the teaching of the past is reflected in test results. This implies some successes and failures that can suggest certain teaching approaches for the future.

Selecting the Right Test

Ideally, the following steps would be taken by the teacher committee in selecting the most appropriate standardized test to be used in any given situation:

1. Examine the children's permanent record folders to determine what testing they have had.
2. Gather all other regular evaluation data from the classroom teacher about the children. See what areas need reinforcing by a standardized instrument (test).

3. Examine tests directly that purport to measure what is needed. This could be done by reference to Buros' [9] description of the tests and reviews, by ordering specimen sets of the tests, and by studying those on hand in the reading clinic or office. Before a test is finally approved, the teacher should read the manual thoroughly and the reviews of Buros and take the test himself.

If all factors are favorable—cost, validity, reliability, availability of norms, appropriate forms, machine-scoring answer sheets, and so on—then the test may be selected and used.

Interpreting Standardized Tests

The first rule in interpreting the test results is that one must be cautious and not jump to conclusions with insufficient data. Scores from tests should always be related to other evaluative material, inasmuch as the test is only a sampling of the child's behavior. If there are subtest scores, the profile of these should be studied carefully for clues to the way the child works in reading or related areas. Sometimes the standardized test results show only that further testing would be desirable for measuring the performance of the child in specialized areas, and therefore a diagnostic rather than a survey test is needed.

Usually, a range of abilities in a group of children can adequately be tested by one level of a standardized test. However, if the test is too difficult, the child will not be adequately tested; he or she will get discouraged quickly and guess at answers or give up entirely. If the test is too easy for a child he or she will not be adequately challenged. In looking over test results from a group of children, the teacher should realize that a bunching of scores near the top or bottom of the scale should be suspect.

For determining the seriousness of retardation in reading from testing, a sliding scale should be used and comparisons between tests made. A test of mental ability may be used for establishment of the expectancy level of performance. The reading test score may be compared with the expectancy level. In the primary level the child's reading at a full grade below expectancy would indicate that remedial help is advisable. Otherwise, some corrective work in the classroom could probably bring him or her up to expectancy. At the upper elementary level, a discrepancy of two grade levels would result in similar conclusions. Reading test results are often compared with arithmetic test results as a discrepancy technique. Another discrepancy may be noted between the problem-solving section and computation section of arithmetic tests, because the problem-solving section is more closely related to reading ability.

[9] Oscar K. Buros, *Reading Tests and Reviews* (Highland Park, NJ: The Gryphon Press, 1968); and *Reading Tests and Reviews,* II (1975).

If children are to move in the direction of self-evaluation in order to set their own goals and to work toward their goals, they should know the purpose of the testing. They are then more inclined to do their best with the test items. The results are apt to be a truer picture of their performance, whether the test is a maximum performance test (intelligence, achievement, aptitude) or a typical performance test (interest, temperament, personality, values).

Dangers to Be Considered in Interpreting Tests. Probably the greatest danger is the unexamined assumption. The most common one is that the test measures the skills that have been taught in the local curriculum and that it measures the most important aspects of reading. The best way to examine this assumption is to do an item analysis—to determine exactly what the items do test. Another danger that frequently occurs is the assumption that the items are timely and not outdated. In a vocabulary test the item *Mars* (a planet) suddenly starts yielding the answer "chocolate bar"; and the response for *cougar* (a cat) suddenly becomes "a car." According to the standardization, each answer is marked wrong until a manual revision appears, whereas they are both perfectly correct, logical, and timely.

In test-retest situations, failure to correct for regression toward the mean is especially serious where children have been selected because of their low reading ability. If this correction is not made, the interpretation may be wrong.

Too many of the current reading tests have items that can be answered from the child's experience and background information rather than from the reading selection. This is often overlooked even when the teacher studies the test items directly. All of the above factors affect the validity of the test.

There is a danger where a single test result is used as a single criterion for grouping or for instruction or for labeling a child for a year or for characterizing his or her total reading achievement. The higher level processes such as critical thinking are seldom adequately sampled in a single test. When setting up experimental and control groups a school system has frequently used the standardized test as a single criterion to measure gains, whereas there are other factors that should be considered along with this criterion. Age, sex, the teacher, the previous type of instruction are among those factors that enter the learning situation and may help to reduce the variables to a single measurable variable.

Finally, listed among the dangers must be the practice of overtesting, or the wasteful practice in time, effort, and money of testing and filing the results, without making any use of them. Except for the diagnostic clinical setting, tests of mental ability should not be given yearly. One in early primary, upper elementary, and secondary school should suffice. Standardized tests of reading should be used only when needed to supplement regular classroom evaluation procedures, not regularly duplicating them. Reading survey tests are measures too gross to be used annually. Diagnostic achievement tests may be helpful at the beginning of the school year, serving a specific use in the program along with other evaluative data.

Types and Representative Standardized Tests

Reading Readiness Tests. The reading readiness test is used to determine the degree of readiness of the child for beginning formal reading instruction. It is usually given at the end of the kindergarten or the beginning of first grade, although it is sometimes administered earlier when, in the teacher's judgment, the child is ready for beginning reading. Because teacher judgment is a good predictor of success in beginning reading, the test should be used to complement the teacher's judgment. If the child is ready, formal instruction in reading should begin. If he or she is not ready, further experiences in verbal, auditory, visual, and motor activities should be continued until the child is ready. Following are some representative examples of standardized reading readiness tests:

American School Reading Readiness Test, 1964 revision.* Vocabulary, visual discrimination, recognition of words, following directions, memory for geometric forms. The Bobbs-Merrill Co., Inc.

Clymer-Barrett Prereading Battery, 1966–67. Visual discrimination, auditory discrimination, visual-motor, total. Personnel Press, Inc.

Early Detection Inventory, 1967. School readiness tasks, social-emotional behavior responses, motor performance, total. Follett Publishing *Company.*

Gates-McGinitie Reading Tests: Readiness Skills, 1969. Listening comprehension, auditory discrimination, following directions, letter recognition, visual-motor coordination, auditory blending, word recognition, total. Teachers College Press, Columbia University.

Lee-Clark Reading Readiness Test, 1962 revision. Letter symbols, concepts, word symbols, total. California Test Bureau.

Lippincott Reading Readiness Test (including Readiness Checklist), 1973. J. B. Lippincott Company.

Macmillan Reading Readiness Test, rev. ed., 1963–70. Rating scale, visual discrimination, auditory discrimination, vocabulary and concepts, letter names, total; visual-motor (optional). Macmillan Publishing Co., Inc.

McHugh-McParland Reading Readiness Test, 1968. Rhyming words, beginning sounds, visual discrimination, identifying letters, total. Cal State Bookstore.

Metropolitan Readiness Tests, 1969. Word meaning, listening, matching, alphabet, numbers, copying, total, drawing a man (optional). Harcourt Brace Jovanovich, Inc.

---

* Only the latest revised copyright date is listed.

Murphy-Durrell Reading Readiness Analysis, 1965. Sound recognition, letter naming, learning words, total. Harcourt Brace Jovanovich, Inc.

Perceptual Forms Test, 1967. Visual development. Winter Haven, Lions Research Foundation.

School Readiness; Behavior Tests Used at the Gesell Institute, 1971. Readiness to start school. Programs for Education.

School Readiness Survey, 1967. Ages 4–6. To be administered by parents with school supervision. Consulting Psychologists Press, Inc.

Screening Test of Academic Readiness, 1966. Ages 4–6.5. Picture vocabulary, letter, picture completion, copying, picture description, human figure drawings, relationships, numbers, total (IQ). Priority Innovations, Inc.

The Steinback Test of Reading Readiness, 1966. Letter identification, word memory, auditory discrimination, language comprehension, total. Scholastic Testing Service, Inc.

Valett Developmental Survey of Basic Learning Abilities, 1966. Ages 2–7. Motor integration and physical development, tactile discrimination, language development, and verbal fluency, conceptual development. Consulting Psychologists Press.

The Reading Achievement Test. There are reading achievement tests, and there are reading sections of general achievement tests that measure achievement in several academic areas. Some yield part scores only; others yield part and total reading scores. Many of them give conversion tables for raw scores into percentiles, stanines, and grade level. When one is choosing the correct achievement test for a particular group of children the factors that are important are (1) appropriate knowledges and skills for the local program and graded similarly; (2) scores available for the areas desired; (3) levels included whereby children will test relatively near the middle (for example, children about fifth grade in reading ability would suitably take a level 4–6 test). Following is a selected list of elementary reading achievement tests, some having levels above sixth grade:

American School Achievement Tests: Part I, Reading, 1963. Grades 2–3, 4–6. Sentence and word meaning, paragraph meaning, total. The Bobbs-Merrill Co., Inc.

Burnett Reading Series: Survey Test, 1968. Grades 1.5–2.4, 2.5–3.9, 4.0–6.9. Word identification, word meaning, comprehension, total. Scholastic Testing Service, Inc.

California Reading Test, 1972. Grades 1–2, 2.5–4.5, 4–6. Vocabulary, comprehension, total. California Test Bureau.

Comprehensive Primary Reading Scales, 1960. Grade 1. Reading comprehension, picture-reading vocabulary, meaning-reading vocabulary, word recognition vocabulary scale. Van Wagenen Psycho-Educational Research Laboratories.

Comprehensive Tests of Basic Skills: Reading, 1973. Vocabulary, comprehension, total. McGraw-Hill Book Company.

New Developmental Reading Tests, 1968 Grades 1–2.5, 2.5–3, 4–6. Vocabulary, general comprehension, specific comprehension, total. Lyons & Carnahan.

Gates-MacGinitie Reading Tests, 1972. Grades 1, 2, 3, 2–3, 4–6. Vocabulary, comprehension, and (4–6) speed and accuracy. Teachers College Press, Columbia University.

Iowa Test of Basic Skills, 1978. Grades 3–9. Vocabulary, reading comprehension, language, methods of study. Houghton Mifflin Company.

Metropolitan Achievement Tests: Reading, 1971. Grades 2, 3–4, 5–6. Word knowledge, word discrimination, reading. Harcourt Brace Jovanovich, Inc.

The Nelson Reading Test, rev. ed., 1962. Grades 3–9. Vocabulary, paragraph comprehension, total. Houghton Mifflin Company.

Primary Reading Survey Test, 1973. Grades 2, 3. Scott, Foresman and Company.

Progressive Achievement Tests of Reading, 1969–70. Comprehension, vocabulary, levels of achievement. New Zealand Council for Educational Research.

SRA Achievement Series: Reading, 1967. Grades 1–2, 2–4, 3–4, 4–9. Vocabulary, comprehension, total. Science Research Associates, Inc.

Sequential Tests of Educational Progress: Reading, 1972. Grades 4–6. Cooperative Test Division.

Stanford Achievement Test: Reading Tests, 1974. Grades 1.5–2.5, 2.5–4.0, 4.0–5.5, 5.5–6.9. Word meaning, paragraph meaning. Harcourt Brace Jovanovich, Inc.

Tests of Reading: Inter-American Series, 1973. Grades 1–2, 2–3, 4–6. (Parallel tests and manuals in English and Spanish.) Vocabulary, level-speed-total comprehension, total. Guidance Testing Associates.

Diagnostic Reading Tests. Diagnostic reading tests are needed when the general achievement tests and teacher's judgment indicate that further testing is needed to identify specific areas of weakness in the child's skills or knowledge. In some cases, the test can be administered by the classroom teacher; in others, the reading specialist or clinician would do the intensive testing. The classroom teacher should know some of these tests and what they can contribute to the evaluation picture. This information is helpful in deciding whether a referral is desirable or not. Following is a list of selected diagnostic reading tests:

Classroom Reading Inventory 2d ed. 1973. Grades 2–8. Word recognition, independent reading level, instructional reading level, frustration level, hearing capacity level, spelling. William C. Brown Company, Publishers.

The Denver Public Schools Reading Inventory, 1968. Grades 1–8. Instructional level, independent level (strengths and weaknesses on selections from the *Sheldon Basic Reading Series*). Denver Public Schools.

Diagnostic Reading Scales, rev. 1972. Grades 1–8. Word recognition, instructional level (oral), independent level, rate, potential level (auditory comprehension), consonant sounds, vowel sounds, consonant blends, common syllables, blending, letter sounds. California Test Bureau.

Diagnostic Reading Tests, 1972. Grades—all. Readiness-relationships, eye-hand coordination, visual discrimination, auditory discrimination, vocabulary, grades 2, 3–4, above; word recognition, comprehension, total. Committee on Diagnostic Reading Tests, Inc.

Doren Diagnostic Reading Test of Word Recognition Skills, 1973. Grades 1–9. Letter recognition, beginning sounds, whole word recognition, words within words, speech consonants, ending sounds, blending, rhyming, vowels, sight words, discriminate guessing, total. American Guidance Service, Inc.

Durrell Analysis of Reading Difficulty, new ed., 1955. Grades 1–6. Comprehensive analysis. Harcourt Brace Jovanovich, Inc.

Durrell-Sullivan Reading Capacity and Achievement Tests, 1945. Grades 2.5–4.5, 3–6. Word meaning, paragraph meaning, total, spelling, written recall. Harcourt Brace Jovanovich, Inc.

Gates-McKillop Reading Diagnostic Tests, 1962. Grades 2–6. Comprehensive test that yields twenty-eight different scores. Teachers College Press, Columbia University.

Gillingham-Childs Phonics Proficiency Scales, 1973. Grades 1–6. Cambridge, MA, Educational Publishing Service.

McCullough Word-Analysis Tests, 1963. Grades 4–6. Initial blends and digraphs, phonetic discrimination, matching letters to vowel sounds, sounding whole words, phonetic symbols, phonetic analysis, total, dividing words into syllables, root words in affixed forms, structural analysis total, total. Personnel Press, Inc.

Phonics Knowledge Survey, 1964. Grades 1–6. Fifteen parts. Teachers College Press, Columbia University.

Reading Miscue Inventory, 1972. Grades 1–7. Oral reading inventory with miscue analysis. Macmillan Publishing Co., Inc.

Standard Reading Inventory, 1966. Grades 1–7. Independent reading level, minimum instruction level, maximum instruction level, frustration level, plus checklists. Pioneer Printing Company.

Stanford Diagnostic Reading Test, 1971. Grades 2.5–4.5, 4.5–8.5. Comprehension, vocabulary, auditory discrimination, syllabication, beginning and ending sounds, blending, sound discrimination. Harcourt Brace Jovanovich, Inc.

Woodcock Reading Mastery Tests, 1973. Grades K–12. Letter identification, word identification, word attack, word comprehension, passage comprehension. American Guidance Service, Inc.

Oral Reading Tests. The classroom teacher may want to use a standardized oral reading test to supplement the informal reading inventory and to complement judgment based on the day-to-day reading by the child. In addition to the oral reading sections of the previously listed diagnostic tests, the following are listed as selected oral reading tests:

Flash-X Sight Vocabulary Test, 1961. Grades 1–2. Sight vocabulary, experience vocabulary. Educational Developmental Laboratories, Inc.

Gilmore Oral Reading Test, 1968. Grades 1–8. Accuracy, comprehension, rate. Harcourt Brace Jovanovich, Inc.

Gray Oral Reading Test, 1967. Grades 1–16. The Bobbs-Merrill Co., Inc.

Slosson Oral Reading Test, 1963. Grades 1–8. Slosson Educational Publications.

Study Skills Tests. A complete evaluation program would include a measure of the children's study skills to assess the habits developed and pursued. Because the crux of the situation is actually the use to which the child puts reading skills, this is an important area. It is sometimes overlooked because the teacher gets so engrossed in the specific skills of reading that he or she fails to look up to the ultimate golas. Following are three selected study skills tests that can be used in the elementary school:

New Comprehensive Tests of Basic Skills: Study Skills, 1971. Atlases, almanacs, library catalog cards, indexes, encyclopedias, maps, graphs, charts. California Test Bureau/McGraw-Hill.

SRA Achievement Series: Work Study Skills, 1969. Grades 4–6, 6–9. References, charts, total. Science Research Associates, Inc.

Survey of Study Habits and Attitudes, 1967. Grades 7–12. (Although this test is for high school students, it could be used with some upper elementary groups as a self-study analysis.) Study habits and attitudes. Psychological Corporation.

Work-Study Skills: Iowa Every-Pupil Tests of Basic Skills, Test B, 1947. Grades 3–5, 5–9. Map reading, use of references, use of index, use of dictionary, alphabetizing, total. Houghton Mifflin Company.

Specialized Tests. There are many specialized tests for the measurement of factors that are related to the child's learning success in varying degrees. If there is a possibility one might help the teacher understand his or her children better, he or she should investigate its potential use. A few representative tests of the many available are listed:

Basic Sight Word Test, 1942. Grades 1–2. 220 sight words. Garrard Publishing Company.

Botel Reading Inventory, 1978. Grades 1–12. Free reading level, highest instructional level, highest potential level, frustration level. Follett Publishing Company.

Gilliland Learning Potential Examination, 1966. Grades 1–6. (For use with remedial readers and the culturally disadvantaged.) Nonreading and noncultural, predicted comprehension, total, visual memory. Montana Reading Clinic Publications.

Illinois Test of Psycholinguistic Abilities (ITPA), 1968. Ages 2½–9. Can the child learn by decoding, association, encoding, automatic, and sequencing. Institute for Research on Exceptional Children, University of Illinois.

Learning Methods Test, 1964. Grades K, 1, 2, 3. Comparative effectiveness of methods of teaching new words: visual, phonic, kinesthetic, combination of three. Mills Center, Inc.

The Reading Eye, II, 1969. Grades 1–16. An eye-movement camera with materials for testing reading vision: fixations, regressions, average span of recognition, average duration of fixation, rate and comprehension. Educational Developmental Laboratories, Inc.

Screening Tests for Identifying Children with Specific Language Disability, 1967. Children with average or above IQ in Grades 1–2.5, 2–3.5, 3.5–4. Visual copying—near point and far point, visual perception memory for words, visual discrimination, visual perception memory with kinesthetic memory, auditory recall, auditory perception of beginning and ending sounds, auditory associations. Educators Publishing Service, Inc.

The New Classroom Reading Inventory, 2d ed., 1973. Grades 2–10. Informal Reading inventory, three forms. William C. Brown Company, Publishers.

Other Tests. The teacher should familiarize himself with other types of tests, such as group and individual tests of mental ability, personality tests, projective devices, visual and auditory screening, and others that may be used by the clinician or other school personnel. Other types of tests may be a direct or indirect source of information that will help the teacher understand the instructional needs of each child. Many children are not referred for special testing when they need it. The reasons may be that the teacher does not know of the availability of the test, has not been encouraged to make referrals, or does not recognize the need that might be exposed through a thorough testing. How can a teacher know tests and what they can and cannot do? Here are some possibilities: (1) get specimen sets and study them, (2) read about them in Buros's *Reading Tests and Reviews,* (3) enroll in a tests and measurements or a statistics course, (4) enroll in a course in orientation to psychological testing, (5) participate in evaluation studies in the school system, (6) request in-service programs, and (7) run your own personal in-service programs.

Criterion-Referenced Tests

The "Right to Read" thrust of the 1970s brought into focus another broad objective concerning schools' accountability for educational growth or improvement for all pupils. When teachers ask themselves, "Have Tom's skills in reading and arithmetic improved? How much has he learned in his content area subjects this year?" they need measuring instruments that will give them reliable answers. Their decision as to a choice between norm-referenced and criterion-referenced tests should be influenced by their up-to-date knowledge concerning each type of test. Only then can they be certain that they are relating their measuring devices to their objectives.

Some of the differences between norm-referenced and criterion-referenced tests have been summarized in Figure 22. When purposes for test

Figure 22. Norm- vs. Criterion-Referenced Tests

NORM-REFERENCED TESTS	CRITERION-REFERENCED TESTS
TEST DESIGN	
For comparing pupils' relative standing on a variable such as computation in mathematics, reading comprehension, etc.	For measuring certain behaviors and determining pupils' mastery of a specific skill, such as decoding words with certain consonant blends in the initial position
TEST PERFORMANCE	
Stated in terms of age or grade norms, percentiles, stanines	Stated in terms of measured attainment of behavioral objectives
THE PUPIL'S STATUS	
Determined in relation to others; where the individual is, according to the mean established for a large norming group	Determined in relation to some criterion; how well the individual performs in a skills-test situation
INSTRUCTIONAL OBJECTIVES	
Low degree of relationship; broad, nationwide objectives may be detected in analysis of standardized test items	Complete relationship, as the objectives are the referents; local, specific objectives determine the nature of the test items
ADVANTAGES	

Related to purposes
  Measurement of continuous growth
 	
  Measurement of variability in areas of development
 	
  Comparisons with national norms
  Compilation of local norms
	Related to purposes
	  Measurement of the pupil's current status in relation to objectives of the curriculum
	  Emphasis on the individual's progress rather than on his rank in a group
	  Prerequisite to, and follow-up for, diagnostic-prescriptive teaching

DISADVANTAGES	
Too much reliance may be put on the total score rather than on an analysis of the items that determined the score Sampling procedures may be challenged as biased	Possibility of too much attention to the "mastery of a skill" rather than to its application and use Some learning objectives are difficult to measure with written test items

Figure 22. *Norm- vs. Criterion-Referenced Tests* (Continued)

NORM-REFERENCED TESTS	CRITERION-REFERENCED TESTS
Results are often used merely to label the child rather than to fashion his or her instructional program	Difficulty of determining the number of items that will let the teacher judge the pupil's attainment of mastery
Testmakers may be controlling the curriculum when instruction is geared to "teaching for the test"	Possibility that instruction may become narrowly tied to skills objectives rather than become varied and creative
Tests may become the total program of evaluation, going beyond the true scope of their usefulness	Misinterpretation of results could lead to accelerated vertical instruction and/or lack of subsequent reinforcement of supposedly "mastered" skills

selection have been well defined, the school personnel will be in a good position to make their choices. The types listed on the table are not mutually exclusive, however. A few standardized tests have appeared with the publisher's advertisement to the effect that the items have been developed to measure behavioral objectives and that a print-out will be made available to help teachers form instructional groups based upon the skills deficiencies noted. Some companies offer to construct test items based upon statements of behavioral objectives sent to them by a school or school system.

Blachford [10] pointed out a number of pitfalls for unwary developers of criterion-referenced tests. When tests include items from easy to hard, when minimum competency levels and critical scores are set, the interpretation of results may parallel some of the unfavorable features of norm-referenced tests, which from the viewpoint of some teachers would be statistical ranking and labeling of students. She indicated that many teachers would need specific instructions for the preparation of objectives and for the construction of the test items that will measure the attainment of the objectives.

How the teachers of one school system developed their own criterion-referenced tests was reported by Royal.[11] The Bangor, Michigan, school was asked to write tests for kindergarten and first grade. Teachers first listed all performance objectives they hoped children would accomplish by the end of the year. These were broken down into behavioral objectives that could be measured by specific test questions. Reporting on the effects of the project, Royal stated:

[10] Jean S. Blachford, "A Teacher Views Criterion-Referenced Tests," *Today's Education* (March-April 1975), p. 36.
[11] Mildred Royal, "Performance Objectives and C-R Tests—We Wrote Our Own!" *The Reading Teacher*, 27:701–703 (April 1974).

They [educators] became more alert to the teaching techniques advocating praise and building a good self-concept, pretests and prescription teaching, posttests and reteaching. They were introduced to many new materials using record players, filmstrip machines, tape recorders, reading machines, and individualized self-checking workbooks. And the most exciting part of the whole thing was that we learned not to be frightened by any of it, but to just dive in and have fun learning with the children.[12]

A movement in the direction of helping teachers use objectives as a departure toward individualizing instruction is found in the Crofts In-Service Program (see publishers listed in Appendix). A study of its Reading Comprehension Skills program shows that it includes objectives, instructional guides, pretests, and posttests. A class record chart identifies the specific objectives and the test item developed to test it. The student's response to each item is checked so that the teacher may determine his or her achievement and needs. Under "Paragraph Reading Objectives," the following is an example of a stated objective and the notation of the item in the test related to it:

The learner will recognize and select the detail taken directly from the paragraph that best completes a sentence. (Class Record Form, Test A, Item 1)[13]

After pretest data have been gathered, teachers have the information needed to plan an instructional program geared to individual needs in reading comprehension. The manual carefully states that the tests are not standardized, do not indicate grade-level performance, but *do* help the teacher determine what skills the student needs to improve. A posttest with a similar breakdown of the relationship between test items and objectives is provided.

The *Prescriptive Reading Inventory*[14] is a criterion-referenced test geared to the elementary school, grades 1.5 to 6.5. From the information compiled in its "Class Diagnostic Map" and the "Class Grouping Report," teachers can prescribe instruction for groups, the whole class, or individuals needing remedial help. The manual describes the development of the reading objectives, which were based upon an analysis of five widely used basal reading series. The instructional materials were reviewed to determine behaviors that could be described in stating reading objectives. The inventory includes ninety cognitive objectives, stated in such terms as "The student will . . . identify, employ, demonstrate, recognize, define . . ." An individual study guide for each of the four levels of the inventory helps teacher

---

[12] Ibid., p. 703.
[13] Marion L. McGuire and Marguerite J. Bumpus, *The McGuire-Bumpus Diagnostic Comprehension Test* (New London, CT: Croft Educational Services, Inc., 1972).
[14] *Prescriptive Reading Inventory, A, B, C, D* (Monterey, CA: McGraw Hill, Inc., 1972).

and student pinpoint areas of weakness and locate textbook and workbook references applicable to improvement. Suggestions for classroom activities are incorporated in the handbook, with prescriptive page references. Among the reading skills stated in behavioral objectives are phonic and structural analysis, as well as literal, interpretative, and critical comprehension.

The *High Intensity Learning Systems—Reading* [15] includes skills of word study, vocabulary, and comprehension and study skills. Tests for proficiency in a skill, such as recognizing a compound word, indicate to the teacher which children are in need of further instruction. Commercial materials such as textbooks and workbooks that provide practice are listed, with suggestions that teachers add other sources as they locate them. An example follows:

To form compound words:

SUGGESTED SOURCES	OTHER SOURCES FOUND BY TEACHER
SRA I–C	_____
Mr. Launch	_____

The Wisconsin plan [16] and IGE are terms used interchangeably in many school systems. Individually guided education (IGE) is the broader concept. The Wisconsin Design is a system that conforms to the concept in that, after identifying instructional objectives, it provides for the individual with suggestions for appropriate instructional materials, and it groups children with common needs. Skills and objectives of word attack, comprehension, and study skills are outlined for seven levels. The plan provides for preassessment of skills, monitoring student progress, criterion-referenced tests, and feedback to the teacher and pupil. The Wisconsin Research and Development Center has developed curriculum materials utilizing a criterion-reference approach to evaluation in which a level of mastery of 80 per cent is specified for each student. A record of each pupil's reading skill development can be kept beginning in kindergarten and continuing through sixth grade.

Teacher-made Criterion-Referenced Tests. When the teacher has clearly defined an objective, such as "to be able to decode compound words made up of words previously known by the child," and has taught the technique, he or she next locates practice exercises for the child's reinforcement. How much practice the child will need is an individual matter, but the teacher must measure the child's attainment of the skill. The teacher, therefore, develops a criterion-referenced test, with each item related to the

[15] *High Intensity Learning Systems—Reading* (New York: Random House Inc., 1971).
[16] Wayne Otto and Eleanor Askov, *The Wisconsin Design for Reading Skill Development* (Minneapolis, MN: National Computer Systems, Inc., 1972).

stated objective. He or she needs to define the conditions of the test: "Given (x number) words, the child will be able to encircle the parts of any compound words he or she finds (as in *mailbox, orange, after, houseboat*) with (x per cent) accuracy." The development of such statements poses several problems for the teacher, who must decide upon the number of items to be included. What percentage of accuracy shall he or she expect? When exactly has the child demonstrated mastery of the skill? Does mastery, so determined, mean that the child will remember this skill and use it in any reading situation that he or she meets, as in content area books, library books, and reading outside of school? Obviously, one criterion-referenced test will not furnish all of the answers. The teacher must provide opportunities for transfer of the practiced skill to ensure its ultimate effectiveness.

Whether they are commercially available or teacher-made, as in the preceding examples, criterion-referenced tests are useful in providing information about students' reading achievement. They focus on an individual's performance rather than ranking him or her with other students at his or her age or grade level. Teachers need to be aware of some limitations, inasmuch as only certain behaviors can be assessed with this type of instrument. Although many skills in the cognitive domain lend themselves to this paper-and-pencil type of test, many desirable learning objectives in the affective and psychomotor domain do not. Some that are not readily tested are students' attainment of such objectives as preference, commitment, or set, to name a few that differ according to an individual's total background. Unfortunately, not all learning can be translated into terms suitable to the form of criterion-referenced test items.

RELATING EVALUATION TO OBJECTIVES

Currently, developments in the field of education evaluation reflect a more analytic approach than had previously been in practice. Educators have given renewed attention to relationships among objectives and assessment procedures. They have gained new perspectives as they formulated behavioral objectives, analyzed the teaching-learning process, and developed new techniques for evaluating the students' attainment of realistic objectives. In every area of the curriculum teachers are encouraged to consider objectives, evaluate pupil competencies, provide appropriate instruction, and assess the pupils' attainment of the predetermined general and specific objectives.

OTHER INFORMAL EVALUATION TECHNIQUES

Ratings

There are two general classifications of techniques that are used in the classroom and that involve the use of instruments developed by the teacher for a particular group of children. They should be revised from time to time to improve their effectiveness and to develop the kinds of records that will be helpful in planning the instructional program. They are informal, although the teacher may develop normative data from their continued use. The first falls under the heading of *ratings,* for these indicate the degree to which the child possesses a given trait or skill. The second comes under the heading of *rankings,* for they yield a ranking order of position within the specified group with regard to the characteristic or skill. Each of these processes is discussed briefly, and then the cumulative reading record folder is discussed from the standpoint of what should be done with the findings.

Checklists. The first of the ratings commonly used is the checklist. The teacher builds a checklist in order to record quickly specific aspects of the child's behavior in different reading situations—such as the fluency, interpretation, posture, and accuracy skills in oral reading or the vocabulary, perception, and comprehension difficulties encountered by the child in silent reading. One important aspect of the use of checklists is that the reading material should be at the appropriate level for the child; otherwise, the checklist will only indicate that the material is too easy or too difficult for the child and will not yield a good measure of performance. Checklists usually have categories to be checked by the teacher—such as *inadequate, improved,* and *adequate;* or a group such as *yes, no, sometimes.* Checklists should be dated and notes affixed summarizing their findings. Sometimes examples of specific item-errors are helpful for future use as a recheck.

Questionnaires. The second of the ratings is a form called the *questionnaire.* The interest inventory is a good example. Open-end questions call for the child's response as he or she sees fit. These are useful in getting quickly acquainted with the child and his background. Typical questions are (1) "Do you like to read?" (2) "How many books did you read last summer?" (3) "Do you have a library card for the public library?" (4) "What kind of books do you like best?" and so on. Discussion of responses with the child can often point the way for beginning the reading program. Note that the preceding questions are trying to get answers that relate to the very basic objectives of the reading program.

Interviews. Third of the ratings is the interview. This should be structured so that the teacher can observe the child in a face-to-face situation without the peer group and can draw conclusions that supplement the other aspects of the valuation program. After gaining rapport with the child, the teacher raises open-ended questions that encourage the child to talk about his or her reading confidentially. This way the child will be encouraged to express his or her feelings as well as convey his or her knowledge and skills. Teachers should give the child the feeling that they are really interested in what the child has to say and end with the impression that there will be further opportunities for this kind of discussion. Immediately following the interview the teacher should record the salient points of the discussion for future reference. If the child's interests and tastes and attitudes are the purpose of the interview, the question, "Why?" must be asked several times for a thorough assessment of choices and decisions.

Diaries. A fourth form of ratings may be obtained from the child's own record keeping and diaries. This usually results in considerable motivation, where the child records free reading choices—title, source, and reaction to the story or book and the characters. The record keeping should be kept relatively simple, not laborious, so that sustained interest will be maintained. The diary is a little different in that it should be the pupil's confidential record. It is most useful where it deals with peer-and-parent relationships outside the school. Because the diary is unstructured by the teacher, it will tend to deal with those instances that are most interesting to the child. The diary must be interpreted carefully by the teacher because the child may tend to report only acceptable school-type behavior or may try to shock the adult (teacher) into giving additional attention. The motive is often hidden.

Rankings

Rankings represent the assignment of a relative rank-order position within the specific group with respect to the stated characteristic. This, of course, can be done with any kind of objective data made up of a continuous variable. However, ranking is most commonly used in the informal group of sociometric devices that are developed to get preferences among the peer group in order to determine the social structure. A sociogram can be developed after informing the group, "We are going to divide into work groups to act out this story." The questions would be (1) "With whom would you like to work?" (2) "Who would be your second choice?" and (3) "Who would be your third choice?"

Another form that yields similar results is the "guess who" technique, where characteristics or personal descriptions are arranged from complimentary to unfavorable ones and the child is asked to put someone's name in the blank. An example of one statement might be "Here is someone who has lots of friends because he is so nice to everybody. _____."

Sociometric information may help the teacher understand some of the children better and thus be able to help them more; it may help the teacher identify causal factors in reading that had not been apparent. The latter is illustrated by the fact that occasionally a teacher is surprised to find that a pupil's lack of response in oral situations was due as much to a self-concept in peer-group relationships as to a degree of understanding and skill in the reading material being discussed.

Anecdotal Records

The best way to get a true picture of a child's overall performance in perspective is for the teacher to keep regular anecdotal records. These are actual recordings of what the child said or did—not interpretations. The interpretation should come only at selected intervals during the year after a series of anecdotal recordings are available. Samples of anecdotal records are given here by way of illustration:

> Bill reads for a few minutes and then gazes out of the window.
> Susie does not volunteer an answer in a group situation.
> Eddy says he has read _____ (a book), but he cannot discuss any character or the plot of the story. He did know that it took place on the Mississippi River.
> Tommy helps Fred with hard words whenever Fred gets stuck.

Regular, systematic recording should be a part of the teacher's daily routine. The records should go into the child's cumulative reading record folder for later use.

The Cumulative Reading Record Folder

The classroom teacher should have in a file a folder for each child. In the folder should be kept

1. Standardized tests administered through the year.
2. Analysis of the preceding tests.
3. Regularly accumulated anecdotal records.
4. Informal tests, checklists, IRI's.
5. Periodic assessments done at reporting time.
6. Results of parent interviews and reports.
7. Records of books read and work accomplished by the child.
8. Samples (representative) of the child's work.
9. Pertinent facts from the child's history.
10. Predictions needed for instructional planning, based on performance to date.

The cumulative reading record folder should be put in good order and completed at the end of the year, before it goes to the principal for filing in the office, with recommendations for the next year. It should reside in the office files over the summer—available to the principal, supervisor, reading specialist, or other concerned personnel. The next September it should be released to the child's next teacher, to be kept in the classroom file for reference and continued use. In this way the file grows along with the child, providing a continuous picture of progress. Too great an emphasis cannot be placed on this record. The first step the new teacher of a child takes is studying the folder to get a complete picture of the child's background to date before working with the child in a learning program. How else can the teacher truly gear the program to the child rather than gear the child to an already structured program?

MATERIALS

The good classroom teacher keeps another kind of file up to date. This is a file of reading instruction materials to which he or she can refer whenever necessary—a different approach is needed, some children are not being challenged with current materials, or it is time to requisition materials for budget preparation. The situation may arise at any time where knowledge is needed quickly to meet the reading objectives. It is, therefore, suggested that the teacher keep a file including

1. Material on different sets of basal readers—publishers' advertisements, comparative level-by-level charts of presentation of skills.
2. Annotated lists of trade books with recommended levels. The teacher may want to run a readability check on the ones available or even on the textbooks with the Spache formula for primary grade materials or the Lorge or Dale-Chall formulas for upper grades or the quicker Fry formula.
3. A listing of multilevel programs and supplementary programs, indicating their comprehensiveness, expense, level, and type and purpose. Examples of these would be the multilevel SRA program, the Frosting Visual-Perceptual program, the McGraw-Hill Programed Reading, the Economy Phonetic Keys to Reading.
4. A list of diagnostic tools that have been reported as successful in the literature of the professional journals and textbooks and at conferences.

Teachers are faced almost daily with brand new materials for reading instruction. How are these new materials to be evaluated? Too much is often left to chance in our schools. Some criteria should be determined, and the choices made on the bases of those criteria. Each teacher could establish his or her own criteria—for instance (1) the face value (good for my students, meet my objectives in reading instruction, look interesting); (2) recommendations of the authors and publishers; (3) sampling of opinions of colleagues who have tried the materials; (4) fit with the scope and sequence of my program; (5) teacher competency to handle this program; (6) will it work, for whom, under what circumstances? and (7) whatever other criteria are important to the children and program. A good filing system is a mark of a well-organized teacher, one who can put his or her hands on the needed data quickly when the time is propitious.

PROGRAM

A number of checklists have been published for evaluating a reading program. Instead of simply asking, "Are the children reading effectively?" "Do they like to read?" and "Do they read?" the checklists actually get into the component specific aspects of the program. They ask that judgments be based on

1. Pertinent goals of the program.
2. Administrative and supervisory help in the program.
3. The classroom environment for reading.
4. Variety of activities pertinent to reading.
5. Quality teaching.
6. A differentiated program—reaching all pupils.
7. Sequence—the experiences that fit into a vertical organization of the total program.
8. Intensive skills in the program.
9. Scope—pleasurable attitudes, interests, broad values.
10. Full parental support of the program.
11. A continuous evaluation program.
12. Quality materials of instruction.

Under each heading may be listed many subpoints for determining how good a program is. The classroom teacher plays an important role in the total program. One might say that the chain is as strong as its weakest link, for once a child falls behind in normal progress in reading, it is extremely expensive in time and effort and money to try to get him or her back to an appropriate level. It may be accomplished, but usually at a terrific cost to the child and the educational tutors.

ACCOUNTABILITY

Educational accountability has implied the concept of educators' responsibility for curriculum, instruction, and evaluation of students' progress. In the decades of the sixties and seventies society showed a growing interest in the schools. Consumerism put demands upon schools, as the citizen wanted proof that educational dollars were producing reasonable results. The focus of attention upon accountability can be traced to taxpayers' concern for the increasing cost of education and to citizens' and educators' concern for the effectiveness of education for all pupils, especially in basic skills.[17] An evaluation of student achievement appeared to be an answer to the public's demands.

In the 1960s a series of court decisions influenced the trend to accountability. The Exploratory Committee on the Assessment of Progress in Education was formed in 1964 and eventually resulted in the establishment of the National Assessment program. In 1965 the passing of the Elementary and Secondary Education Act required school systems to assess by objective means the achievement of those students who were in federally funded programs for the educationally deprived. Needs assessment became part of the program when schools requested federal funds. The Coleman Act on Equality of Educational Opportunity in 1966 reported an attempt to assess the quality of school services by testing pupil achievement. Thus in the 1960s attention was focused on the accountability of the schools, on the evaluation of educational services and the educational product, with the stated purpose of assuring equal educational opportunity for all students.

Accountability has had and will have a strong influence on educational practices. It has highlighted the significance of educating the individual. It has spawned a systems approach to the progress of that individual through the recommendation of needs assessment, goals, specific instruction, and continuous evaluation of his achievement.

Strain[18] pointed out teachers' responsibility for the assessment of learners' needs in reading; determination of objectives of instruction; individualization of reading instruction; development of attitudes and interests in reading; evaluation of processes and products of reading instruction; and overall knowledge, understandings, and skills of reading instruction. In other words, accountability in reading instruction refers to the teacher's thorough understanding of the reading process and his or her ability to use the varied tools of assessment of each pupil's status and progress in becoming an accomplished reader.

That accountability has become of wide concern is evident in the development of national and state assessment programs, and the passage of educational accountability laws in several states (See the 1978 IRA publication on Reading and the Law).

[17] Frank Sciara and Richard Jantz, *Accountability in American Education* (Boston: Allyn & Bacon, Inc., 1972).
[18] Lucille B. Strain, *Accountability in Reading Instruction* (Columbus, OH: Charles E. Merrill Publishing Company, 1976), pp. 12–15.

NATIONAL AND STATE ASSESSMENT

Studies of educational achievement by the National Assessment of Educational Progress (NAEP) were begun in the 1970s. The purpose of the surveys was to assess the literal comprehension, inferential comprehension, and reference skills of nine-, thirteen-, and seventeen-year-old students. The first survey was conducted in the school year of 1970–1971 with subsequent technical reports on skills and knowledge of reading and literature. The second nationwide survey in the school year 1974–1975 was reported in 1976. Among the findings reported by NAEP were the following:

> Nine-year-olds, during the second assessment, read significantly better than did nine-year-olds four years earlier.
> Black nine-year-olds improved more dramatically than did nine-year-olds as a whole.
> Girls continued to read better than boys at all age levels.
> The reading ability of thirteen- and seventeen-year-olds changed little in the four-year period.
> Both thirteen- and seventeen-year-olds improved slightly in literal comprehension, but declined in inferential comprehension.
> In study skills nine-year-olds improved, but thirteen-year-olds declined.[19]

The parts of the report that showed a statistically significant increase in reading ability of some of the children tested were considered as encouraging. Venezky [20] pointed out, however, that the differences in the scores should be interpreted only when compared to a sufficient and desirable level of performance and anticipated changes. He felt that implications should not be made without a complete study of the validity of the test items and the classification of those items. He considered unfortunate the fact that NAEP could not show relationships between special reading programs and the improvement in reading shown by some of the test scores. One of the strengths of the NAEP cited by Venezky was the provision of an alternative to norm-referenced tests by their establishing procedures for selecting and validating objective test items over a wide range of abilities.

Several studies have appeared that make the findings of the NAEP studies useful for teachers who are not experts in statistics and measurement.[21] These studies reported procedures, examples of items, and the results shown by the tests in reading, writing, and literature. Two examples

[19] Diane Lapp and Robert Tierney, "Reading Scores of American Nine-Year-Olds: NAEP's Tests," *The Reading Teacher,* 30:756–760 (April 1977).
[20] Richard L. Venezky, "NAEP: Should We Kill the Messenger Who Brings Bad News?" *The Reading Teacher,* 30:750–755 (April 1977).
[21] J. Stanley Ahmann, *How Much Are Our Young People Learning? The Story of the National Assessment* (Bloomington, IN: Phi Delta Kappa Educational Foundation, 1976); John C. Mellon, *National Assessment and the Teaching of English* (Urbana, IL: National Council of Teachers of English, 1975).

of findings useful to the classroom teacher as shown in an analysis of the items scored by nine-year-olds follow: [22]

1. More than two thirds can comprehend literal facts in simple, brief stories.
2. Less than one third can determine the main idea in a reading passage.

Applebee [23] reported highlights of the various interpretive summaries made by the National Assessment staff, Phi Delta Kappa, Carnegie Corporation, and the National Council of Teachers of English. As they peruse these analyses, teachers can learn about the achievement of the children tested in the surveys and make appropriate adjustments in the planning of programs and materials for the children in their own classrooms. For example, they can make opportunities for children to find the main idea in a paragraph or other reading selection when they find that children need that particular skill (as indicated for nine-year-olds in the NAEP study). Teachers can also be alert to discovering future analyses of NAEP data in state and national reading publications. See "Journals," in the Appendixes.

Some states have established assessment plans modeled after NAEP. Others have developed their own programs in order to provide equal educational opportunities for every child. At the beginning of 1978 twenty-six states had enacted some form of competency-proficiency standards. Factors stressed in many of the programs are needs assessment, standards, objectives, goal indicators, and program budgeting.

In the New Jersey Thorough and Efficient (T&E) program for language arts, reading, and mathematics, the State Department works with teachers to develop standards, identify goals, and set up a working model. There are six centers in the state, staffed by reading specialists who work with local schools on needs assessment, on program development, and on a budget based on that program. One basic goal, such as the acquiring of adequate communication skills, for example, would have specific goal indicators: to be able to speak fluently, to be able to read effortlessly. An assessment design is formulated to determine the extent to which goals are being met and to delineate how skills achievement are measured. Citizen involvement in the T&E program is mandated by the state.

A helpful tool for local school districts' planning for thorough and efficient education was the publication of the source book *Modelog.*[24] Models

[22] Ina Mullis, Susan Oldefendt, and Donald Phillips, *What Students Know and Can Do: Profiles of Three Age Groups* (Denver: Education Commission of the States (Tests and Measurements Clearing House 006 076), 1977.

[23] Arthur N. Applebee, "Perspectives on the National Assessment of Educational Progress," *The Reading Teacher,* 31:250–53 (Nov. 1977).

[24] Fred G. Burke, commissioner, *Modelog: A Catalog of Comprehensive Educational Planning Component Models* (Trenton, NJ: New Jersey Department of Education, 1975).

were included from other states, such as the Sarasota County Needs Assessment Process from Florida, Objectives for Instructional Programs from California, Developing a Large-Scale Assessment Program from Colorado, and Individually Prescribed Instruction: Reading and Math from Pennsylvania.

In order to give educational planners an overview of the components of each model the following was presented with one or more of the components highlighted for each.

Figure 23. *Educational Planning Component Model*

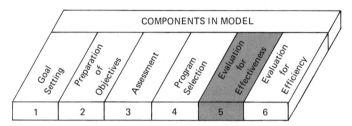

For example, the planning category, component 5, Evaluation of Effectiveness, was highlighted for "Criterion-Referenced Test Concepts, EPIC Criterion-Referenced Tests," on pages 200 and 201. The developers, source, and cost of the 1975 paperback book were given, with a note that consultant services costs vary by contract. The book answered such questions as, "What is a criterion-referenced test?" "How does it differ from a norm-referenced test?" "How is it constructed, and how are the results reported?" EPIC could supply the school district with criterion-referenced items or provide technical assistance to develop new items for the school system.

SUMMARY

Behavioral objectives, individualized instruction, criterion-referenced tests, and accountability are among the terms educators will continue to encounter in the future. The concepts are older than the terms. Conscientious teachers have always taught individuals with different goals in mind for each student. Their tests were closely related to the lessons devised for each pupil. In the course of a school year, they were accountable for the educational growth of all pupils.

On the large-scale basis of today's educational systems, needs assessment, behavioral objectives, and varied appraisal instruments are all part of the process of evaluation. National and state assessment programs attest to the interest of the public—taxpayers, employers, parents—in accountability on the part of the school. Measurement of pupil achievement is considered as an indication of the success or failure of the schools.

Appraisal should be an ongoing process of preassessment, continuous evaluation, and postassessment in all areas of the curriculum. Purpose should be the key to the selection of appraisal instruments, teacher-made, criterion-referenced, and/or standardized. Appraisal of reading progress is the process that should help the child and the teacher in their efforts to maintain the greatest potential learning rate in all reading activities.

SELECTED READINGS

Ahmann, J. Stanley; Marvin D. Glock; and Helen L. Wardeberg. *Evaluating Elementary School Pupils*. Boston: Allyn & Bacon, Inc., 1967.

Austin, Mary C.; Clifford L. Bush; and Mildred H. Huebner. *Reading Evaluation, Appraisal Techniques for School and Classroom*. New York: The Ronald Press Company, 1961.

Bleismer, Emory. "Informal Teacher Testing in Reading." *The Reading Teacher* 26,268–272 (Dec. 1972).

Bloom, Benjamin S.; Thomas Hastings; and George Madaus. *Handbook on Formative and Summative Evaluation of Student Learning*. New York: McGraw-Hill Book Company, 1971.

Buros, Oscar K., ed. *Reading Tests and Reviews, II*. Highland Park, NJ: The Gryphon Press, 1975.

Farr, Roger. *Reading: What Can Be Measured?* Newark, DE: The International Reading Association. 1969.

——— and Nancy L. Roser. "Reading Assessment: A Look at Problems and Issues." *Journal of Reading,* 17,592–599 (May 1974).

Kaufman, Maurice. "Measuring Oral Reading Accuracy." *Reading World,* 15,4, 216–226 (May 1976).

Pikulski, John. "A Critical Review: Informal Reading Inventories." *The Reading Teacher,* 28,141–145 (Nov. 1974).

Prescott, George A. "Criterion-Referenced Test Interpretation in Reading." *The Reading Teacher,* 25,347–354 (Jan. 1971).

Strain, Lucille B. *Accountability in Reading Instruction*. Columbus, OH: Charles E. Merrill Publishing Co., 1976.

Chapter 14

Challenging Every Reader

OBJECTIVES

To gain an acceptance of the role of individual differences in the reading program

To provide for the needs of each child in reading

To recognize the significance of "knowing" each child before planning his instruction

To recognize, and be able to help, children with different reading backgrounds and potential, such as the gifted

To understand, and be prepared for, the concept of mainstreaming

INTRODUCTION

When a teacher has acquired a good background of knowledge concerning the nature of individual differences as well as optimum teaching procedures and instructional materials, he still faces the challenge of getting each pupil to *read* and to read as well as he can. The greatest percentage of the knowledge children acquire in their schooling is gained through reading. Knowing this, the teacher faces the responsibility of providing for everyone the most appropriate instruction in skills as well as the best materials available for utilizing these skills for the process of learning or acquiring an education.

The types of learners and readers who typically appear in elementary classrooms include the average, slow, and gifted learners; the reluctant reader; the disadvantaged learner; and the retarded reader. Separate sections in this chapter will spotlight the characteristics of these children, their learning problems, and implications for their reading instruction.

The teacher's aspirations for the child will need to be based upon the best information available as to his potential. At any time during the child's school years the teacher can ask, "How is Tom doing? Is he achieving as well as he can? Am I providing appropriate reading material in all his subject areas? Or is he being frustrated by materials and concepts beyond his present abilities?"

In order to have a point of reference for answers to these questions, the teacher can use a chart such as Figure 24. He will need to know Tom's mental ability as assessed by an individual intelligence test (his IQ), his chronological age, and the number of his previous years in school. Figure 24 is meant to be a composite picture of *relative* potential, not a specific guide line, certainly not a positive or final picture. The teacher could make the following type of interpretations: A child of ten, with four previous years in school, where *all* previous teachers understood his problems and provided effective instruction, could be expected to achieve

1. At kindergarten level, if an individual test of mental abilities showed about 50 IQ.
2. At third grade level, if his individual IQ of 85 showed the child to be in the slow but normal range.
3. At fifth grade level, if the child was noted to be about average on an individual test of mental ability.

Figure 24. Potential Academic Achievement of Children with Various Intelligence Quotient Levels *

PREVIOUS YEARS IN SCHOOL	CHRONO-LOGICAL AGE	SLOW-LEARNING RANGE			SLOW NORMAL RANGE			AVERAGE			ABOVE AVERAGE
BINET OR WISC IQ		50	60	70	75	80	85	90	100	110	120
0	6	Pre K	P K K	K	K	K	K	K	K,1	1	1,2
1	7	P K	P K	K	K	K	K	K,1	1,2	2	2,3
2	8	K	K	K	K,1	K,1	1	1,2	2,3	3	3,4
3	9	K	K	K,1	1	1,2	2	2,3	3,4	4	4,5
4	10	K	K,1	1,2	2	2,3	3	3,4	4,5	5	5,6
5	11	K	1	2	2,3	3	3,4	4	5,6	6,7	6,7
6	12	K,1	1,2	2,3	3,4	3,4	4,5	5	6,7	7,8	7,8
7	13	1	2	3,4	4	4,5	5,6	6	7,8	8,9	8,9
8	14	1,2	2,3	4	5	5,6	6	7	8,9	9,10	9,10
9	15	2	3,4	5	5,6	6,7	7	8	9,10	10,11	10,11
10	16	2,3	4	5,6	6,7	7	8	9	10	12	11,12
11	17	−3	4+	−6	−7	7+	8+	9+	10+	12+	12+

* This chart was developed in the reading clinic at Southern Connecticut State College, using some original data prepared by Samuel Kirk † for slow-learners, and by the state department of special education in Ohio.
† Samuel Kirk, *Teaching Reading to Slow-Learning Children*. (Cambridge, MA: Houghton-Mifflin Company, 1940), p. 28.

Note that if the teacher enters the chart and reads downward, the expectancy level for a child within a certain learning range shows the possibility of improving, as long as his teachers understand his strengths and weaknesses and make adequate teaching provisions. Thus a child with a very low IQ—50—can be expected to do as well as low third grade (reading, writing, and arithmetic) if he or she remains in school for twelve years. A child with an IQ of 80 needs ten years in school to reach a seventh grade level of academic performance. A child of 100 IQ will do acceptable work at grade ten or above after twelve years in school. Above average children can be expected to do grade level and better in each grade.

Another way to interpret these rows and columns would be to look at the reading score made by a pupil, age thirteen, whose IQ was about 90 (average). The *most* the teacher could expect would be a grade six level of achievement. When a child's reading score is grade five or below, the child would be retarded (for him or her) in reading. Similarly, a child of thirteen with an IQ of 70 could not be expected to achieve better than third or fourth grade. Another with an IQ of 110 could be retarded if he or she did not achieve at eighth or ninth grade levels.

The slow learner in the middle grades, aged approximately nine to fourteen, will show reading scores as indicated in the box—provided that instruction has been geared to his or her needs up to the point of testing. Also, of course, other things must be in the child's favor—health, personality and other psychological factors, and so on. Otherwise, even lower scores will be made on achievement tests.

Finally, relatively speaking, the chart anticipates *growth* for everyone —a slower pace for some, average to above average for others. Knowing where the child is and providing the right books at the right time—these are the keys to diagnostic teaching. Teachers who enter this chart with a knowledge of a child's age, previous years in school, and individually assessed level of mental ability will have a starting point for determining both the amount and rate of growth that might be expected for the pupil's educational achievement.

THE AVERAGE LEARNER

On a continuum from very low to very high, it has been found statistically that the greatest number of cases tends to cluster near the mean (or average) of the distribution. When all learners are plotted on such a continuum, we find the greatest number to be *average* learners. Traditionally, we have defined the average learner in terms of our expectancy for him or her. This fact calls our attention to the variable that determines our level of expectancy—the child's native ability as measured by available intelligence tests.

Here we encounter another concept of *average*—the tasks achieved and the abilities of other children at a given age provide norms upon which we can base a judgment concerning the capabilities of each child of the same age. When one child achieves at a level different from that which we expected, knowing his or her age, we attempt to quantify the difference. We first state that the child is below average or above average and then attempt to show how much below or above he or she is. When we are studying many children of a given age, we find fewer children the farther we get on either side of the mean or average. So the teacher is concerned with a relatively small number when slow learners and gifted learners are detected in the classroom. The teacher is dealing with the majority of children when he or she undertakes to challenge the average learners in the typical classroom.

Our graded classrooms and graded textbooks have been based upon the concept that children usually develop in increments of a year's growth in a year's time. Thus the average child is expected to cover a year's work in various curricular areas—entering fifth grade after a year in the fourth grade, and so on. If only the variables of mental ability and chronological age are considered, it is possible to anticipate about a year's growth in achievement each year. Teachers, however, have learned that those who fall within the average range of intelligence, with IQ's from 90 to 110, exhibit many variations in other areas—health, interests, environment, attitudes, emotional stability, and so on. The children's school achievement may be influenced by any combination of factors other than intelligence and chronological age. For example, at a given age children have certain interests in common. Teachers capitalize on this bit of information in making curriculum choices, book and story selections, and other decisions. They also need to recognize individual variations in interest—Polly's preoccupation with horses, Tom's strong interest in stamp collecting, or Henry's interest in everything mechanical. Sometimes these interests can be tapped to provide an incentive, otherwise lacking, to further learning in the classroom—a springboard to other areas of the curriculum.

Careful assessment is required to determine which are the average learners. They can be expected to make normal progress through school, about twelve grades in twelve years. Because programs have typically been geared to their needs, they presumably will exhibit no great problems in terms of their materials, methods, assignments, and so on. Experienced teachers, however, recognize individual differences and group differences among the so-called average. When this group is viewed as a band rather than a point on a continuum, the concepts of *low average* and *high average* begin to cloud the above picture. All of the varied factors influencing an individual at a given time prevent clear-cut decisions concerning a group of low-average pupils or another of high-average pupils. If five average classes were assigned to five teachers, the teachers would find five *different* groups of children.

The challenge to the teacher of average children, then, is (1) to determine the skills or lack of skills that caused the scores that led to this designation; (2) to know as much about each individual as possible—background of knowledge and experience, interests, and effective techniques for instruction; (3) to provide methods and materials appropriate to current level of functioning; and (4) to encourage each child to perform sometimes at optimum level of performance.

THE SLOW LEARNER

There are a few children in every heterogeneous classroom whose mental ability, as measured by existing intelligence tests, falls within the range from 70 IQ to 90 IQ. At levels below 70 children in some states are candidates for special classes for slow learners. Some school systems have no extra provisions for these children, who must struggle along in a regular classroom.

Teachers need to recognize the fact that the mental ages of these children lag behind their chronological ages. When they attain a mental age of about six and one-half years, these children will usually respond favorably to initial reading instruction if previous learning experiences had been within their capabilities—that is, reading readiness activities taken at a slow pace. They may be eight to ten years old, with two to four years of prereading experiences before they are ready for formal instruction in reading. The slowest will progress at about a half-year rate each year, to an achievement level of approximately fourth grade after twelve years in school—all other factors being in his or her favor. The best in this group will also make slow progress but can be expected to achieve at about eighth grade level after twelve years in school. See Figure 26. Again, all things must be in his favor—teachers who understand learning problems, good health, a minimum of family mobility, small class size allowing for individual attention to his or her needs, and so on.

These children profit from concrete experiences preceding and during any reading. They need their attention drawn to facts—the main points they will need to remember. Comprehension in reading materials will progress slowly from simple recognition of basic facts to sequence and some critical reading skills when they are adolescents. Their current reading achievement level will need to be known when reading materials are being selected. The slow child of fourteen after eight years of careful instruction, may be able to read books of fourth and fifth grade difficulty by himself. The very slowest, circa 60 IQ, will be doing well *for him* if he is reading in second or third grade materials with good comprehension. If he has been promoted in regular classrooms he will be sitting with ninth grade boys and girls. Some of his interests will be similar to those of others his own age. For peer group status he will need to make contributions to group projects. His classroom teacher, with the help of the school librarian, can give him reading material geared to his reading level with content that will provide some answers to class projects in science, social studies, literature, and other content areas.

If a child should be in a special class for slow learners, the regular classroom teacher should recognize this potentiality and recommend testing for this placement. The child will probably make the best progress when with a group under a teacher specially trained to handle the needs of slow learners. Mainstreaming qualifies this generalization.

The prognosis for all of the children in the slow-learning range is for yearly improvement in their skills and overall achievement. Teachers need to realize the slow pace of such improvement. They need to provide appropriate skills instruction and appropriate reading materials so that the child's learning can continue throughout the school years, whether placed in a special class or in regular classrooms.

THE GIFTED LEARNER

Certain children in any classroom appear to be better motivated, to learn faster, and to retain more than do other children. Depending upon the criteria used for their identification, it is possible to find from 1 to 20 per cent of the school population to be intellectually gifted. When above average intelligence quotients are the criterion used, the gifted are those within the range of superior (above 120 IQ) to genius levels (above 180 IQ).

In the elementary classroom the pupils with potential for high cognitive reasoning abilities need to be challenged so that their giftedness may be developed to the fullest extent. The teacher is challenged, therefore, not only to detect the highly gifted, but to provide "encouragement, intensive instruction, continuing opportunity as he advances, a congruent stimulating social life, and cumulative success experiences." [1]

Detection of these children may be by the teacher's and parents' observation of certain types of behavior, such as verbal fluency, self-motivation, and creativity, for example. These observations need to be supplemented by the results of group and individual intelligence tests, because some of these children may not be exhibiting a classroom performance consistent with their mental abilities. Some of the same factors that influence adversely the

[1] S. L. Pressey, "Concerning the Nature and Nurture of Genius," *Educating the Gifted,* ed. Joseph L. French, (New York: Holt, Rinehart and Winston, 1960), p. 14.

average and the slow child may also affect the educational level attained by the gifted. Thus foreign-language background, emotional disturbance, poor physical development, poor health, family problems, and so on may prevent the child from performing academically as well as he is able.

Teachers can make use of several lists that have been developed to identify intellectually capable children.[2,3] Among the characteristics noted are such abilities as learning easily and rapidly, recognizing and exploring cause-and-effect relationships, retaining information, using a large vocabulary, early interest in clocks and calendars, asking many questions, and early development in learning to read and in upper grade classrooms reading books a grade or more above others.

Providing an effective program for these children in the regular classroom is imperative. A stimulating classroom environment encourages individual discovery and effort, makes creative expression possible, and causes intellectual activities of the classroom to be both successful and rewarding to the individual.

The gifted learner at the earlier levels can profit from an individualized reading program. Thus, when the teacher has ascertained the independent and instructional reading levels and has administered an interest inventory, he or she may help the gifted pupil with appropriate books and materials. At the some time, the teacher will provide opportunities for social growth through experiences in the planning and executing of group projects, as well as through sharing of the child's own creative projects.

Extensive materials within the reading range of gifted pupils may be found by the teacher and librarian working together, once the interests of gifted children are known. Good practical projects that are recognized by these pupils as worthwhile must be devised. An example is the writing, editing, and publishing of a class or school newspaper or monthly magazine. Another is the development of an auditorium program with a panel discussion or debate on a current topic. Sometimes these children suggest their own projects. Teachers need to be alert to such suggestions and capitalize upon them, for they are keys to the motivation of the gifted.

The gifted profit from early lessons on the various uses of the library. They may be introduced to the card catalog, reference books, almanacs, and atlases before other children their age are ready for them. Thus they are prepared to pursue their individual interests independently as soon as possible.

Marion Scheifele has compiled many practical suggestions for teaching

---

[2] Jack Kough and Robert DeHaan, *Teacher's Guidance Handbook,* I. *Identifying Children Who Need Help* (Chicago: Science Research Associates, Inc.), 1955.
[3] Paul Witty, "Gifted Children—Our Greatest Resource," *Nursing Outlook,* 3:499 (Sept. 1955).

Leisure reading time

the gifted in a handbook for teachers.[4] She lists extensive suggestions for school-and-community activities, other activities integrated with group projects, and independent and creative activities for the gifted in the classroom. Among the activities that are highly correlated with their reading achievement are (1) reading or telling stories to younger children, (2) locating and collecting materials for a class project, (3) reading and reporting on books on advanced levels, (4) writing dramatizations of historical events, and (5) illustrating stories or poems.

The teacher who finds gifted students in the class will need to re-examine methods and techniques of instruction. Gearing instruction to individual needs is of utmost importance. These children need early independence in word recognition skills. Because they learn more and faster than the average, they typically do not require the longer period for the sequential development of skills needed by other students.

Teachers need to give these children opportunities to develop creative reading skills, imagination, and insights. High level comprehension skills of creative and critical reading may be initiated at primary grade levels, as outlined in Chapter 5.

With adequate direction, superior students take a great deal of interest in semantics. They will enjoy the study of words and their origins.[5] They learn to take pride in unlocking the multiple meanings of words from con-

[4] *The Gifted Child in the Regular Classroom* (New York: Bureau of Publications, Teachers College, Columbia University, 1953), pp. 51–64.
[5] *Picturesque Word Origins* (Springfield, MA: G. and C. Merriam Company, 1933).

text. At the same time, they get much satisfaction from using dictionaries for improving their vocabulary, for pronunciation, for synonyms, and so on.

Because the gifted can do much independent reading for both recreation and information, they profit from early attention to study skills and such library techniques as the use of research and reference sources. It is not unusual to find a student who wishes to exhaust the subject. This child wants to know all that he can about a certain topic—in the primary grades he may become an expert on prehistoric animals; in the middle grades, on astronomy or engines; in the upper grades, on early American exploration or the life and inventions of a man like Thomas Alva Edison. The gifted pupil needs, therefore, the skills to read the books from which to get the information he wants—often at a level considerably above that in which his age and schooling would place him.

Teachers need to provide curriculum enrichment for the superior students. Both horizontal and vertical enrichment would be suggested. Textbooks that are basic to the school's curriculum usually suggest sources and activities beyond the regular assignments. Alert teachers can keep records from year to year of the additional materials students themselves discover in their quest for more information on topics of interest. Thus teachers can build resource units and programs broad enough for the individual needs of future classes.

Teachers are gearing reading instruction to the gifted when they provide opportunities for independent research projects, when they organize their teaching in broad units, and when they encourage the superior to specialize. Research projects can be undertaken in conjunction with curriculum-based units or with outside interests. A topic of interest that is held over a period of years can result in a specialist—stamp collections that expand into keen interest in geographical areas, coin collections that span an historical era, and so on. The gifted student thus gains both from self-satisfaction and from the esteem of peers, who look upon him as a specialist.

Upon occasion the teacher will discover a potentially capable student who has reading disabilities. The student will exhibit the characteristics of the remedial reader. Instruction geared to his or her improvement will be usually not very different from that provided other remedial readers. One point of difference, however, is that the prognosis may include some indication of improvement sooner or faster than that of an average or slower learning pupil. Basic to the improvement of the disabled but gifted reader is an evaluation that detects reading strengths and weaknesses.

These students can be helped to evaluate their own reading achievement. Because of their interests and self-motivation they usually will be eagerly receptive to suggestions for improvement in reading and study skills.

The issue with respect to gifted children in the elementary school is how they should be treated to further their maximum progress in reading. There have been three distinct ways of doing this:

1. Ability grouping—in specialized schools, in special classes in regular schools, in special out-of-school activities such as Saturday morning classes or grouped within the classroom.
2. Acceleration (vertical)—skipping grades, early admission to school, or advancing the child faster in an ungraded organization.
3. Classroom enrichment (horizontal)—individualized reading, flexible environment, individualized study materials, or supplementary materials.
4. Extra-classroom enrichment program—special room or school where a specially-trained teacher works with the children in a highly motivating environment.

Gifted children need instruction in reading; they cannot just be turned loose to read on their own. Ideally, they would be given enrichment material and be allowed or encouraged to read at as high a level as they can. The typical stumbling block has been the traditional rigid grade-level thinking of teachers and administrators, so that the child is held back with the rest of the students. For this child, a special grouping would be best, for he could then read at an independent level and profit therefrom.

The authors favor an enrichment program as the best solution to this child's needs. Acceleration should be considered only if the child is socially, physically, and emotionally mature enough, and then only if gifted in all of the cognitive areas of the school's program.

THE RETARDED READER

When a disparity exists between a pupil's mental ability and the current level of achievement, he or she exhibits retardation. Thus, if a teacher knows a pupil's mental age, chronological age, years in school, previous academic level, and current academic level, the teacher may make certain interpretations that will enable him to provide appropriate instruction geared to what can be expected of the pupil at this point. When a child of average learning ability is found to be reading at third grade level in fifth grade, he or she is considered a retarded reader. When the superior learner in the fifth grade is reading at high fourth or low fifth grade level, he or she may be assumed to be a retarded reader—he should be capable of above-grade-level reading achievement. When the slow learner in grade five is reading in a primer, he also is retarded, for he should be able to read at second or third grade level. All three children in these examples are retarded readers, achieving below expectancy levels.

The teacher's first responsibility is to determine why pupils are reading at a level that is low for them. Next the teacher analyzes the pupils' reading performance to discover their strengths and weaknesses. Armed with answers concerning each pupil's reading problems, the teacher can plan a remedial program for each one. The second step usually uncovers specific reading difficulties, such as word analysis difficulties, comprehension problems, or vocabulary difficulties. The first step may uncover such personal problems as lack of interest in reading, poor attitudes toward school or toward books, or emotional or neurological blocks that prevent normal learning. A common problem is a combination of low interest and poor word analysis ability, resulting in little comprehension of reading material. Teachers can try to build interest in a topic through pictures, motion pictures, trips, discussions, provision of real objects, tape recordings, and so on. They can locate material that will be easy to read so that the child can absorb content while reading. They can provide meaningful activities for each child to use the knowledge gained in reading. Such activities might include participation in the work of a school or class newspaper, frieze, mural, or "movie," writing and editing chapters for a class book, and other real projects. The teacher's goals are to get the pupils to read as widely as possible, to experience success, and to learn to enjoy reading.

How will the realization of these goals differ for each of the learners mentioned in these examples? When their problems have been recognized, they will progress at their own rates toward their own reading improvement. Thus it is possible to predict for gifted learners who are retarded that they will attain the level expected of them in a relatively short time. It will take the average reader longer to attain the level expected of him or her. The slow learner will also improve, but at a much slower pace.

The degree of each pupil's reading retardation will need to be discovered in order for the school to make appropriate adjustments. When a child has fallen behind in achievement, an evaluation of his or her reading may indicate a lack of reading skills, which can be corrected by the classroom teacher, using the techniques of diagnostic test-teach-test indicated earlier. Occasionally, such pretesting reveals some severe retardation. The pupil may have serious deficits in vocabulary or comprehension development. He or she may have severe learning problems or exhibit serious deficits in other developmental areas, such as language, health, personality, perceptual and neurological factors, and so on. Teachers need to know when to refer children to the school's specialists for further testing. They also need to know which children should be selected for remedial instruction. It has been suggested that children be selected for remedial teaching when the difference between reading age and mental age is at least six months in the primary grades, nine months in grades four and five, and a year in grades six and over. Thus children whose reading is below expectation for their intelligence level will profit from the help of intensified reading instruction in addition to the careful daily instruction of the classroom teacher.

A special remedial teacher is often available in elementary schools.

He or she may work with small groups of children who need similar skills instruction. Such groups may range from two to seven children. The remedial teacher occasionally works with the severely retarded reader on an individual basis. The child needing individual help may be the older nonreader, one who is handicapped emotionally or neurologically, the non-English-speaking pupil, and so on. Children who need more attention than the regular classroom teacher can give can be cared for by the reading specialist—in the school setting or in a remedial clinic.

Many hire remedial reading teachers who spend most of their time working with children individually or in small groups. The city of St. Louis organizes the "Room of Twenty," where the children get a strong concentrated emphasis on reading for a full year and then go back to their regular classrooms. In the clinic setting specialists, such as the medical doctor, the social worker, and the psychologist, may be used for referral for special difficulties that are suspected to be interfering with the child's reading. School systems have to assess their needs with respect to retarded readers and then staff and equip a program to meet those needs. Because such programs are expensive, the system should be working to improve its developmental program constantly as a preventive measure. Education is shortchanged if both are not done simultaneously.

Children with Language Difficulties

Bilingual and non-English-speaking children come to the English-speaking school from a home where the language and customs are entirely foreign to the school's setting. Many of them have had little or no contact with the English language. They do not understand the abstractions of the language. They fail to reach the achievement level of their capacities. They fail to keep up with the English-speaking children. They represent a different culture with its own values and beliefs. When they encounter the letter *o* in words such as *come, book, go, not, to,* and *down,* they are confused by the sound-symbol relationships. The foregoing illustrates only one of the many problems these children face when they attempt to read words in English.

There are several possible approaches to this type of problem. One is the establishment of a bilingual school such as that in Dade County, Florida.[6] Another method is that of supplementing classroom instruction with audiovisual aids, such as films, filmstrips, slides, records, and pictures, with an emphasis on vocabulary and common experiences verbalized. The teacher necessarily must study the children's cultural values and linguistic background in order to understand their behavior and responses. Skills must be taught linguistically in a systematic fashion in order of their sound-

[6] Paul W. Bell, "The Bilingual School," *Reading and Inquiry.* IRA Proceedings 10 (1965), pp. 271–74.

symbol relationship. The following sequence is the most workable: (1) hearing, (2) repeating orally, (3) seeing, (4) reading, and (5) writing. If children are mixed as to English-speaking and non-English-speaking, they could be paired so that they learn from each other. Current journals on reading contain articles relating the experiences of teachers in classrooms and their helpful suggestions for teaching bilingual children and for teaching English as a second language. The teacher who is in this situation for the first time should study these articles carefully and adapt methodology and materials accordingly.

Feeley [7] recommended the language experience approach as the child who speaks another language learns a new vocabulary in English and generates sentences to be written down by the teacher. She saw this approach as a procedure for developing readers who would be getting meaning from print rather than doing surface level decoding without thinking about meaning.

Onativia and Donosa [8] developed parallel sets of cards to help beginning readers differentiate between the structures of their native language and English. Cards were color coded for parts of speech. Picture cards were also used.

Spanish: | el | | pato | | nada |

English: | the | | duck | | swims |

The position of the adjective was noted first as it was said in Spanish, then as it occurred in English. An example follows:

| Mary | | had | | toys | | beautiful |

| Mary | | had | | beautiful | | toys |

The card system served the purpose of enabling the students to internalize the structure of verbal statements in a bilingual manner.

The foregoing summaries of articles from an issue of *The Reading Teacher* are examples of the kinds that teachers can study when they encounter the bilingual child for the first time. They can adapt methodology and materials to the needs of individual children. There are complete pro-

---

[7] Joan T. Feeley, "Bilingual Instruction: Puerto Rico and the Mainland," *The Reading Teacher,* 30:741–44 (April 1977).

[8] Oscar V. Onativia and Maria Alejandra Reves Donosa, "Basic Issues in Establishing a Bilingual Method," *The Reading Teacher,* 30:727–34 (April 1977).

grams for bilingual settings and complete programs for English As A Second Language (ESL) settings. They are not within the province of this book. Teachers in these settings need a strong aptitude for, and ability in the languages and cultures represented.

THE DISADVANTAGED

In the decades of the fifties and sixties the nation's school systems became aware that increasing numbers of children with limited backgrounds were swelling school populations at all levels, primary through secondary. Geographically, they were appearing in depressed urban areas; in the inner city; in Appalachia; in rural areas of California, Georgia, and other far-flung sections of the country. They were children of migrant workers and of low-income families. They included Indian, Puerto Rican, Mexican, black, and white children as well as others.

As these children were studied, various terms were commonly used to describe them—*disadvantaged, underprivileged, impoverished,* to name a few. They were found to be different in a number of ways—culturally, economically, socially, emotionally, and educationally. The educational deficits characteristic of these children were their nonstandard language patterns, poor self-concept and self-image, lack of motivation and aspiration, low conceptual abilities, and meager backgrounds of experience. Their problems were often compounded by their parents' poverty and/or frequent movement to a new residence and school.

Schuman [9] has found that inner-city children do not have a firm language base for abstract thinking and cannot achieve class-inclusion until late in academic life. Class inclusion is one of the levels of thinking in Piaget's theory of intelligence—one of the steps in the onset of concrete operational intelligence.

There have been various large-scale studies. The Great Cities School Improvement Project [10] was a nationwide educational experiment aimed at improving the education of children with limited backgrounds. Initiated in the fifties, it focused upon children's speaking vocabulary, oral language usage, and improved overall English programs. In 1965 the Task Force of the National Council of Teachers of English made a nationwide study of projects and programs for the disadvantaged. As a result of their study of over sixty elementary programs they identified the following characteristics of disadvantaged elementary school children: language retardation, lack

[9] Davida Schuman, "Class-Inclusion in the Inner-City Child: Analysis of Task Presentation." Paper presented at the Seventh Annual International Interdisciplinary Conference on Piagetian Theory and the Helping Professions, Children's Hospital, Los Angeles and the University of Southern California, January 28, 1977.
[10] Clarence W. Wachner, "Detroit Great Cities School Improvement Program in Language Arts," *Elementary English,* 41:734–42 (1964).

of the experiences needed for academic learning, inability to postpone immediate satisfaction for longer-term goals, aggressive behavior, lack of a time concept, a tendency to be slow in learning, a need to pursue one idea at a time, lack of interest in academic achievement, inability to generalize, dialects that differ from informal standard English, lack of self-concept, a feeling of being unable to succeed, and a feeling of rejection by society.[11]

What can be done to compensate for impoverished backgrounds? The Economic Opportunity Act of 1964 was an attempt to minimize the impact of poverty. Project Head Start, one of several community action programs, was initiated in the summer of 1965. It represented a concept of a child development center to which the family, the community, and the professional services would contribute their resources on the home front. In the first summer over half a million preschool children were involved in twenty-five hundred Head Start programs. Osborn[12] reported that the programs were designed to stimulate children's thinking, with a curriculum geared to their interests and abilities. Activities included art, stories, science, creative play, and visits to community facilities. The success of these community-centered projects has led many educators to propose downward extension of school programs, so that three- and four-year-olds might profit from language experiences appropriate to their ages, preparing them for the more formal instruction of the primary grades and ensuring success when they are faced with typical educational experiences.

Bereiter identifies as culturally or educationally disadvantaged those children who have not learned at home or in preschool those things they need to know before they can learn what is offered in the program of the first grade. He states that what they need is not the "abstract enrichment and experiences" but rather a straightforward educational instruction program. He claims success in a preschool program of three daily twenty-minute sessions of language learning, arithmetic, and reading, characterized by (1) fast pace, (2) reduced task-irrelevant behavior, (3) strong emphasis on verbal responses, (4) carefully planned small-step instructional units with continual feedback, and (5) heavy work demands with rewards for thinking. He says that, contrary to the educator's worries of stress and anxiety being created, the children were tired but relaxed and cheerful. The children were ready for reading instruction upon entry to first grade. Although Bereiter's program does seem especially strenuous for preschoolers, it does get educational and personal development results of a favorable nature. It, therefore, could be a model for others to examine carefully. He gives guidelines for planning and acquiring the right teachers, and any

[11] Richard Corbin and Muriel Crosby, co-chairmen, *Language Programs for the Disadvantaged* (Champaign, IL: National Council of Teachers of English, 1965), pp. 76–77.
[12] D. Keith Osborn, "A Look at Child Development Centers—Operation Head Start," *The Reading Teacher,* 19:332–34 (Feb. 1966).

groups working with the educationally disadvantaged would do well to study the whole program.[13]

Thus, in their programs preceding formal instruction in the basic educational skills of reading, writing, and arithmetic, the preschool disadvantaged children are provided many firsthand experiences. They become personally acquainted with many facets of their environment—their peers, the adults around them, the materials and equipment of their classroom, interaction with other children and adults, and manipulation of the many objects they meet daily. These experiences have been carefully planned to give them positive feelings of adequacy in dealing with people and materials, success in the tasks they undertake, and a positive self-image. With a program that has been carefully structured to overcome the differences in their backgrounds, disadvantaged children can approach their first formal lessons with wholesome attitudes about themselves and their schooling. They can attain the *will to learn,* which is so essential in readiness for instruction in reading, mathematics, social studies, science, and the appreciation of music and the other arts.

Not all disadvantaged children exhibit all of the characteristics delineated earlier, yet these children are found to have many educational problems in common. These include language problems, such as nonstandard dialects, bilingualism, or even nonexperiences with language usage; meager experiential backgrounds to prepare them for reading and for absorbing content area subject matter in textbooks; and a predilection toward being reality-bound rather than prepared for the abstract type of thinking associated with reading words in print. In order to be successful, reading programs for the disadvantaged need to be based upon teachers' knowledge of the characteristics of these children combined with teaching strategies geared to the children's current level of functioning.

Before beginning formal reading instruction, teachers need to analyze all individuals in regard to their readiness—their span of attention, their ability to differentiate among symbols, to associate sight with sound, to recall related information, to retain information, to conceptualize, and to do abstract thinking. As children move into reading, their teachers need to plan for individual growth through carefully selected, structured increments of learning. Learning a sequential pattern of skills is of benefit to these children, whether teacher-developed or commercially developed as in programed learning kits. Here the teacher's objective is to help all pupils to

[13] Carl Bereiter, Ontario Institute for Studies in Education, Toronto, Canada. Speech given at Rutgers University Spring Reading Conference, March 25, 1969. Additional sources of information: Carl Bereiter, "Are Pre-School Programs Built The Wrong Way?" *The Nations Schools* 92:55–56 (June 1966); and Carl Bereiter and Siegfried Engelmann, "Observations on the Use of Direct Instruction with Young Disadvantaged Children," *Journal of School Psychology,* IV:55–62 (Spring 1966).

be on their own in reading as soon as they are able. When they compete with themselves, there is no occasion for urgency to catch up with others in the class or to feel inferior because of comparisons with others. Success may come slowly, but personal failure is never a part of this picture.

Once reading skills have been introduced, much reinforcement at current achievement levels is the order of the day. Thus, teachers and librarians supply many books reflecting the pupil's interests at his or her current reading level. Early success with easy-reading material is essential so that these children learn a positive attitude toward reading. One disadvantaged adolescent remarked to Daniel Fader, "Like reading, man. You know—it ain't so bad." Yet many of this boy's counterparts have been apathetic toward any reading or writing in or out of school. Fader's book is a documented testimonial to the value of professional dedication to the ideal of literacy for everyone—that "reading ain't so bad, and it's time more people learned how good it is." [14] To the extent that teachers make reading an enjoyable and worthwhile experience, *all* children will read.

Disadvantaged children can be taught to read efficiently in the content areas. They can be taught study skills for silent, independent reading with good comprehension. They can be taught to take part in class discussions with their peers (disadvantaged and otherwise!) so that they recognize that they have worthwhile contributions that can be appreciated by others. (See the section in this chapter on the "Reluctant Reader" for further suggestions for adequate instruction of disadvantaged, reluctant readers.)

Numerous approaches to the initial teaching of reading have been tried with disadvantaged children. These include basal readers (traditional orthography), i.t.a. (Initial Teaching Alphabet), language experience, linguistic, visual (sight), phonics training, audiovisual methods, programed instruction, and various combinations. Children from impoverished backgrounds lack the types of experiences that prepare them for reading—such as reacting to auditory and visual stimuli. Their skills of auditory and visual discrimination may be retarded. Tests that indicate the child's ability to make gross and fine distinctions in these areas would help the teacher decide when a child can begin his or her reading program. A lack in any area (as indicated, for example, by the Wepman Test of Auditory Discrimination) would indicate the need for emphasis on further experiences in auditory or visual discrimination before embarking on any teaching technique. See the tests in Chapter 13.

Teachers will probably continue to ask themselves, "What is the *best* approach to teaching reading to disadvantaged children?" Studies to date have not given conclusive proof that any one approach is better than others for these children when they are ready for reading instruction. One of the

[14] Daniel N. Fader and Elton B. McNeil, *Hooked on Books: Program and Proof* (New York: Berkley Publishing Corporation, 1968), p. 19.

most ambitious studies of the past decade was the five-year study of the CRAFT Project (Comparing Reading Approaches in First Grade Teaching with Disadvantaged Children). In a final report, Harris and Morrison [15] considered the effectiveness of the use of two basic approaches, skills-centered and language experience. The first included two methods—the use of conventional basal readers and the combined use of basal readers with a phonovisual system. The second included the language experience method leading into individualized reading as well as a language-experience audio-visual method. No significant differences were found between the approaches or between the various methods. The writers recommended that efforts be made in the future to determine which combination of instructional components will prove most suitable for these children. They indicated that results showed the teacher to be far more important than the method. They suggested that further research is needed to clarify the teacher behavior associated with optimal results.

Becker [16] described the main points of the University of Oregon's Direct Instruction Model, one of the programs of Project Follow Through. That project was organized in 1967 to select and evaluate promising educational programs in the first three grades for disadvantaged children. Significant program gains were shown by the DIM in measures of basic skills, cognitive skills, and positive effect. The program DISTAR, published by Science Research Associates and designed by Siegfried Engelmann, utilized small-group instruction with daily sequenced instruction in reading, arithmetic, and language. Three tests were used—Wide Range Achievement Test, Metropolitan Achievement Test, and the Slosson Intelligence Test. Positive findings on performance levels of the children tested confirmed the original assumptions that poor children can succeed in school, that the basic education of economically disadvantaged children can be improved. Becker concluded that as schools are established today, they are not preparing low performing children for the vocabulary they will meet in the fourth grade. To improve this situation, he pointed out that language learning must be continuous throughout the grades.

Guthrie [17] reviewed a comparative study of Follow Through, the large-scale teaching program for disadvantaged children. Thirteen programs that were matched with non-Follow Through programs in the same schools and communities were evaluated to learn which were most successful models. In the top half of models consistently superior to the control groups was Direct Instruction, described earlier.

[15] Albert J. Harris and Coleman Morrison, "The CRAFT Project: A Final Report," *The Reading Teacher,* 22:335–40 (Jan. 1969).
[16] Wesley C. Becker, "Teaching Reading and Language Arts to the Disadvantaged," *Harvard Educational Review.* 47:518–543 (Nov. 1977).
[17] John T. Guthrie, "Follow Through: A Compensatory Education Experiment," *The Reading Teacher,* 31:240–44 (Nov. 1977).

Perceptive teachers who can supply diversified approaches to instruction based upon their analysis of individual needs would seem to be in the best position to provide adequate prereading and reading instruction for disadvantaged children. In summary, strategies for teaching disadvantaged children to read include

1. Recognition of the characteristics of disadvantaged children.
2. Supplying the lacks in their prereading developmental needs.
3. Provision of a carefully paced, firsthand language experience program.
4. Structuring of concrete learning experience.
5. Gradual introduction of abstract reading experiences.
6. Built-in success at every step.
7. Reinforcement with easy-reading, interesting materials.
8. Convincing these children that they *are* learning and that adults are interested in their successful development: "Someone cares."

Whether the children come from the city slums, Appalachia, Indian reservations, or migrant labor camps, they are a problem in America because their achievement in reading is typically below that of others. Attempts have been made to help them through federally sponsored programs, adjusted teaching materials, new teaching materials, experimental programs, and changes in methods of instruction. Of one point we are sure—they need strong, creative, good teachers, working with appropriate materials and a variety of approaches to meet the needs of the children. Some approaches that have been reported with varying degrees of success are corrective feedback, building upon the child's existing language and conceptual structures, a continued readiness program, having the child imitate the teacher's speech, teaching standard English as a second language, the individual diagnose-and-teach sequence, raising the aspirations of the child, presenting minority characters in a favorable light in stories, teaching social aims as well as skills, extending language experiences through trips, giving extra auditory practice, building a sense of personal worth, teaching values and attitudes, and special programs, such as Head Start. As the evidence accumulates, desirable practices along with good materials will be spelled out so that schools can plan complete programs for these children and can fully prepare teachers to help them.

THE RELUCTANT READER

Reluctant readers do not achieve as well as expected, for they show little or no interest in reading. In the early grades they show no interest in books and in learning to read. Their attention seems to be on other things—frequently big muscle activities, games, and hobbies. In the upper grades they have become adept at sidestepping reading activities. Some, but not all, have managed to sharpen their listening skills. Thus they appear for a while to be keeping up with their content area subjects. Usually, when they enter the secondary school, their lack of independent reading ability causes failing marks and even dropouts.

As the reluctant readers are detected, their teachers are challenged to provide appropriate instruction. Their independent and instructional reading levels must first be determined. Their current interests may provide some clues as to the types of reading materials that would snag their reading attention. Enough material must be found—the task of teachers and librarians, as well as the students themselves. Charles Spiegler's account of a book fair,[18] which captured the reading interest of urban secondary boys, showed that boys themselves can choose the reading materials that will eventually lead them to improved reading skills.

Teachers who have determined instructional reading levels will note that these children are penalized by very inadequate skills. They typically have no independence in attacking words. Some can unlock words to the extent of pronouncing them but cannot grasp the meaning of paragraphs and longer selections. Their reading, whether oral or silent, is slow and laborious, with very little comprehension.

What can teachers do to help the reluctant readers? They need to be aware of the role of motivation. If possible, they need to locate a reading model that these children can emulate. Older boys and girls may be led to note the part reading played in the success of a community helper or other well-known person whom they admire. Younger children may be led to the point that they want to finish an exciting story started by the librarian or teacher.

The teacher's preparation is extremely important. Skillful questions will arouse interest and keep interest alive. Class discussion needs to be encouraged—to the point that it may involve more time than the reading itself. Self-involvement and peers' experiences recounted are often keys to eventual reading improvement for these children.

Teachers can use a modified form of the SQ3R technique to help these students with their reading in content areas. See Chapter 6. Although they may be reluctant readers at the outset, they usually want to be like the others and take part in class discussions. Therefore, over and over the teacher will introduce the topic as a whole in an overview better readers could achieve for themselves. They can encourage these children to read just far

---

[18] Charles G. Spiegler, "As the Bee Goes to the Flower for Its Nectar," from J. Allen Figurel, ed., *Reading as an Intellectual Activity,* Conference Proceedings of IRA (Englewood Cliffs, NJ: Scholastic Book Services, 1963), pp. 155–59.

enough to answer a question. After some discussion of several answers, the teacher can pose another question for which they will read again. Reluctant readers profit from keeping records of their own progress—typically on short selections for which several questions of comprehension have been developed.

Teachers of reluctant readers may compare notes as to methods and techniques that have proved successful. The language-experience technique has been used to good advantage with some of these children. Accounts of their personal life after school and on vacations may be typed and used as reading material. A group may bind some of the accounts into book form. A combination of telling, writing, editing, and reading has been successful with many who showed a distaste for regular books.

When a number of reluctant readers appear in the same classroom, they may be reached through a greater emphasis than usual upon socialization. Teachers provide the casual setting by letting them talk, discuss reactions, and take a large part in their own lessons. These students often gain insights into their own shortcomings and subsequently show a greater interest in learning how they can improve their reading skills.

An approach that has been very practical has been the provision for *real* projects. Examples, depending upon the age and interests of the pupils, include telephone conversations, job applications, newspaper items, illustrating paperbacks, role-playing, reading for parts in plays, putting a television play on tape, and so on. These require reading in their preparation, so teachers find reading material adapted to their levels, as well as time to go over, polish, and refine the product into a finished work of which the students can be proud. Teachers are providing practice, children are experiencing a positive purpose for reading and writing.

More specialized techniques that have been used include a listening-viewing center, the overhead transparency technique, and teaching by tape. In the listening-viewing center teachers have gathered appropriate filmstrips and recordings, headphone sets, and a screen. Children listen while viewing a story on film. Follow-up may include oral discussion or worksheets to check comprehension and progress to date.

Transparency overhead projection is finding its way into many modern classrooms. Transparencies lend themselves to many types of lessons—phonics, poetry, and directions for worksheets, to name a few. Oral storytelling is enhanced with a sequential projection of parts of a story. Children volunteer answers when comic strips are projected with empty balloons. Children's compositions can be analyzed by peers when projected for a group to evaluate.

Tape recording has proven a boon to the busy classroom teacher. Lessons for individual and small groups may be prepared in advance, to be played when the teacher may be occupied with other lessons. Children's conversations may be recorded, typed, and read back; listen-and-learn tapes are commercially made with topics such as comprehension skills, study skills, and building a better vocabulary.

Thus, filmstrips, transparencies, and tapes sometimes snag the interest of certain pupils, just as the small increment of lessons in programed learning kits (see Chapter 11) has captured some pupils who would not attempt a whole chapter or book. Teachers need to be ready to capitalize upon any device or technique that will provide a springboard to reading for the reluctant reader.

When the reluctant reader has progressed to the point of attaining some security in his or her reading and some interest in books, materials must be located that are centered around familiar people and situations. For some, this will mean family and neighbors. For the inner-city child the Jimmy series developed for Detroit children will provide a familiar vocabulary and content. The girl with a Puerto Rican family may wish to read a book like Lewiton's *Candita's Choice.*[19] In the middle grades the student who has become interested in his or her country's neighbor would enjoy *Canada and the U.S.A.*[20] Here again the school librarian can give assistance to the classroom teacher who knows the students, their current achievement, and their interests. Books with captivating titles and jackets can appear like magic on the library table at just the right time for reluctant readers to turn into eager readers.

THE LEARNING DISABLED CHILD

According to the federal law on educating the handicapped (PL 94–142), children are designated as learning disabled when they have such disorders as perceptual handicaps, brain injury, minimal brain dysfunction, dyslexia, and developmental aphasia. Such disorders may be manifested in imperfect ability to listen, think, speak, read, write, spell, or do mathematical calculations.

Unfortunately in the past, learning disabled children may have remained undetected throughout their school years. Because their special problems have often not been diagnosed before they entered school, they may have sat in regular classrooms mistakenly considered to be mentally retarded, passive, hyperactive, unmotivated, or even discipline problems. Their early identification is imperative in order that they may learn to compensate for their problems. They may be given adaptive measures and thus benefit from their education.

When it is suspected that a child has a learning disability, the regular

[19] Mina Lewiton, *Candita's Choice* (New York: Harper & Row, Publishers, 1959).
[20] Richard J. Walton, *Canada and the U.S.A.* Parents Magazine Press.

elementary or secondary teacher may refer him or her to the school psychologist and/or the learning disability specialist. The teacher should be alert to the child who exhibits several of the following characteristics:

Has short attention span
Is easily distracted
Is constantly active
Shows lack of coordination
Confuses left and right
Lacks ability to follow oral directions
Shows poor verbal ability
Has poor self-expression
Reverses letters, words, digits
Confuses similar letters and words
Mixes capital and lower case letters
Confuses letters and sounds in writing and spelling
Mixes manuscript and cursive writing

The National Education Association devoted a section in the journal *Today's Education* to the child with learning disabilities. Bonnie Jones [21] provided teachers with sensible suggestions for identification and referral of LD children, for understanding their problems, and for teaching techniques.

Another publication, *Readings in Learning Disabilities,* [22] gives the experienced teacher and the new teacher some insights into the characteristics and diagnosis of learning disabled children and offers suggestions for helping them. The suggestions are based upon understanding the children's specific problems and then adapting instruction to their particular needs. For example, sessions should be short, interesting, not boring, with less written work than for the regular child, and with few or no distractions. These are some of the ways the classroom teacher may adapt instructional procedures when handicapped children are mainstreamed.

MAINSTREAMING

Educators have long maintained that every child has a right to an education. Some schools have had classes for the gifted, the slow learners, the children with poor vision or hearing, and so on. In the seventies certain state and federal laws have indicated that school systems should provide for all handicapped children.

The Education for All Handicapped Children Act, PL 94–142, was

[21] Bonnie Jones, "Helping Teachers Teach the LD Student," *Today's Education,* 66: 46–48 (Nov.-Dec. 1977).
[22] Herbert Goldstein, et al., *Readings in Learning Disabilities* (Guilford, Conn.: Special Learning Corporation, 1978).

passed by Congress in 1975. According to this act, handicapped children are those who are identified as

> Mentally retarded
> Hearing impaired—deaf or hard-of-hearing
> Sight impaired—blind, partially sighted
> Health impaired
> Speech impaired
> Emotionally disturbed
> Multihandicapped
> With specific learning disabilities

The federal law requires that handicapped children be identified and provided with a free appropriate public education (FAPE). It mandates that handicapped children be educated in the least restrictive environment, such as in the regular classroom (mainstreaming) unless, because of the severity of the handicap, the child could not receive a satisfactory education there.

An individualized education program (IEP) must be completed for each child who needs special education. The IEP is expected to be a statement of educational goals, objectives, and services appropriate to the child. The law anticipates that handicapped children will benefit from an educational environment appropriate to their needs. As the law is implemented, certain handicapped children will be taught in the regular classroom. Others will need the provision of specialized supportive services.

Teachers who were prepared as elementary or secondary educators will need to keep up-to-date concerning research findings and innovative practices for the handicapped through in-service training and resources, college courses, and personal research.

DIALECT SPEAKERS

Among the children who appear in the modern classroom are those who are dialect speakers. They are speakers of nonstandard English.

In the typical American classroom, teachers have sometimes misinterpreted this child's reading errors. They have expected the child to learn to speak standard English before he or she could be taught to read.

In the seventies a number of studies showed that children with nonstandard dialects had the same chance of learning to read as those who spoke standard English.[23] Linguists have reported that nonstandard dialects are structured systems.

[23] Walter Gantt, Robert Wilson, and C. Mitchell Dayton, "An Initial Investigation of the Relationship Between Syntactical Divergencies and the Listening Compre-

The implications for the classroom teacher are that Black dialect has very little effect on black children's reading achievement. They point out that Black English is different rather than deficient. Although differences between Black dialect and standard English do exist, they apparently do not greatly interfere with black children's learning to read. Other nonstandard speech was found to have a minimal effect on the reading of Spanish-speakers and those with a Newfoundland dialect.[24] Garcia [25] said that the Chicanos' difficulty with reading would be related to factors other than their bilingualism.

SUMMARY

Any reading program that is completely effective meets the needs of each child. This is an ambitious undertaking because needs are not always observable in the overt behavior of children. A cooperative effort among teachers, parents, librarians, and administrators will help to identify the true needs of the children.

Practically all children can learn to read when the school knows how to motivate them to learn the skills and knowledges they need and creates a completely favorable environment for reading. This chapter has shown that teachers will accomplish more by adjusting the materials and program to the child than by labeling the child and trying to fit him or her into a preconceived mold.

SELECTED READINGS

Andelman, Frederick. "Mainstreaming in Massachusetts Under Law 766." *Today's Education,* 65,2 (March-April 1976), 20–22.
Becker, Wesley C. "Teaching Reading and Language Arts to the Disadvantaged." *Harvard Educational Review,* 47,4 (Nov. 1977), 518–43.

hension of Black Children," *Reading Research Quarterly,* 10,2:193–211 (1974–1975); Leona Foerster, "Language Experience for Dialectically Different Black Learners," *Elementary English,* 51:193–97 (Feb. 1974); William Rupley and Carol Robeck, "Black Dialect and Reading Achievement," *Reading Teacher,* 31, 5:598–601 (Feb. 1978).

[24] Groves Mathewson and Denise Pereya-Suarez, "Spanish Language Interference with Acoustic-Phonetic Skills and Reading," *Journal of Reading Behavior,* 7:187–96 (1975).

[25] Ricardo Garcia, "Mexican American Bilingualism and English Language Development," *Journal of Reading,* 17:467–73 (March 1974).

Brooke, Edward. "PL 94–142—Getting the Money to Make It Work." *Today's Education,* 66,4 (Nov.-Dec. 1977), 50–52.

Cawley, John F., et al. *The Slow Learner and the Reading Program.* Springfield, IL: Charles C Thomas, Publisher, 1972.

Dupuy, H. F. *The Rationale, Development and Standardization of a Basic Vocabulary Test.* Washington, DC: U.S. Government Printing Office, 1974.

Fader, Daniel. *The New Hooked on Books.* New York: Berkeley Publishing Corporation, 1976.

Foerster, Leona. "Language Experiences for Dialectically Different Black Learners." *Elementary English,* 51 (Feb. 1974), 193–97.

Gantt, Walter N.; Robert Wilson; and C. Mitchel Dayton. "An Initial Investigation of the Relationship Between Syntactical Divergencies and the Listening Comprehension of Black Children." *Reading Research Quarterly* 10,2 (1974–75), 193–211.

Goldstein, Herbert, et al. *Readings on Learning Disabilities.* Guilford, CT: Special Learning Corporation, 1978.

Goodman, Kenneth S., and Catheline Buck. "Dialect Barriers to Reading Comprehension Revisited." *The Reading Teacher,* 27,1 (Oct. 1973), 6–12.

Heilman, Arthur. *Principles and Practices of Teaching Reading.* Columbus: OH: Charles E. Merrill Publishing Company, 1977.

Horn, Thomas D., ed. *Reading for the Disadvantaged: Problems of Linguistically Different Learners.* New York: Harcourt Brace Jovanovich, Inc., 1970.

Hunt, Barbara. "Black Dialect and Third and Fourth Graders' Performance on the Gray Oral Reading Test." *Reading Research Quarterly,* 10 (1974–75), 102–23.

Jones, Bonnie. "Helping Teachers Teach the LD Student." *Today's Education,* 66,4 (Nov.–Dec. 1977), 46–48.

Joyce, William W., and James A. Banks, eds. *Teaching the Language Arts to Culturally Different Children.* Reading, MA: Addison-Wesley Publishing Co., Inc., 1971.

Knapp, Margaret. "Black Dialect and Reading: What Teachers Need to Know." *Journal of Reading,* 19,3 (Dec. 1975), 231–36.

Labuda, Michael, ed. *Creative Reading for Gifted Learners: A Design for Excellence.* Newark, DE: International Reading Association, 1972.

Mathewson, Grover, and Denise Pereya-Suarez. "Spanish Language Interference with Acoustic-Phonetic Skills and Reading." *Journal of Reading Behavior,* 7 (1975), 187–96.

Niensted, Serena. "Talking With LD Teachers." *The Reading Teacher,* 28,7 (April 1975), 662–65.

Pflaum-Connor, Susanna, ed. *Aspects of Reading Education,* Berkeley, CA: McCuthan Publishing Corporation, 1978.

Rupley, William H., and Carol Robeck. "Black Dialect and Reading Achievement." *The Reading Teacher,* 31,5 (Feb. 1978), 598–601.

"Schooling the Handicapped." *NEA Reporter,* 16,7 (Oct. 1977), 4–5.

Siegel, Ernest. *Special Education in the Regular Classroom.* New York: The John Day Co., Publishers, 1969.

Swiss, Thom, and Turee Olson. "Reading and Slow Learners." *The Reading Teacher,* 29,7 (April 1976), 732–35.

Walker, Laurence, "Newfoundland Dialect Interference in Oral Reading." *Journal of Reading Behavior,* 7 (1975), 61–78.

Witty, Paul A., ed. *Reading for the Gifted and the Creative Student.* Newark, DE: International Reading Association, 1972.

Wolfram, Walt. "Sociolinguistic Alternatives in Teaching Reading to Nonstandard Speakers." *Reading Research Quarterly,* 6 (1970), 9–33.

Appendices

Appendices

SERIES **r**™
The New Macmillan Reading Program

The skills program of SERIES **r**: The New Macmillan Reading Program represents a logical and carefully maintained sequence of introduction, development, evaluation, reinforcement and maintenance. At primary levels the important word attack skills were computer analyzed to obtain the most beneficial progression. At these levels, each subsequent skill reinforces and maintains skills taught previously in the sequence. It is not necessary—or beneficial—therefore to test for mastery of all word attack skills introduced at each level. At intermediate levels, comprehension skills receive important emphasis, particularly in their relationship to reading in the content areas.

A guide to symbols used in this Scope and Sequence

‡   Skill introduced and taught prior to the level in which
     it is tested
•   Skill tested within the level—corresponds to the level focus
     skills within the Teacher's Edition lesson plans
*   Skill taught but not tested within level
✔   Review and maintenance or further applications of skills
     taught at previous levels
•✔   Review, development and testing in greater depth of skill
     taught in previous levels

A chart of traditional grade level designations

SERIES r Levels	Traditional Grade Placement
Levels 1, 2	Kindergarten Program
Levels 3,3+	Reading Readiness (K or Grade 1)
Levels 4-6	Preprimers
Levels 7, 8	Primers
Levels 9, 10	First Reader
Levels 11, 12	2¹ Reader
Levels 13, 14	2² Reader
Levels 15, 16	3¹ Reader
Levels 17, 18	3² Reader
Levels 19-24	Fourth Reader
Levels 25-30	Fifth Reader
Levels 31-36	Sixth Reader

Contents

Scope and Sequence, Levels 1-3+ (Kindergarten/Readiness)

Scope and Sequence, Levels 4-18 (Primary Grades)

    Word Recognition
    Comprehension
    Study Skills
    Language Skills
    Oral Language Skills
    Listening, Attitudes, Creative Activities

Scope and Sequence, Levels 19-36 (Intermediate Grades)

    Comprehension
    Attitudes, Language Skills
    Oral Language
    Word Recognition
    Literary Skills
    Study Skills
    Listening Skills, Creative Activities

Program Materials, Levels 1-3+ (Kindergarten/Readiness)

Program Materials, Levels 3-18 (Primary Grades)

Program Materials, Levels 19-36 (Intermediate Grades)

Solo Book Titles, Levels 1-36

Scope and Sequence, Levels 1-18 Kindergarten–Primary Grades

Kindergarten—Levels 1, 2

	LEVEL 1/Read-It-Yourself Books A&B
ORAL LANGUAGE	•Using vocabulary appropriate for level
	•Using complete simple sentences
	•Using correct verb form with noun
	‡
	‡
	*Naming animals, family members, foods, and community workers
	*Recognizing and naming body parts
	*Dictating sentences and stories
	*Telling stories
	‡
	*Using correct singular or plural noun form
LANGUAGE CONCEPTS	•Knowing that words are read and written from left to right
	‡
	*Understanding that oral language can be written
	*Understanding that words are made of letters
	*Understanding that words serve a purpose
	‡
VISUAL SKILLS	•Matching a letter to an initial letter in a word
	•Matching and recognizing colors, sizes, and shapes

‡Development of skill tested at later level
•   Skill taught and tested within level
*   Skill taught but not tested within level

Kindergarten–Readiness

Readiness – Levels 3,3+

LEVEL 2/Read-It-Yourself Books A&B	LEVEL 3/Read-It-Yourself Books A&B
✔	✔
✔	✔
✔	✔
•Using parts of speech	✔
•Using basic sentence transformations	•✔
✔	✔
✔	✔
✔	✔
✔	✔
•Telling story with a beginning, middle and end	✔
‡	•Retelling story in own words
✔	✔
	*Distinguishing between singular and plural nouns
✔	✔
‡	•Showing left-to-right progression by reading and printing
✔	✔
✔	✔
✔	✔
•Distinguishing between letter, word, and sentence	✔
	*Following top-to-bottom progression
*Recognizing purpose of marks of punctuation	✔
✔	✔
✔	✔

Kindergarten—Levels 1, 2

	LEVEL 1/Read-It-Yourself Books A&B
VISUAL SKILLS (Continued)	•Matching and recognizing letters and numerals
	‡
CONCEPT DEVELOPMENT	•Ordering a sequence
	*Associating numerals with number of objects
	*Counting objects
	*Recognizing textures, temperatures and relative size
CRITICAL THINKING	•Making inferences and predicting outcomes
	•Classifying
	*Solving problems
	‡
COMPREHENSION	•Following directions
	•Naming object by hearing description
	‡

✔ Review and maintenance or further development   •✔ Review and maintenance with further testing

Readiness – Levels 3,3+

LEVEL 2/Read-It-Yourself Books A&B	LEVEL 3/Read-It-Yourself Books A&E
↙	↙
•Matching words	↙
	•Recognizing word forms that are the same and different
↙	↙
↙	↙
*Identifying number/numeral correspondence	↙
	*Recognizing numerals
↙	↙
↙	↙
•Relating picture of concept to its opposite	↙
•Describing cause and effect	↙
*Distinguishing between fantasy and reality	↙
	*Understanding locational concepts
*Understanding time concepts	↙
↙	↙
↙	↙
•Naming two classifications for an object	↙
↙	↙
‡	*Drawing conclusions
↙	↙
	•Following four-part directions
↙	↙
•Completing an oral statement with spoken word that fits context	•↙

Kindergarten–Readiness

	Kindergarten—Levels 1, 2
	LEVEL 1/Read-It-Yourself Books A&B
COMPREHENSION (Continued)	‡
	‡
AUDITORY SKILLS	•Discriminating whether word sounds are the same or different
	•Listening to a story read aloud
	*Listening for a purpose
	•Naming common sounds after hearing them
	‡
	‡
	‡
	‡
	‡
AUDITORY-VISUAL SKILLS	
LETTER-NAME KNOWLEDGE	•Recognizing and naming capital and small letters
	*Reciting the alphabet
	*Recognizing the same letter shape in different sizes
	*Using the words capital and small to describe letters
	‡

‡Development of skill tested at later level • Skill taught and tested within level

Kindergarten–Readiness   * Skill taught but not tested within level

Readiness – Levels 3,3+

LEVEL 2/Read-It-Yourself Books A&B	LEVEL 3/Read-It-Yourself Books A&B
‡	•Recalling sequence of oral story
‡	•Recognizing main idea of a story
	*Recalling details
✔	✔
✔	✔
✔	✔
✔	✔
•Recognizing objects that have the same beginning sound	✔
•Recognizing words that rhyme	✔
‡	•Naming objects that begin with the same sound as a given word
‡	•Naming words that rhyme with given words
‡	•Selecting pictures of objects that have the same beginning sound
*Preview—recognizing the phoneme-grapheme correspondences for initial /b/b, /k/c, /d/d, /f/f, /g/g, /h/h, /j/j, /l/l, /m/m, /n/n, /p/p, /r/r, /s/s, /t/t, /v/v, /w/w, /y/y, /z/z	✔
	*Recognizing the phoneme-grapheme correspondences for initial /b/b, /k/c, /d/d, /f/f, /g/g, /h/h, /j/j, /k/k, /l/l, /m/m, /n/n, /p/p, /kw/q, /r/r, /s/s, /t/t, /v/v, /w/w, /y/y, /z/z
✔	✔
✔	✔
*Putting letters in alphabetical order	✔
✔	✔
✔	✔
‡	•Naming and printing capital and small letters

Kindergarten—Levels 1, 2

	LEVEL 1/Read-It-Yourself Books A&B
MOTOR SKILLS	•Drawing a line from left to right
	*Drawing or coloring within boundaries
	*Tracing letters and numerals
	*Using scissors
	‡
	‡
WORD RECOGNITION	
ATTITUDES	•Handling book with care
	‡
	*Recognizing the importance of weather, food, clothing, and shelter
	*Understanding what a community is and how it functions
	*Recognizing the roles of community workers
	*Understanding that machines make work easier

✔ Review and maintenance or further development

Readiness – Levels 3,3+

LEVEL 2/Read-It-Yourself Books A&B	LEVEL 3/Read-It-Yourself Books A&B
✔	✔
✔	✔
✔	✔
✔	✔
•Printing name	✔
•Printing letters Aa-Za	✔
*Printing words	✔
	*Copying sentences
	*Printing name and address
*Recognizing specific words: a, boy, boys, girl, girls, I, man, the	✔
	*Recognizing basic sight words: a, and, boy, boys, can, can't, down, girl, girls, I, in, jump, jumps, man, out, ride, run, runs, to, the, up, walk, walks
✔	✔
•Naming ways language can be helpful	✔
‡	•Selecting a book independently
✔	✔
✔	✔
	*Understanding that cities depend upon the country for food, water, and raw materials
✔	✔
✔	✔
*Developing sense of pride in doing things	✔
*Developing sense of own likes and dislikes	✔
*Recognizing safe behavior	✔

Kindergarten–Readiness

	WHO CAN? LOST & FOUND HATS & BEARS
	LEVELS 4-6
WORD RECOGNITION **CONSONANTS** **INITIAL**	•Recognizing the phoneme-grapheme correspondences for /b/b, /k/c, /d/d, /f/f, /g/g, /h/h, /j/j, /k/k, /l/l, /m/m, /n/n, /p/p, /r/r, /s/s, /t/t, /v/v, /w/w, /y/y
CONSONANTS **FINAL**	•Recognizing the phoneme-grapheme correspondences for /b/b, /d/d, /g/g, /n/n, /s/s, /t/t
CONSONANT CLUSTERS **INITIAL**	

Primary Grades   •Skill taught and tested within level   *Skill taught but not tested within level

AMIGOS **UPS & DOWNS**	**COLORS** **BEING ME**
LEVELS 7-8	**LEVELS 9-10**
	✓
•Recognizing the phoneme-grapheme correspondences for /z/*z*	
✓	✓
•Recognizing the phoneme-grapheme correspondences for /m/*m*, /p/*p*, /ks/*x*	✓
•Recognizing the phoneme-grapheme correspondences for /br/*br*, /kr/*cr*, /dr/*dr*, /fl/*fl*, /gl/*gl*, /gr/*gr*, /pl/*pl*, /pr/*pr*, /st/*st*, voiceless /sh/*sh*, /th/*th*	✓
	•Recognizing the phoneme-grapheme correspondences for /bl/*bl*, /kw/*qu*, /tr/*tr*, /hw/*wh* *Recognizing the phoneme-grapheme correspondences for /ch/*ch*, /kl/*cl*, /sl/*sl*, voiced /th/*th*

	BELIEVE IT! FEELINGS
	LEVELS 11-12
WORD RECOGNITION **CONSONANTS** **INITIAL**	✔
	✔
CONSONANTS **FINAL**	✔
	✔
CONSONANT CLUSTERS **INITIAL**	✔
	✔
	• Recognizing the phoneme-grapheme correspondences for /fr/*fr*, /sm/*sm*, /skr/*scr*, /sp/*sp*, /str/*str*, /thr/*thr*

✔ Review and maintenance or further development

STAND TALL A SECOND LOOK	SECRET SPACES GOOD NEWS
LEVELS 13-14	**LEVELS 15-16**
✔	✔
✔	
•Recognizing the phoneme-grapheme correspondences for /s/c, /j/g	✔
✔	✔
✔	✔
✔	✔
✔	✔
✔	✔
•Recognizing the phoneme-grapheme correspondences for /n/kn, /r/wr	✔
	•Recognizing the phoneme-grapheme correspondences for /f/ph, /s/sc, /sk/sch, /spl/spl, /skw/squ, /sw/sw, /tw/tw

	BEGINNINGS ENDINGS
	LEVELS 17-18
WORD RECOGNITION **CONSONANTS** **INITIAL**	✔
	✔
CONSONANTS **FINAL**	✔
	✔
CONSONANT CLUSTERS **INITIAL**	✔
	✔
	✔
	✔
	✔
	•Recognizing the phoneme-grapheme correspondences for /shr/*shr*, /spr/*spr* *Recognizing the phoneme-grapheme correspondences for /sk/*sk*, /sn/*sn*

Primary Grades

	WHO CAN? LOST & FOUND HATS & BEARS
	LEVELS 4-6
WORD RECOGNITION (Cont.) **CONSONANT CLUSTERS** **FINAL**	
VOWELS **MEDIAL**	•Recognizing the phoneme-grapheme correspondences for /a/a, /i/i, /o/o
VOWELS **MEDIAL WITH THE** *e* **MARKER**	
VOWELS **INITIAL**	
VOWELS **FINAL**	
VOWEL CLUSTERS **(INITIAL, MEDIAL** **AND FINAL)**	

Primary Grades   •Skill taught and tested within level   *Skill taught but not tested within level

AMIGOS UPS & DOWNS	COLORS BEING ME
LEVELS 7-8	**LEVELS 9-10**
	•Recognizing the phoneme-grapheme correspondences for /ch/*ch*, /ch/*tch*, /nd/*nd*, /ng/*ng*, /ngk/*nk*, /st/*st*
✔	✔
•Recognizing the phoneme-grapheme correspondences for /e/*e*, /u/*u*	✔
•Recognizing the phoneme-grapheme correspondences for /a/*a*, /ĭ/*i*	✔
*Recognizing the phoneme-grapheme correspondences for /ē/*e*, /ō/*o*, /yoo/*u*	✔
	•Recognizing the phoneme-grapheme correspondences for /a/*a*, /u/*u*
	•Recognizing the phoneme-grapheme correspondences for /ī/*y*
	*Recognizing the phoneme-grapheme correspondences for /ē/*y*
	•Recognizing the phoneme-grapheme correspondences for /ā/*ai*, /ā/*ay*, /ē/*ea*, /ē/*ee*, /ī/*ie*, /ō/*oa*

	BELIEVE IT! FEELINGS LEVELS 11-12
WORD RECOGNITION (Cont.) **CONSONANT CLUSTERS FINAL**	✔
	•Recognizing the phoneme-grapheme correspondences for /k/*ck*, /ld/*ld*, /l/*ll*, /nt/*nt*, /sh/*sh*, /s/*ss*, voiceless /th/*th*
VOWELS MEDIAL	✔
	✔
VOWELS MEDIAL WITH THE *e* MARKER	✔
	✔
VOWELS INITIAL	•✔
	•Recognizing the phoneme-grapheme correspondences for /e/*e*, /i/*i*, /o/*o*,
VOWELS FINAL	✔
	✔
VOWEL CLUSTERS (INITIAL, MEDIAL AND FINAL)	•Recognizing the phoneme-grapheme correspondences for /oi/*oi*, /o͞o/*oo*, /oo/*oo*, /ou/*ou* •Recognizing different spellings for /ā/, /ē/, /ī/, /ō/ •Recognizing /ur/ spelled as *er, ir, or, ur*

Primary Grades   ✔Review and maintenance or further development

STAND TALL A SECOND LOOK	SECRET SPACES GOOD NEWS
LEVELS 13-14	**LEVELS 15-16**
✓	✓
✓	✓
	•Recognizing the phoneme-grapheme correspondences for /lk/*lk*, /lp/*lp*
✓	✓
✓	✓
✓	✓
✓	✓
✓	✓
✓	✓
✓	✓
✓	✓
•Recognizing the phoneme-grapheme correspondences for /ô/*al*, /är/*ar*, /ô/*au*, /ô/*aw*, /ôr/*or* •Recognizing different spellings for /oi/, /ou/ •Recognizing the phoneme-grapheme correspondences for /ôl/*al*, /ôl/*all*, /er/*ear*, /ur/*ear*	•Recognizing the phoneme-grapheme correspondences for /ar/*air*, /ar/*ear*, /ā/*ei*, /ā/*eigh*, /ar/*eir*, /ē/*ie*, /ī/*igh*, /īld/*ild*, /īnd/*ind*, /ō/*oe*, /ōld/*old*, /ō/*ow* *Recognizing the phoneme-grapheme correspondences for /ar/*are*, /er/*ere*, /yo͞o/*ew*, /īr/*ire*, /yo͝or/*ure*

•✓Review and maintenance with further testing

	BEGINNINGS **ENDINGS**
	LEVELS 17-18
WORD RECOGNITION (Cont.) **CONSONANT CLUSTERS** **FINAL**	✔
	✔
	•Recognizing the phoneme-grapheme correspondences for /ft/*ft*, /f/*gh*, *gh* as in *sigh*, /lt/*lt*, /mp/*mp*, /sk/*sk*, /sp/*sp*
VOWELS **MEDIAL**	✔
	✔
VOWELS **MEDIAL WITH THE** *e* **MARKER**	✔
	✔
VOWELS **INITIAL**	✔
	✔
	•Recognizing the phoneme-grapheme correspondences for the schwa sound /ə/
VOWELS **FINAL**	✔
	✔
VOWEL CLUSTERS **(INITIAL, MEDIAL** **AND FINAL)**	•Recognizing the phoneme-grapheme correspondences for /ē/*ea*, /e/*ea*, /ē/*ei*, /o͞o/*ew*, /ē/*ey*, /o͞o/*ou* •Recognizing the phoneme-grapheme correspondences for /o͞o/*ue*

Primary Grades

	WHO CAN? LOST & FOUND HATS & BEARS
	LEVELS 4-6
WORD RECOGNITION (Cont.) **SYLLABICATION**	
WORD BASES	•Recognizing the graphemic bases with initial consonant substitution -*an*, -*ig*, -*it*, -*ob*, -*ot* *Recognizing the phonemic base /an/
WORD ENDINGS	•Recognizing the plural ending -*s*
	•Recognizing the verb ending -*s*
WORD FORMATION	

Primary Grades •Skill taught and tested within level   *Skill taught but not tested within level

AMIGOS UPS & DOWNS	COLORS BEING ME
LEVELS 7-8	**LEVELS 9-10**
	•Hearing syllables in words
•Recognizing the graphemic bases with initial consonant substitution -*ut, -un* *-en*	✔
✔	✔
✔	✔
•Recognizing the possessive ending -*'s*	✔
•Recognizing the verb endings -*ed, -ing*	✔
•Recognizing compound words •Recognizing hyphenated words	✔

	BELIEVE IT! **FEELINGS**
	LEVELS 11-12
WORD RECOGNITION (Cont.) **SYLLABICATION**	✔
WORD BASES	✔
WORD ENDINGS	✔
	✔
	✔
	✔
	•Recognizing the comparative endings -er, -est
WORD FORMATION	✔
	•Dropping final e before adding -ed, -ing
	•Doubling final consonant before adding -ed, -ing

Primary Grades   ✔Review and maintenance or further development

STAND TALL A SECOND LOOK	SECRET SPACES GOOD NEWS
LEVELS 13-14	**LEVELS 15-16**
*Hearing syllables in one-, two-, and three-syllable words	•Using vowel sounds as clues to number of syllables in words •Syllabication between prefix and root, and between suffix and root *Dividing compound words into syllables
✔	✔
✔	✔
✔	✔
✔	✔
✔	✔
✔	
	*Recognizing the ending -es with words ending in f
✔	✔
✔	✔
✔	✔

	BEGINNINGS ENDINGS
	LEVELS 17-18
WORD RECOGNITION (Cont.)	✔
SYLLABICATION	✔
	•Recognizing the double medial consonant as a clue to syllabication
	•Recognizing *le* as a syllable
	•Hearing and marking accented syllables
	•Dividing words between schwa sound and accented syllable
	*Recognizing the ending *-ed* as a separate syllable after words ending in *t* or *d*
WORD BASES	✔
WORD ENDINGS	✔
	✔
	✔
	✔
	✔
	✔
	*Recognizing the ending *-es* with words ending in *ss, x,* or *ch*
WORD FORMATION	✔
	✔
	✔

Primary Grades

	WHO CAN? LOST & FOUND HATS & BEARS
	LEVELS 4-6
WORD RECOGNITION (Cont.) **WORD FORMATION** (Continued)	
CONTRACTIONS	
PREFIXES	
SUFFIXES	
COMPREHENSION	•Finding the main idea
	•Recalling details
	‡
	‡
	‡
	‡
	‡

Primary Grades   •Skill taught and tested within level   *Skill taught but not tested within level
‡Development of skill tested at later level

AMIGOS UPS & DOWNS	COLORS BEING ME
LEVELS 7-8	**LEVELS 9-10**
	•Recognizing contraction with *n't*
•✔	✔
•✔	✔
•Developing sequence	✔
•Understanding characters	✔
*Relating a story to personal experience	✔
‡	•Distinguishing between fact and fantasy
‡	•Drawing conclusions
‡	•Predicting outcomes
‡	•Understanding cause and effect

	BELIEVE IT! FEELINGS
	LEVELS 11-12
WORD RECOGNITION (Cont.) **WORD FORMATION** (Continued)	
CONTRACTIONS	✔
PREFIXES	•Recognizing the prefix *un-*
SUFFIXES	
COMPREHENSION	✔
	✔
	•✔
	•✔
	✔
	✔
	✔
	•✔
	✔

Primary Grades   ✔Review and maintenance or further development

STAND TALL A SECOND LOOK	SECRET SPACES GOOD NEWS
LEVELS 13-14	**LEVELS 15-16**
•Recognizing changing *y* to *i* before adding *-ed* or *-es*	✔
•Recognizing changing *y* to *i* before adding the comparative endings *-er* or *-est*	✔
•Recognizing doubling the final consonant before adding the comparative endings *-er* and *-est*	✔
✔	✔
•Recognizing contractions with *'ll, 'm, 're,* and *'ve*	✔
'd, 's	✔
✔	✔
•Recognizing the prefix *re-*	✔
	•Recognizing the prefixes *in-, dis-*
	be-
•Recognizing the suffixes *-ful* and *-less*	✔
-ish, -ly, -ment, -ness, -ship, -ward	•Recognizing the suffixes *-ous, -ion*
	-able, -hood, -y
✔	✔
✔	✔
✔	✔
✔	✔
✔	✔
✔	✔
✔	•✔
✔	✔
✔	✔

•✔Review and maintenance with further testing

	BEGINNINGS ENDINGS
	LEVELS 17-18
WORD RECOGNITION (Cont.)	✔
WORD FORMATION (Continued)	✔
	✔
CONTRACTIONS	✔
	✔
	✔
PREFIXES	✔
	✔
	✔
	*Recognizing the prefixes *im-, micro-, mis-, non-, pre-, semi-, sub-, super-, tele-, tri-, uni-,*
SUFFIXES	
	✔
	*Recognizing the suffixes *ist, -teen*
COMPREHENSION	✔
	✔
	✔
	✔
	✔
	✔
	✔
	✔
	✔

Primary Grades

	WHO CAN? LOST & FOUND HATS & BEARS
	LEVELS 4-6
COMPREHENSION (Cont.)	‡
	‡
	‡
STUDY SKILLS	•Contents page
	•Left-to-right progression
	•Speech balloons to indicate speakers
	*Alphabetizing
	*Classifying
	*Studying illustrations
	‡

Primary Grades •Skill taught and tested within level   *Skill taught but not tested within level

‡Development of skill tested at later level

	BELIEVE IT! FEELINGS
	LEVELS 11-12
COMPREHENSION (Cont.)	*Recognizing the author's purpose
	‡
	‡
	‡
	‡
	‡
	‡
STUDY SKILLS	✔
	✔
	•Alphabetizing to the second letter
	✔
	✔
	✔
	✔
	•Adjusting reading rate
	•Following written directions
	•Using public signs

Primary Grades   ✔Review and maintenance or further development

AMIGOS UPS & DOWNS	COLORS BEING ME
LEVELS 7-8	**LEVELS 9-10**
‡	‡
	‡
‡	‡
‡	‡
•✔ (author identification)	✔
✔	✔
✔	
✔	
✔	✔
✔	✔
•Summarizing information	✔
	•Classifying units of measure
‡	•Following oral directions
	‡
‡	‡

STAND TALL A SECOND LOOK	SECRET SPACES GOOD NEWS
LEVELS 13-14	**LEVELS 15-16**
	✔
•Comparing and contrasting feelings and story themes	✔
•Evaluating the reality of a story (Distinguishing between fiction & nonfiction)	✔
•Following reasons to a conclusion	✔
•Listing major events leading to a main idea	✔
•Understanding cause and effect of character's feelings	✔
	•Organizing to show sequence
‡	•Reading to locate specific information
‡	•Understanding literary forms
‡	‡
‡	‡
‡	‡
✔	✔
✔	✔
•Alphabetizing to the third letter	*Alphabetizing to the fourth letter
✔	✔
✔	✔
✔	
✔	✔
✔	✔
✔	✔

•✔ Review and maintenance with further testing

	BEGINNINGS ENDINGS
	LEVELS 17-18
COMPREHENSION (Cont.)	✔
	✔
	✔
	✔
	✔
	✔
	✔
	✔
	✔
	•Interpreting figurative language
	•Recognizing the author's plan
	•Using context to determine meaning of words
STUDY SKILLS	✔
	✔
	✔
	✔
	•✔
	✔
	✔
	•✔

Primary Grades	Primary Grades

	WHO CAN? LOST & FOUND HATS & BEARS
	LEVELS 4-6
STUDY SKILLS (Cont.)	*Making a class dictionary
LANGUAGE SKILLS	*Enjoying literature (fairy tales, poetry, stories)
	*Reading with expression
	*Understanding marks of punctuation (! ? " ")
	*Understanding rhymes
	*Using words in sentences
	*Writing (dialogue, poetry, rhymes, sentences, stories)

Primary Grades   •Skill taught and tested within level   *Skill taught but not tested within level

‡Development of skill tested at later level

AMIGOS UPS & DOWNS	COLORS BEING ME
LEVELS 7-8	**LEVELS 9-10**
*General use of the dictionary	✔
‡	‡
	‡
(Books, poetry, stories)	✔
✔	✔
(' - ! ? " ") ✔	(' : ( ) ?) ✔
✔	✔
✔	✔
(titles) ✔	(captions) ✔
*Understanding pronouns	
	*Using adjectives
*Understanding word opposites (antonyms)	✔

	BELIEVE IT! FEELINGS
	LEVELS 11-12
STUDY SKILLS (Cont.)	
	*Understanding library procedure
	‡
	‡
LANGUAGE SKILLS	✔
	✔
	✔
	✔
	✔
(ads, diaries, letters)	✔
	✔
	✔
	✔

Primary Grades

✔Review and maintenance or further development

‡Development of skill tested at later level

STAND TALL A SECOND LOOK	SECRET SPACES GOOD NEWS
LEVELS 13-14	**LEVELS 15-16**
•Finding definitions of words in a children's dictionary •Finding words in a dictionary alphabetized to the third letter	✔
•Categorizing personal interests for book selection •Using library for self-selection of books and materials	✔
	•Interpreting simple diagrams
	•Reading globes
‡	•Reading simple maps
	•Using the glossary
‡	‡
✔	✔
✔	✔
✔	✔
✔	✔
✔	✔
(reports) ✔	(descriptions) ✔
✔	✔
✔	✔
✔	✔

	BEGINNINGS ENDINGS
	LEVELS 17-18
STUDY SKILLS Cont.)	✔
	✔
	✔
	✔
	✔
	✔
	•Interpreting simple line and picture graphs
	•Making simple outlines
	•Using abbreviations
	•Using capital letters as initials
	•Using scanning as a technique for finding information
LANGUAGE SKILLS	✔
	✔
	✔
	✔
	✔
(paragraphs, plays)	✔
	✔
	✔
	✔

Primary Grades

	WHO CAN? LOST & FOUND HATS & BEARS
	LEVELS 4-6
LANGUAGE SKILLS (Continued)	
ORAL LANGUAGE SKILLS	*Giving personal opinions
MAKING ORAL **RESPONSES**	*Responding to specific questions
	*Retelling stories
PARTICIPATING IN **GROUP DISCUSSION**	✔
USING ORAL LANGUAGE **CREATIVELY**	*Dramatizing and role-playing
	*Playing word games
	*Using one's imagination

Primary Grades   •Skill taught and tested within level   *Skill taught but not tested within level

‡Development of skill tested at later level

AMIGOS UPS & DOWNS	COLORS BEING ME
LEVELS 7-8	**LEVELS 9-10**
✔	✔
✔	✔
✔	✔
*Defending an opinion or answer	✔
*Verbalizing generalizations	
‡	‡
✔	✔
✔	✔
✔	✔
*Using descriptive words	✔
	*Expressing feelings
✔	✔

	BELIEVE IT! FEELINGS
	LEVELS 11-12
LANGUAGE SKILLS (Continued)	*Understanding synonyms
	*Understanding homographs
ORAL LANGUAGE SKILLS	✔
MAKING ORAL RESPONSES	✔
	✔
	*Defining words and phrases
	✔
	‡
PARTICIPATING IN GROUP DISCUSSION	✔
USING ORAL LANGUAGE CREATIVELY	✔
	✔
	✔
	✔
	✔

Primary Grades   ✔Review and maintenance or further development

STAND TALL A SECOND LOOK	SECRET SPACES GOOD NEWS
LEVELS 13-14	LEVELS 15-16
✔	✔
	✔
*Understanding homophones	✔
	*Understanding personification
✔	✔
✔	✔
	✔
✔	✔
✔	✔
✔	✔
•Relating self-identity issue to personal experience	✔
✔	✔
✔	✔
✔	✔
✔	✔
✔	✔
✔	✔

	BEGINNINGS ENDINGS
	LEVELS 17-18
LANGUAGE SKILLS (Continued)	✔
	✔
	✔
	✔
	*Understanding similes
ORAL LANGUAGE SKILLS	✔
MAKING ORAL RESPONSES	✔
	✔
	✔
	✔
	✔
	✔
PARTICIPATING IN GROUP DISCUSSION	✔
USING ORAL LANGUAGE CREATIVELY	✔
	✔
	✔
	✔
	✔

Primary Grades

	WHO CAN? LOST & FOUND HATS & BEARS	AMIGOS UPS & DOWNS	COLORS BEING ME
	LEVELS 4-6	LEVELS 7-8	LEVELS 9-10
LISTENING	*Listening for comprehension	✔	✔
	*Hearing rhymes		
	*Noting details	✔	✔
	*Listening to recordings	✔	✔
ATTITUDES	*Developing awareness of careers	✔	✔
CREATIVE ACTIVITIES			
CONSTRUCTING	*Bulletin board displays	✔	✔
	*Collages	✔	✔
	*Puppets		✔
DRAWING	*Maps		
	*Pictures	✔	✔
	*Picture Stories	✔	
ILLUSTRATING	*Poems	✔	✔
	*Stories	✔	✔
PUTTING TOGETHER	*Booklets	✔	✔

Primary Grades   *Skill taught but not tested within level

✔Review and maintenance or further development

BELIEVE IT! FEELINGS	STAND TALL A SECOND LOOK	SECRET SPACES GOOD NEWS	BEGINNINGS ENDINGS
LEVELS 11-12	LEVELS 13-14	LEVELS 15-16	LEVELS 17-18
✔	✔	✔	✔
✔	✔	✔	✔
✔	✔	✔	✔
✔	✔	✔	✔
✔	✔	✔	✔
		✔	
✔	✔	✔	
✔	✔		✔
	*Costumes	✔	✔
	*Props	✔	✔
			✔
✔	✔	✔	✔
			✔
✔	✔	✔	✔
	*Reports	✔	✔
✔	✔	✔	✔
✔			
			*Preparing "television shows"

Scope and Sequence, Levels 19-36 Intermediate Grades

	GROWING PASTIMES MESSAGES	CYCLES IMPRESSIONS A VISIT WITH ROSALIND	MOMENTS BIRDS & BEASTS SIGNALS
	LEVELS 19-21	LEVELS 22-24	LEVELS 25-27
COMPREHENSION	•Identifying cause and effect	✓	✓
	•Noting author's word choice	✓	✓
	•Recognizing the author's purpose	✓	✓
	‡	•Distinguishing among fact, fiction & opinion	✓
	‡	•Using context to determine word meaning	✓
	‡	•Visualizing from a written description	✓
	‡	‡	•Drawing conclusions
	‡	‡	•Following sequence
	‡	‡	•Locating answers to specific questions
			‡
			‡
	‡	‡	

Intermediate   ‡Development of skill tested at later level   •Skill taught and tested within level

WONDERS OUTLETS MOONBALL	AWAKENING JOURNEYS DIALOGUES	INROADS EXPRESSIONS A HORSE CAME RUNNING
LEVELS 28-30	LEVELS 31-33	LEVELS 34-36
✔	✔	✔
*Understanding metaphors	*Recognizing mood through author's choice of words	✔
✔	✔	•✔
✔	✔	✔
•✔	✔	✔
•Noting sensory images	✔	✔
✔	✔	*Making inferences
✔	*Developing time sequences	*Making time lines
✔	✔	✔
•Comparing sources of information and detecting discrepancies		✔
•Following the organizational pattern of writing in the content area	•✔	
•Noting details	✔	✔
•Noting sensory images	*Understanding figurative language	*Understanding descriptive language

	GROWING PASTIMES MESSAGES	CYCLES IMPRESSIONS A VISIT WITH ROSALIND	MOMENTS BIRDS & BEASTS SIGNALS
	LEVELS 19-21	LEVELS 22-24	LEVELS 25-27
COMPREHENSION (Continued)	‡	‡	‡
	‡	‡	‡
	‡	‡	‡
	‡	*Categorizing	✔
	‡	‡	‡
	‡		‡
	*Setting the purposes for silent reading	✔	✔
		•Recognizing one's own personal bias and preconceptions	✔
ATTITUDES	*Developing career awareness	✔	✔
	*Recognizing similarities among cultures		
	*Responding to emotions of story and/or story characters	✔	✔
LANGUAGE SKILLS	‡	•Extending ideas and topics	✔
	‡	•Identifying homographs	✔

*Skill taught but not tested within level   ✔Review and maintenance   •✔Review with further testing

WONDERS OUTLETS MOONBALL	AWAKENING JOURNEYS DIALOGUES	INROADS EXPRESSIONS A HORSE CAME RUNNING
LEVELS 28-30	LEVELS 31-33	LEVELS 34-36
•Predicting outcomes	✔	*Making inferences
	•Identifying main ideas	✔
✔	•Making comparisons	✔
		•Applying personal standards
✔	✔	•Classifying
	‡	•Identifying motives
‡	‡	•Making generalizations
✔	✔	✔
		✔
✔	✔	✔
✔	✔	
✔	✔	✔
✔	✔	✔
✔	✔	

Intermediate

	GROWING PASTIMES MESSAGES	**CYCLES IMPRESSIONS A VISIT WITH ROSALIND**	**MOMENTS BIRDS & BEASTS SIGNALS**
	LEVELS 19-21	**LEVELS 22-24**	**LEVELS 25-27**
LANGUAGE SKILLS (Continued)	‡	•Identifying homophones	✔
		•Identifying picturesque language	✔
	‡	•Interpreting figurative language	✔
		•Recognizing alliteration	✔
	‡		•Identifying antonyms
			‡
	‡	‡	‡
	‡	‡	‡
	*Reading with expression	✔	✔
	*Recognizing the origin and evolution of words		✔
	*Using marks of punctuation (general, : ;)	(apostrophe, hyphen)	✔

Intermediate　　‡Development of skill tested at later level　•Skill taught and tested within level

WONDERS OUTLETS MOONBALL	AWAKENING JOURNEYS DIALOGUES	INROADS EXPRESSIONS A HORSE CAME RUNNING
LEVELS 28-30	**LEVELS 31-33**	**LEVELS 34-36**
✔	✔	✔
✔	✔	✔
✔	✔	✔
	✔	✔
✔	✔	✔
•Identifying word function: verbs, adjectives, nouns	✔	✔
•Distinguishing between definite & indefinite terms	✔	✔
‡	•Distinguishing between concrete & abstract terms	✔
‡	‡	•Identifying synonyms
‡	‡	•Recognizing multiple meanings
✔	✔	✔
✔	✔	✔
✔	✔	✔ (quotation marks)

	GROWING PASTIMES MESSAGES	CYCLES IMPRESSIONS A VISIT WITH ROSALIND	MOMENTS BIRDS & BEASTS SIGNALS
	LEVELS 19-21	LEVELS 22-24	LEVELS 25-27
LANGUAGE SKILLS (Continued)	*Using words in sentences	✔	✔
	*Writing (diaries, letters, poems, stories)	✔ (descriptions, plays, directions, letters, paragraphs, poems, related stories, reports, sentences)	✔ (descriptions, letters, paragraphs, poems, sentences, stories)
			*Recognizing personification
ORAL LANGUAGE SKILLS	*Defending an opinion or answer	✔	✔
MAKING ORAL RESPONSES	*Defining words	✔	✔
	*Giving personal opinions	✔	✔
	*Relating to personal experience	✔	✔
RESPONDING TO SPECIFIC QUESTIONS	*Giving answers	✔	✔
	*Responding to thought questions	✔	✔
	*Using words in sentences	✔	✔
	*Verbalizing generalizations	✔	✔
PARTICIPATING IN GROUP DISCUSSION	✔	✔	✔
USING ORAL LANGUAGE CREATIVELY	*Dramatizing	✔	✔
	*Making oral reports	✔	✔

*Skill taught but not tested within level   ✔Review and maintenance or further development

WONDERS OUTLETS MOONBALL	AWAKENING JOURNEYS DIALOGUES	INROADS EXPRESSIONS A HORSE CAME RUNNING
LEVELS 28-30	LEVELS 31-33	LEVELS 34-36
✓	✓	✓
✓	✓	✓
✓	✓	
✓	✓	✓
✓	✓	✓
✓	✓	✓
✓	✓	✓
✓	✓	✓
✓	✓	✓
✓	✓	✓
✓	✓	✓
✓	✓	✓
✓	✓	✓
✓	✓	✓

Intermediate

	GROWING PASTIMES MESSAGES	CYCLES IMPRESSIONS A VISIT WITH ROSALIND	MOMENTS BIRDS & BEASTS SIGNALS
	LEVELS 19-21	LEVELS 22-24	LEVELS 25-27
USING ORAL LANGUAGE CREATIVELY (Continued)	*Playing word games	✔	✔
	*Telling stories	✔	✔
	*Using descriptive language	✔	✔
		*Expressing feelings	✔
WORD RECOGNITION	•Identifying accented syllables: primary stress	✔	✔
	•Identifying and analyzing compound words	✔	✔
	•Recognizing basic sight words in the content area	•✔	•✔
	•Recognizing -le ending as a clue to syllabication		✔
		•Recognizing and using common prefixes	✔
		•Recognizing and using common suffixes	✔
	‡	‡	
			‡

Intermediate   ‡Development of skill tested at later level •Skill taught and tested within level

WONDERS OUTLETS MOONBALL	AWAKENING JOURNEYS DIALOGUES	INROADS EXPRESSIONS A HORSE CAME RUNNING
LEVELS 28-30	LEVELS 31-33	LEVELS 34-36
✔	✔	✔
✔	✔	✔
✔	✔	✔
✔	✔	✔
✔	✔	
✔	✔	✔
✔	•✔	✔
	*Identifying accented syllables: primary and secondary	
✔		✔
✔	✔	✔
•Recognizing possessives	✔	
	•Changing adjectives to adverbs	
	•Changing root words to nouns	

	GROWING PASTIMES MESSAGES	CYCLES IMPRESSIONS A VISIT WITH ROSALIND	MOMENTS BIRDS & BEASTS SIGNALS
	LEVELS 19-21	LEVELS 22-24	LEVELS 25-27
WORD RECOGNITION (Continued)			‡
			‡
REVIEW OF PRIMARY SKILLS	*Phoneme-grapheme correspondences for initial and final consonant clusters		
	*Phoneme-grapheme correspondences for long and short vowels and the schwa	✔	✔
	*Common spelling patterns	✔	
LITERARY SKILLS	•Identifying different types of fiction (fable, historical fiction, myth)	•✔	•✔
	Recognizing story elements: •Plot	✔	✔
	•Characterization	✔	✔
	•Setting	✔	✔
			*Recognizing theme
			•Recognizing climax

*Skill taught but not tested within level   ✔Review and maintenance   •✔Review with further testing

WONDERS OUTLETS MOONBALL	AWAKENING JOURNEYS DIALOGUES	INROADS EXPRESSIONS A HORSE CAME RUNNING
LEVELS 28-30	LEVELS 31-33	LEVELS 34-36
	‡	•Analyzing words through prefix meaning
‡	‡	•Analyzing words through suffix meaning
‡		•Changing root words to adjectives
	✔	
	*Reviewing phoneme-grapheme correspondence	✔
✔		
✔	✔	
	•✔	
•✔	✔	✔
	✔	•✔
	✔	
✔	✔	✔

Intermediate

	GROWING PASTIMES MESSAGES	CYCLES IMPRESSIONS A VISIT WITH ROSALIND	MOMENTS BIRDS & BEASTS SIGNALS
	LEVELS 19-21	LEVELS 22-24	LEVELS 25-27
LITERARY SKILLS (Continued)	‡	‡	•Recognizing mood through author's word choice
	‡		
	‡	‡	
	*Appreciating poetry	✔	✔
	*Distinguishing between fiction and nonfiction		✔
		*Distinguishing between fact and fiction	
			*Recognizing different types of poetry
STUDY SKILLS DICTIONARY SKILLS	•Finding appropriate meanings	✔	*General use
	•Using the main entry; using guide words and illustrations	✔	✔
			•Recognizing and using different types of dictionaries
READING STUDY AIDS			•Charts
			•Diagrams
	•Graphs		•✔

Intermediate   ‡Development of skill tested at later level   •Skill taught and tested within level

WONDERS OUTLETS MOONBALL	AWAKENING JOURNEYS DIALOGUES	INROADS EXPRESSIONS A HORSE CAME RUNNING
LEVELS 28-30	LEVELS 31-33	LEVELS 34-36
	✔	✔
	•Identifying style	✔
‡	‡	•Identifying different types of nonfiction
✔	✔	✔
	✔	✔
	✔	✔
✔		✔
✔	✔	✔
✔	✔	✔
✔	✔	✔
✔		✔
✔	✔	✔

	GROWING PASTIMES MESSAGES	CYCLES IMPRESSIONS A VISIT WITH ROSALIND	MOMENTS BIRDS & BEASTS SIGNALS
	LEVELS 19-21	LEVELS 22-24	LEVELS 25-27
READING STUDY AIDS (Continued)	•Maps	✔	•✔
	•Tables		✔
	•Developing time sequences		✔
	•Outlining		
	‡	•Keeping simple records	
	‡	•Summarizing	✔
ENCYCLOPEDIA		•Using the encyclopedia	✔
		•Using the pronunciation key	✔
LIBRARY	•General understanding and use		•Using the Dewey Decimal System
REFERENCE BOOKS			•Using the newspaper
			‡
			‡
		‡	‡
	*Adjusting reading rate to reading purpose	✔	✔

*Skill taught but not tested within level. ✔Maintenance and review •✔Review with further testing

WONDERS OUTLETS MOONBALL	AWAKENING JOURNEYS DIALOGUES	INROADS EXPRESSIONS A HORSE CAME RUNNING
LEVELS 28-30	LEVELS 31-33	LEVELS 34-36
✔	✔	✔
	✔	
•✔	✔	✔
✔	✔	•✔
✔	•✔	✔
✔	✔	✔
•Following cross references in the encyclopedia		
	✔	✔
✔	•✔	
✔	✔	✔
•Using an almanac		✔
‡	•Using an atlas	
‡	‡	•Taking notes
✔	✔	

Intermediate

	GROWING PASTIMES MESSAGES	CYCLES IMPRESSIONS A VISIT WITH ROSALIND	MOMENTS BIRDS & BEASTS SIGNALS
	LEVELS 19-21	LEVELS 22-24	LEVELS 25-27
REFERENCE BOOKS (Continued)	*Alphabetizing	✔	✔
	*Doing research	✔	✔
	*Studying and using illustrations	✔	✔
		*Categorizing	✔
LISTENING SKILLS	*Listening to recordings	✔	✔
	*Listening to speakers	✔	✔
CREATIVE ACTIVITIES CONSTRUCTING	*Bulletin board displays	✔	✔
	*Models	✔	✔
DRAMATIZING & RELATED AREAS	✔	✔	✔
DRAWING	*Pictures	✔	✔
	*Posters	✔	✔
ILLUSTRATING		✔	✔ (scenes from stories, word meanings)
MAKING THINGS	*Booklets	✔	✔

Intermediate   *Skill taught but not tested   ✔Review and maintenance or further development

WONDERS OUTLETS MOONBALL	AWAKENING JOURNEYS DIALOGUES	INROADS EXPRESSIONS A HORSE CAME RUNNING
LEVELS 28-30	LEVELS 31-33	LEVELS 34-36
✔	✔	✔
✔	✔	✔
✔	✔	✔
✔	✔	✔
✔	✔	✔
✔	✔	✔
✔		✔
		*Displays
✔	✔	✔
✔	✔	✔
✔		✔
✔ (poems, stories, words)	✔	✔ (poems, stories)
	✔	✔

Program Materials, Levels 1-36

Kindergarten/Readiness
Materials: Levels 1-3+

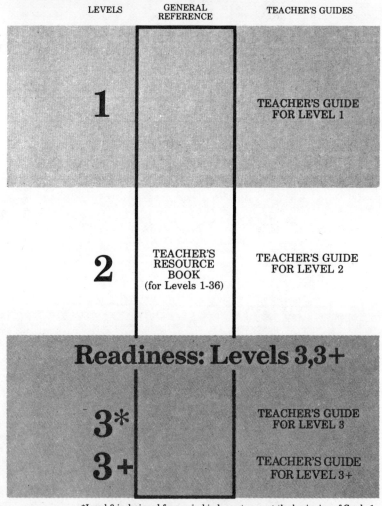

LEVELS	GENERAL REFERENCE	TEACHER'S GUIDES
1		TEACHER'S GUIDE FOR LEVEL 1
2	TEACHER'S RESOURCE BOOK (for Levels 1-36)	TEACHER'S GUIDE FOR LEVEL 2

Readiness: Levels 3,3+

3*		TEACHER'S GUIDE FOR LEVEL 3
3+		TEACHER'S GUIDE FOR LEVEL 3+

*Level 3 is designed for use in kindergarten or at the beginning of Grade 1.
**All cards—except alphabet—are printed on both sides.

INTRODUCTION OF CONCEPTS		MANIPULATIVES**
READ AND TELL 1		**1 SET UPPER- AND LOWER-CASE ALPHABET ON CLEAR PLASTIC** **1 SET UPPER- AND LOWER-CASE ALPHABET CARDS, WITH FLOCKED LETTERS**
READ AND TELL 2	2 INSERTABLE POCKET CARDS (LAMINATED FOR WRITING AND ERASING ON ONE SIDE) (for Levels 1-3)	**42 PICTURE CARDS (INCLUDING TV SEQUENCE CARDS)** **63 PICTURE AND WORD CARDS** **20 WORD CARDS**
READ AND TELL 3		**20 PICTURE CARDS** **30 WORD CARDS** **11 SENTENCE CARDS**

PUPIL BOOKS	PRACTICE	ACTIVITIES	PARENT INVOLVE-MENT
READ-IT-YOURSELF 1 BOOK A	*DO-IT-YOURSELF 1*		
READ-IT-YOURSELF 1 BOOK B	*SOMEMORE 1*		
		24 PICK 'n PLAYS (AND STAND)	PARENT LETTERS ON SPIRIT DUPLICATING MASTERS
READ-IT-YOURSELF 2 BOOK A	*DO-IT-YOURSELF 2*		
READ-IT-YOURSELF 2 BOOK B	*SOMEMORE 2*		
READ-IT-YOURSELF 3 BOOK A	*DO-IT-YOURSELF 3*	25 ACTIVITY SHEET SPIRIT DUPLICATING MASTERS	
READ-IT-YOURSELF 3 BOOK B	*SOMEMORE 3*		
	DO-IT-YOURSELF 3+		

LEARNING TO USE BOOKS	REINFORCE- MENT	ASSESSMENT	SKILLS MANAGE- MENT	
SOLO BOOKS 2 SOFTBOUND BOOKS—WITH PICTURES AND/OR WORDS*	*EXTRA!* 1	LEVEL 1 PRE- ASSESSMENT LEVEL 1 POST- ASSESSMENT		
SOLO BOOKS 2 SOFTBOUND BOOKS—WITH PICTURES AND/OR WORDS*	*EXTRA!* 2	LEVEL 2 PRE- ASSESSMENT LEVEL 2 POST- ASSESSMENT PERIODIC ACHIEVEMENT TEST, LEVELS 1-2	McBEE CARDS OR CLASS PLAN SHEET (for Levels 1-3)	
SOLO BOOKS 2 SOFTBOUND BOOKS—WITH PICTURES AND/OR WORDS*	*EXTRA!* 3	LEVEL 3 PRE- ASSESSMENT** LEVEL 3 POST- ASSESSMENT		

*For list of titles, see page 38.
**(Reading Readiness Test)

Primary Grade
Materials: Levels 3+-18

LEVELS	GENERAL REFERENCE	LESSON PLANS

Gr.1		
3*,3+ 4 5 6		TEACHER'S EDITION *WHO CAN? LOST AND FOUND* AND *HATS AND BEARS*
7 8	TEACHER'S RESOURCE BOOK (for Levels 1-36)	TEACHER'S EDITION *AMIGOS* AND *UPS AND DOWNS*
9 10		TEACHER'S EDITION *COLORS* AND *BEING ME*
Gr.2 11 12		TEACHER'S EDITION *BELIEVE IT!* AND *FEELINGS*
13 14		TEACHER'S EDITION *STAND TALL* AND *A SECOND LOOK*
Gr.3 15 16		TEACHER'S EDITION *SECRET SPACES* AND *GOOD NEWS*
17 18		TEACHER'S EDITION *BEGINNINGS* AND *ENDINGS*

*Inclusion of Levels 3,3+ in Grade 1 is optional. See preceding pages for a description of the materials.
**Available in softbound editions for each level or in hardbound editions combining two levels, at Levels 7-18.
***Teacher's Edition of each workbook is provided.

BASIC READERS**	SKILLS PRE-ASSESSMENT AND PRACTICE***
WHO CAN? *LOST AND FOUND* *HATS AND BEARS*	WORKBOOK FOR *WHO CAN?* *LOST AND FOUND* AND *HATS AND BEARS*
AMIGOS *UPS AND DOWNS*	WORKBOOK FOR *AMIGOS* WORKBOOK FOR *UPS AND DOWNS*
COLORS *BEING ME*	WORKBOOK FOR *COLORS* WORKBOOK FOR *BEING ME*
BELIEVE IT! *FEELINGS*	WORKBOOK FOR *BELIEVE IT!* WORKBOOK FOR *FEELINGS*
STAND TALL *A SECOND LOOK*	WORKBOOK FOR *STAND TALL* WORKBOOK FOR *A SECOND LOOK*
SECRET SPACES *GOOD NEWS*	WORKBOOK FOR *SECRET SPACES* WORKBOOK FOR *GOOD NEWS*
BEGINNINGS *ENDINGS*	WORKBOOK FOR *BEGINNINGS* WORKBOOK FOR *ENDINGS*

INDEPENDENT READING*	VOCABULARY AND SKILLS REINFORCEMENT	
2 SOFTBOUND BOOKS (SOLOS) AT EACH LEVEL, LEVELS 4-10	EXTRA! 4 EXTRA! 5 EXTRA! 6 EXTRA! 7 EXTRA! 8 EXTRA! 9 EXTRA! 10	**SKILLS RESERVOIR BOX A**
4 SOFTBOUND BOOKS (SOLOS) AT EACH LEVEL, LEVELS 11-18	EXTRA! 11 EXTRA! 12 EXTRA! 13 EXTRA! 14	**SKILLS RESERVOIR BOX B**
	EXTRA! 15 EXTRA! 16 EXTRA! 17 EXTRA!.18	**SKILLS RESERVOIR BOX C**

*For a list of titles, see page 38.
**One two-record album or four cassettes for each grade.

ENRICHMENT**	POST-ASSESSMENT	SKILLS MANAGEMENT
READINGS, DRAMATIZATIONS, AND SONGS LEVELS 4-10	LEVEL 4 POST-ASSESSMENT LEVEL 5 POST-ASSESSMENT LEVEL 6 POST-ASSESSMENT LEVEL 7 POST-ASSESSMENT LEVEL 8 POST-ASSESSMENT LEVEL 9 POST-ASSESSMENT LEVEL 10 POST-ASSESSMENT PERIODIC ACHIEVEMENT TEST	CROSS-REFERENCE CHARTS FOR SKILLS AT EACH LEVEL
READINGS, DRAMATIZATIONS, AND SONGS LEVELS 11-14	LEVEL 11 POST-ASSESSMENT LEVEL 12 POST-ASSESSMENT LEVEL 13 POST-ASSESSMENT LEVEL 14 POST-ASSESSMENT PERIODIC ACHIEVEMENT TEST	McBEE CARDS OR CLASS PLAN SHEET
READINGS, DRAMATIZATIONS, AND SONGS LEVELS 15-18	LEVEL 15 POST-ASSESSMENT LEVEL 16 POST-ASSESSMENT LEVEL 17 POST-ASSESSMENT LEVEL 18 POST-ASSESSMENT PERIODIC ACHIEVEMENT TEST	

Intermediate Grade Materials: Levels 19-36

LEVELS	GENERAL REFERENCE	LESSON PLANS
Gr.4 19 20 21 22 23 24		TEACHER'S EDITION *GROWING, PASTIMES* AND *MESSAGES* TEACHER'S EDITION *CYCLES, IMPRESSIONS* AND *A VISIT WITH ROSALIND*
Gr.5 25 26 27 28 29 30	TEACHER'S RESOURCE BOOK (for Levels 1-36)	TEACHER'S EDITION *MOMENTS BIRDS AND BEASTS* AND *SIGNALS* TEACHER'S EDITION *WONDERS, OUTLETS* AND *THE MOONBALL*
Gr.6 31 32 33 34 35 36		TEACHER'S EDITION *AWAKENING, JOURNEYS* AND *DIALOGUES* TEACHER'S EDITION *INROADS, EXPRESSIONS* AND *A HORSE CAME RUNNING*

*Softbound Edition. Also available as hardbound, Three-In-One Editions.
**Teacher's Edition of each workbook is provided.

BASIC READERS*	SKILLS PRE-ASSESSMENT AND PRACTICE**
GROWING *PASTIMES* *MESSAGES* *CYCLES* *IMPRESSIONS* *A VISIT WITH ROSALIND*	WORKBOOK FOR *GROWING,* *PASTIMES* AND *MESSAGES* WORKBOOK FOR *CYCLES,* *IMPRESSIONS* AND *A VISIT WITH ROSALIND*
MOMENTS *BIRDS AND BEASTS* *SIGNALS* *WONDERS* *OUTLETS* *THE MOONBALL*	WORKBOOK FOR *MOMENTS,* *BIRDS AND BEASTS* AND *SIGNALS* WORKBOOK FOR *WONDERS,* *OUTLETS* AND *THE MOONBALL*
AWAKENING *JOURNEYS* *DIALOGUES* *INROADS* *EXPRESSIONS* *A HORSE CAME RUNNING*	WORKBOOK FOR *AWAKENING* *JOURNEYS* AND *DIALOGUES* WORKBOOK FOR *INROADS,* *EXPRESSIONS* AND *A HORSE CAME RUNNING*

INDEPENDENT READING*	VOCABULARY AND SKILLS REINFORCEMENT	
2 SOFTBOUND BOOKS (SOLOS) AT EACH LEVEL, LEVELS 19-24	EXTRA! 19 EXTRA! 20 EXTRA! 21 EXTRA! 22 EXTRA! 23 EXTRA! 24	SKILLS RESERVOIR BOX D
2 SOFTBOUND BOOKS (SOLOS) AT EACH LEVEL, LEVELS 25-30	EXTRA! 25 EXTRA! 26 EXTRA! 27 EXTRA! 28 EXTRA! 29 EXTRA! 30	SKILLS RESERVOIR BOX E
2 SOFTBOUND BOOKS (SOLOS) AT EACH LEVEL, LEVELS 31-36	EXTRA! 31 EXTRA! 32 EXTRA! 33 EXTRA! 34 EXTRA! 35 EXTRA! 36	SKILLS RESERVOIR BOX F

*For a list of titles, see page 38.
**One two-record album or four cassettes for each grade.

ENRICHMENT**	POST-ASSESSMENT	SKILLS MANAGEMENT
READINGS, DRAMATIZATIONS, AND SONGS LEVELS 19-24	LEVEL 19 POST-ASSESSMENT LEVEL 20 POST-ASSESSMENT LEVEL 21 POST-ASSESSMENT LEVEL 22 POST-ASSESSMENT LEVEL 23 POST-ASSESSMENT LEVEL 24 POST-ASSESSMENT	CROSS-REFERENCE CHARTS FOR SKILLS AT EACH LEVEL
READINGS, DRAMATIZATIONS, AND SONGS LEVELS 25-30	LEVEL 25 POST-ASSESSMENT LEVEL 26 POST-ASSESSMENT LEVEL 27 POST-ASSESSMENT LEVEL 28 POST-ASSESSMENT LEVEL 29 POST-ASSESSMENT LEVEL 30 POST-ASSESSMENT PERIODIC ACHIEVEMENT TEST	McBEE CARDS OR CLASS PLAN SHEET
READINGS, DRAMATIZATIONS, AND SONGS LEVELS 31-36	LEVEL 31 POST-ASSESSMENT LEVEL 32 POST-ASSESSMENT LEVEL 33 POST-ASSESSMENT LEVEL 34 POST-ASSESSMENT LEVEL 35 POST-ASSESSMENT LEVEL 36 POST-ASSESSMENT PERIODIC ACHIEVEMENT TEST	

Solo Book Titles

Grade	Level	Title
Kindergarten	1	**The Box:** Bottner
	1	**The Can:** Gelman
	2	**EEK-A Monster:** Bottner
	2	**Shapes:** Engquist
Readiness	3,3+	**Fat and Thin:** Marzollo
	3,3+	**From Start to Finish:** Haven
Preprimer	4*	**Ride Ride Ride:** McClanahan
	4**	**Can We Eat Now?:** Marzollo
	5*	**Pony Bird:** Marzollo
	5**	**Small Circus:** Hopkins
	6*	**Come On In:** McClanahan
	6**	**The Sun Book:** Bass, Goldman
Primer	7*	**What Things Are Funny?:** Thurman
	7**	**The King in the Window:** Weiner
	8*	**In the Old Days:** Haven
	8**	**Fun City:** Gelman
Gr. 1²	9*	**Queen Minna:** Rabinowich
	9**	**A Poem Can Say It:** Moore, Ed.
	10*	**The Breakfast Buffalo:** McClanahan
	10**	**The Mission of PAIDES I:** Rokoff
Gr. 2¹	11*	**The Milk Box Mystery:** Weiner
	11**	**The House That Dreams Painted:** Marzollo
	11*	**What Grandma Did on Her Birthday:** Bottner
	11**	**Feeling Shy:** Widmer
	12*	**Who Is Francis?:** Steiger
	12**	**Growing Wild:** Bass, Goldman
	12*	**The Robber Child:** Rokoff
	12**	**No-Cook Book:** Goldman

*Controlled Vocabulary   **Extended Vocabulary*

Grade	Level	Title
Gr. 2²	13*	**If Wishes Were Fishes:** Gluckin
	13**	**The Goober and Gull Club:** Boegehold
	13*	**Pen Pal from Another Planet:** Brenner
	13**	**Poem Time Is Now:** Moore, Ed.
	14*	**Nobody Knows Me:** Myers
	14**	**Shaped by Hands: Indian Art of North America:** Katz
	14*	**Nadir of the Streets:** Alexander
	14**	**The Electrical Helper:** Morey, Hood
Gr. 3¹	15*	**Ride a Painted Horse:** Benjamin
	15**	**The Bunny Who Wanted to Be a Tap Dancer:** ito
	15*	**The Magic Pot:** McGovern
	15**	**You Look, Too:** Moore, Ed.
	16*	**Sea Otters Come Home:** Franchere
	16**	**Tracks:** Brenner
	16*	**The Trouble with Bubbles:** Tobin
	16**	**Underground Tales:** Mehdevi
Gr. 3²	17*	**Spinning in Space:** Levy
	17**	**Josita's Dancing Cleaners:** Walborn
	17*	**Uncle Max's Secret:** Whitney
	17**	**Boxes, String, Shells & Things:** Katz
	18*	**Margaret Mead: A Life in Science:** Hoobler
	18**	**The Flowers of Mallorca:** Mehdevi
	18*	**Judge Pao and the Mystery of the Dream:** Andrews
	18**	**Frontier Diary:** Hoobler
Gr. 4	19	**How to Earn Money If You're Under 12:** Gelman
	19	**Mr. Harry Know-It-All:** Froman
	20	**John's Secret Treasure:** Steele
	20	**How Otto Ringling Became King of the Circus:** Kinney
	21	**The Camera:** Moore
	21	**Grant Wood: Farm Boy with an Artist's Eye:** Kinney

Grade	Level	Title
	22	**The Invention That Wouldn't Fly:** Cavanna
	22	**A Museum of Time:** Anastasio
	23	**The Land of the E*erf:** Tobin
	23	**Poets Notice Everything:** Moore, Ed.
	24	**The Ghost Boy:** Mann, Houlton
	24	**The Case of the Missing Hoopaland:** Levy
Gr. 5	25	**Growing Up in Kenya:** Reimann
	25	**Tell About Someone You Love:** Heide
	26	**Henry Aaron and Babe Ruth: Home-Run Champions:** Devaney
	26	**Last Road to Safety: A True Story:** Mann
	27	**My Dog Zeke:** Sonnett
	27	**Lost:** Gray
	28	**Living with Wolves:** Jones
	28	**No Roads for the Wind:** Heide
	29	**Comits: A Book of Comic Skits:** Gelman
	29	**Poets Go Wishing:** Moore, Ed.
	30	**Mud Fight Diamond:** Mitchell
	30	**The Secret of the Gourmandy:** Martel
Gr. 6	31	**The Me I Am:** Gelman
	31	**Handwriting: A Secret Way to "Look Inside":** Mann
	32	**Coming of Age: The Hopi Way:** Monjo
	32	**Jinjero, The Scar-Faced Baboon:** Jolly
	33	**And, Now, a Word from Our Sponsor:** Kinney
	33	**The Dreaming Mind:** Kettlekamp
	34	**The Stuff of You:** Froman
	34	**The Bermuda Triangle: Fact or Fiction?:** Vecsey
	35	**Louis, Elvis, and Ludwig:** Noble
	35	**Each in a Different Voice:** Moore, Ed.
	36	**Don't Bite Your Grandmother's Ear:** Cavanna
	36	**Captain Logic and the Jewel Thief:** Orkin

Glossary

Academic (Scholastic) Aptitude. The combination of native and acquired abilities needed for schoolwork or the likelihood of success in academic work as estimated from a measure of the necessary abilities.

Accent. To give stress or prominence to a syllable or word.

Accountability. The responsibility of educators to do their job, which is to help learners achieve specified and measurable results of the educational endeavor.

Achievement Test. A test that measures the extent to which a person has acquired information or mastered certain skills.

Affix. A sound attached to the beginning or end of a word, such as a prefix or suffix; in some languages, inserted within a word.

Age Norms. Values representing average or typical performance for persons of various age groups.

Ambidexterity. Proficient use of both hands.

Anomaly. Deviation from the common rule or type or form; an abnormality.

Antonym. A word having the opposite meaning of another word, as *hot–cold.*

Aphasia. Sensory or motor disability of language functions caused by brain injury, an alexia or agraphia.

Articulation. The formation of speech sounds; the sequential development of curricular offerings.

Aspirate. A breathed sound such as the *h* in *hot.*

Audiometer. A device for testing hearing.

Auditory Discrimination. Ability to discriminate between sounds of different characteristic frequencies.

Auditory Perception. The mental awareness of sounds.

Basal Reading. The type of reading usually done during a directed reading period with a basic reader book, one of a series.

Battery. A group of several tests standardized on the same population so that results on the several tests are comparable (when the term is used correctly).

Bibliotherapy. Selected books used for their therapeutic effect on children who are mentally or emotionally disturbed.

Bilingualism. The speaking of two languages.

Blend. The fusion of two or more sounds in a word without loss of identity of each sound.

Breve. The short arc placed over a vowel to indicate a short sound, as *mĕt.*

Cadence. Rhythmic flow of language; rhythm.

Caldecott Award. Yearly medal awarded by the ALA to the artist who excelled in illustration of children's books in the preceding year.

Capacity Reading Level. Comprehension level of 75% or better on material read aloud by the examiner.

Case Study. An intensive diagnostic analysis of an individual's reading abilities to determine the nature of the difficulties and causes and possible solutions.

Ceiling. The upper limit of ability measured by a test.

Choral Reading. A group reading in unison.

Chunking. The process of combining units in thought, resulting in fewer units to be remembered.

Cloze Procedure. Technique used to evaluate pupil performance and determine readability level, involving the deletion of every fifth (or *n*th) word from running text; the learner is expected to complete the thought.

Cognition. The process of perceiving or knowing.

Configuration. The general form or shape of a word.

Congenital. Present in the individual at birth, but not necessarily hereditary.

Context Clue. Identification of a new word by anticipation of the meaning owing to the words and ideas adjacent to the word.

Control. Any procedure in an experimental design that eliminates the effect of a factor or that insures that it remains constant in its effect on the responses measured.

Correlation, Coefficient of (r). The degree of relationship between two variables, varying between -1.00 for a perfect negative correlation (highest on one test, lowest on other) through 0.00 (no relationship) to $+1.00$ (highest on one test, highest on the other).

Criterion. A standard by which a test may be judged; a set of scores, ratings, and so on.

Cybernetics. The comparative study of the human and electromechanical control systems or the reciprocal interactions between the individual and the instruments in his or her environment.

Decibel. Minimum perceptible change in intensity of sound.

Decoding. Understanding the relationship between the writing system and the more familiar sound system; phonic analysis.

Deductive. Making specific application from the general principle.

Derived Sentence. Any sentence generated by following transformational principles applied to the basic sentence.

Dextral. Right-handed or pertaining to the right side.

Diacritical Marks. Small signs that designate a particular sound of a letter or letters, as ă, ā, ä.

Diagnostic Test. A test used to locate specific areas of weakness or strength or to determine the nature of weakness, yielding subparts of some larger body of knowledge or skills.

Dialect. The sectional or local modifications of language, including the distinguishing features of pronunciation, grammar, and vocabulary.

Digraph. Two successive letters representing one phoneme, as *ch* in *child* or *ai* in *rain.*

Diphthong. A glide from one vowel sound to another in the same syllable, as *ow* in *cow* or *ui* in *suite.*

Directed Reading. A reading lesson with basal reading material, including orientation, silent reading, vocabulary and comprehension development, oral reading, and follow-up.

Dyslexia. Inability to read or to understand what one reads silently or orally, a condition generally associated with brain dysfunction.

Echolalia. Repetition of words or phrases spoken by others without intent to convey meaning.

Encoding. Interpreting oral language in symbols or writing.

Enrichment. Curricular experiences that broaden an individual's understanding of instructional goals.

Enunciate. Pronounce with distinctness.

Etiology. Deals with the causes of a disorder.

Etymology. A branch of linguistics that deals with the origin and derivation of words.

Euphony. Agreeableness of sound; easily pronounced speech sound.

Experience Approach. The development of beginning reading through direct language-type and reading-like experience.

Extrapolation. The process of estimating values of a function or curve beyond the range of available data.

Extrinsic. Outward or external; a reward such as a gold star.

Eyedness. The preference or dominance of one eye in perceptual-motor tasks.

Eye-Voice Span. The distance between the point where the eyes are seeing and the voice is reporting in oral reading.

Factor. A condition that is presumed to influence the results on two or more tests and thus cause the scores to be related.

Family (Word). A group of rhyming words containing identical word elements, as *mat, sat, hat, bat.*

Flash Cards. Small cards on which letters or words or phrases are printed and that are exposed briefly for rapid recognition.

Formal English. The form of language that is used in literature, official documents, and all formal speech and writing, as contrasted to the vernacular or colloquial forms.

Format. The general appearance and physical makeup of a book.

Framing Words. Designating a group of words by placing the hands at each end.

Free Reading. Independent reading for information or pleasure.

Frontispiece. The illustrative page preceding the title page of a book.

Frustration Reading Level. On an IRI, the student scores no less than 75% in word recognition and 50% in comprehension (approximately); interpretation: the student has great difficulty in reading; needs help.

Generative Grammar. A language model that shows by a sequence of applied rules how language operates to form all the grammatical sentences.

Generic. Broadly applicable to members of a genus or class.

Glides. A rapid movement of the articulatory organs of speech to or from the position they take for the articulation of a vowel; that is, *y* in *yoga, w* in *wad,* or the vowel-consonant glides /ou/ and /oi/. Unglided vowels: *i* in *sit.*

Grade Equivalent. The grade level for which a given score is the real or estimated average.

Grammar. The science or the study of the system and structure of language.

Grapheme. A minimum unit of the writing system, not able to be subdivided, as the letter *d* or the letter *g* in *dog;* sometimes combinations of letters, as in digraphs, *sh* in *ship.*

Group Test. A test that may be administered to a number of individuals at the same time by one examiner.

Guide Words. Words printed in boldface at the top of a page in the dictionary for quick selection of the page on which a word may be found.

Hetergeneous. Distributed with wide variability; the opposite of *homogeneous.*

Homogeneous. Distributed with small or regular variability.

Homographs. Written forms of words similar in their orthography, but having different meanings, as *bow* (to bend) and *bow* (a tie).

Homonym. A word having the same pronunciation as another word, but differing in meaning and spelling, as *bear* and *bare.*

Hornbook. A paddle-shaped wood on which the alphabet appeared, covered with transparent horn; used in teaching reading in Colonial America.

Hyperopia. Farsightedness.

Idiom. A peculiar syntactical pattern that, understood as a whole, has a different meaning from that of its component parts, often incapable of literal translation in another language, as "Hop to it!" and "Get busy!"

Imagery. The imagining of events or mental pictures.

Independent Reading Level. On an IRI, the student scores no less than 99% in word recognition and 90% in comprehension (approximately); interpretation- the highest level the individual can read on his own.

Individual Test. A test that can be administered to only one person at a time.

Inflection. Rise and fall of the pitch of the voice in speech.

Informal Reading Inventory. IRI- a test in which the individual reads a graded series of selections, easy to difficult, until reaching frustration level; the teacher records all errors in pronunciation, vocabulary, and comprehension; from the results the teacher determines independent, instructional, and frustration levels.

Instructional Reading Level. On an IRI, student scores no less than 95% in word recognition and 75% in comprehension (approximately); interpretation-the student will need the help of the teacher to make progress in reading development.

Intelligence Quotient (IQ). A measure of brightness that takes into account the score on an intelligence test and age.

$$IQ = \frac{MA}{CA} \times 100$$

Intonational Pattern. A unit of a language's speech melody characterized by juncture, pitch, and stress occurring in the total utterance meaning.

i.t.a. Initial Teaching Alphabet, the augmented Roman alphabet of forty-four symbols used in a beginning reading program.

Juncture. A pause in the flow of oral language that indicates meaning.

Kinesthetic. Connecting sensations with body movements.

Language. An established system of communication by means of written or spoken symbols.

Learning. Changes in performance (behavior) resulting from experience.

Learning, Rote. Memorization through repetition with little or no attention to meaning.

Lexicographer. An author or compiler of a dictionary.

Linguistics. The scientific study of human language or of human speech and its recorded forms.

Macron. A short horizontal mark over a vowel to indicate its long sound, as *āte.*

Mainstreaming. Placing handicapped children in the regular classroom for all or a portion of their instruction.

Manuscript. A handwritten document or a writing program typically primary and characterized by printed symbols.

Matched Groups. Two equated groups (usually on sex, age, intelligence, and so on); a control and an experimental group.

Maturity. The quality of being fully developed in form and function with regard to a trait or a number of traits.

Mean. Arithmetic mean—the sum of a set of scores divided by their number.

Media, Instructional. Classroom materials used to enhance teaching—texts, reference books, kits, films, slides, globes, maps, microfilm, transparencies, and so on.

Median. The point on a scale of measurement arranged in order of size that divides the distribution into two equal groups.

Mental Age. The age for which a given score on an intelligence test is average or normal.

Miscue. Unexpected response to written language resulting from the reader's grammatical system interacting to his experience with the environment and the printed page.

Mode. The value of a distribution of scores that occurs the greatest number of times.

Morphology. The study of word formation, including derivation, inflection, and the adding of prefixes and suffixes.

Myopia. Nearsightedness.

Newberry Award. Annual medal awarded to the author of the most distinguished contribution to American literature for children published during the preceding year.

Nonreader. An individual who cannot read, even after considerable instruction.

Normal Curve. The symmetrical, bell-shaped curve of a normal distribution.

Oculomotor. Moving the eyeballs.

Onomatopoeic Words. Words formed by imitating a natural sound, as *buzz* and *hiss.*

Ophthalmograph. A device for photographing eye movements during reading.

Overt. Outward; easily observed.

Pacing. Controlling the rate of reading; also, providing each child with materials at a tempo that insures success at current stage of maturity.

Percentile. A point on a scale of scores in a distribution below which the given per cent of scores occur; 20 per cent of the scores are below the twentieth percentile.

Perception. Recognition or awareness of sensation through any sense organ.

Perseveration. Abnormal persistence of an activity after the stimulus or need is removed.

Phoneme. A minimum distinctive sound unit in speech or a group of variants of one speech sound, as the spoken words *fat* and *sat* are distinguished by the initial consonant phonemes /f/ and /s/.

Phonemics. The study of language structure in terms of its phonemes or units of sound.

Phonetics. The study and classification of sounds used in human communication.

Phonics. The study of sound-letter relationships in reading and spelling.

Phonogram. A printed letter or group of letters forming a speech sound.

Pocket Chart. A container or holder for flash cards.

Population. Any group of individuals who are alike in at least one specific way, as all the fifth graders in the school system.

Power Test. A test with no time limit that measures level of performance rather than speed of response.

Prefix. An affix in front of the root word that changes or modifies its meaning, as /un/ in *unlike.*

Profile. A diagram that shows the relative position of an individual or a group in several traits or test scores to show variation from trait to trait.

Program. The subject matter that is to be learned by the student via machine or other device.

Random Sample. A portion of the members of the population with an equal chance of every member of the population being included, in order to preclude bias in selection.

Range. The distance between the highest and the lowest measures of a distribution.

Rapport. Mutually harmonious working relationships.

Raw Score. The original score obtained from a test or other measurement.

Readability. The objective measure of the difficulty of a book or article.

Readiness Test. A test that measures the extent to which an individual has achieved a degree of maturity or acquired certain skills or information needed in order to undertake successfully some new learning activity.

Realia. Real things as opposed to abstractions; objects or materials that typically represent a period of time in history or a geographical region.

Regressive. Backward.

Reinforcement. The strengthening of a response through reward or satisfaction.

Retention. Learning that permits later recall or recognition.

Rhetoric. The study of the art of speaking and writing effectively the principles of communication.

Root. An original word form from which words have been developed by the addition of affixes.

Sample. A group drawn from a larger population.

Schwa. An indistinct unstressed vowel, as the e /ə/ in *problem.*

Semantics. The study of the meaning of words and phrases.

Sight-Saving Materials. Usually printed in 24- or 32-point type to be more easily seen.

Sight Word. A word that has been memorized or is recognized as a whole.

Sinistral. Innately left-handed.

Skewness. An unsymmetrical curve.

Skimming. A very rapid reading of a selection for a specific purpose, excluding unimportant details.

Standard Deviation. A measure of variability of scores around the mean; the more the scores cluster around the mean, the smaller the standard deviation.

Standard Score. Any of a variety of transformed scores in terms of which raw scores may be expressed for convenience, comparability, ease of interpretation, and so on.

Standardized Test. A systematic sample of performance obtained under prescribed conditions, scored according to definite rules, and capable of evaluation by reference to normative information. Evidence of validity and reliability should be provided.

Stanine. One of the steps in a nine-point scale of normalized standard scores with a mean of 5 and a standard deviation of 2.

Statistic. A value, such as the mean, that characterizes a specific series of scores.

Strabismus. Squint or cross-eyes.

Strephosymbolia. Twisted symbols, as the reversing of *was* and *saw.*

Suffix. An affix added to the end of a root word to change or modify the meaning, as /ful/ in *harmful.*

Supplementary Reading. Reading assigned to reinforce or maintain some learned ability in the basic reading lesson or other subject.

Survey Test. A group-status test that measures general achievement in a given subject or area.

Syllabication. Division of words into syllables, usually for pronunciation, as *de-light-ful.*

Syndrome. A constellation of symptoms of a given condition.

Synonym. A word that has the same, or nearly the same, meaning as another word, as *theory–hypothesis.*

Tachistoscope. A device that controls the exposure time and illumination while flashing figures, letters, words, or other material on a screen.

Tactile. Pertaining to the sense of touch.

Taxonomy. Scientific classification of an area specifying its component parts.

Theory. An hypothesis for which there is usually some verification, which remains to be proved or put to practical use.

Transformational Grammar. One kind of generative grammar; beginning with a simple sentence and showing changes as a word to a clause, active to passive, and so on.

Validity. The extent to which a test does the job for which it is used.

Variability. The dispersion of scores in a distribution; the spread above and below the mean.

Variable. A condition in a scientific investigation that may affect the observation or measurement.

Visual Memory Span. The number of items that can be recalled immediately after seeing them presented.

Vocalization. Movement of the lips or vocal apparatus during reading.

Vowel. An open, unobstructed sound, as /a/, /e/, /i/, /o/, /u/, and sometimes /y/ and /w/.

Word Analysis. Analyzing a new word into known elements for the purpose of identification.

Word Blindness. A label indicating the alleged inability to interpret words owing to a pathological condition, either congenital or acquired.

Word Caller. An individual who does not group words meaningfully, but pronounces each word individually and slowly.

Word Discrimination. The distinguishing of the form and configuration of words.

Word Variant. A root and an inflectional ending, as *read* + *s,* or *reads.*

Journals

Journals Devoted Entirely to Reading

Epistle, published by the Professors of Reading Teacher Educators, 309 Aderhold Building, University of Georgia, Athens, GA 30602.

Journals of the International Reading Association, Newark, DE 19711:

> *The Reading Teacher,* elementary level
> *Journal of Reading,* middle school, secondary, college, adults
> *Reading Research Quarterly,* scholarly research

*Journal of Reading Behavior, published by the National Reading Conference, Inc., Indiana University, Bloomington, IN 47401.

New England Reading Association Journal, Westfield State College, Westfield, MA 01085.

*Query, publication of the Saskatchewan Reading Council and the only reading journal published in Canada, the Saskatchewan Teachers Federation, P.O. Box 1108, Saskatoon, Saskatchewan, Canada.

Reading, national journal of the United Kingdom Reading Association. St. Paul's College, Newbold Revel, Rugby, Warwickshire, England CV230JS.

Reading Clinic, published monthly by the Center for Applied Research in Education in New York. School of Education, Illinois State University, Normal, IL 61761.

*Reading Horizons, Reading Center and Clinic, Western Michigan University, Kalamazoo, MI 49008.

Reading Improvement, Project Innovation, 1402 West Capitol Drive, Milwaukee, WI 53206.

*Reading World (formerly *Journal of the Reading Specialist*), College Reading Association, Elementary Education Department, Shippensburg State College, Shippensburg, PA 17257.

Journals Frequently Containing Reading and Related Topics

Bulletin of the Orton Society, Route 12, Box 31, Frederick, MD 21701.

Childhood Education, Association for Childhood Education, 3615 Wisconsin Ave NW, Washington, DC 20016.

The Clearing House, Fairleigh Dickinson University, Teaneck, NJ 07666.

Education, The Bobbs-Merrill Co., Inc., 4300 W. 62 St., Indianapolis, IN 46208.

Educational Research, National Foundation for Educational Research in England and Wales, Slough, Bucks, England.

Educational X-Change, Westhill Middle School, 4860 Onondaga Road, Syracuse, NY 13215.

Elementary School Journal, The University of Chicago Press, 5835 Kimbark Ave., Chicago, IL 60637.

English Journal, National Council of Teachers of English, Champaign, IL 61820.

* Indicates a quarterly publication; all others are monthly.

Harvard Educational Review, Longfellow Hall, 13 Appian Way, Cambridge, MA 02138.
High Points (published irregularly), N.Y.C. Board of Education, 110 Livingston St., Brooklyn, NY 11201.
The Instructor, F. A. Owen Publishing Co., Dansville, NY 14437.
Journal of Education, 765 Commonwealth Ave., Boston, MA 02115.
Journal of Educational Psychology (bimonthly), American Psychological Association, Inc., 1200 17 St. NW, Washington, DC 20036.
Journal of Educational Research, Dembar Educ. Research Services, Inc., 2018 N. Sherman Ave., Madison, WI 53701.
Language Arts (formerly *Elementary English*), National Council of Teachers of English, 508 S. Sixth St. Champaign, IL 61820.
Teacher, 23 Leroy Ave., Darien, CT 06820.

Other Reading Journals

Alabama Reader, Alabama Reading Association, semiannual, 5002 Haley Center, Auburn University, Auburn, AL 36830.
California Reader, quarterly, Education Department, California Polytechnic State University, San Luis Obispo, CA 93407.
Georgia Journal of Reading, Georgia Council of the IRA, semiannual, Box 218, Georgia State University, University Plaza, Atlanta, GA 30303.
Illinois Reading Council Journal, a yearbook, Northern Illinois University, De Kalb, IL 60115.
Indiana Reading Quarterly, Indiana State Council of IRA, 318 Teachers College, Ball State University, Muncie, IN 47306.
Michigan Reading Journal, Michigan Reading Association, three times a year, Central Michigan University, 52 Benton Road, Saginaw, MI 48602.
Minnesota Reading Quarterly, Minnesota Reading Association, P.O. Box 29023, Minneapolis, MN 55429.
Missouri Reader, Missouri State Council of IRA, annually, 503 East Clark Street, Warrensburg, MO 64093.
Reading Instruction Journal, New Jersey Reading Teachers Association, Jersey City State College, Jersey City, NJ 07305.
Reading in Virginia, Virginia State Reading Association, Longwood College, Farmville, VA 23901.
Tennessee Reading Teacher, twice yearly, Route 11, Sycamore Drive, Jonesboro, TN 37659.
Wisconsin State Reading Association Journal, United Scholars Association, three times yearly, 704 Bauman, Oshkosh, WI 54901.

* Indicates a quarterly publication; all others are monthly.

Publishers

Agency for Instructional Television, Box A, Bloomington, IN 47401. 812–339 2203.

Allyn & Bacon, Inc., 470 Atlantic Avenue, Boston, MA 02210. 617–482 9220.

American Book Company, Division Litton Educational Publishing, Inc., 450 W. 33rd Street, New York, NY 10001. 212–594 8660.

American Guidance Service, Inc., Publishers' Building, Circle Pines, MN 55014. 612–786 4343.

Appleton-Century-Crofts, 292 Madison Avenue, New York, NY 10017. 212–532 1700.

A/V Concepts Corporation, 756 Grand Blvd., Deer Park, L.I., NY 11792.

Barnell Loft, Ltd., 958 Church Street, Baldwin, NY 11510. 516–868 6064.

Basic Books, Inc., 10 E. 53rd. Street, New York, NY 10022. 212–593 7057.

Belknap Press. See Harvard University Press.

Benefic Press, Division of Beckley-Cardy Co., 10300 W. Roosevelt Road, Westchester, IL 60153. 312–287 7110.

Berckley Publishing Corporation, Affiliate of G. P. Putnams Sons, 200 Madison Avenue, New York, NY 10016. 212–883 5500.

Bobbs-Merrill Co., Inc., A Thomas Audel Co., 4300 W. 62nd Street, Indianapolis, IN 46206. 317–291 3100.

Borg-Warner Educational Systems, 600 W. University Drive, Arlington Heights, IL 60004.

Bowker, R. R., Co., A Xerox Publishing Company, 1180 Avenue of the Americas, New York, NY 10036. 212–764 5100.

Bowmar, P.O. Box 5225, Glendale, CA 91201.

Brown, William C., Co., Publishers, 2460 Kerper Blvd., Dubuque, IA 52001. 319–588 1451.

C-B Films, Inc. 7934 Santa Monica Blvd., Los Angeles, CA 90046.

California Test Bureau, Division of McGraw-Hill, q.v.

Chandler Publishing Co., Division of Intext Educational Publishers, 10 E. 53rd Street, New York, NY 10022. 212–593 7000.

Chester Electronic Laboratories, Chester, CT 06412.

Columbia University Press, 562 W. 113th Street, New York, NY 10025.

Committee on Diagnostic Reading Tests, Inc. Mountain Home, NC 28758. 704–693 5223.

Communacad, Box 541, Wilton, CT 06897.

Consulting Psychologists Press, Inc., 577 College Avenue, Palo Alto, CA 94306. 415–326 4448.

Cooperative Test Division, Educational Testing Service, Princeton, NJ 08540. 609–921 9000.

Coronet Instructional Media, 65 E. South Water Street, Chicago, IL 60601. 312–332 7676.

Creative Learning Systems, Inc., Park Centre Suite 9A, 1701 E. 12th Street, Cleveland, OH 44114. 216–621 6488.

Croft Educational Services, 100 Garfield Avenue, New London, CT 06320. 204–442 8501.

Crowell, Thomas Y., Company, 10 E. 53rd Street, New York, NY 10022. 212–593 7000.

Curriculum Associates, Inc. 6 Henshaw Street, Woburn, MA 01801.

Davidson Films, Inc., 165 Tunstead Avenue, San Anselmo, CA 94960. 415–457 1203.

Denver Public Schools, 414 Fourteenth Street, Denver, CO 80202.

Developmental Learning Materials, 7440 Natchez Avenue, Niles, IL 60648.

Doubleday & Company, Inc., 245 Park Avenue, New York, NY 10017. 212–953 4561.

Dreier Educational Systems, Box 1291, Highland Park, NJ 08904. 201–572 2112.

Dutton, E. P., & Co., Inc., 201 Park Avenue, South, New York, NY 10003. 212–674 5900.

Educational Development Corporation, 4900 S. Lewis, Tulsa, OK 07415. 918–749 6831.

Educational Development Laboratories, Inc., Div. McGraw-Hill, q.v.

Educational Recording Sales, 157 Chambers Street, New York, NY 10007.

Educational Test Bureau. See American Guidance Service.

Educators Publishing Service, Inc., 75 Moulton Street, Cambridge, MA 02138. 607–547 6706.

Encyclopedia Britannica Educational Corporation, 425 N. Michigan Avenue, Chicago, IL 60611. 312–321 6711.

ERIC Document Reproduction Service, P.O. Box 190, Arlington, VA 22210. (For microfilm and microfiche.)

Essay Press, Inc., P.O. Box 5, Planetarium Station, New York, NY 10024.

Eye Gate House, 146–01 Archer Avenue, Jamaica, NY 11435. 212–291 9100.

Fearon Publishers, Inc., Div. of Pitman Publishing Corp., 6 Davis Drive, Belmont, CA 94002. 415–592 7810.

Field Enterprises Educational Corp., 510 Merchandise Mart Plaza, Chicago, IL 60654. 312–341 2424.

Films Incorporated, 1144 Wilmette Avenue, Wilmette, IL 60091.

Follett Publishing Co., Div. of Follett Corp., 1010 W. Washington Blvd., Chicago, IL 60607. 312–666 5858.

Garrard Publishing Co., 107 Cherry Street, New Canaan, CT 06840. 203–966 4581.

Ginn & Co., A Xerox Publishing Co., 191 Spring Street, Lexington, MA 02173. 617–861 1670.

Globe Book Co., Inc., 175 Fifth Avenue, New York, NY 10010, (Minisystems.)

Golden Press, Inc. See Western Publishing Co.

Grolier Educational Corp., Subs. of Grolier Inc., Danbury, CT; 575 Lexington Ave, New York, NY 10022. 212–751 3600.

Grossett & Dunlap, Inc., 51 Madison Avenue, New York, NY 10013. 212–689 9200.

Gryphon Press, 220 Montgomery Street, Highland Park, NJ 08904. 201–247 7506.

Harcourt Brace Jovanovich, Inc., 757 Third Avenue, New York, NY 10017. 212–754 3100.

Harper & Row Publishers, 10 E. 53rd Street, New York, NY 10022. 212–593 7000.

Harvard University Press, 79 Garden Street, Cambridge, MA 02138. 617–495 2600.

Hayes School Publishing Co., Inc., 321 Pennwood Avenue, Wilkinsburg, PA 15221. 412–371 2373.

Heath, D. C., & Company, 125 Spring Street, Lexington, MA 02173. 617–862 6650.

Highsmith Company, Inc. Highway 106E, Fort Atkinson, WI 53538.

Holt, Rinehart and Winston, 383 Madison Avenue., New York, NY 10017. 212–688 9100.

Houghton Mifflin Company, 2 Park Street, Boston, MA 02107. 617–725 5000.

Indiana University Audio Visual Center, Bloomington, IN 47401. 812–337 2853.

Instruction Communications Technology, Inc., 10 Stepar Place, Huntington Station, NY 11746.

Instructional Fair, Inc., 4158 Lake Michigan Drive, Grand Rapids, MI 49504.

International Reading Association, 800 Barksdale Road, Newark, DE 19711. 302–731 1600.

The JAB Press, Inc., Box 315, Franklin Lakes, NJ 07410. 201–891 8240.

Jamestown Publishers, P.O. Box 6743, Providence, RI 02940. 401–351 1915.

Jam Handy, Scott Educational Services, Lower Westfield Road, Holyoke, MA 01040.

Johns Hopkins Press, Baltimore, MD 21218. 301–366 9600.

Charles A. Jones, Worthington, OH.

Kenworthy Educational Service, Inc., P.O. Box 3031, Buffalo, NY 14205. 716–886 5700.

Keystone View, Div. of Mast Development Co., 2212 E. 12th Street, Davenport, IA 52803. 319–326 0141.

Knopf, Alfred A., Inc., Subs. of Random House, Inc., 201 E. 50th Street, New York, NY 10022. 212–757 2600.

Lansford Publishing Company, P.O. Box 8711, 1088 Lincoln Avenue, San Jose, CA 95155.

Learning Associates, Inc., P.O. Box 561167, Miami, FL 33156.

Learning Concept, 2501 N. Lamar, Austin, TX 78705. 800–531 5004.

Learning Resources Division of Educational Development Corporation, 202 Lake Merean Dr., Lakeland, FL 33803. 813–643 5705.

Learning Systems/Coronet, Instructional Media, Department A123B, 60 Connolly Parkway, Hamden, CT 06514. 203–288 8807.

Learning Through Seeing, Inc. Sunland, CA 91040.

Learning Tree Filmstrips, 434 Pearl Street, Box 1590, Department 400, Boulder, CO 80306.

Lippincott, J. B., Company, E. Washington Square, Philadelphia PA 19105. 215–574 4200.

Littlefield, Adams and Co., 81 Adams Dr., Totowa, NJ 07511. 201–256 8600.

Lyons & Carnahan. See Rand McNally and Company.

McGraw-Hill Book Company, 1221 Avenue of the Americas, New York, NY 10020. 212–997 1221.

McKay, David, Co., Inc., 750 Third Avenue, New York, NY 10017. 212–661 1700.

Macmillan Publishing Co., Inc., 866 Third Avenue, New York, NY 10022. 212–935 2000.

Media Five, 3211 Cahuenga Blvd., West, Hollywood, CA 90068. 213–851 5166.

Media Materials, Inc., Department K8, 2936 Remington Avenue, Baltimore, MD 21211.

Merriam, G. & C., Company, Subs. of Encyclopaedia Brittanica, Inc., 47 Federal Street, Box 281, Springfield, MA 01101. 413–734 3134.

Merrill, Charles E., Publishing Company, Div. of Bell & Howell Co., 1300 Alum Creek Dr., Columbus, OH 43216. 614–258 8441.

Miller-Brody Productions, Inc., 342 Madison Avenue, Department 78, New York, NY 10017.

Mills Center, Inc., 1512 E. Broward Blvd., Ft. Lauderdale, FL 33301.

M.I.T. Press, The, 28 Carleton Street, Cambridge, MA 02142. 617–253 7297.

MKM, 809 Kansas City Street, Rapid City, SD 57701.

Montana Reading Clinic Publications, 517 Rimrock Road, Billings, MT 59102.

NEA Division of Press, 1201 Sixteenth Street, S.W., Washington, DC 20036.

New York University Film Library, 22 Washington Place, New York, NY 10003. 212–598 2250.

New York University Press, 21 W. Fourth Street, New York, NY 10012. 212–598 2886.

Noble & Noble Publishers, Inc., One Dag Hammarskjold Plaza, 245 E. 47th Street, New York, NY 10017. 212–832 7300.

Ohio State University Press, Hitchcock Hall, Room 316, 2070 Neil Avenue, Columbus, OH 43210. 614–422 6930.

Owen, F. A., Publishing Company, Dansville, NY 14437.

Oxford University Press, Inc., 200 Madison Ave., New York, NY 10016. 212–679 7300.

Pacific Productions, Inc., 20217 Shattuck Avenue, Berkeley, CA 94705. 415–848 3785.

Pacifica Tape Library, 5316 Venice Blvd., Los Angeles, CA 90019. 213–931 1625.

Parker Publishing Co., subs. of Prentice-Hall, Inc., q.v.

Penguin Books, Inc., 625 Madison Avenue, New York, NY 10022. 212–755 4330.

Penn State University Audio-Visual Services, 17 Willard Building, University Park, PA 16802. 814–865 0291.

Personnel Press, Div. Ginn and Company, 191 Spring Street, Lexington, MA 02173. 617–861 1670.

Phi Delta Kappa, Eighth and Union, Box 789, Bloomington, IN 47401. 812–339 1156.

Phonovisual Products, Inc., P.O. Box 5625, Friendship Station, Washington, DC 20016.

Pioneer Printing Co., 306-B Flora, Bellingham, WA 98225.

Pitman Publishing Corp., 6 Davis Drive, Belmont, CA 94002. 415–592 7810.

Prentice-Hall, Inc., Englewood Cliffs, NJ 07632. 201–592 2000.

Priority Innovations, Inc., P.O. Box 792, Skokie, IL 60076.

Professional Educators Publications, Inc., P.O. Box 80728, Lincoln NE 68501.

Programs For Education, Box 85, Lumberville, PA 18933.

Psychological Corporation, 757 Third Avenue, New York, NY 10017. 212–888 3500.

Public School Publishing Co. See Bobbs-Merrill.

Rand McNally & Company, P.O. Box 7600, Chicago, IL 60680. 312–673 9100.

Random House, Inc. (Singer School Division), 201 E. 50th Street, New York, NY 10022. 212–751 2600.

Readers Digest Educational Division, Pleasantville, NY 10570. 914–769 7000.

Regnery, Henry Co., Subs. Contemporary Books Inc., 180 N. Michigan Avenue, Chicago, IL 60601. 312–782 9181.

Ronald Press Company, The Division of John Wiley, Inc., 79 Madison Avenue, New York, NY 10016. 212–683 9070.

Scholastic Testing Service, Inc., 480 Meyer Rd., Bensenville, IL 60611. 617–383 1526.

Science Research Associates Inc., Subs. of IBM, College Division, 1540 Page Mill Road, Palo Alto, CA 94304. 415–493 4700.

Scott, Foresman and Company, 1900 East Lake Avenue, Glenview, IL 60025. 312–729 3000.

Silver Burdett Company, Div. of General Learning Co., 250 James St., Morristown, NJ 07960. 201–385 8100.

Singer, L. W. Co. See Random House.

Slosson Educational Publications, 140 Pine Street, East Aurora, NY 14052. 716–652 0930.

Society for Visual Education, Inc., 1345 W. Diversey Parkway, Chicago, IL 60614. 800 621 1900.

Special Learning Corporation, 42 Boston Post Road, Guilford, CT 06437. 203–453 6525.

Spencer International Press, Inc., Subs. Grolier, Inc., Danbury CT; and 575 Lexington Avenue, New York, NY 10022. 212–751 3600.

Steck-Vaughn Co., P.O. Box 2028, Austin, TX 78767. 512–476 6721.

Stoelting, C. H., Co., 424 N. Homan Avenue, Chicago, IL 60624. 312 522 5400.

Sunburst Communications, 41 Washington Avenue, Pleasantville, NY 10570. 800–431 1934.

Syracuse University, 1455 East Colvin Street, Syracuse, NY 13210. 315–479 6631.

Teachers College Press, Columbia University, 1234 Amsterdam Avenue, New York, NY 10027. 212–870 4078.

Teachers Publishing Corporation, 23 Leroy Avenue, Darien CT 06820

Thomas, Charles C, Publishers, 301 E. Lawrence Avenue, Springfield, IL 62717. 217–789 8980.

Transcontinental Film Center, 244 West 27th Street, New York, NY 10006. 212–989 3330.

University Microfilms, 300 North Zeeb Road, Ann Arbor, MI 48106. (For microfilm editions.)

University of Chicago Press, 11030 South Langley Avenue, Chicago, IL 60628.

University, Harvard, Press. See Harvard University Press.

University of Illinois Press, Urbana, IL 61801. 217–333 0950.

University of Iowa Press, 203 Graphic Services Bldg., Iowa City, IA 52242. 319–353 3181.

New York University Press, 21 W. Fourth Street, New York, NY 10012. 212–598 2886.

Ohio State University Press, Hitchcock Hall, Rm. 316, 2070 Neil Avenue, Columbus, OH 43210. 614–422 6930.

Van Nostrand, D., Company, 450 W. 33rd Street, New York, NY 10001. 212–594 8660.

Van Wagenen Psycho-Educational Research Laboratories, 1729 Irving Avenue, South, Minneapolis, MN 55411.

Viking Press, Inc., The, 625 Madison Avenue, New York, NY 10022. 212–755 4330.

Wagner Co., Dist. by: Borden Publishing Co., 1855 W. Main Street, Alhambra, CA 91801. 916–967 6988.

Watts, Franklin, Inc., Subsidiary of Grolier Inc., 730 Fifth Avenue, New York, NY 10019. 212–757 4050.

Wayne State University, 5448 Cass Avenue, Detroit, MI 48202. 313–577 1980.

Webster, Div. of McGraw-Hill Book Company, 1221 Avenue of the Americas, New York, NY 10020. 212–997 2073.

Western Psychological Services, Div. of Manson Western Corp., 12031 Wilshire Blvd., Los Angeles, CA 90025. 213–478 2061.

Western Publishing Co., Inc., 1220 Mound Avenue, Racine, WI 53404. 414–633 2431.

Wiley, John, & Sons, Inc., 605 Third Avenue, New York, NY 10016. 212–867 9800.

Winter Haven Lions Research Foundation, Inc., P.O. Box 111, Winter Haven, FL 33881. 813–294 1775.

Note: Many of the selected publishers listed in this section have branch or regional offices in addition to the main office listed. Some have offices in other countries. A letter or phone call to the office would result in informing one of a closer source.

Name Index

Ahman, J. Stanley, 359, 362
Allen, Amy, 305
Allen, Roach Van, 256
Almy, Millie, 143
Ames, Louise, 22, 33, 41, 55, 56, 59, 251
Andelman, Frederick, 387
Anderson, Robert, 318
Andrews, Robert, 112
Applebee, Arthur, 360
Aquinas, Margaret, 53
Arbuthnot, May H., 32
Armstrong, David, 315
Arnstein, P. A., 5
Arthur, Grace, 42
Ashley, L. F., 218
Askov, Eleanor, 351
Aukerman, Robert, 272
Auerback, Irma, 44
Austin, Mary C., 18, 19, 46, 59, 86, 104, 192, 197, 222, 238, 249, 253, 309, 314, 323, 362
Ausubel, David P., 40

Banathy, Bela H., 313
Banks, James, 170, 388
Bannister, Gladys, 51
Barnard, Douglas, 112
Barnhart, Clarence, 260
Barrett, Katherine, 53
Barrett, Thomas, 328
Becker, Wesley, 380, 387
Bell, Paul, 374
Bereiter, Carl, 378
Berger, Allen, 179
Bettelheim, Bruno, 299
Billig, Edith, 272
Blachford, Jean, 349
Blair, Susan M., 48
Blanton, William, 336
Bliesmer, Emory, 362
Bloom, Benjamin, 176, 177, 328, 362
Bloomfield, Leonard, 260

Bolvin, J. O., 321
Bond, Guy L., 24, 222
Boraks, Nancy, 305
Bourke-White, Margaret, 141
Bowler, Mike, 280
Bracken, Dorothy K., 216
Bresnahan, Mary, 210, 288
Brooke, Edward, 388
Brown, James, 299
Bruner, Jerome S., 59, 251, 270
Brunner, Joseph, 215
Buck, Catherine, 388
Budin, Marilyn, 50
Bumpus, Marguerite, 350
Burg, Leslie, 253
Burke, Fred, 350
Buros, Oscar K., 111, 112, 340, 362
Burros, Arnold, 179
Bush, Clifford L., 112, 192, 197, 222, 249, 362
Byers, Loretta, 216

Calfee, R. C., 272
Camp, Bonnie, 218
Carlson, Thorsten, 249, 253
Carnine, Douglas, 85
Carroll, J. B., 71
Casteneda, Alberta, 44
Cawley, John, 388
Chall, Jean, 59, 132
Chambers, Dewey, 32
Chan, Julie, 197
Chomsky, Noam, 272
Claybough, Amos, 179
Clegg, Ambrose, 170
Cole, Luella, 99
Connor, John W., 33
Corbin, Richard, 376
Cox, Mary B., 48
Criscuolo, Nicholas, 323
Crosby, Muriel, 377
Curl, David, 299
Curry, Robert, 218

Dale, Edgar, 132
Daniel, Patricia, 49
Darling, Richard, 303
Dayton, C. Mitchell, 386, 388
DeGracie, James, 112
DeHaan, Robert, 369
de Hirsch, Katrina, 59
Deichman, J. W., 50
Della-Piana, G., 307
DeStafano, J. S., 272
Dolch, Edward, 71, 72, 105
Donosa, Maria A. R., 375
Dorfman, N., 50
Downing, John, 59, 143, 259
Drever, James, 112
Duffy, Gerald, 197, 299, 305, 313
Dupuy, H. F., 388
Durkin, Dolores, 22, 43, 46, 59, 87,
     112

Earle, Richard, 179
Elkins, Deborah, 32
Emery, F. E., 323
Engelmann, Siegfried, 378
Erickson, Carlton, 299
Estes, Eleanor, 141

Fader, Daniel, 379, 388
Farnham-Diggery, Sylvia, 5
Farr, Roger, 336, 362
Fay, Leo, 253
Feeley, Joan, 216, 375
Figurel, J. Allen, 8, 382
Fisher, Margery, 32
Fitzgerald, Mildred, 253
Foerster, Leona, 209, 387, 388
Ford, David, 253
Forgan, Harry, 323
Fraenkel, Jack, 170
Francis, W., 71
Frazier, Alexander, 315, 323
Freeland, Alma, 9, 222
Fries, Charles, 260
Friesen, Doris, 43
Froese, Victor, 108
Fry, Edward B., 72, 132
Furth, Hans, 59

Gantt, Walter, 386, 388
Garcia, Ricardo, 387
Gates, Arthur, 42, 59, 74
Gates, Doris, 141
Gattegno, Caleb, 259
Gaynor, Barbara, 53
Gerace, Rita, 133
Gerhard, Christian, 144
Gibson, Eleanor, 74, 75, 81, 85, 89,
     112, 261, 267, 272
Gillespie, Margaret, 33
Glock, Marvin, 362
Goldstein, Herbert, 385, 388
Goodlad, John, 318
Goodman, Kenneth, 260, 388
Goodman, Yetta, 197
Graham, Lorenz, 288
Gray, Lillian, 222
Gray, Susan, 43
Greenblatt, E. L., 218
Grotberg, Edith, 9, 222
Guthrie, John T., 380

Haber, Ralph, 19
Hafner, Lawrence, 237, 272
Hall, Maryanne, 48
Harcleroad, Fred, 299
Harris, Albert J., 44, 74, 197, 222,
     237, 380
Harris, Theodore, 165
Harrow, Anita, 329
Hastings, Thomas, 362
Heilman, Arthur, 87, 112, 192, 197,
     237, 388
Heiss, Warren, 215
Henry, George, 144
Higgenbotham, Dorothy, 64
Hillerich, Robert, 59
Hood, Joyce, 71
Hopkins, Carol, 71
Hopper, Robert, 59
Horn, Ernest, 63
Horn, Thomas, 59, 388
Howes, Virgil, 179, 323
Huck, Charlotte, 33
Huebner, Mildred, 192, 197, 222, 249,
     362
Hull, Marion, 112

Hunt, Barbara, 388
Hunt, Linda, 223
Hunt, Lyman, 272

Ilg, Frances I., 22, 33, 41, 55, 56, 59, 251
Iverson, William J., 33, 223

James, Helen, 273
Jansky, Jeanette, 59
Jantz, Richard, 358
Johns, Jerry, 71, 220, 223, 332
Johnson, Dale, 71
Johnson, Lois, 219
Jolly, Hayden, 237, 272
Jones, Bonnie, 385, 388
Joyce, William, 388
Jung, R., 205, 218

Kachuk, Beatrice, 304
Kahn, Michael, 71
Karl, Jean, 223
Karp, Etta, 107, 112
Katz, Bobbi, 288
Kaufman, Maurice, 196, 197, 253, 362
Kemp, Jerrold, 313, 323
King, Ethel, 43
Kirk, Sam, 364
Kirkland, Eleanor, 59
Klare, George, 132, 144
Klaus, Robert, 43
Knapp, Margaret, 388
Korngold, Blanche, 253
Kottmeyer, William, 179
Kovner, Albert, 253
Kough, Jack, 369
Krathwohl, David, 328
Kucera, H., 71
Kuhn, Doris Young, 33
Kujoth, J. S., 223

Labuda, Michael, 388
Ladley, Winifred, 214
Laffey, James, 179
Lamb, Pose, 112
Lamme, Linda, 323
Landeck, Beatrice, 223
Lane, Patrick, 305

Lapp, Diane, 359
Larson, Martha, 188, 197
Latham, William, 59, 253
Lawson, Robert, 78
Lee, Dorris, 256
Lee, Nancy, 223
Lefevre, Carl, 260
Leonard, Laurence, 112
Levin, Harry, 74, 75, 81, 85, 89, 112, 261, 267, 272
Lewis, Richard B., 299
Lewiton, Mina, 384
Liberty, C., 5
Lindvall, C. M., 321
Lloyd, Bruce, 165
Lloyd, Rosalin, 165
Loree, Ray, 137
Lorge, Irving, 74, 75, 132

Madaus, George, 362
Mager, Robert, 328
Malaregna, Ralph, 306
Mangieri, John, 71
Mangrum, Charles, 323
Marcus, Albert, 304
Martin, Clyde, 44
Martuano, Arlene, 255
Masia, Bertram, 328
Maslow, A. H., 202
Mathewson, Grover, 387, 388
Mazurkiewicz, Albert J., 112
McCann, Donnarae, 33
McCormick, Sandra, 314, 323
McGuire, Marion, 350
McKee, Barbara, 53
McManus, Anastasia, 43
McNally, D. W., 59
McNeil, Elton, 379
Meehan, T., 49
Mellon, John C., 359
Merritt, John, 179, 253
Meshover, Leonard, 87
Meyers, Charles, 221
Michaelis, John, 150, 170, 171
Miller, Clyde, 126
Mills, Robert E., 73
Mitchell, Johnny, 84
Moe, Alden, 71

Morphet, Mabel V., 42
Morrison, Coleman, 18, 19, 44, 46, 59, 86, 104, 238, 253, 309, 314, 323, 380
Mour, Stanley, 19
Mullins, Jane, 210, 223
Mullis, Ina, 360

Natalico, Diana, 59
Neuwirth, Sharyn, 97
Newman, Thelma, 317
Niensted, Serena, 388
Norvell, G. W., 214, 219

O'Connell, Carol, 314, 324
Oldefendt, Susan, 360
Ollila, Lloyd, 59
Olson, Duree, 388
Onativia, Oscar, 375
Osborne, D. Keith, 377
Otto, Wayne, 253, 351

Pagan, Judith, 132
Page, William, 187, 197
Painter, Helen, 300
Peebles, James, 179
Pereya-Suarez, Denise, 387, 388
Pflaum-Connor, Susanna, 388
Phillips, Donald, 360
Pikulski, John, 362
Pollack, Cecilia, 305
Powell, Barbara, 305
Prescott, George, 362
Pressey, S. L., 148, 368
Putnam, Lillian, 335

Ramsey, Wallace, 219
Rauch, J. Sidney, 250, 323
Richard, Olga, 33
Richman, B., 71
Rinsland, F. W., 63
Robeck, Carol, 387, 388
Roberts, Kathleen, 49, 59
Robinson, Francis, 29, 147, 155, 179
Robinson, Helen, 49, 50, 220, 328
Robinson, H. Alan, 170, 179, 250
Roeder, Harold, 223
Rogers, Janette, 315

Roggenbuck, Mary, 210, 223
Root, Shelton L., 33
Rosenberg, Judith K., 33
Rosenberg, Kenyon, 33
Rosner, Jerome, 47
Roth, Bea, 84
Royal, Mildred, 349
Ruddell, Robert B., 19, 112, 179, 260, 272, 323
Rufsvold, Margaret, 300
Rupley, William, 47, 59, 215, 223, 387, 388
Russell, David, 24, 107, 112, 117

Sabatino, D. A., 50
Sadker, David, 223
Sadker, Myra, 223
Sandberg, Herbert, 207
Sartain, Harry W., 226, 272, 320
Schaefer, Paul J., 143
Schulwitz, Bonnie, 179
Schwartz, Elaine, 139
Schuman, Davida, 376
Sciara, Frank, 358
Scriven, Michael, 328
Sea, Marcella, 221
Seashore, Robert H., 64
Sebesta, Sam L., 33, 223
Seegars, J. C., 64
Shane, Robert, 32
Shatkin, Eva, 133
Sheff, Alice, 139
Sher, Norman, 305
Sherk, John J., 72
Sherman, George, 197, 299, 305, 313
Shipley, Joseph, 103
Siegel, Ernest, 388
Silvaroli, Nicholas, 332
Silverston, R. A., 50
Simmons, Beatrice, 215
Simon, H. A., 5
Simon, Norma, 210, 223
Simpson, G. O., 221
Singer, Harry, 19
Sipay, Edward, 197, 222, 237
Skrypa, Aldon, 317
Sloan, Glenna D., 33
Smith, Dora V., 33

Smith, Frank, 19, 64, 116, 144, 179
Smith, James, 272
Smith, Karl, 146
Smith, Margaret, 146
Smith, Nila B., 69
Smith, Richard, 253
Snow, Lawrence, 323
Spache, Evelyn, 144, 192, 197, 237
Spache, George, 132, 144, 192, 197, 237, 288, 300
Spiegler, Charles, 382
Stake, Robert, 328
Stanchfield, Jo M., 44, 219
Standing, E. Mortimer, 255
Stauffer, Russell, 144
Steinberg, Zena, 258
Stoddard, George, 319
Stone, Clarence, 74
Strain, Lucille, 323, 358, 362
Sutherland, Zena, 32
Sutton, Marjorie, 44
Swiss, Thom, 388

Tacker, Robert S., 49
Tanyzer, Harold, 223
Taylor, Mark, 216
Tewksbury, John L., 319
Thackray, D. V., 59
Thelan, Judith, 179
Thomas, Ellen L., 170
Thorndike, Edward L., 63, 74
Thorndike, Robert L., 176, 179
Thorpe, Louis, 221
Tierney, Robert, 359
Tinker, Miles B., 24
Tinsley, Drew C., 143

Trela, Thaddeus, 223
Trow, William, 270
Tuinman, J. J., 336
Tyler, Ralph, 328

Van Leeuwen, Jean, 288
Venezky, Richard, 273, 359

Wachs, Harry, 59
Wachner, Clarence, 376
Wagner, Eva B., 222
Walker, Lawrence, 389
Wallach, Lise, 307
Wallach, Michael, 307
Walter, Richard, 132
Walton, Richard, 384
Wardeberg, Helen, 362
Wardhaugh, Ronald, 260
Washburne, Carleton, 42
Waynant, Louise, 317, 323
Weintraub, Samuel, 220
Weiss, M. Jerry, 215, 240
Wepman, Joseph, 49
West, Gail, 179
Wetmore, Cora, 53
Williams, Frederick, 59
Wilson, Richard, 273
Wilson, Robert, 317, 323, 386, 388
Witty, Paul, 9, 218, 219, 222, 369, 389
Wolf, Suzanne, 210, 223
Wolfram, Walt, 389
Wright, Robert, 316

Zimet, Sara, 218

Subject Index

Accent, 93
Accent marker, 95
Accountability, 357–58
Administration and organization of programs, 301–23
Administrators, 248–49
Affix, 88
Aides, 306–307
Alphabet, 69, *see also* Dictionary
  practical use, 161
  sounds of consonants, 77–8
  sounds of vowels, 77–8
Alternative schools, 321–22
Anecdotal records, 355
Appraisal, 327–62
Arithmetic, 174–75
Assessment, national and state, 359–61
Assigning reading material, 290–99
Associations, professional, 240–41
Audio-visual aids, 216
Auditory discrimination, 109
Average learner, 365–67

Basal reader, 263–65
  approach, 263–65
  materials, 277–78
  series, 74
  vocabulary control, 73–5
  word count lists, 74
Beginning reading instruction
  oral reading, 180–97
  vocabulary development, 61–112
Bilingual child, 374–76
Books, children's, 288–89

CAI, 313
Cards, word, 104–106
Case study, 335
Challenging the learner, 363–87
  average learner, 365–67
  dialect speakers, 386–87
  disabled, 384–85
  disadvantaged, 376–81

gifted, 368–72
handicapped, 385–86
language difficulties, 374–81
mainstreaming, 385–86
reluctant readers, 381–84
retarded readers, 372–74
slow learners, 367–68
Checklists
  child development, 25–8
  common prefixes, 91
  common roots, 92
  common suffixes, 91–92
  dictionary skills, 94
  efficient readers, 29–30
  informal evaluation, 353
  oral reading, 194–95
  parents, 62
  personal growth record, 52–3
  reading comprehension skills, 120–21
  signs of readiness, 67–8
Child development, 20–32
  Piaget's stages, 20–21, 48–49
Children's literature, 25–28, 48–49, 288–89
Children's thinking, 116–117
Choral reading, 187–88
Chunking, 97
Classroom, self-contained, 308–10
Cloze, 75
College influences on programs, 251
Committee, reading, 302
Communication skills, 3
Community, 9–15
  federal support, 15
  private institutions, 11–14
Comprehension, reading
  basic factors, 113–65
  cybernetic principles, 146–51
  definitions, 115–16
  external factors, 131–33
    reading program, 131
    reading materials, 131–32
    readability of materials, 132–33

Comprehension, reading (*cont.*)
   meaningful vocabularies, 118
   nature of, 113–16
   personal factors, 128–30
     emotional adjustments, 130
     experiential background, 129
     intelligence, 123–29
     interests, 130
     physical factors, 129–30
     purpose for reading, 130
   questions, 139–142
   rate of, 161–65
   stratified concept, 117
Comprehension skills, *see* **Reading**
   comprehension skills
Computer assisted instruction, 313
Conferences
   teacher, 240–41
   pupil-teacher, 334–35
Configuration, 75, 87
Consonants, 78
Consultants, Reading, 249–50
Content areas, 99, 165–79, 303–305
   analysis, 165–67
   English, 167–69
   literature, 176–78
   mathematics, 174–75
   science, 172–74
   social studies, 169–72
   vocabulary, 99–100
Context clues, 75, 97–98
Continuous progress plan, 320
Courses of study, 238
Cross-age tutoring, 305–306
Cumulative reading record folder,
   355–56
Curriculum planning, 229–30
Cybernetic principles, 146–51
   instrument analysis, 147–49
   task analysis, 149–51

Decoding, 5, 6, 23
Departmentalization, 317–18
Derivative, 88
Dictionary, 94–6
   development tasks, 94
   examples, 96–7
   skills, 94–5

Disadvantaged, 376–81
   evaluation, 337–38
   language, 65–6
Discussion, classroom, 175–76
Dramatization, 188

Efficient reader, 29–32
   checklists, 29–30
English, 167–69
Experience charts, 39, 67, 72

Federal support, 15
Figurative language, 98
Fixations, 47

Games, 69
Grapheme, 85
Grouping, 310–12
   homogeneous, 310–312
   heterogeneous, 312

Hallmarks of mature reader, 24
High Intensity Learning Systems–
   reading, 351
Home, 8–9
Homographs, 101
Homonyms, 101

Individualized reading, 261–63
Inflectional form, 88–9
Influences on reading
   administrators, 248–49
   colleges, 251
   consultants and specialists, 249–51
   librarians, 248
   parents, 246
   professional associations, 251
   research, 251
   school study councils, 252
   teachers, 244–45, 247–48
   U.S. Office of Education, 252
Informal classroom techniques of evaluation, 330–38
Informal reading inventory, 331–33
Information processing, 5–6
   cognitive process, 6
   input stage, 6
   output stage, 6

Initial Teaching Alphabet, i.t.a., 259
Inservice programs, 238–40
Interests, 201–23
    culture and society, 204–206
    evaluation, 217–22
    materials and media, 211
    psychological bases, 202–204
    reading instruction, 206–10
International Reading Association, 15
Interview rating, 353–54
IQ and reading potential, 363–65

Kindergarten, 43, 50, 55, 58
Kits, 283

Language acquisition, 61
Language arts, 3, 4, 7–8
Language difficulties, 374–81
Language experience approach, 256–58
Language of the disadvantaged, 65–66
Language Master, 84
Language production
    orthographic rules, 61
    phonological rules, 62
Learner, the
    average, 365–67
    disabled, 384–85
    gifted, 368–72
    retarded, 372–74
    slow, 367–68
Learning centers, 316–17
Learning theory, 133–39
Librarian, 161, 248
Library-media center, 287–88
Linguistics, 62–3, 114, 260–61
Literature, *see* Children's literature
Locational skills, 160–61
    library techniques, 160–61

Magazines, 213
Mainstreaming, 385–86
Materials of instruction, 131–33, 274–99
    assigning reading material, 290–99
    library-media center, 287
    readability of, 132
    sources, 275–76

supplementary, 281–87
    films and filmstrips, 284–85
    games, 283–84
    kits, 283
    programed, 283
    reference works, 285–87
    workbooks, 282
teachers' manuals, 278–79
textbooks, 278–81
types, 276
Mathematics, 174–75
Media use, 303
Modalities, 49–50
Montessori method, 255, 488

Newspapers, 215
Nongraded classrooms, 318–19

Objectives, 327–30
Observations of children's performance, 333–34
Oral reading, 180–97
    checklist for teachers, 194–95
    evaluation, 191–96
    examples of good practice, 197–90
    purposes, 181–84
    recordings, 189–90
    skills, 184–87
    standardized tests, 193, 195, 196
Organization and administration of reading program, 301–23
    content areas, 303–305
    grouping, 310–12
    instructional systems, 312–22
    media use, 303
    pupils as tutors, 305–306
    reading committee, 302
    self-contained classroom, 308–10
    use of aides, 306–307
    ways of organizing for teaching, 307–308

Paraprofessionals, 306–307
Parents, 8–9, 61
Parents and teachers, 246–47
Perception, 5
Perceptual-conceptual process, 5

Perceptual skills, 47
    auditory, 48
    visual, 48
Personal growth record, 52–3
Personnel, 15–6
Physical factors, 129–30
Phonic analysis, 77–87
Phonic elements, 78–81
Phonics instruction, 77
Phonics, practice, 84
Phonics principles, 82–84
Phonics program, 77
Phoneme, 85
Planning, teachers', 231–53
    daily lesson, 232–34
    long range, 231
    teacher-pupil, 234–36
    unit, 231–32
PLATO, 313
Prefix, 88
    common prefixes, 91
Preprimary rooms, 50–55
Prereading activities, 54–55
Prereading programs, 255–65
Preschool reading, 42–45
Prescriptive Reading Inventory, 350
Professional associations, 15
Professional influences on reading pro-
        grams, 251
Programed
    approaches, 265–71
    materials, 283
Programs, reading, 224–72
    adult influences, 251–52
    basal readers, 263–65
    curriculum planning, 229–30
    growth of effective, 243–53
        definition, 245–46
    individualized, 261–63
    i.t.a., Initial Teaching Alphabet,
        259
    language experience, 256–58
    linguistic, 260–61
    Montessori, 255
    prereading, 255–65
    programed and systems approaches,
        265–71

scope and sequence, 227–28
sources of help, 236–43
teacher's planning, 231–36
Words-in-Color, 259–60
Proofreading, 169
Propaganda devices, 125–28
Purpose for reading, 130

Questionnaires, 353
Questions, 23, 139–43
    for clarification, 139–42
    formulating new questions, 141
    preceding reading, 139
    to promote thinking, 142–43

Ranking scales, 354–55
Rate of comprehension, 161–65
    appropriate materials, 161–63
    flexibility, 163–65
    scanning, 163
    skimming, 163
Rating scales, 353–54
Readability, 132–33
    application of formulas, 132
Readiness, 22, 37
    chronological age, 39–42
    developmental appraisal, 56
    definitions, 38–39
    identification, 55–8
    keys, 38–47
    personal growth record, 52–53
    research implications, 47
    techniques of appraisal, 56–58
Reading
    definitions, 6, 7
    developmental charts, 25–28
    environment, 18–19
    in the social studies, 99
    motivation, 6, 7
    process, 4
Reading comprehension skills
    analysis during reading, 123
    author's pattern of writing, 123
    author's purposes, 125
    challenging writer's authority, 124–
        25
    chart of skills, 120–21

comparisons, 124
drawing conclusions, 122–23
evaluating content, 124
feeling and mood, 121
following directions, 121
locating information, 122
main ideas, 118–19
outcomes, 119–21
personal associations, 124
propaganda devices, 125–28
pupil's preparation, 151–52
sequence, 119
specific details, 119
teacher's preparation, 147–151
Reading environment
children's theater, 10
the classroom, 16–17
the community, 9–15
the home, 8–9
the school, 15–17
Reading in the Language Arts, 3–4, 7–8
Reading Journals, *see* Appendix
Reading specialist, 16
Reading vocabulary, *see* Vocabulary
Recordings, 189
Records, reading, 355–57
Reluctant readers, 381–84
Research, 251
Retarded readers, 372–74
Roots, word, 87
common word roots, 92–93

Saccade, 47
School study councils, 251–52
Science, 172–74
Sequence of skills, 89–93
Sight words, 70–73
Dolch Basic Sight Vocabulary, 71
Mills Learning Methods Test, 73
Studies, 71–2
Slow learner, 367–68
SRA Reading Laboratories, 162, 164
Strategies for
developing interest in words, 102–104
developing reading readiness, 45–6

diversifying questions, 139–43
evaluating oral reading, 191–96
improving rate of comprehension, 161–65
teaching comprehension skills, 147–51
teaching the disadvantaged, 376–81
teaching reading in content areas, 165–78
Stress, 93
Structural analysis, 87–93
clues, 75
common generalizations, 88–9
common prefixes, 91
common roots, 92
common suffixes, 91–2
syllabication, 89
Suffix, 88
common suffixes, 91–2
Syllabication, 81–2, *see also* Structural analysis
Syntactic clues, 97
Synonym, 97
Systems approach, Programed instructional, 312–22

Teacher, 16–17
as a reader, 17–18
authorities in the field, 241–42
beginning, 281
conferences, 240–41
courses of study, 238
helps, 236–43
inservice programs, 238–40
manuals, 278–79
materials, 237
personnel, 236
professional associations, 240–41
responsibility, 244–45
role in comprehension, 143
role in readiness, 46–7
self-evaluation, 337
sources for children's books, 288–89
special services, 242
Teaching comprehension skills, *see also* Cybernetic principles
concentration, 158–59

Teaching comprehension skills (*cont.*)
   locational skills, 160–61
   motivation, 151–52
   rate of comprehension, 161–65
   SQ3R, 155–60
   study techniques, 156
   work habits, 152–55
Team learning, 316
Team teaching, 314–15
Tests
   achievement, 343–44
   criterion-referenced, 347–52
   diagnostic, 344–45
   informal, 335–36
   interpreting, 340–42
   oral, 193–96, 345–46
   purpose for use, 339
   reading readiness, 56–57, 342–43
   reliability, 338
   selecting, 339
   specialized, for reading use, 346–47
   standard, 338–52
   study skills, 346
   validity, 338
   vocabulary
      primary, 110
      readiness, 109
      elementary, 110–11
Textbook
   beginning teachers, 281, 288
   content areas, 278
   selection, 279–81
Thinking, *see* Children's thinking
Transitional rooms, 50–55
Tutors, pupils as, 305

Unit planning, 231–32
United States Office of Education, USOE, 252

Vocabulary, *see also* Reading comprehension skills
   control, 73–5
   evaluation, 108–111
   figurative expressions, 101
   foreign language, 102
   games, 106–107
   intelligence, 65
   meaningful practice, 104–106, 118
   misconceptions, 101
   omissions, 101
   parents' role, 61–2
   readiness, 66–70
   reversals, 101
   size, 61
   substitutions, 100
   types, 63
   word calling, 100
Vocabulary tests
   primary, 110
   elementary, 110–11
Vowels, 78–84

Will to learn, 45–6
Wisconsin Design, 313
Word analysis, 75–99
Word-by-reading, 108
Word calling, 100
Word counts, 62–5
Word, interest in, 102–104
Word lists, graded, 330–31
Word meanings
   context clues, 97–8
   figurative language, 98, 101
   idiomatic expression, 98
   word origins, 102–104
Words in Color, 259–60
Workbooks, 282
Work habits, 152–55
   chart, 154
Work samples, 336–37